# EXTERNAL DEBT
# OF DEVELOPING
# COUNTRIES

## *1983 SURVEY*

ORGANISATION FOR ECONOMIC CO-OPERATION AND DEVELOPMENT

Pursuant to article 1 of the Convention signed in Paris on 14th December, 1960, and which came into force on 30th September, 1961, the Organisation for Economic Co-operation and Development (OECD) shall promote policies designed:

- to achieve the highest sustainable economic growth and employment and a rising standard of living in Member countries, while maintaining financial stability, and thus to contribute to the development of the world economy;
- to contribute to sound economic expansion in Member as well as non-member countries in the process of economic development; and
- to contribute to the expansion of world trade on a multilateral, non-discriminatory basis in accordance with international obligations.

The Signatories of the Convention on the OECD are Austria, Belgium, Canada, Denmark, France, the Federal Republic of Germany, Greece, Iceland, Ireland, Italy, Luxembourg, the Netherlands, Norway, Portugal, Spain, Sweden, Switzerland, Turkey, the United Kingdom and the United States. The following countries acceded subsequently to this Convention (the dates are those on which the instruments of accession were deposited): Japan (28th April, 1964), Finland (28th January, 1969), Australia (7th June, 1971) and New Zealand (29th May, 1973).

The Socialist Federal Republic of Yugoslavia takes part in certain work of the OECD (agreement of 28th October, 1961).

*In order to achieve its aims the OECD has set up a number of specialised committees. One of these is the Development Assistance Committee, whose Members have agreed to secure an expansion of aggregate volume of resources made available to developing countries and to improve their effectiveness. To this end, Members periodically review together both the amount and the nature of their contributions to aid programmes, bilateral and multilateral, and consult each other on all other relevant aspects of their development assistance policies.*

*The Members of the Development Assistance Committee are Australia, Austria, Belgium, Canada, Denmark, Finland, France, the Federal Republic of Germany, Italy, Japan, the Netherlands, New Zealand, Norway, Sweden, Switzerland, the United Kingdom, the United States and the Commission of the European Economic Communities.*

Publié en français sous le titre:

ENDETTEMENT EXTÉRIEUR
DES PAYS EN DÉVELOPPEMENT

ETUDE 1983

This Survey has been compiled by the OECD
Development Co-operation Directorate and is
published under the responsibility
of the Secretary-General.

*Also available*

**DEVELOPMENT CO-OPERATION: 1983 REVIEW.** Efforts and Policies of the Members of the Development Assistance Committee (December 1983)
(43 83 05 1) ISBN 92-64-12533-7   250 pages                                   £12.00   US$24.00   F120.00

**INVESTING IN DEVELOPING COUNTRIES.** 5th Revised Edition (March 1983)
(43 83 02 1) ISBN 92-64-12424-1   122 pages                                   £7.60   US$15.00   F76.00

**GEOGRAPHICAL DISTRIBUTION OF FINANCIAL FLOWS TO DEVELOPING COUNTRIES 1978-1981** – Disbursements, Commitments, External Debt, Economic Indicators (March 1983)
(43 82 02 3) ISBN 92-64-02355-0   bilingual   278 pages                       £11.00   US$22.00   F110.00

*Prices charged at the OECD Publications Office.*

*THE OECD CATALOGUE OF PUBLICATIONS and supplements will be sent free of charge on request addressed either to OECD Publications Office,*
*2, rue André-Pascal, 75775 PARIS CEDEX 16, or to the OECD Sales Agent in your country.*

# TABLE OF CONTENTS

The debt statistics presented in this Survey are compiled by the OECD Secretariat from a number of sources:

-- The OECD Creditor Reporting System (CRS);

-- The World Bank Debtor Reporting System (DRS);

-- Other official sources and OECD Secretariat estimates.

Combining and cross-checking data from these various sources provide as complete a picture as possible of the total debt and debt service of all developing countries, including 4 Southern European countries (Greece, Portugal, Turkey and Yugoslavia) but excluding China PR. In all, 157 countries and territories (LDCs) are included in the Survey. (For details, see the Technical Note.)

The comprehensive scope of this Survey means that the aggregates differ from those presented in other published debt studies, notably by the World Bank and the International Monetary Fund (IMF), and show larger volumes of outstanding debt and debt-service payments. However, there is no inconsistency between the figures published by the OECD and the other sources, once the different coverage of debtors is taken into account. This Survey thus supplements similar studies by the World Bank and IMF, making a number of particular contributions:

a) The data for debt and debt service linked to OECD creditors are presented under three main categories of particular analytical relevance:

-- Official Development Assistance;

-- Export credits (both from official sources and officially guaranteed private, including bank-financed, export credits);

-- Capital-market finance (including bonds and bank credits other than export credits);

-- Hence total bank lending is _split_ between "financial credits" and "export credits".

b) Debt and debt service paid to different creditor groups are split into non-concessional and concessional.

c) Average interest paid on the outstanding stock of debt is shown for various categories of financing and for major categories of developing countries.

d) Information on short-term assets and liabilities as well as floating-interest debt and impact of exchange-rate changes is provided.

At the time the statistical compilations were completed (November 1983), there was still considerable uncertainty regarding the extent to which large shortfalls in current debt-service payments by several large debtors would result, by the end of 1983, in arrears or in restructuring of maturities. This applies particularly to payments on short- and long-term debt to banks. Hence projections for 1983 of debt and debt service to banks remain uncertain.

Except for the Tables in Chapter II, the data in this Survey concern essentially debt and debt service. A full statistical analysis of the flows underlying the data on debt stocks is contained in separate OECD publications, notably the annual DAC Chairman's Report and the annual report on the Geographical Distribution of Financial Flows to Developing Countries. The forthcoming new BIS/OECD series on external claims of banks and guaranteed trade-related claims of non-banks in the BIS reporting area is not, at present, used in the compilation of this Survey (see Section 5 in Chapter I).

It is recalled that the names or geographical classifications of countries or territories shown in this, as in any other OECD publication, do not imply any expression of view regarding juridical status. The designation "developing countries" (LDCs) is used as a generic term which does not carry any special meaning as to the political or legal classifications of the recipients concerned.

Chapter I

OVERVIEW

## 1. INTRODUCTION

In the mid-1970s, the growing complexity of financial flows to developing countries created a need to keep track of the rate of increase and the composition of the debt stock and the debt-service obligations of developing countries. It was in recognition of this need that the Development Co-operation Directorate of the OECD began to collect the statistical series on which this annual Survey of the external debt of developing countries (LDCs) is based.

It cannot be emphasized too strongly that debt statistics, like any other statistical series, are constructs. Their meaning and implications have to be assessed in the context of the underlying conceptual and statistical framework. Within this framework, however, the financial magnitudes and structures which are thus "constructed" reflect the institutional and economic realities which have shaped the financial history of the developing world. In the current situation, interpreting the statistics and understanding the nature and scope of the debt problem have become closely interrelated. Hence this introductory Chapter treats some of the current analytical and policy issues regarding developing-country debt problems, while Chapter II attempts to show how the pattern of financial flows to developing countries over the past decade or so relates to the current debt picture and discusses some of the problems involved in interpreting aggregate debt statistics. Chapter III, "Salient Trends and Facts", provides commentary on and analysis of the basic statistical material contained in the 22 major summary Tables. The Technical Note and the Note on Coverage (preceding this Chapter) set out the basic conceptual, definitional and statistical elements which are essential to the proper understanding of this Survey.

Given the great complexity of the subjects treated, the commentary in this Survey cannot and does not aim to constitute a full analysis of the debt problem. It is hoped, however, that it will make some contribution to improved comprehension of the situation, and especially of two fundamental aspects:

-- The diversity and the particularity of the external financial structures and situations of individual developing countries;

7

-- The importance of the dynamics of debt situations and of major switches in their domestic and international economic context which, much more than the magnitudes of what are composite and complex debt and debt-service aggregates, determine the nature and extent of debt problems.

## 2. THE CURRENT DEBT PICTURE

### A. General Assessment

In 1983, the full scope of the current debt problems among developing countries became evident. An unprecedented number of countries had to re-schedule their debts and there are still others who, currently or prospec-tively are having to reschedule. The cumulative total of the amounts involved represent a large portion of the outstanding stocks of bank debt in particu-lar. And it has become clear that the major problem cases, especially, are complex, both individually and with respect to their wider systemic, economic and political implications. It seems evident, from the more detailed analysis which follows, that the major fall in interest rates from the autumn of 1982 came just in time to prevent what remains a serious but still manageable situ-ation from becoming an international financial impasse.

The basic assessments emerging from this Survey are that, while the foundations for greater stability were laid in 1983, much remains to be done in 1984 and beyond to bring debt problems adequately under control; and that, while a significant measure of progress appears feasible in the aggregate over the course of this year, much will depend on the specifics of individual cases.

Although there is no doubt that the situation overall has introduced into the international economic system a new source of fragility and vulnera-bility that may not dissipate for some time, important progress has been made in containing and managing both individual problems and the actual or poten-tial systemic consequences. The complexity of the current debt situation and the present economic context poses particular difficulties in making an over-all assessment, or even judging the significance of movements in the relevant economic and financial aggregates. Nevertheless, the available evidence seems to indicate that a substantial consolidation is underway, helped by the fact that some of the fundamental domestic and international elements in the debt situation are now stabilizing.

A major feature of the last year was the demonstrated commitment of the authorities in key creditor countries, working with the major international financial institutions [particularly the International Monetary Fund (IMF) and the Bank for International Settlements (BIS)] and the authorities of debtor countries, to resolve individual problems and to keep the overall situation under control. Leadership and co-operation among the private banking communi-ty have also played a vital role. An implicit commitment among all the par-ties involved to continue this co-operation is the basic guarantee that the international financial system can underpin world recovery and assist the resumption of economic growth and development progress in debtor countries.

Important challenges remain for creditors, debtors and the international community in general. Major rescheduling agreements and coherent adjustment programmes have yet to be put in place in some significant cases. The course of events in the period ahead cannot by any means be predicted with certainty. However, much has been learned on all sides in the past year. There are real achievements to build upon in the further efforts needed in 1984 and beyond, to achieve a more viable, assured position for individual problem countries and for the financial system as a whole.

On the broader international economic scene, the immediate outlook is encouraging, even if not problem-free. World trade growth is reviving and some improvement of the terms of trade of developing countries is currently in train. This improving environment will assist the major debt-problem countries, but they will need to continue working hard to lay the basis for resumed growth in their economies. The difficulties -- political, social and economic -- of getting back to adequate growth rates in some, if not most, of these countries remain daunting. The poorer debt-problem countries, with mainly official debt, have not been so directly affected by interest rates, but they have suffered radically from the adverse terms of trade and declining trade growth of the last few years, which exposed their underlying economic vulnerability and institutional weaknesses. These countries should be significantly helped by resumed trade growth and rising terms of trade during the coming year. Nevertheless, they will not easily throw off the legacy of several years of international recession -- nor will stronger external conditions solve their fundamental development problems, which are essentially domestic in nature.

Important as it will be to further resolve individual problems, there is a broader task which must be advanced in 1984, but with a time horizon stretching through the rest of the decade. This more fundamental task is to ensure that trade and finance flow in the world economy in a dynamic and sustainable way, providing the incentives and the scope for investment, growth and adjustment in all countries. International economic co-operation should focus on this task, which is vital to the well-being of the advanced countries and essential to the ability of the developing countries to confront successfully the development challenges which they face.

B. The Evolution of the Debt Situation and the International Economic Context, 1978-84

In Tables A and B, a selected set of data has been assembled, with the aim of helping to clarify how the debt situation and the international economic context have evolved and interacted since 1978, and to assess the complicated transitions which are presently occurring. This analysis may help to throw some more light on the main issues for 1984 and beyond.

The approach is a dynamic one, with the focus on changes in relevant aggregates, and on some of the critical relationships between aggregates, rather than on the absolute values of particular aggregates. In addition, on the debt-service side, only the interest element is brought into the picture. Leaving out the practically important, but in economic terms secondary, problems of amortization, roll-over and rescheduling both simplifies the analysis and helps to illuminate the evolution of the debt situation. The aggregate debt stocks of developing countries are best regarded as a perpetuity,

Table A

EVOLUTION OF MEDIUM- AND LONG-TERM DEBT STOCKS, CURRENT-ACCOUNT
BALANCES, BANK LENDING AND TRADE, 1978-84

| | 1978 | 1979 | 1980 | 1981 | 1982 | 1983 | (1984) (a) |
|---|---|---|---|---|---|---|---|
| | Annual increase in stocks of medium- and long-term debt (b) $ billion | | | | | | |
| Low-income countries | 13 | 11 | 12 | 9 | 10 | 12 | .. |
| Lower middle-income countries | 9 | 9 | 9 | 10 | 10 | 10 | .. |
| Upper middle-income countries | 47 | 40 | 33 | 37 | 31 | 33 | .. |
| All LDCs | 69 | 60 | 54 | 56 | 51 | 54 | .. |
| of which: Non-OPEC, Non-OECD | 47 | 40 | 43 | 53 | 44 | 42 | (55) |
| | Non-OPEC, non-OECD current account and bank financing $ billion | | | | | | |
| Current-account balance | -26 | -39 | -60 | -76 | -65 | -45 | (-40) |
| Net borrowing from banks | 24 | 29 | 32 | 44 | 32 | 20 | (22) |
| of which: Long-term | 12 | 15 | 16 | 26 | 23 | 27 | (24) |
| Short-term | 12 | 14 | 16 | 18 | 9 | -7 | (-2) |
| Increase in reserves | 13 | 10 | 1 | 4 | -6 | 8 | (14) |
| | OPEC current account and bank financing $ billion | | | | | | |
| Current-account balance | -1 | 65 | 111 | 52 | -16 | -31 | (-32) |
| of which: "Low absorbers" | 8 | 34 | 87 | 57 | 0 | -24 | (-22) |
| "High absorbers" | -10 | 31 | 23 | -5 | -17 | -8 | (-10) |
| Net borrowing from banks | .. | 6 | 4 | 5 | 8 | 12 | (18) |
| of which: Long-term | .. | 4 | 1 | 2 | 3 | 8 | (25) |
| Short-term | .. | 2 | 3 | 3 | 5 | 4 | (-7) |
| | Trade volumes and prices per cent change from previous year | | | | | | |
| Non-OPEC, Non-OECD LDC trade | | | | | | | |
| Export volumes | 7 | 9 | 8 | 9 | 3 | 4 | (7) |
| Import volumes | 5 | 10 | 5 | 6 | -5 | -1 | (6) |
| Export prices | 8 | 18 | 17 | -4 | -7 | -3 | (4) |
| Import prices | 14 | 19 | 23 | 0 | -5 | -4 | (2) |
| OPEC countries | | | | | | | |
| Export volumes | -4 | 3 | -15 | -18 | -19 | -8 | (7) |
| Import volumes | 5 | -12 | 15 | 25 | 5 | -8 | (3) |
| of which: "Low absorbers" | 7 | 8 | 9 | 30 | 8 | 1 | (4) |
| "High absorbers" | 4 | -23 | 24 | 21 | 3 | -15 | (2) |

10

Table B

EVOLUTION OF INTEREST PAYMENTS, AVERAGE INTEREST COSTS
AND INTEREST/EXPORT RATIOS, 1978-84

| | 1978 | 1979 | 1980 | 1981 | 1982 | 1983 (c) | (1984) (a) |
|---|---|---|---|---|---|---|---|
| | Annual increase in gross interest payments on medium- and long-term debt $ billion | | | | | | |
| Low-income countries | 0.7 | 0.7 | 0.3 | 0.4 | 0.6 | 0.0 | (0.5) |
| Lower middle-income countries | 0.5 | 1.3 | 1.4 | 1.0 | 1.5 | -0.3 | (0.9) |
| Upper middle-income countries | 3.5 | 6.1 | 8.0 | 6.7 | 4.9 | -1.9 | (4.9) |
| All LDCs | 4.7 | 8.1 | 9.7 | 8.0 | 7.1 | -2.2 | (6.3) |
| of which: Non-OPEC, Non-OECD | 2.9 | 5.1 | 7.6 | 6.0 | 5.4 | -0.8 | (4.1) |
| | Average interest costs on medium- and long-term disbursed debt per cent | | | | | | |
| Floating-interest debt | 8.4 | 12.3 | 15.5 | 17.4 | 17.1 | 12.7 | (12.5) |
| Total LDC debt | 6.3 | 7.7 | 9.0 | 9.7 | 10.0 | 8.7 | (9.0) |
| of which: LICS | 3.4 | 3.8 | 3.8 | 3.8 | 4.0 | 3.7 | (3.7) |
| LMICs | 5.2 | 7.3 | 8.7 | 9.0 | 9.8 | 8.3 | (8.4) |
| UMICs | 7.8 | 9.3 | 11.0 | 12.1 | 12.2 | 10.6 | (11.0) |
| | Total gross interest payments (including short-term) as percent of total exports of goods and services per cent | | | | | | |
| Non-OPEC, Non-OECD LDCs | 8 | 9 | 11 | 13 | 17 | 15 | (14) |
| 4 largest debtors: | | | | | | | |
| Brazil | 24 | 31 | 32 | 39 | 50 | 39 | (40) |
| Mexico | 20 | 21 | 20 | 26 | 31 | 31 | (35) |
| Argentina | 11 | 14 | 22 | 34 | 52 | 42 | (44) |
| South Korea | 6 | 8 | 12 | 14 | 14 | 14 | (13) |
| All others | 6 | 6 | 7 | 8 | 10 | 9 | (8) |

Tables A and B

a.  1984 figures are conjectural, based on projections in the OECD Economic Outlook 34 and on Secretariat projections regarding interest payments, based on interest costs and debt build-up in 1984, but making no allowance for payment of substantial amount of interest arrears now outstanding (see text).

b.  The annual nominal increases in medium- and long-term debt must be seen in conjunction with changes in short-term borrowing from banks and changes in reserves. They also have to be assessed with the statistical impact of exchange-rate changes in mind, as explained in the text. All 1984 figures in Tables A and B assume no change from November 1983 exchange rates.

c.  Reflects mainly fall in interest rates, but also some further net accumulation of interest arrears during 1983.

Notes: Current-account balances include ODA grants as a current receipt. (IMF Balance-of-Payments Statistics treat ODA grants as a capital receipt and therefore show larger current deficits for developing countries.)

Net borrowing from banks includes change in arrears of interest as a form of bank finance.

increasing in size over time. While action to keep outstanding debt stocks in place during a crisis is of course vital, as the events of the past eighteen months have shown, the real determinant of debt burdens and debt-carrying capacity is the interest bill.

As will be clear from the analysis, an assessment of the current position is impossible without constructing some picture of 1984. The Secretariat has taken the approach of calculating the increase in interest payments that may be expected in 1984, given assumptions about interest costs and growth in the debt stock. The resulting figure takes no account of payment during 1984 of the substantial arrears of interest which were outstanding at the end of 1983. To the extent that debt negotiations in 1984 are successful in dealing with arrears, actual interest payments will be higher and possibly much higher, by several billion dollars, than shown in Table B. This procedure has the merit, however, of giving some impression of the "underlying" dynamics of interest payments at current interest rates.

The main features in the build-up of debt problems also can be identified in Tables A and B. From a comparatively strong and stable position in 1978 (reflecting a largely complete adjustment to the first oil shock) the effect of the second oil shock on the balance-of-payments situation in 1979 and 1980 is apparent, while the interest-rate shock already shows a major impact in 1979, continuing until 1982. The sustained trade growth of non-members of the Organisation of Petroleum Exporting Countries (non-OPEC) and non-OECD developing countries until 1981 in the face of declining terms of trade and rising interest rates, remarkable in retrospect, was associated with escalating current-account deficits, rapid build-up of bank borrowing, both short- and long-term, and declining growth in reserves. An important background factor running through all the different sections of both Tables is the strong rise in the dollar from 1979 to the present (1).

What is of most significance in Tables A and B however, is the perspective provided on the adjustment process and particularly the developments involving interest costs and interest payments. The current-account adjustment in developing countries, while it may have been too long delayed, has been extremely rapid and now seems, with the up-turn in world trade, to be largely complete, at least in the aggregate. It is apparent that the associated fall in bank financing of non-OPEC, non-OECD developing countries from the 1981 peak was indeed of major proportions. However it is also obvious, on the one hand, that the 1981 level of bank financing was well beyond any sustainable level, and on the other hand, that the current level of bank financing far from represents a wholesale withdrawal by the banks from developing-country lending. It should be said that the real tests for both the external viability of debtor countries and the level of bank lending lie in the future, and will be determined by basic medium-term trends rather than the short-run exigencies which dominated in 1983.

A new phenomenon is the appearance of a significant deficit among the "low-absorbing" oil-producing developing countries. It appears that these countries are absorbing the fall in their oil revenues by running deficits rather than cutting import levels. The bank-financing projection for OPEC assumes that the "low-absorbers" will make some recourse to bank loans rather than finance all their deficits by liquidating financial or other assets.

The interest-payments scene depicted in Table B is the most striking aspect of the picture. It is clear that above all, the debt crisis has been about the inability of the major debtor countries to maintain the rapidly mounting interest payments in conditions characterised by high real interest rates, falling terms of trade and stagnating world trade, against a background of massive borrowing in the same period, and in some cases, significant capital flight.

Between end-1978 and end-1982, the rise in interest rates, together with the massive increase in borrowing over the same period, brought about a doubling of interest payments on medium- and long-term debt alone, from some $25 billion in 1979 to $50 billion in 1982 for all developing countries, and from $17 billion to $35 billion for non-OPEC, non-OECD developing countries (see Tables 2 and 10). In this situation the annual increases in the interest bill for medium- and long-term debt of developing countries were running, as shown in Tables A and B, at around $8 billion on average for all LDCs and $6 billion for non-OPEC, non-OECD countries. The bulk of these increases was of course accounted for by a few major borrowers paying the highest interest rates (see Table 22). The turn-around between 1982 and 1983 was thus of quite major proportions. The origin of this crucial break in the strong upward trend of interest payments was obviously the fall in interest rates on floating-interest debt, itself due to developments in United States (US) interest rates. The "saving" for non-OPEC, non-OECD developing countries in interest on medium- and long-term debt alone is estimated at some $7 billion in 1983 and, including the saving on short-term debt, may have reached a total of something like $9 billion. This major reduction in interest costs was particularly crucial for the major debt-problem countries. Indeed, in retrospect it seems difficult to imagine that their debt problems could have remained manageable in 1983 without the fall in floating interest rates.

As it was, interest arrears did build up in 1983, even more than in 1982, and the fall in interest payments recorded in 1983 reflects this accrual of interest arrears as well as the fall in interest rates. In 1984, it is estimated that clearing up outstanding arrears could entail a once-and-for-all addition to interest payments of several billions of dollars, and would result in some adjustment to the bank-financing and current-account projection shown in Table A.

The Secretariat's estimate is that, leaving aside any change in outstanding interest arrears between end-1983 and end-1984, the increase in the on-going (i.e. current) interest bill of all developing countries in 1984 would be in the $5 to $6 billion range, and for non-OPEC, non-OECD countries alone, around $4 billion. In the context of an improving world economy this, in aggregate, would represent a more stable situation in which the major debtor countries could make headway in combining adjustment with growth. However the manageability of interest payments, including arrears, can only be assessed in the context of individual debtor-country situations, which differ significantly from case to case.

Although the interest burdens look to be more stable, they are still heavy and interest payments must inevitably increase as the debt stock grows. Moreover, real interest rates, however measured, are still high. A further fall in world interest rates of one percentage point would save $2 billion for the major holders of floating-rate debt. A fall of two and one-half percentage points would thus provide savings equal to the estimated "underlying" increase in the LDC interest bill for 1984. This, in combination with the improved outlook for stable growth in the world economy that such a fall in interest rates would imply in the current context, would obviously be of very major assistance, even if not necessarily critical, to the adjustment efforts of the major debtor countries. Prospects of a further fall in interest rates would, in addition, greatly help the resolution, in the course of debt negotiations, of the problems posed for banks and some debtor countries by the existence of still large amounts of arrears. The arrears problem indicates that the debt situation will require further intensive management and cooperation in 1984, while the real interest-rate problem suggests that debt pressures on major developing countries will not soon vanish.

## 3. SITUATING THE DEBT PROBLEM

Three factors combined to produce the unforeseen number and scope of the debt problems now having to be managed and resolved:

-- The major transformations in the world economic environment over the 1979-83 period, deriving inter alia from the shift in policy priorities in major industrial countries towards medium-term stabilization and growth objectives, with largely unforeseen short-term consequences, including an extended recession and a sharp disinflation, which reflected the extent of contemporary economic and financial interdependence;

-- The "overborrowing" from banks by some developing countries and correspondingly, "overlending" by the banks to those developing countries following the second oil shock;

-- Unsustainable economic strategies in many developing countries, combined at times, especially in some of the major borrowing countries, with sudden policy lapses and chaotic financial developments.

Although it is not the purpose of this Survey to present a detailed account of the build-up to the problems of 1982-83, there are certain points, sometimes overlooked, which deserve rather to be kept in mind when consequences and lessons are being drawn from recent experience.

A. Developing-country debt problems are not all the same, and not all developing countries have debt problems.

The debt problems of some of the major Euro-currency market borrowers facing high interest costs are very different from those of the poorer developing countries holding mainly official or officially guaranteed debt and with low average interest costs. Moreover, within each of these two main groups of problem cases, there are major differences in the nature and causes of debt difficulties. Among the major problem countries the Mexican problem seems to have erupted particularly suddenly, as a result of the loss of control of fiscal policy in 1981 and the abrupt turn-around of oil market conditions. Argentina began from what was a relatively comfortable debt position in 1978, but the deterioration in its situation proceeded rapidly in the subsequent four years until 1982, when its interest/export ratio exceeded even that of Brazil. In both Mexico and Argentina, as with some other major problem countries, capital flight on a significant scale is understood to have occurred. In Brazil this was not so much the case until the later stages. The problem in Brazil seems to have been one of overly ambitious and insufficiently productive investment, inefficient and costly resource-allocation policies and a scale of foreign borrowing inherently out of line with an economy where exports are less than 10 per cent of GNP, leaving little room for manoeuvre in the face of a rise in interest rates or adverse trade conditions. In Chile, the promising economic recovery of the second half of the 1970s was aborted and reversed in a very short space of time by an untenable combination of exchange-rate and other policies. Generally speaking, in most of the debt-problem countries, whether relatively advanced or very poor, there is a background of major policy failures which, added to the sudden change in the world economy, produced unmanageable situations.

The list of developing countries which do not have significant debt problems in current circumstances is as impressive in its own way as the list of those that do. Such a list is headed by South Korea, with the fourth largest volume of debt outstanding. The comparative interest payments/exports ratios in Table B speak for themselves regarding the relative position of South Korea. In part this position is due to the favourable average interest costs (see Table 22), but this reflects to some degree South Korea's own credit standing. The basic reason for South Korea's success in using debt financing productively has been its economic strategy, together with a willingness to adjust at an early stage, as for example in 1980. Other major borrowing countries who have avoided problems because of strong economic management include Algeria (where a change in economic and financial strategy in the late 1970s was probably vital in averting a debt crisis in 1982), Indonesia (where adjustment in 1982-83 to falling oil revenues has been vigorous and India [where the bulk of external financing has been provided by Official Development Assistance (ODA) and early recourse was made to the IMF]. Malaysia, Thailand and Taiwan are other countries whose external economic position and credit rating have remained strong. The case of Turkey, which suffered a major debt crisis in 1979-80, shows what can be achieved in a relatively short space of time through well orchestrated international support based on rigorous adjustment measures and the adoption of medium-term policy orientations for a more productively functioning economy. Finally, China has a remarkable financial record in the last two years. Following retrenchment in 1980-81 from what appeared to be a too rapid expansion of imports, China has increased its foreign reserves from about $3 billion at end-1980 to an estimated $15 billion at end-1983 and is now a sizable net creditor.

The differences in country situations clearly owe much to country-specific factors, but there are also some key generic factors in play in debt situations. First, there is the problem of "contagion", whereby the Mexican crisis for example helps to generate the Brazilian crisis and the whole region falls under a shadow. Second, there are some basic economic policy orientations which tend to lead towards debt problems, while others tend to foster a high degree of resilience. The nature of these policy alternatives and their influence on debt situations are discussed in the section "Debt, Trade and Finance" later in this Chapter.

B. Bank lending to developing countries began to accelerate a whole decade prior to the second oil shock and was generally soundly based; the major mistakes following the second oil shock involved new factors.

It is commonly believed that the growth of bank lending to developing countries was a phenomenon associated essentially with "recycling" of oil surpluses following the first and second oil shocks. This is a mistaken interpretation of recent financial history. In fact, the major part of the expansion of the role of the banks in the financing of developing countries took place in the late 1960s and early 1970s, before the first oil shock. This phenomenon was associated with three major factors. First, there was the expansion of the Euro-markets and international bank lending in general in that period. Second, there was the improvement in the terms of trade of developing countries, culminating in the commodity-price boom of 1972-73. Third, there was the background of outstanding development progress in many developing countries and the emergence of a growing number of credit-worthy developing-country borrowers. The strong financial position of developing countries at the time of the first oil shock, together with the expansion of other forms of finance, enabled them to stablize their call on bank finance between 1974 and 1976. The next major expansion of bank financing then took place in 1977 and 1978, again before the second oil shock and in a context of strong improvement in terms of trade, signs of balance-of-payments adjustment and continuing strong growth potential, and a healthy build-up of foreign exchange reserves. Medium- and long-term bank lending to developing countries then declined in real terms in 1979 and 1980, but in 1980 this decline was more than offset by strong expansion of short-term bank finance. In 1981 another burst of medium- and long-term lending occurred while short-term lending continued unabated. This expansion of both short- and long-term lending continued until mid-1982, setting the scene for the crisis which "suddenly" emerged afterwards.

This background can be traced in Tables C and D in Chapter II, particularly in Table D, which provides a "real-terms" series of financial flows to developing countries (2).

A correct understanding of the history seems important if a considered and more widely agreed view of the future role of bank lending is to evolve. The major errors in the post-1978 period can be briefly characterised. As is evident in Tables A and B, the expansion of bank lending, short- and long-term, after 1978 took place in a context of escalating interest rates on floating-rate debt and deteriorating terms of trade. Furthermore, as indicated above, economic strategies and policies in some major borrowing countries were quite clearly at odds with the productive use of such volumes of foreign borrowing. In mitigation, it is also true that the extent and duration of the international recession were not foreseen and the significance of the increase in real interest rates was also not widely appreciated. The generally satisfactory record of bank lending to developing countries in the 1970s and its relatively very important contribution to bank profits no doubt also contributed to overconfidence.

At the same time, the evidence suggests that insufficient control was exercised over bank exposure to a number of countries, with a large amount of short-term lending simply "happening" rather than being part of bank policies. Insufficient attention to the qualitative dimensions of the expansion of Euro-market activity, and the inter-bank market in particular, on the part of both participants and supervisors, seems in retrospect at least, to be

16

implied. The evidence also suggests that country-risk assessments did not sufficiently focus on the overall coherence of economic strategies and economic policies in the major borrowing countries as fundamental determinants of debt-servicing capacity in developing countries. These failures are perhaps the most important lessons for the future, in respect of bank lending to developing countries.


C. Disinflation and other recent transformations in the world economy have changed the economics of debt financing and produced a pattern of international balances which differs radically from the experience in the 1970s.

The sharp reversal in the prevailing world economic conditions which took place at the turn of the decade -- from an inflationary to a disinflationary environment -- has had major consequences for the developing countries and major implications for resource-transfer processes. Disinflation has had its classic effects on debt burdens, commodity prices and borrowing costs. If, as indeed intended, the reduction in world inflation proves lasting and sets the scene for sustained growth in the world economy, then the current intense difficulties posed for many developing (and developed) countries will begin to ease. However, if the current situation were to develop beyond being a healthy, if drastic, readjustment of economic policies among the major countries and came to constitute a constellation of key exchange rates, real interest rates and commodity prices that was unhelpful to growth, international adjustment and open trade, the consequences would be extremely damaging and current debt and financing problems would quickly escalate.

Obviously, the present juncture is a critical one. New and curious situations are a feature of the current international economic scene. Governments in OECD Member countries have found themselves funding large cyclical deficits at high real interest rates, and in some countries large structural deficits are continuing through the recovery period. As in the case of the large developing-country debtors, these governments are facing an inexorably increasing interest bill, which threatens to reduce their budgetary flexibility in the future. On the international scene, the seemingly perverse situation has emerged where the two largest net creditors -- the United States and the Gulf oil-producing states -- are currently large importers of capital. Their combined current-account deficits in 1984 are expected to reach over $100 billion. Even allowing for an important degree of overstatement in this amount, which cannot however be assessed because it is not currently possible to allocate the world current-account discrepancy, it represents a very significant absorption of foreign savings. It is fair to say that the major transfers of current real savings are presently taking place among the rich countries -- in particular from Japan to other OECD Members, principally the United States.

This new pattern of international balances may be only transitional and, if it provides the route back to stable world economic growth, it in fact will help the developing countries to restore their trade balances and financial positions. But the persistence of such a pattern for too long would, as the current situation on international financial markets indicates, produce a prolonged squeeze in developing countries relying on non-concessional finance. Considering their development situation, the Gulf countries may well need to run sizable deficits for some time and they can afford to do so. The case of the United States is different, in both its domestic and international dimensions. At the present time, international financial flows, interest rates and the strength of the dollar reflect the capital-importing needs of the United States resulting from divergent trends in that country between investment and savings. (It should be noted that the "savings gap" in the United States is a result not only of the budget deficit, but stems also from the household savings rate, which should recover somewhat in 1984 but remains historically low.) (3)

An essential part of finding the way out of current developing-country debt problems will therefore be to achieve a pattern of savings-investment balances and international capital flows which is more appropriate and more sustainable. The developing countries have enormous capital needs for physical and human infrastructure and an economic potential to match. The challenge ahead is for both developed and developing countries to work towards policies in which capital flows from the rich countries to the advancing countries at moderate real interest rates through an appropriate mix of market processes and official financing mechanisms. On the side of the developed countries this means reducing the claims of the public sector on total savings and stimulating household savings. In the developing countries, policies need to ensure that resource allocation and use is efficient, that domestic savings are adequate, that the economic climate is attractive to foreign investors and that domestic capital is encouraged to stay in the country rather than be placed abroad.


## 4. SOME ANALYTICAL AND POLICY ISSUES


### A. Capital Inflows, Debt and Development

The debt crisis, coming after a decade or more of marked growth in resource flows to developing countries, has refocused attention on the underlying conditions and concepts of the transfer process. Whether and to what extent a capital inflow enhances economic development can only be judged in a broad macro-economic perspective. Efficient resource-allocation policies are crucial (as has become even clearer from the last decade's policy experiences), but equally critical are the maintenance and growth of domestic savings, the efficiency of the governmental and commercial infrastructure, and the stability of the social and political framework.

Much of the post-war thinking about development centered on the problem of the "savings gap" and the consequent need for large capital inflows to developing countries. An old concept, the "net financial-transfer" concept, has recently reappeared in the debate. In terms of this concept, "net financial transfers" are calculated by starting with gross capital inflows and deducting amortization and interest payments. The fact which has caught attention in recent months is that whereas net capital inflows exceeded net interest payments, and by a very considerable margin, in the 1970s, in 1983 this relationship turned around for some large debtors, with interest payments exceeding net capital inflows. In terms of the "net financial-transfer" concept, an inflow of finance became an outflow of finance. This of course holds only on an aggregate basis because the debt-service payments of the major borrowing countries dominate the picture. For the many developing countries relying on concessional finance (see Chapter II), the equation looks entirely different.

It is certainly true that major developing-country borrowers have been caught in a squeeze as bank lending has returned to more sustainable levels and real-interest burdens have risen, but the "net financial-transfer" concept is essentially erroneous. As a matter of definition, the transfer of resources to developing countries, i.e. their imports of foreign savings, is measured by nothing other than the current-account deficit in their balance of payments. (In practice, there is a measurement problem connected with the statistical discrepancy in the global current-account balance, but only a very small share of this is thought to affect the current balance of non-oil developing countries. Inflation, through its impact on interest rates and the rate of real amortization of debt stocks, also distorts the relationship between the current account and the capital account.) The current deficit, in turn, is matched by the net inflow of capital (gross flows less repayments), and not by the so-called net transfer (net capital inflow less interest payments). As long as a country records a significant current-account deficit, it has a positive transfer of resources -- whatever the amount of interest payments recorded in its current account. Developing countries should normally run current-account deficits, financed by net imports of capital; and over time the growing volume of interest payments may require a growing trade surplus, i.e. the structure of the current account may need to adjust. The real question is whether external and internal factors are such that this evolution is part of well-functioning growth process or whether it reflects unsustainable domestic trends and policies and a malfunctioning of the international economy. It is disturbing therefore that the "net financial-transfer" concept, which confuses the capital and current accounts, is again enjoying some currency, while the real policy implications of the capital-transfer process are in danger of not being properly comprehended, either in capital-exporting countries or capital-importing countries.

When the capital-transfer process works effectively, higher output and income growth provide the means whereby interest payments can be met, leaving a net income gain for the capital-importing country or at least allowing consumption increases to be shared more evenly between present and future generations, while the economic structure adjusts progressively to produce a growing external debt-servicing capacity. This analysis holds, whether the imported capital comes in the form of debt finance or equity finance (direct foreign investment), although the external servicing requirments of the latter are of a different character. When the process does not work effectively because of inappropriate policies or major distortions in the domestic or international economy, the result is an income loss which reduces present or prospective consumption levels and may provoke an eventual balance-of-payments crisis.

In fact, during the 1970s, the capital-transfer process worked rather well in a considerable number of cases, marginally well in some and poorly in others, the results depending on how individual developing countries performed in terms of the policy and other factors cited at the outset of this Section. A generally favourable feature was the strong rise in savings and investment rates in many developing countries through the 1960s and 1970s. Developing countries have been (over the last decade) commonly saving and investing higher proportions of their gross domestic product than developed countries and producing higher absolute and per capita income growth. The main exceptions here have been the least developed countries (LLDCs), where indeed, especially in Africa, development progress has been extremely disappointing, per capita incomes declining and aid dependence increasing. But there have been other exceptions also, and very often a fall in domestic savings and investment has been one of the factors behind the emergence of debt problems. Not uncommonly the cause has been a widening of public sector deficits, financed by foreign borrowing, at the same time as public sector institutions have performed poorly and resource-allocation policies generally have deteriorated.

It ought to be said that some smaller OECD capital-importing countries have borrowed significant amounts of foreign capital over the last decade while their domestic savings, investment and growth performance have all been declining. While none of these countries is likely to suffer a debt crisis as such, there is no doubt that their debt burdens are putting pressure on budgets and external balances.

The recent change in the relationship between net capital inflows and interest payments does however have a real significance, although not of the kind implied by the "net financial-transfer" concept. In the mid-1970s, real interest rates were negative and inflation brought about a situation where debt stocks were falling in real terms. (High nominal interest rates represented a premature repayment of principal.) These conditions justified and made possible high rates of nominal net capital imports, while interest payments presented little problem. Present conditions are exactly the reverse. High real interest rates and low inflation have increased debt burdens. Large new net borrowing in these circumstances is neither possible nor economically rational. Interest payments on the now much higher debt stocks are, as shown above, very significant. Thus the current situation of high real interest rates and apparently low growth in debt stocks is the mirror image of the earlier period of negative real interest rates and high rates of nominal debt accumulation.

The policy challenge is not to get back to any particular level of "net financial transfer", but rather to ensure, in a broad sense, that the capital-transfer process is working effectively. More moderate real interest rates, sustainable growth in the world economy and the preservation of stable but responsive financial markets and official financing mechanisms are the main requirements on the international front. On the domestic front, the central need is for economic policies which attract and effectively use capital inflows in appropriate forms and at the lowest possible premiums above market rates. In many debt-problem countries such policies would also help to secure the return of domestic capital lost through capital flight.

If the capital-transfer process is put back into better working order by the adoption of improved domestic and international policies, the result may or may not be a positive "net financial transfer" but it will certainly assist the development process in the capital-importing countries, raising incomes there and in the capital-exporting countries.

B. The Management of Debt Problems

Of the 157 countries and territories covered in this Survey, some 35 were involved, in 1983, in discussions with creditor groups regarding delays or non-payment of debt service. More significantly, these 35 countries represented around one-half of the total number of countries with outstanding debt of more than $1 billion in 1983. Sixteen rescheduling agreements were

20

concluded with private creditor groups and 15 with official creditor groups by a total of 20 countries. These agreements covered, in many cases, amounts due between 1982 and 1984. (It is not necessary or appropriate here to describe in any detail the processes and practices of debt rescheduling; this subject has been comprehensively covered in a recent IMF publication.) (4). The current extent of debt-rescheduling and refinancing operations, together with the major transitions in the world economy and relative creditor/debtor positions described earlier, strongly suggests that formal debt negotiations are likely to become a more important and permanent part of international financial co-operation. While generalised debt-relief mechanisms have, for good reasons, been rejected as a way through the current and possible future difficulties, a definite evolution seems now to be taking place towards an integrated and broadly agreed set of approaches to handling debt problems individually and to strengthening the ability of the financial system to contain and respond to the general systemic risks. The evolution has in part been underway for some time, starting with the banking crises of the early 1970s. Rather than ever arriving at a settled "system", however, what is happening may best be described as a process of continuous evolution and adaptation. The elements include the various aspects of bank supervision and prudential management; IMF quota increases and the enlargement and recasting of the General Agreement to Borrow; World Bank structural adjustment lending and co-financing innovations; ad hoc collective aid efforts in low-income debtor countries; and of course the private and public sector debt-reorganisation "Clubs".

This may all be seen as a new phase in the continuing evolution of the post-World War II international financial system -- a system which has now become pluralistic, global and integrated, with a critical degree of inter-dependence between the official sector and the private sector and between major borrowers and major lenders. As events have shown, this system is complex, dynamic (driven simultaneously by competition and by regulatory factors) and highly sensitive to new opportunities and unforeseen shocks alike.

A critical but subtle balance is required between a reasonable degree of stability and a reasonable degree of risk, if the financial system is to function effectively. Current efforts to find ways of dealing with the debt problems of developing countries represent essentially a search for such a balance. It is important, when seeking to stabilize the situation, that no major party, whether borrower or lender, government or private, should be able to take everything for granted. This implies that residual elements of risk and uncertainty are not only likely, but necessary features of the system. They provide the pressures required to bring about responsible policies and practices on the part of both lenders and borrowers.

In the circumstances of the last eighteen months, exceptional actions have been essential on all sides. The initiative of the IMF in stipulating new bank-lending requirements as part of rescue packages prevented financial collapses in which the banks would have lost substantial amounts of their assets and large fractions, or even all, of their own capital. Major creditor countries in conjunction with the BIS have provided critical bridging finance. IMF operations have reached an historic peak. The large decline in interest rates and the often sweeping cuts in imports by debtor countries were also crucial but non-repeatable events.

The key question now is how the future can be managed towards a more stable, self-sustaining financial situation. As has been implied earlier, private bank finance has a definite role to play in developing-country financing and probably cannot fall below a certain minimum. However banks, individually and collectively, will have to see their role and interests in a broader perspective than in the past. Their ability to avoid losses and cultivate profitable business will depend on their becoming investors in country situations as a whole, including the social and institutional framework, rather than simply providers of project finance or trade finance, essential as these are. It is now abundantly clear that the banks cannot be assured of repayment and interest unless the borrowing country is on a sound development track. Recent developments suggest that banks and borrowing countries are able to meet on this common ground. Debt-reorganisation conditions, interest spreads, fees and new maturities may best be determined in this longer term perspective with the aim of securing social, political and financial viability as a whole.

## C. Debt, Trade and Finance

It is appropriate to conclude this overview by looking at the most general and, in a basic sense, most important of the lessons for economic policy and international co-operation that the debt crisis has revealed. Events in 1983 brought home the close linkages between trade and finance in the form of a concentrated, dramatic downward spiral as lenders and debtors simultaneously contracted financial and trade flows. While much effort had to be quickly focused on the particular actors involved in this situation, the real lessons for the trade and finance systems and relations between debtors and creditors are much wider.

The essential message is that both lending and borrowing countries must direct their efforts to ensuring that conditions are right for the expansion of mutually beneficial trade, and for the efficient allocation of world savings to investment where the returns are highest. Financial and trade flows generated in that kind of policy environment will lead to the gradual disappearance of current debt problems, and new debt crises will be less likely. It follows directly from this view that it would be wrong to attempt to relate trade policies directly to the debt of particular countries; rather, these policies must be seen in relation to the overall flow of funds between debtor and creditor countries, now and in the future. Similarly, the aim cannot be to use the financial leverage that exists vis-à-vis the indebted countries to extract "concessions" in the trade or investment area. Rather, the greater sense of realism that the debt crisis has engendered (both in debtor countries and in creditor countries) should be used to engage in a broader dialogue on the policies needed to bring back satisfactory flows of savings, and their efficient deployment, to the benefit of both lenders and borrowers.

As regards trade, the essential point to emerge from recent experience is that policies aiming to encourage the development of internationally competitive industries, through market-oriented domestic policies and more liberal trade policies, have served not only the interests of the world economy but also the self-interest of countries that move in this direction. It is not accidental, for instance, that those developing countries which have pursued market-oriented policies to make themselves competitive and flexible have come through the debt crisis in a relatively satisfactory way. Many of them have moved in this direction unilaterally, with policies based on their own self-interest rather than externally applied disciplines.

Outward-looking approaches are risky for developing countries to maintain, however, without secure markets for their goods and a conviction of expanding trade opportunities in areas where they have comparative advantage. The industrial countries therefore also have important obligations: to avoid arbitrary and discriminatory use of safeguard actions -- which tend to come into force just where developing countries are most successful in competing; to strengthen the pace of their own structural adjustment out of areas of declining comparative advantage; and to refrain from using subsidies that unfairly deny markets to producers in developing countries. This having been said, it is important to note that countries which have pursued outward-looking approaches have generally fared better during the recent turmoil than those that have pursued a more insulated strategy. Apparently, the greater resiliency and dynamism that come from competition in world markets and the adoption of policies oriented towards international competition bring to a country benefits that outweigh the costs of being more exposed to fluctuations in demand abroad.

In the field of investment, policies which are conducive to improving the allocation of resources domestically and internationally will create new and more viable investment opportunities. The world economy can begin to reap benefits from better structural and trade policies even in the fairly short run because policies that offer more secure trade in the future create incentives for investment today.

The key element is a country's domestic policy environment. There is a strong complementarity between the policies necessary to strengthen the trade environment and those that promote investment, whether funded domestically or from abroad. Developing countries that move toward greater integration into international markets on a more diversified basis can expect to gain increasing access to both equity and debt finance. Their prospects of rising exports will enhance the capacity to service both their existing debt and the new credit that growth demands.

Trade and finance policies along these lines need of course to be supported by appropriate monetary and fiscal policies and, as noted earlier, by international policy co-operation designed to secure a set of key exchange rates and interest rates conducive to growth, adjustment and open trade. In turn, trade and finance policies have their own input to make in creating satisfactory macro-economic and adjustment performance.

While it is inevitable that short-term ad hoc approaches will continue to play a role in resolving current debt problems, it should be clear that their contribution to a fundamental solution is limited. The need is also for long-term systemic policies which improve the functioning of the world economy in the interest of securing a sustainable worldwide recovery. Active dialogue and initiatives for international co-operation between developed and developing countries are essential -- and the focus must be on these medium-term principles if the debt problem is to be handled effectively and positively rather than ineffectively and with damage to the longer-term performance of the world economy.

# 5. DEBT STATISTICS AND THE DEBT SITUATION

Continuing and sustainable inflows of capital to developing countries and, as a consequence, continued but sustainable accumulation of debt is essential to the development process and to the health and security of the world economy in general. It is clear that important rearrangements of the financial and economic patterns which evolved in the last decade or so are now taking place. In this context a crucial and shared policy concern must be to ensure that the new patterns which emerge allow, and enable, the dynamic relationship between capital flows, debt accumulation and development to operate in a positive, rather than in a negative mode.

This is of course a question of economic policy and economic management in both developed and developing countries. But improved and more timely information on the evolving financial flows and structures has an important contribution to make to policy discussions and analyses. The OECD is actively co-operating to this end with other agencies concerned, such as the World Bank, the BIS and the IMF. Agreement has been reached with the BIS on new procedures which will enable the guaranteed export-credit lending of commercial banks to non-BIS borrowers, including the developing countries, to be identified at six-monthly intervals. This clearly policy-relevant figure has hitherto been estimated by the OECD Secretariat alone in the context of this annual Survey. The resulting six-monthly statistical report will not only allow banks' guaranteed trade-related claims to be separated from their other claims, it will also inter alia show the evolution of total trade-related lending, whether provided through banks as "financial trade credits" or through non-banks in the form of "supplier credits". The new series will be derived by combining data in existing BIS and OECD reporting systems using new methodology. At this stage there will be no information on debt service. Further development of the new series and its relationship to this annual Survey are presently under consideration.

There is little doubt that there is still further scope for co-operation of this kind among the agencies concerned and their member countries to reduce reporting lags, harmonize concepts and definitions and generally to ensure that debt and related financial statistics are comprehensive, comprehensible and relevant in a period when financial instruments and institutions as well as the patterns and structures of the world economy are changing rapidly.

24

## Chapter II

## FINANCIAL FLOWS TO DEVELOPING COUNTRIES AND THE INTERPRETATION OF AGGREGATE DEBT STATISTICS

### 1. FINANCIAL FLOWS, 1970-82

It is important, when assessing the debt aggregates, to keep in mind that they are the outcome of the historical volume and pattern of financial flows to developing countries and that they are the sum not of all these flows, but only of the net flows of debt-creating forms of finance. The four Tables presented in this Chapter, taken from the 1983 Development Assistance Committee (DAC) Chairman's Report, provide some perspectives on the size and character of the financial flows (5).

The organising concepts for the various categories of financial flow and debt and for the country groups are those developed in the framework of the Development Assistance Committee and therefore reflect a development-finance and policy perspective (6). An important concept is that of "financial-resource transfers", defined as financial flows with an original maturity of one year or more, the implicit assumption being that original maturities of less than one year indicate borrowing for working balances of one kind or another.

Short-term bank lending is not, by this definition, included in the aggregates presented in the Tables. However, a significant amount of short-term lending to a number of developing countries occurred from the late 1970s, which was in practice a more permanent accumulation of debt. One of the elements in the debt-restructuring operations of the past year has been the transformation of part of such lending into longer term lending. The third chapter in this Survey, "Salient Trends and Facts", contains some Secretariat estimates and comments on this phenomenon, which has played a significant role in recent major debt problems.

Also excluded from the "financial-resource transfer" concept is IMF lending, on the grounds that it is essentially a smoothing operation, using revolving funds, rather than a permanent transfer which will add to the normal secular increase in the stock of outstanding liabilities.

Finally, there are two recognised forms of "financial-resource flow" which do not create "debt". These are first, Official Development Assistance grants, and second, foreign direct investment, which creates a stock of foreign-owned equity rather than foreign-owned debt and which has no fixed servicing obligations attached.

Tables C and D (III-1 and III-2 in the Chairman's Report) show the evolution of the full range of financial flows to developing countries over the period 1970-82, including net IMF purchase and for later years, estimated short-term bank lending. Of the total net financial-resource receipts of over $90 billion in 1982, which constitute "financial-resource transfers" as defined previously, about one-third were "non-debt-creating", i.e. the direct investment flows plus the approximately 55 per cent of ODA from all sources that was disbursed in the form of outright grants. (The proportion of grant ODA in the total ODA from DAC countries alone was much higher at about 75 per cent.)

In Table E (III-3), a more summary picture of the changing structure of financial flows in the 1970-82 period is presented. This period can be regarded as a particular episode in the history of developing-country financing. The beginning of the 1970s witnessed the rapid expansion of international bank lending to developing countries (the actual take-off of this expansion, in fact, occurred in the mid- to late 1960s) and a major lift in the rate of increase of ODA flows in real terms compared with the 1960s. The multilateral development financing institutions also moved into a growth phase in both concessional and non-concessional lending. OPEC aid entered the picture in a major way in the mid-1970s and has remained an important though declining (in real terms) flow.

In summary, the decade of the 1970s witnessed a very major expansion of financial transfers to developing countries with significant changes in the pattern of transfers. (The switch in the proportions of private flows provided by bank lending and foreign direct investment, respectively, deserves special note.) This all took place in a particular historical context, marked by: considerable evolution in financial institutions and mechanisms, large payment imbalances associated with the oil shocks, the relative resilience of developing-country growth, and persisting world inflation. This historical episode may now be seen to have reached a culmination in the early 1980s, with 1982 marking the end of an era and the beginning of a phase in which new problems and conditions presented major and immediate challenges.

A snapshot of the developing-country financing scene at the end of this period already described is contained in Table F (III-4) on the concessional/non-concessional financing mix of developing countries. This Table organises developing countries into five categories (three principal categories, two with sub-categories) according to the proportions of ODA in their total receipts of medium- and long-term financial resources. The scale runs from 90 per cent or more ODA to 10 per cent or less ODA in total receipts. India and China are excluded from these categories and shown separately since, as is clear from the Table, their massive population size combined with their relatively low involvement in external financing make them very much cases apart.

The main features emerging from this analysis may be thus summarised:

-- The 102 ODA-reliant and middle-position countries, with 14 per cent of developing-country GNP and 22 per cent of developing-country population, receive 74 per cent of all ODA;

Table C

TOTAL NET RESOURCE RECEIPTS OF DEVELOPING COUNTRIES FROM ALL SOURCES, 1970-82 -- CURRENT PRICES

$ billion at current prices

| | 1970 | 1971 | 1972 | 1973 | 1974 | 1975 | 1976 | 1977 | 1978 | 1979 | 1980 | 1981 | 1982 |
|---|---|---|---|---|---|---|---|---|---|---|---|---|---|
| 1. Official Development Assistance | 8.23 | 9.14 | 9.84 | 12.68 | 16.50 | 20.95 | 20.35 | 20.98 | 28.10 | 31.93 | 37.33 | 36.63 | 34.24 |
| A. Bilateral | 7.16 | 7.84 | 8.46 | 10.72 | 13.68 | 17.11 | 16.49 | 16.15 | 22.09 | 25.69 | 29.54 | 28.70 | 26.79 |
| DAC countries | 5.66 | 6.31 | 6.61 | 7.08 | 8.23 | 9.79 | 9.50 | 10.08 | 13.12 | 16.33 | 18.11 | 18.28 | 18.53 |
| OPEC countries | 0.39 | 0.44 | 0.66 | 2.03 | 4.15 | 5.68 | 5.17 | 4.28 | 6.90 | 6.96 | 8.73 | 7.61 | 5.51 |
| CMEA and other donors | 1.11 | 1.09 | 1.19 | 1.61 | 1.30 | 1.64 | 1.81 | 1.79 | 2.07 | 2.40 | 2.70 | 2.81 | 2.75 |
| B. Multilateral agencies | 1.07 | 1.30 | 1.38 | 1.96 | 2.82 | 3.84 | 3.87 | 4.83 | 6.01 | 6.24 | 7.79 | 7.93 | 7.45 |
| 2. Grants by private voluntary agencies | 0.86 | 0.91 | 1.04 | 1.37 | 1.22 | 1.34 | 1.35 | 1.49 | 1.65 | 1.95 | 2.31 | 2.02 | 2.31 |
| 3. Non-concessional flows (a) | 10.95 | 11.83 | 13.30 | 19.86 | 19.81 | 34.31 | 34.89 | 44.56 | 57.91 | 57.72 | 56.41 | 69.27 | 56.63 |
| A. Official or officially supported | 3.96 | 4.92 | 3.75 | 4.86 | 7.64 | 10.53 | 12.66 | 15.74 | 19.21 | 18.72 | 22.49 | 22.14 | 22.63 |
| Private export credits (DAC) | 2.09 | 2.71 | 1.44 | 1.16 | 2.40 | 4.42 | 6.74 | 8.84 | 9.70 | 8.85 | 11.12 | 11.33 | (9.00) |
| Official export credits (DAC) | 0.59 | 0.72 | 0.74 | 1.13 | 0.80 | 1.20 | 1.39 | 1.44 | 2.22 | 1.73 | 2.46 | 2.01 | (2.45) |
| Multilateral | 0.71 | 0.92 | 1.01 | 1.31 | 1.81 | 2.53 | 2.54 | 2.69 | 3.09 | 4.16 | 4.85 | 5.68 | (6.68) |
| Other official and private flows (DAC) | 0.25 | 0.28 | 0.45 | 1.02 | 0.83 | 0.75 | 0.80 | 0.63 | 1.36 | 1.14 | 2.24 | 1.96 | (3.00) |
| Other donors (b) | 0.32 | 0.29 | 0.11 | 0.24 | 1.80 | 1.63 | 1.19 | 2.14 | 2.84 | 2.84 | 1.82 | 1.16 | (1.50) |
| B. Private | 6.99 | 6.91 | 9.55 | 15.00 | 12.17 | 23.78 | 22.23 | 28.82 | 38.70 | 39.00 | 33.92 | 47.13 | 34.00 |
| Direct investment | 3.69 | 3.31 | 4.23 | 4.72 | 1.89 | 11.36 | 8.31 | 9.82 | 11.59 | 13.42 | 10.54 | 16.13 | (11.00) |
| Bank sector (a) | 3.00 | 3.30 | 4.80 | 9.70 | 10.00 | 12.00 | 12.70 | 15.80 | 23.20 | 24.90 | 22.00 | 29.00 | 21.00 |
| Bond lending | 0.30 | 0.30 | 0.52 | 0.58 | 0.28 | 0.42 | 1.22 | 3.20 | 3.91 | 0.68 | 1.38 | 2.00 | 2.00 |
| Total Receipts (1 + 2 + 3) | 20.04 | 21.88 | 24.18 | 33.91 | 37.53 | 56.60 | 56.59 | 67.03 | 87.66 | 91.60 | 96.05 | 107.92 | 93.18 |
| Memorandum items: | | | | | | | | | | | | | |
| Short-term bank lending | .. | .. | .. | .. | .. | .. | .. | 16.00 | 17.00 | 16.00 | 26.00 | 25.00 | 17.00 |
| IMF purchases, net (c) | 0.34 | 0.05 | 0.30 | 0.36 | 1.74 | 3.24 | 2.98 | -0.43 | -0.85 | 0.52 | 2.61 | 6.40 | 6.70 |

a. Excluding bond lending and export credits extended by banks which are included under private export credits. Including loans by branches of OECD banks located in offshore centres, and for 1980, 1981 and 1982 participations of non-OECD banks in international syndicates.

b. Other official flows from OPEC countries, Ireland, Luxembourg, Spain, Yugoslavia, India, Israel and China.

c. All purchases minus repayments including reserve tranches but excluding loans by the IMF Trust Fund included under multilateral ODA above.

Note: Figures concerning non-DAC Member countries are based as far as possible on information released by donor countries and international organisations, and completed by OECD Secretariat estimates based on other published and unpublished sources. They may therefore not comply in all respects with the norms and criteria used by DAC Members in their statistical reports made directly to the OECD Secretariat.

Table D

TOTAL NET RESOURCE RECEIPTS OF DEVELOPING COUNTRIES FROM ALL SOURCES, 1970-82 -- CONSTANT PRICES

$ billion (1981 prices)

| | 1970 | 1971 | 1972 | 1973 | 1974 | 1975 | 1976 | 1977 | 1978 | 1979 | 1980 | 1981 | 1982 |
|---|---|---|---|---|---|---|---|---|---|---|---|---|---|
| 1. Official Development Assistance | 21.30 | 22.18 | 21.48 | 24.72 | 29.10 | 32.03 | 30.19 | 28.82 | 33.53 | 33.79 | 36.21 | 36.62 | 34.97 |
| A. Bilateral | 18.45 | 19.03 | 18.47 | 20.90 | 24.13 | 26.16 | 24.45 | 22.18 | 26.36 | 27.19 | 28.65 | 28.70 | 27.37 |
| DAC countries | 14.58 | 15.31 | 14.43 | 13.80 | 14.51 | 14.97 | 14.09 | 13.85 | 15.66 | 17.28 | 17.56 | 18.28 | 18.93 |
| OPEC countries | 1.00 | 1.07 | 1.44 | 3.96 | 7.32 | 8.69 | 7.67 | 5.88 | 8.23 | 7.36 | 8.47 | 7.61 | 5.63 |
| CMEA and other donors | 2.86 | 2.65 | 2.60 | 3.14 | 2.29 | 2.51 | 2.69 | 2.46 | 2.47 | 2.54 | 2.62 | 2.81 | 2.81 |
| B. Multilateral agencies | 2.86 | 3.16 | 3.01 | 3.82 | 4.97 | 5.87 | 5.74 | 6.63 | 7.17 | 6.60 | 7.56 | 7.93 | (7.61) |
| 2. Grants by private voluntary agencies | 2.22 | 2.21 | 2.27 | 2.67 | 2.15 | 2.05 | 2.00 | 2.04 | 1.97 | 2.06 | 2.24 | 2.02 | 2.36 |
| 3. Non-concessional flows (a) | 28.22 | 28.71 | 29.04 | 38.71 | 34.94 | 52.46 | 51.77 | 61.21 | 69.11 | 61.08 | 54.71 | 69.27 | (57.84) |
| A. Official or officially supported | 10.20 | 11.94 | 8.19 | 9.47 | 13.47 | 16.10 | 18.78 | 21.62 | 22.92 | 19.81 | 21.81 | 22.14 | 23.12 |
| Private export credits (DAC) | 5.39 | 6.58 | 3.14 | 2.26 | 4.23 | 6.76 | 10.00 | 12.14 | 11.58 | 9.37 | 10.79 | 11.33 | (9.19) |
| Official Export Credits (DAC) | 1.52 | 1.75 | 1.62 | 2.20 | 1.41 | 1.83 | 2.06 | 1.98 | 2.65 | 1.83 | 2.39 | 2.01 | (2.50) |
| Multilateral | 1.83 | 2.23 | 2.21 | 2.55 | 3.19 | 3.87 | 3.77 | 3.70 | 3.68 | 4.40 | 4.70 | 5.68 | 6.82 |
| Other official and private flows (DAC) | 0.64 | 0.68 | 0.98 | 1.99 | 1.46 | 1.15 | 1.19 | 0.86 | 1.62 | 1.21 | 2.17 | 1.96 | (3.07) |
| Other donors (b) | 0.82 | 0.70 | 0.24 | 0.47 | 3.18 | 2.49 | 1.76 | 2.94 | 3.39 | 3.01 | 1.77 | 1.16 | (1.53) |
| B. Private | 18.01 | 16.77 | 20.86 | 29.24 | 21.46 | 36.36 | 32.98 | 39.59 | 46.18 | 41.27 | 32.90 | 47.13 | 34.73 |
| Direct investment | 9.51 | 8.03 | 9.24 | 9.20 | 3.33 | 17.37 | 12.33 | 13.49 | 13.83 | 14.20 | 10.22 | 16.13 | (11.24) |
| Bank sector (a) | 7.73 | 8.01 | 10.48 | 18.91 | 17.64 | 18.35 | 18.84 | 21.70 | 27.68 | 26.35 | 21.34 | 29.00 | (21.45) |
| Bond lending | 0.77 | 0.73 | 1.14 | 1.13 | 0.49 | 0.64 | 1.81 | 4.40 | 4.67 | 0.72 | 1.34 | 2.00 | 2.04 |
| Total Receipts (1 + 2 + 3) | 51.75 | 53.11 | 52.79 | 66.10 | 66.19 | 86.54 | 83.96 | 92.07 | 104.61 | 96.93 | 93.16 | 107.92 | 95.18 |
| Memorandum items: | | | | | | | | | | | | | |
| Short-term bank lending | .. | .. | .. | .. | .. | .. | .. | 21.98 | 20.29 | 16.93 | 25.22 | 25.00 | 17.36 |
| IMF purchases, net (c) | 0.88 | 0.12 | 0.66 | 0.70 | 3.07 | 4.95 | 4.42 | -0.59 | -1.01 | 0.55 | 2.53 | 6.40 | 6.86 |
| GNP deflator (1981 = 100) | 38.8 | 41.2 | 45.8 | 51.3 | 56.7 | 65.4 | 67.4 | 72.8 | 83.8 | 94.5 | 103.1 | 100.0 | 97.9 |

a. Excluding bond lending and export credits extended by banks which are included under private export credits. Including loans by branches of OECD banks located in offshore centres, and for 1980, 1981 and 1982 participations of non-OECD banks in international syndicates.

b. Other official flows from OPEC countries, Ireland, Luxembourg, Spain, Yugoslavia, India, Israel and China.

c. All purchases minus repayments including reserve tranches but excluding loans by the IMF Trust Fund included under multilateral ODA above.

Note: Figures concerning non-DAC Member countries are based as far as possible on information released by donor countries and international organisations, and completed by OECD Secretariat estimates based on other published and unpublished sources. They may therefore not comply in all respects with the norms and criteria used by DAC Members in their statistical reports made directly to the OECD Secretariat.

## Table E

### COMPONENTS IN THE INCREASE IN RESOURCE TRANSFERS OF DEVELOPING COUNTRIES FROM ALL SOURCES, 1970-82

Grants, direct investment of other official and private financial flows
with maturities of more than one year
(real terms: 1981 prices and exchange rates)

| | 1970 $ billion | 1970 % of total | 1982 $ billion | 1982 % of total | Increase $ billion | Increase % of total | Increase in each component % |
|---|---|---|---|---|---|---|---|
| 1. ODA | 21 | 41 | 35 | 36 | 14 | 30 | 67 |
|     DAC (bilateral) | 15 | 29 | 18 | 18 | 3 | 6 | 20 |
|     OPEC (bilateral) | 1 | 2 | 6 | 6 | 5 | 11 | 500 |
|     Other donors | 2 | 4 | 3 | 3 | 1 | 2 | 50 |
|     Multilateral | 3 | 6 | 8 | 8 | 5 | 11 | 167 |
| 2. Private grants | 2 | 4 | 2 | 2 | x | x | x |
| 3. Non-concessional | 28 | 55 | 61 | 62 | 33 | 70 | 118 |
|   A. Private | | | | | | | |
|     Direct investment (a) | 10 | 20 | 14 | 14 | 4 | 9 | 40 |
|     Capital market finance (bank sector + bonds) | 8 | 16 | 23 | 23 | 15 | 32 | 188 |
|   B. Official or officially supported | | | | | | | |
|     Export credits (DAC) | 7 | 14 | 12 | 12 | 5 | 11 | 71 |
|     Other | 1 | 2 | 5 | 5 | 4 | 9 | 400 |
|   C. Multilateral | 2 | 4 | 7 | 7 | 5 | 11 | 250 |
| Total | 51 | 100 | 98 | 100 | 47 | 100 | 92 |
| Memorandum items: | | | | | | | |
| Official sector + private grants (1 + 2 + 3B + 3C) | 33 | 64 | 61 | 62 | 28 | 60 | 85 |
| Private sector (3A) | 18 | 36 | 37 | 38 | 19 | 40 | 105 |
| Total DAC ODA (bilateral + multilateral) | 17 | 34 | 27 | 28 | 8 | 17 | 59 |

a. For direct investment the 1982 figure is in fact an average of 1981 and 1982. Direct investment flows have fluctuated considerably in the last few years and the 1981-82 average seems a reasonable representation of the trend level in the recent period.

Table F

THE "FINANCING MIX" OF DEVELOPING COUNTRIES AND TERRITORIES FROM ALL SOURCES, 1980-81 ANNUAL AVERAGES

| | % of total ODA | % of total non-concess. | % of total receipts | % of total debt | Memorandum items: | | |
| --- | --- | --- | --- | --- | --- | --- | --- |
| | | | | | Number of countries | % of total GNP | % of total pop. |
| 1. ODA-reliant countries | 48 | 5 | 19 | 11 | 69 | 7 | 15 |
| Completely reliant (over 90 % ODA) | 23 | 1 | 8 | 3 | 41 | 2 | 8 |
| Highly reliant (66-90 % ODA) [excluding India; see below] | 25 | 4 | 11 | 8 | 28 | 5 | 7 |
| 2. Middle-position countries (33-66 % ODA) | 26 | 13 | 17 | 16 | 33 | 7 | 7 |
| 3. "Market-terms" countries | 16 | 79 | 59 | 69 | 45 | 67 | 26 |
| ODA significant (10-33 % ODA) [excluding China; see below] | 12 | 22 | 19 | 21 | 20 | 16 | 12 |
| ODA not significant (less than 10 % ODA) | 4 | 57 | 40 | 48 | 25 | 51 | 14 |
| 4. India and China | | | | | | | |
| India (81 % ODA) | 9 | 1 | 3 | 4 | 1 | 7 | 21 |
| China (11 % ODA) | 1 | 3 | 2 | 1 | 1 | 12 | 30 |
| Total | 100 | 100 | 100 | 100 | 149 | 100 | 100 |

-- The 46 "market-terms" countries, with 67 per cent of developing-country GNP and 26 per cent of developing-country population, absorb 79 per cent of the non-concessional flows;

-- India and China, with 19 per cent of developing-country GNP and 51 per cent of developing-country population, absorb only 5 per cent of the total resource flow.


## 2. PROBLEMS IN THE INTERPRETATION OF AGGREGATE DEBT STATISTICS

The debt Tables which form the centre-piece of the present Survey need to be interpreted in the light of this analysis of financial flows. For the reasons outlined in Section 1, the debt-stock and debt-service data do not, by definition, encompass foreign direct investment and the share (over one-half) of ODA flows disbursed as grants. What the Survey focuses on, therefore, is those financial stocks which generate on-going, contractual debt-service obligations in the form of amortization and interest payments.

The debt-stock magnitudes themselves need to be assessed with due regard to a number of considerations, already implicit in the preceding flow analysis.

## A. Heterogeneity of the Components of the Debt Stock

The aggregate numbers are composed of funds borrowed on quite disparate terms and conditions, ranging from ODA loans at very low interest rates and with long repayment periods, to multilateral non-concessional loans at market interest rates but with lengthy amortization, to export credits at (hitherto and in some cases still) subsidised interest rates and medium repayment terms, to commercial fixed-interest loans at market interest rates and medium-term repayment, to floating-interest-rate syndicated credits. The loans may involve, variously, official entities on both the borrowing and lending sides, either as primary participants or guarantors; they may be bilateral or multilateral; they may involve official entities lending to private entities; private entities lending to official entities; or they may be purely private transactions. Even these distinctions are subject to degrees of shading, overlapping or even transformation. As is clear in Table F, the composition of the debt stock of different categories of developing countries will vary greatly according to the "financing mix". This is evident in a comparison of the debt-stock composition shown in Tables 3, 5 and 7 of this Survey. It perhaps needs to be more widely appreciated that the real significance of the debt-stock data lies not so much in the aggregates, which tend to attract most attention, but more in the composition of the debt stock, which needs careful study.

## B. Country Coverage

The magnitudes of developing-country debt numbers vary considerably according to the country coverage. The country coverage and the country categories used in this Survey are shown in Annex 2 (7). Apart from the "all-developing-countries" definition, another aggregate debt stock shown in this Survey is "non-OPEC, non-OECD developing countries", a category comparable to the more generally known "non-oil developing countries" but excluding the three OECD Member countries (Greece, Portugal and Turkey) and Yugoslavia. The aggregate debt stock for this group (see Tables 9 and 10) is some $146 billion less and aggregate debt service some $34 billion less than the aggregates for "all developing countries". The OPEC countries alone account for $104 billion and $24 billion of the 1983 debt stock and debt service, respectively. The rationale for paying attention to aggregates which exclude OPEC countries made sense in the conditions following 1973. It remains meaningful now in the new oil market and economic context because, as Table A already indicates, the debt situations of OPEC and non-OPEC countries will continue to evolve in divergent directions for some time, but in a rather different way than previously. The problem of defining country categories which do have policy relevance, and adjusting such categories when economic conditions change, is not of course confined to the presentation of debt statistics. This Survey does contain other categorisations, including the "largest-borrowers" concept (Tables 21 and 22). The "Low-Income Countries" (LICs), "Lower Middle-Income Countries" (LMICs) and "Upper Middle-Income Countries" (UMICs) analysis presented in many of the Tables continues to offer some of the most interesting insights. It reveals in particular the extent to which the interest cost of carrying debt rises with income level, reflecting the "financing-mix" position (shown in Table F earlier in this Chapter) through both the interest-cost differentials and the pattern of debt stocks. Nevertheless, within these broad groups the situation of just a few countries can dominate the group averages.

## C. Exchange Rates

Measuring the statistical and economic impact of exchange-rate changes on the LDCs' indebtedness and economies can take place at several levels.

First -- and this Survey provides indications in this respect only -- one can measure the statistical impact of exchange-rate changes on reported gross indebtedness of LDCs. The impact can vary widely from one country to another, reflecting differences in the currency composition of their respective debt: in particular the share of their dollar-denominated debt in their total debt varies from virtually zero (e.g. Cuba) to under 25 per cent (e.g. many African LICs), to over 70 per cent (e.g. Argentina, Brazil, Mexico). The Secretariat's estimates of the impact of dollar appreciation in recent years is set out in Chapter III. These estimates illustrate a little-appreciated feature -- that a rising dollar lowers the dollar value of the debt stock and debt-service payments, since the considerable amount of non-dollar-denominated stocks and service payments are in effect devalued. A future fall in the dollar would conversely, as in previous dollar depreciations, increase the debt-stock and debt-service figures. A 10 per cent fall in the value of the dollar, for example, would increase the dollar value of currently outstanding debt stocks of developing countries by some $30 billion and debt-service obligations by some $4 billion.

Second, the statistical net impact on the overall balance of payments of a debtor country is generally much smaller because the respective effect on the sources of foreign exchange (exports plus new capital inflows) and on the uses of foreign exchange (imports and debt-service payments) tend to offset each other.  Also, the impact is minimal for countries whose external trade and finance are essentially denominated in US dollars:  this is the case of many large debtors, in particular amongst oil exporters and newly industrialising countries.

Third, measuring the impact of exchange-rate changes on the full and real economic cost of external borrowing is a much more complex issue since beyond statistical impacts it involves such issues as terms of trade, domestic inflation, local exchange-rate management practices and policies, etc.  The question is too complex and its effects too differentiated for any general conclusion to be drawn without lengthy empirical analysis.  Moreover, the general economic context, policy adjustments and financial-market reactions associated with the particular change or trend in the value of the dollar would have a critical bearing on whether debt-carrying capacities were lightened or increased.

Further commentary and estimates of exchange-rate impacts on debt statistics are contained in Chapter III, Section 3, and in the Technical Note, Section D.

## D. Relationships between Aggregates

The "total debt" of developing countries can be defined in various ways, which may differ by $100 billion or more   This Survey focuses mainly on gross long-term debt;  but data on short-term debt are included in various places, in particular in Tables 13, 14 and 15.  The aggregation of short-term and long-term debt into a "total gross debt" is a tempting calculation but it can be misleading.  For developing countries as a whole, and for the majority of individual debtors, short-term assets are generally higher than short-term liabilities (the main exceptions being the large debtors of Latin America). Current developments, including a major restructuring of short-term debt into long-term debt and a build-up of reserves, will further increase the number of debtors whose total net debt is no higher than their gross long-term debt.

What this Chapter illustrates essentially is the need to place the parameters of the debt situation in the context of a complicated financial and economic backdrop and to recognise that the statistical constructs and problems must be adequately appreciated for the Survey material to be properly assessed.

Chapter III

SALIENT TRENDS AND FACTS

1. TOTAL DEBT, DEBT STRUCTURE AND DEBT SERVICE

The estimated external debt of all developing countries and territories (LDCs) on the DAC list (see Annex 2) stood at $606 billion at the end
of 1983. This is the outstanding disbursed amount of medium- and long-term
lending from all sources (see Table 1). Selected data on short-term assets
and liabilities of non-OPEC, non-OECD developing countries are shown in Tables
13 and 14.

The aggregate figures in this Survey are not directly comparable with
those in the 1982 Survey. Spain is no longer included in the debt data for
developing countries. Moreover, in the 1982 Survey, estimates for 1982 were
made on the basis of 1981 exchange rates whereas in this Survey, 1982 data are
based on 1982 exchange rates. (Estimates of 1983 debt figures are based on
mid-October 1983 exchange rates.) Finally, new LDC income groups have been
designed (see Annex 2).

In the course of the debt accumulation during the past ten years, there
was a marked deceleration of the long-term debt build-up since 1978. In that
year, the annual growth rate peaked at 26 per cent, followed by a gradual decline of the growth rate to 10 per cent in 1983. The major reasons for this
deceleration were the slowing down of reserve build-up during 1979-81, the
increase in short-term debt and in IMF lending, and the adjustment in current-
account deficits during 1982-83. However, part of this decrease is also due
to the appreciation during 1981-83 of the US dollar in which all aggregate
totals are expressed: a higher dollar exchange rate reduces the dollar equiv-
alent of non-dollar debt.

Short-term debt is not included in Tables 1 to 10. The figures which
follow recapitulate the estimated share of short-term debt in total (short-
and long-term) debt of non-OPEC, non-OECD developing countries (8). The share
increased during 1972-76, fell during 1977-78, and increased again markedly in
connection with the second oil shock and the London Inter-Bank Offer Rate
(LIBOR) rise. It fell during 1983 along with the fall in imports resulting
from the adjustment efforts of debtors, and also due to the consolidation of
short-term credits and arrears into long-term debt; further consolidation is
expected in 1984.

34

PERCENTAGE OF SHORT-TERM DEBT IN TOTAL DEBT
OF NON-OPEC, NON-OECD LDCs

| 1971-72 | 1973-76 | 1977-78 | 1979 | 1980-82 | 1983 | 1984 |
|---------|---------|---------|------|---------|------|------|
| 10      | 15      | 13      | 18   | 22      | 18   | 15   |

The general, though tempered, increase in long-term debt was accompanied by a steady hardening of the debt structure. The share of concessional debt in total debt fell from 38 per cent in 1971 to 24 per cent in 1980 and to 21 per cent in 1983. This change was to a large part due to the sharp rise of private bank lending (particularly until 1981) and the corresponding increase in the share of private bank debt in total debt -- from 12 per cent in 1971 to 27 per cent in 1975 and to 39 per cent in 1983. The rising share of private bank debt in total debt between 1975 and 1983 was compensated by a fall in the share of DAC Members' ODA debt (from 20 to 10 per cent -- partly due to debt cancellation for lower income LDCs) and of debt due to members of the Council for Mutual Economic Assistance [(CMEA), from 5 to 3 per cent]. Virtually all other categories of lending maintained their share in total debt: export credits (21 per cent), bonds (2 per cent), multilateral lending (14 per cent), and OPEC credits (4 per cent). It should be noted, however, that this share analysis excludes non-debt-creating flows, essentially grants and foreign direct investment.

With respect to developing countries' debt service -- a far more economically relevant feature than debt itself -- the year 1983 witnessed the first decline after a continuous rise during the past decade (see Table 2). Total debt-service payments on medium- and long-term debt dropped from $108 billion in 1982 to $96 billion in 1983. This fall in the absolute amount followed a deceleration of the annual growth in debt service from 38 per cent in 1978 to 8 per cent in 1982 (again partly due to the dollar appreciation). From 1982 to 1983, interest payments dropped by 4 per cent -- to $48 billion, and amortization payments by 16 per cent -- also to $48 billion. Amortization payments were therefore as high as interest payments whereas, until 1978, they were at least twice as high as interest payments. The main reason for the disproportionately large fall in amortization payments was massive debt restructuring.

Debt service (actually paid, rather than "due") in 1983 fell particularly for private debt (from $60 billion in 1982 to $50 billion), mainly due to a drastic reduction in the LIBOR (see Section 2) and massive reschedulings of principal repayments for several debtor countries, as well as unpaid arrears of both interest and amortization payments. Consequently, the decrease in total debt-service payments in 1983 concerned only non-concessional debt whereas debt service on concessional debt continued to increase, raising its share in total debt service again to 7 per cent.

2. THE COST OF EXTERNAL FINANCE

The total external debt of developing countries is made up of different types of lending which vary widely with respect to their terms and

availability for different borrowers. Bilateral and multilateral Official
Development Assistance loans are the least expensive type of external credits
available -- with an interest cost of around 2 per cent on the outstanding
debt. However, these funds are scarce and their distribution is concentrated
on poorer developing countries whose credit standing may not attract more
abundant, but also more expensive commercial credits. At the other end of the
scale, private bank loans, extended essentially at floating interest rates
(usually indexed on the LIBOR), are predominant financial instruments for
higher income developing countries with a good credit rating: until recently
funds were relatively easily available, and their higher cost should in principle be covered through effective use for productive investment. In between
these two extremes are bilateral export credits, multilateral non-concessional
lending and bonds; presently, they all carry a similar current interest cost
(8 to 9 per cent on the outstanding debt) but differ markedly with respect to
their maturities and procurement tying status.

On average, the current interest cost which developing countries paid
on their total outstanding long-term debt rose from 5 per cent in 1972-73 to
10 per cent in 1982. This increase was largely due to the steep rise in the
cost of floating-interest debt (from 8.3 to 17.1 per cent) and the increasing
weight of floating-interest debt in total debt (rising from under 5 per cent
in 1972 to over 40 per cent in 1982). With the sharp drop of the LIBOR since
mid-1982, the current cost of floating-interest debt fell significantly to
12.7 per cent in 1983 -- i.e. with the usual six-month time lag embodied in
floating-interest contracts. This largely overcompensated a slight further
increase in the cost of fixed-interest debt, bringing down the average
interest cost of total debt to 8.7 per cent (for details, see Table 12).

Expressing the current nominal interest cost of lending in "real" terms
involves the problem of choosing an appropriate "deflator". For example,
using the US GNP deflator, real Euro-dollar interest rates were negative in
1975, zero in 1976 and rose to 7 per cent in 1982.

It is important to remember that the recent fall in nominal interest
rates reflected essentially the fall in inflation and did not markedly reduce
real interest rates. In contrast to the preceding decade, real interest rates
stayed above the GNP growth rates of most developing countries during the past
two years.

The difference in the debt structure of various categories of developing countries is reflected in the difference in the average cost which they
pay on their debt. In 1983:

-- Low-income countries paid 3.7 per cent on their outstanding debt;
   this low rate -- hardly more than in 1977-78 -- is mainly due to the
   large share of ODA debt in their external liabilities (and unpaid
   interest arrears in some cases);

-- Lower middle-income countries paid 8.3 per cent interest on their
   outstanding debt (down from 9.8 per cent in 1982);

-- Upper middle-income countries paid 10.6 per cent interest on their
   outstanding debt (against 12.2 per cent in 1982); they were
   markedly affected by the sharp decline of the LIBOR since floating-
   interest debt constitutes a large part of their long-term

36

liabilities (45 per cent for the group and around 70 per cent for Brazil and Mexico).

Relating interest payments to outstanding debt, as shown in the preceding paragraphs, reveals the economic cost of foreign finance which can then be compared to its (marginal) yield. This analysis thus provides a key to test fundamental cost/benefit relationships of external capital. To the extent that costs and benefits can be correctly measured, at the margin and in terms of foreign exchange, it is possible to ascertain if foreign loan capital enriches or impoverishes the borrowing country.

Between 1973 and 1983, the ratio of developing countries' interest payments (on long-term debt) to their export receipts more than doubled, from 3 to 8 per cent (see Table 19). This average increase hides developments for individual countries which are dramatic.

For example, the interest/export ratio in 1982 was about 6 per cent for Nigeria (up from about 1 per cent in 1979), 39 per cent for Brazil (25 per cent in 1979), over 20 per cent for Peru (12 per cent in 1979), around 13 per cent for Colombia and the Philippines (7 per cent in 1979); in contrast, the ratio was 0.2 per cent for Saudi Arabia (the same as in 1979).

Table 19 also shows the ratio of interest payments to GNP. It doubled, on average for all developing countries, from 0.8 per cent in 1973 to 1.6 per cent in 1983 (0.8 per cent for the low-income countries). Here again, the average masks widely divergent country situations.

The analysis in this Chapter has been confined thus far to gross medium- and long-term debt (hence leaving out long-term assets and short-term debt and short-term assets of developing countries). The presentation in Tables 13 and 14, based on Secretariat estimates, includes long- and short-term external assets and liabilities of non-OPEC, non-OECD developing countries in 1980-83. This wider coverage raises the total debt level of these developing countries (due to the inclusion of short-term debt) but reduces the net debt exposure of those numerous developing countries which have more short-term assets than short-term debt. Countries in the latter position can therefore be adversely affected by a decrease, rather than an increase, in floating interest rates. It should also be noted that Tables 13 and 14 exclude debtor countries' assets abroad which result from capital flight. Estimates of such assets for non-OPEC, non-OECD LDCs at the end of 1982 range from $50 billion to over $100 billion.

For non-OPEC, non-OECD LDCs taken together:

-- In 1982-83, 53 per cent of their total liabilities, but 73 per cent of their assets were on floating interest rates. This left, on balance, 55 per cent of their total net debt on fixed interest (compared to 65 per cent in 1980). For the great majority of developing countries, over 80 per cent of their total net debt is still on fixed interest;

-- The total net floating-interest debt of developing countries is still, though decreasingly, concentrated on a few countries: Brazil and Mexico together accounted in 1983 for 62 per cent of the total net floating-interest debt (down from 78 per cent in 1978). Adding

Argentina, South Korea and Chile brings the share in 1983 up to 87 per cent (the same as in 1978);

-- Many developing countries had in 1983 still positive net floating-interest assets; they include several low-income countries and notably China (9) and India. This position is due to the fact that poorer LDCs may have no, or limited, access to private bank lending (other than export credits guaranteed by OECD Governments). At the same time, they may keep significant external reserves, including deposits with international banks. Throughout the last decade, until 1982, low-income countries as a group have been net creditors to the international banking system. For low-income countries as a group, net floating-interest assets of $3 billion in 1978 turned into net floating-interest liabilities of $4 billion in 1983 (essentially due to a fall in external reserves). The weight of India is important in this turnaround;

-- Since the short-term effect of fluctuating interest rates on the debtor's balance of payments manifests itself essentially through the net floating-interest debt, increases in LIBOR rates during 1978-82, and subsequent declines since mid-1982, have therefore dramatically affected countries with the largest absolute or relative amounts of net floating-interest debt.

Table 14 relates, for some individual countries most affected by LIBOR changes, and for country groups, the net floating-interest debt in 1978, 1982 and 1983 to the total net debt (including fixed-interest debt) as well as to the GNP. This presentation not only shows the sharp increase in floating-interest debt but permits a sensitivity analysis of changes in the LIBOR (or in the US Prime Rate).

Taking for example the first column of the 1983 figures, the estimated total net floating-interest debt of non-OPEC, non-OECD developing countries is $186 billion (up from $57 billion in 1978). A 1 per cent increase/decrease in the LIBOR would represent for these countries a change in net interest payments (and thus in their current deficit) of $1.86 billion ($554 million for Mexico, $593 million for Brazil, $202 million for Argentina, $166 million for South Korea and $106 million for Chile). It is recalled, however, that the bulk of net debt is still on fixed interest.

The second column shows the relative importance of net floating-interest debt in total net debt in 1983 and hence the relative vulnerability of individual developing countries to LIBOR changes. For non-OPEC, non-OECD countries, the net floating-interest debt as a share of total net debt has grown from 29 per cent in 1978 to 45 per cent in 1982 and 1983; particularly high proportions have been attained in 1983 by such countries as Mexico (78 per cent), Chile (75 per cent), Argentina (70 per cent), Brazil (71 per cent) and South Korea (55 per cent).

The third column relates the net floating-interest debt in 1983 to GNP. Here again, a sensitivity analysis of LIBOR changes is possible. For example, a 1 per cent increase in the LIBOR rate, in terms of the GNP of all non-OPEC, non-OECD developing countries, amounts to almost 0.1 per cent; the impact is 0.4 per cent for Nicaragua, 0.3 per cent for Chile, Sudan and Jamaica.

The following figures show the influence of the massive rise in floating-interest debt (including short-term debt) and its changing cost for non-OPEC, non-OECD developing countries. The growth in total net interest payments substantially exceeded the growth in total net debt until 1982. In 1983, there has been a sharp reversal of these trends, under the impact of declining LIBOR rates.

| Increase in % | 1979 | 1980 | 1981 | 1982 | 1983 | est. 1984 |
|---|---|---|---|---|---|---|
| Net debt | 17 | 18 | 24 | 12 | 11 | 9 |
| Net interest payments | 39 | 46 | 33 | 39 | -10 | 8 |

## 3. IMPACT OF EXCHANGE-RATE CHANGES

As explained in the Technical Note, the exchange-rate changes in recent years (in particular, the steady appreciation of the US dollar during 1981-83) have had a marked effect on all the figures, expressed in US dollars, which are contained in this Survey.

The impact of exchange-rate changes on any debt or debt-service aggregate depends critically on its currency composition: in particular, the higher the dollar share, the lower the impact. The actual composition varies widely from one type of credit to another; e.g. in 1982, some 90 per cent of international bank loans were expressed in US dollars while only about 30 per cent of DAC countries' export credits were expressed in US dollars. Depending on the composition and destination of these credits, the impact can vary considerably from one debtor (or income group) to another.

Full information on the currency composition of the total external debt of LDCs is not available. It is believed, however, that throughout the 1970s, about one-half of total long-term debt and debt service of LDCs was denominated in US dollars. This share increased in 1980-82 and decreased in 1983. The figures which follow reflect the Secretariat's latest computations and estimates. (They exclude short-term transactions; it is estimated that some 70 per cent of LDC short-term assets and some 80 per cent of LDC short-term liabilities are denominated in US dollars.)

### PERCENTAGE OF LONG-TERM US DOLLAR-DENOMINATED DEBT AND DEBT SERVICE IN TOTAL LONG-TERM DEBT AND DEBT SERVICE

| | | 1980 | 1981 | 1982 | 1983 |
|---|---|---|---|---|---|
| Total LDCs | debt | 51 | 55 | 57 | 56 |
| | debt service | 56 | 60 | 61 | 56 |
| LICs | debt | 33 | 37 | 37 | 37 |
| | debt service | 35 | 39 | 40 | 41 |

The slight decrease in the share of dollar-denominated debt in 1983 is, in fact, significant in the light of the appreciation of the US dollar. It reflects the slowdown in new bank lending and, regarding debt service, the decline in LIBOR and postponement of principal repayments to banks. Any future depreciation of the US dollar would of course result in a decrease in the share of dollar-denominated debt in total debt.

The impact of the dollar appreciation during 1981-83 has been threefold: the data in the Survey tend to "underreport" the increase in indebtedness shown for these three years (the figures below provide an indication of such underreporting); the data similarly tend to reduce the relative share of LIC debt in total indebtedness, as well as the share of DAC export credits in total debt and debt service; Table 12 tends to (slightly) underreport the nominal interest cost to debtors.

The next presentation of figures indicates the estimated overall impact of exchange-rate fluctuations during 1980-83 on total and selected categories of external debt. The sign "-" measures the reduction in reported indebtedness due to exchange-rate changes, other things being equal.

IMPACT OF EXCHANGE-RATE CHANGES
Per cent

|  | | 1980 | 1981 | 1982 | 1983 |
|---|---|---|---|---|---|
| Total LDCs | debt | -0.4 | -6.5 | -4.1 | -3.6 |
|  | debt service | -0.3 | -5.2 | -3.8 | -3.4 |
| LICs | debt | -0.7 | -8.9 | -5.7 | -5.4 |
|  | debt service | -0.4 | -7.7 | -5.6 | -4.6 |
| Total LDC ODA debt | | +1.0 | -6.7 | -4.1 | -3.7 |
| Total LDC export-credit debt | | -1.4 | -10.7 | -7.2 | -6.5 |

These annual percentages entail fairly large absolute amounts. Moreover, the impact of exchange-rate changes over the past four years has been cumulative. The data which follow compare the respective trends in total LDC long-term debt during 1980-83 under (A) actual exchange rates and (B) fictitious constant 1980 exchange rates. The difference for debt outstanding at end-1983 is $84 billion.

DEBT AT YEAR-END

| | $ billion | | | | % increase |
|---|---|---|---|---|---|
| | 1980 | 1981 | 1982 | 1983 | 1983 over 1980 |
| (A) | 445 | 501 | 552 | 606 | 36 |
| (B) | 445 | 536 | 611 | 690 | 55 |

# 4. THE SPECIAL DEBT SITUATION OF LOW-INCOME COUNTRIES (LICS)

The external debt of low-income countries (defined in Annex 2) represents only a minor share of total LDC debt and an even lower share of total LDC debt service. Although they pay on average under 4 per cent interest on their external debt, even this modest charge constitutes a payments burden for many low-income countries, given their weak economies and export bases. The external debt of low-income countries increased to $135 billion at the end of 1983. The increase in 1983 (10 per cent) represented a revival of the annual growth in debt, which had fallen to 8 per cent in 1981 from its earlier level of 13 to 19 per cent per annum during 1976-80 (see Table 3).

Between 1975 and 1983, the share of concessional debt in total debt fell from 71 to 60 per cent. Multilateral debt (three-fourths concessional) raised its share from 15 to 26 per cent and export credits from 14 to 18 per cent. These increases are mirrored by declines in the shares of DAC ODA debt (from 39 to 26 per cent) and of (mainly concessional) CMEA debt (from 9 to 5 per cent). This share analysis of outstanding debt ignores massive grant receipts from which low-income countries have traditionally benefited. Moreover, retro-active terms adjustment of ODA debt for the least developed and some other low-income countries has resulted in a decreasing share of ODA debt in total debt, which gives the spurious impression that their debt composition has hardened.

Contrary to groups of developing countries in higher income brackets, debt-service payments of low-income countries continued to increase in 1983 -- to $12.5 billion -- though at a lower rate (8 per cent) than in previous years. This increase was mainly due to the small share of low-income countries' debt on floating interest rates (thus depriving them from benefits of declining LIBOR rates). Another reason was that none of the large low-income countries (Indonesia, India, Egypt and Pakistan), which account for the bulk of the group's debt, sought debt relief in 1982-83. The growth in debt service from 1975 to 1983 had hardly any effect on the share of concessional debt service in total debt service, which hovered around 28 per cent during this period.

In 1983, debt service on DAC ODA loans accounted for only 11 per cent of total debt service (down from 20 per cent in 1975), while export credits captured 37 per cent (roughly their share in 1975) and private bank loans 18 per cent (up from 12 per cent in 1975). Multilateral debt service (formerly two-thirds and now 40 per cent on concessional terms) accounted for 18 per cent of total debt service.

However, the relatively modest growth of low-income countries' debt-service payments in recent years was accompanied, particularly for the least developed countries, by an abnormally low increase, or fall, in their export earnings. Thus, a rising portion -- though with enormous variations among different countries -- of export earnings was pre-empted for debt service and no longer available to pay for imports. (This "debt-service ratio" has, however, limited analytical significance since it ignores capital inflow and imports.)

As with other developing-country categories, aggregate amounts or ratios for the low-income group conceal wide disparities of individual country situations. In particular, the group of low-income countries is heavily dominated by a few large debtors: Indonesia, Egypt, India and Pakistan. Together, these countries account for more than half of the total debt and debt service of the low-income countries. Their external financial situation has improved throughout the 1970s, due to rising export earnings and external resource receipts, including non-concessional borrowing. Since 1981, however, the external balance for some of these countries has somewhat deteriorated.

On the other hand, a number of (mainly African) low-income countries represent chronic cases, afflicted by: structural development problems, inefficient resource use, policy deficiencies, capital flight, falling exports, arrears build-ups, (in some cases) high interest costs on bank debt, and relatively low ODA receipts. The combination of these factors results in economic difficulties which may manifest themselves as "debt-servicing problems".

In fact, for many individual low-income countries, severe payments difficulties have arisen. An increasing number of them have accumulated substantial arrears of both principal and interest payments and had to seek debt relief, both in the framework of the Paris Club and with non-DAC creditors and private banks (see Section 7).

## 5. THE LARGEST DEBTORS

Tables 21 and 22 show the 20 developing countries with the largest debt service actually paid in recent years. They are ranked by debt service, rather than by debt, because even a large stock of debt on soft terms generates only a small debt service. The data emphasize the sharp concentration of the LDC debt service on a limited number of developing countries. In 1983, Brazil and Mexico together accounted for 25 per cent of the total LDC debt service; adding Argentina, Venezuela and Algeria raises the share of the five largest debtors to 41 per cent. The ten largest debtor countries accounted for 56 per cent of the total LDC debt service, and the 20 largest debtors for 76 per cent.

While the debt of the 20 largest borrowers increased in 1982 by 10 per cent, their external reserves (part of their total assets) decreased by 18 per cent. This adverse development was particularly pronounced for Brazil and Mexico, with an increase in their combined debt of 13 per cent and a drop in reserves of 54 per cent. As much as 62 per cent of their long-term debt at end-1982 was due to private banks. This partly explains why 72 per cent of their 1983 debt service was interest payment.

Other countries with an extremely high share of private bank debt in total long-term debt in 1982 included Venezuela (78 per cent), Chile (63 per cent) and Portugal (57 per cent). On the other hand, this share was under 5 per cent for India and Egypt (both low-income countries), Iran and Iraq (both OPEC Members). For the 20 countries together, the bank share was 45 per cent.

Among the 20 largest borrowers, Argentina, Peru and Turkey were the only countries for which debt-service payments had increased substantially from 1982 to 1983. Mexico was virtually the only debtor which had a major

42

increase in interest payments in 1983, due to the payment of arrears accumulated in 1982. For most of the other 20 countries, the current interest cost on outstanding debt decreased in 1983, notable exceptions being Egypt, Iraq and Saudi Arabia.

The abnormally high ratio of debt service to debt for Saudi Arabia and Kuwait (not shown among the 20 largest borrowers) is due to the relatively short (twelve- to eighteen-month) maturity of export-credit debt which these countries have incurred.

Argentina, Brazil, South Korea and Mexico are the four largest non-OPEC debtors as well as the countries with the highest floating-interest debt. They also have large short-term debt but, except for South Korea, low external reserves. Their estimated total gross external debt from all sources, including short-term, IMF and military debt, is shown here. Of South Korea's total debt, the share of debt owed to private markets was comparatively low at 50 per cent at end-1981, because of large official credits and export credits. However, for the other three countries, about three-quarters of their total debt (compared with under 20 per cent for most developing countries) was due to private markets, at variable interest rates and without official support from OECD Governments. More generally, these four countries represent highly differentiated cases of economic situations and prospects.

The extreme concentration of gross bank lending to these four countries (shown in Table 15) is the result of rapid borrowing from private markets during the 1970s. On the other hand, their debt postures must also be seen in the light of various capital outflows by some or all of these countries, including substantial loans to other countries, the acquisition by domestic banks of national external debt instruments, as well as massive capital flight in certain instances.

### TOTAL GROSS DEBT FROM ALL SOURCES
### $ billion

|  |  | 1978 | 1980 | 1981 | 1982 | 1983 |
|---|---|---|---|---|---|---|
| Argentina | short-term | 4 | 11 | 10 | 9 | 11 |
|  | total | 13 | 28 | 34 | 37 | 42 |
| Brazil | short-term | 7 | 9 | 12 | 14 | 15 |
|  | total | 52 | 66 | 77 | 88 | 97 |
| S. Korea | short-term | 3 | 8 | 13 | 14 . | 13 |
|  | total | 16 | 25 | 33 | 38 | 41 |
| Mexico | short-term | 5 | 10 | 21 | 22 | 12 |
|  | total | 38 | 54 | 74 | 82 | 83 |
| Total four countries |  |  |  |  |  |  |
|  | short-term | 19 | 38 | 56 | 59 | 51 |
|  | total | 119 | 173 | 218 | 245 | 263 |

## 6. LENDING AND EXPOSURE OF PRIVATE BANKS

As shown earlier in this Survey, one of the major transformations in international lending during recent years has been the upsurge in private bank loans at floating, rather than fixed, interest rates. The floating-interest system has introduced both a considerable measure of flexibility and market response in resource transfers, but also uncertainty regarding future debt-service obligations.

### A. Lending: Volume and Interest Cost

In most DAC countries, total international lending by commercial banks to developing countries takes the following main forms:

1. Subsidised and officially guaranteed export credits. On average, about one-third of current new bank lending to non-OPEC LDCs consists of such officially guaranteed export credits and the share is rising. (The ratio is higher for EEC countries and much lower for the United States.) The bulk of these bank-financed export credits is on subsidised and fixed interest rates (currently about 10 per cent) and not denominated in United States dollars (in all the Tables of this Survey, these credits are included, together with supplier credits, in "export credits");

2. "Financial credits", including "Euro-loans" -- shown in the Tables as "bank loans" -- essentially on floating interest rates and mainly denominated in US dollars;

3. Short-term credits with original maturities of under one year (for both trade transactions and balance-of-payments purposes).

During 1972-81, medium- and long-term "financial credits" (net disbursements) to developing countries grew from $5 billion to $30 billion (on average, around 22 per cent per year in nominal terms and 12 per cent per year in real terms). With the exception of the group of OPEC borrowers (whose net borrowing fell sharply following the two major oil-price increases in 1974 and 1979), the growth of bank loans to developing countries continued generally unabated throughout this period.

Following are estimates of the development of bank lending since 1981. These figures are consistent with other published sources, notably the IMF, when based on the same geographical coverage and definitions. They exclude China and Eastern European debtors and bank-financed officially guaranteed export credits, but include participation in international syndicates of non-BIS reporting banks.

The interest cost of syndicated Euro-credits for developing countries increased considerably between 1977 and 1981. Average effective total annual interest charges rose from 8 per cent to 17.5 per cent. Since mid-1982, however, there was a significant drop in the US dollar-LIBOR rate which continued in 1983 and stood at about 10 per cent at the end of this year. This has considerably reduced the interest cost for developing-country borrowers. They continue to pay on average, however, a spread twice as high as borrowers from

44

industrialised countries (with some further "spread of spreads" among developing countries) -- a reflection of the higher lending risk as perceived by banks.

TOTAL NET BANK LENDING TO DEVELOPING COUNTRIES
$ billion

|  | 1981 | 1982 | 1983 |
|---|---|---|---|
| Total LDCs | | | |
| Short- and long-term | 52 | 41 | 34 |
| Long-term | 30 | 26 | 36 |
| Short-term | 22 | 15 | -2 |
| OPEC | | | |
| Short- and long-term | 5 | 8 | 12 |
| Long-term | 2 | 3 | 8 |
| Short-term | 3 | 5 | 4 |
| Non-OPEC | | | |
| Short- and long-term | 47 | 34 | 22 |
| Long-term | 27 | 24 | 28 |
| Short-term | 19 | 10 | -6 |
| Non-OPEC, Non-OECD | | | |
| Short- and long-term | 44 | 32 | 20 |
| Long-term | 25 | 23 | 27 |
| Short-term | 18 | 9 | -7 |

## B. Exposure

Despite its increase, total short- and long-term lending by BIS-reporting commercial banks to all developing countries, as a share of their global (i.e. domestic and international) assets, has remained low throughout the past decade. It increased from 2 per cent in 1973 to some 7 per cent in 1982 (some 6 per cent for non-OPEC LDCs). During this period, the share of total international claims in global assets of commercial banks more than doubled to some 20 per cent. The share of non-oil LDCs in these total international claims increased during the first oil shock and remained virtually unchanged at 30 per cent in recent years. Moreover, this exposure remained heavily concentrated on a few large debtors.

Table 15 provides a synopsis of estimated banks' gross and net exposure to non-OPEC, non-OECD developing countries between 1977 and 1983. Until 1982, the stock of short-term bank credits rose from $31 billion to $104 billion, followed by a drop to $96 billion in 1983, due to substantial consolidations of short-term debt into medium-term debt. Consequently, the stock of banks' medium- and long-term credits continued to grow during the 1977-83 period -- from $64 billion to $216 billion. Bank-financed guaranteed export credits grew faster than non-export-related bank lending but accounted for only 17 per cent of total medium-term bank debt in 1983 (although the ratio on current gross lending is about one-third).

The development of gross exposure of private banks is often measured in terms of annual percentage increases. Table 15 shows that the increase in gross exposure has markedly decelerated between 1980 and 1983, with annual growth rates falling from 22 per cent in 1981 to 14 per cent in 1982 and to some 7 per cent in 1983. The increase in 1984 is expected to remain at around 7 per cent. During the 1975-80 period, the corresponding annual increases in bank exposure had been as high as 23 per cent on average.

The estimated gross exposure of banks of $312 billion to non-OPEC, non-OECD developing countries at the end of 1983 (of which four countries -- Argentina, Brazil, South Korea and Mexico -- account for 62 per cent) has to be seen side by side with non-OPEC, non-OECD developing countries' deposits with BIS banks (including here capital flight deposited with banks). They grew from $70 billion to $120 billion, hence only half as fast as banks' assets (with the four countries accounting for 25 per cent in 1983). As a result, the net exposure of private banks to non-OPEC, non-OECD developing countries grew from $25 billion to $192 billion between 1977 and 1983, by 40 per cent per year, with the four countries accounting for 85 per cent in 1983 (down from 148 per cent in 1977).

This net exposure includes bank-extended export credits which are officially guaranteed in the capital-exporting countries and hence do not constitute the same type of international bank risk as domestically unguaranteed financial credits. Without these export credits, the net bank exposure on domestically unguaranteed lending increased from $17 billion to $156 billion (by over 45 per cent per year), with the four countries accounting for 94 per cent in 1983 (down from 188 per cent in 1977). These figures on net bank exposure confirm both its dramatic increase and extreme (though somewhat declining) concentration on a few borrowing countries.

It should be recalled in this context that measuring the "exposure" of banks to LDCs is a complex matter: a part of short-term credits is also guaranteed by the capital-exporting governments, and a part of long-term loans is guaranteed by multinational corporations.

Moreover, it must be kept in mind that averages conceal individual situations: "exposure" manifests itself as between individual banks to individual (large) borrowers; e.g. a "negative" exposure (i.e. when a debtor has more assets than liabilities) to one country does not protect a bank from potential losses on its positive exposure to other debtors.

In the present situation, a key question is to what extent and under which conditions banks can be expected to meet future credit demands of developing countries. A main pre-condition is normally the creditworthiness of the borrower, as perceived by the creditors. However, this fundamental consideration was sometimes overridden by the need to keep large borrowers in crisis situations financially afloat as well as to protect existing portfolios. This has led to substantial "unspontaneous" lending in various cases.

Still, as a general rule, banks pay increasing attention to the credit risk of developing countries. This policy has resulted not only in growing costs of bank credits for overborrowed countries, but also in a reluctance by banks to participate in syndicated loans and debt rescheduling for some developing countries. Generally, there is evidence of increased differentiation in banks' lending policies.

46

To increase the transparency and surveillance of bank lending, in particular the Euro-credit markets, some Central Banks of OECD Member countries have tightened such provisions as bank reporting on a consolidated basis, limitations on banks' capital adequacy and portfolio concentration. Often, banks also follow self-imposed restrictions; however, these measures are not intended to lead to abrupt reductions in bank credits for particular borrowing countries.

## 7. DEBT RESCHEDULING

A restructuring of a developing country's external debt can take place in many ways: in a bilateral or a multilateral context, covering official or private debt, and being implemented through debt rescheduling and/or debt refinancing. Purely bilateral debt reschedulings, or even cancellations of official credits by OECD Member countries, can take place with individual debtors at the discretion of the creditor country; the bulk of these operations concern low-income countries. Debt-relief operations also take place by CMEA and OPEC creditor countries, but little information is available on these operations. The rest of this Section therefore deals exclusively with multilateral official debt relief by OECD Member countries and private bank restructuring.

Until 1982, debt restructuring of developing countries usually followed a relatively simple pattern. The debtor country agreed to an IMF stabilization programme, then negotiated a restructuring of its official debt in a creditor club -- in recent years essentially the "Paris Club" -- and, when relevant, renegotiated its amortization payments due to private banks. In 1982-83, this process has been enlarged through major multi-billion-dollar rescue packages for some developing countries of central strategic importance to the international monetary system. Such packages have included official and private short-term "bridging loans", IMF agreements, long-term bank reschedulings, new bank loans, Paris Club reschedulings and new export credits. Thus far (January 1984), considering the period mid-1982 to end-1984, the overall package for Mexico included about $36 billion and for Brazil about $29 billion (both amounts excluding bridging loans and further commitments during 1984). These packages involved negotiations among the debtor country, the IMF, BIS, commercial banks and official creditors. The IMF role in this process remained crucial: the Fund has taken responsibility for estimating the total financing gap, for negotiating the required adjustment programme and for monitoring its implementation.

Official multilateral debt renegotiations usually take place in the framework of "creditor clubs" (particularly the Paris Club) as well as, exceptionally, Aid Consortia. The Minutes of the Club Meetings provide common guidelines for a given rescheduling which are implemented through bilateral agreements between creditor and debtor. They cover officially extended and officially guaranteed loans, mainly export credits. Negotiations cover in particular: the "consolidation period" (usually twelve months) of the debt service which should be subject to rescheduling; the extent to which the debt service should be covered (i.e. what "down-payment" -- usually 10 to 15 per cent -- of the debt service should not be fully stretched out but repaid during the grace period); and what maturity (usually six to ten years) and grace period (usually three to five years) should be applied. The (moratorium) interest rate is negotiated bilaterally (10).

The ultimate objective of debt restructuring is to restore the credit-worthiness and growth potential of the debtor country while safeguarding the financial interests of the creditors.

Table 20 provides a synopsis of official multilateral debt renegotiations for developing countries since 1956 (when the Paris Club came into being). As seen here, only a limited, though growing, number of developing countries had to seek debt relief since 1975.

In recent years up to 1982, most of the countries which had to seek multilateral official debt relief were small low-income countries, mainly in Africa. In 1983, however, a number of large- and medium-sized debtors also sought reschedulings. Regarding the small debtors, the amounts involved were often modest in absolute terms. However, for the countries concerned, the debt relief was of critical importance in staving off liquidity crises, in providing time for the needed economic adjustment, in restoring their credit-worthiness and thus permitting the resumption of new lending.

| 1975 | 1976 | 1977 |
|------|------|------|
| Chile | India | India |
| India | Zaire | Sierra Leone |
| | | Zaire |

| 1978 | 1979 | 1980 |
|------|------|------|
| Gabon | Sudan | Liberia |
| Peru | Togo | Sierra Leone |
| Turkey | Turkey | Turkey |
| | Zaire | |

| 1981 | 1982 | 1983 |
|------|------|------|
| Central African Republic | Madagascar | Brazil |
| Liberia | Malawi | Costa Rica |
| Madagascar | Senegal | Cuba |
| Pakistan | Sudan | Ecuador |
| Senegal | Uganda | Liberia |
| Togo | | Malawi |
| Uganda | | Mexico |
| Zaire | | Morocco |
| | | Niger |
| | | Peru |
| | | Senegal |
| | | Sudan |
| | | Togo |
| | | Zaire |
| | | Zambia |

Increasingly, there has also been a restructuring of private bank debt, at market terms. These operations can involve over 500 or even 1000 private banks for a single debtor country. The results of these negotiations are documented in financial reviews and surveys (11).

As the following groups show, there have been, thus far, some 30 significant cases of reschedulings with banks concerning the two-year period from mid-1982 to mid-1984. They include debtors in each income group, and their loans were restructured on market terms. While complete information is not presently available on each transaction, the 30 cases combined are estimated to represent a rescheduling of over $80 billion of principal repayments into long-term obligations. At least one-half of this amount originally due between mid-1982 and mid-1984 concerns long-term obligations; the remainder, short-term debt. In addition, most of these restructurings also provided for new bank lending.

| LICs | LMICs | UMICs |
|---|---|---|
| Bolivia | Cuba | Argentina |
| Liberia | Dominican Republic | Brazil |
| Madagascar | Guyana | Chile |
| Malawi | Ivory Coast | Costa Rica |
| Niger | Jamaica | Ecuador |
| Senegal | Jordan | Mexico |
| Sudan | Morocco | Panama |
| Zaire | Nicaragua | Uruguay |
| Zambia | Nigeria | Venezuela |
| | Peru | Yugoslavia |
| | Philippines | |

The amounts and modalities involved in these restructurings attest to the flexibility and potential of private markets to respond effectively to the international debt crisis.

NOTES AND REFERENCES

1.  Apart from the close association with the interest-rate developments, the progressive appreciation of the dollar explains in large part the apparently relatively low build-up of long-term debt stocks compared with current-account deficits over the period 1979-83. While short-term borrowing explains some of this, a significant amount of the discrepancy is accounted for by the effect of the higher dollar on current dollar value of total outstanding long-term debt stocks. Similarly, the depreciation of the dollar in 1978 explains part of the discrepancy in the opposite direction in that year. Since the whole context, and the evolution of all the variables in the Table, would have been different, there is no basis for "adjusting" the debt-stock numbers for the dollar exchange-rate impact. (The question of the statistical and economic implications of exchange-rate changes for the debt situation is discussed in the following chapters.) For 1984, the technical assumption is that the dollar will remain at its current effective rate. The increase in debt stocks of non-OPEC, non-OECD countries projected for 1984 in Table A is substantially larger than that recorded in 1983 with a roughly similar current-account deficit, partly because the statistical impact of a rising dollar is assumed not to be present.

2.  A fuller account of developing-country financing history since 1970 is contained in Development Co-operation: Efforts and Policies of the Members of the Development Assistance Committee, OECD, Paris, 1983.

3.  See Economic Survey of the United States 1983-1984, OECD, Paris, December 1983.

4.  See Recent Multilateral Debt Restructurings with Official and Bank Creditors, Occasional Paper No. 25, IMF, Washington, DC, December 1983.

5.  For a fuller analysis, see Chapter III, "The Overall Flow of Financial Resources to Developing Countries", in Development Co-operation: Efforts and Policies of the Members of the Development Assistance Committee, OECD, Paris, 1983.

6.  See the section "Technical Note" for a comprehensive presentation of concepts and definitions.

7.  See External Debt of Developing Countries -- 1982 Survey, OECD, Paris, 1982. Figures for end-1982 indebtedness in this Survey are markedly lower than 1982 estimates contained in last year's Survey ($74 billion less for total debt of all LDCs and $24 billion for total debt service). Apart from the exclusion in the new Survey of Spain, the difference is also explained by the fact that 1982 estimates were based on 1981 exchange rates whereas 1982 figures in this Survey use actual 1982 exchange rates. (This lower dollar value accounts for some $24 billion less in debt and $4 billion less in debt service.) The remainder of the difference is the "estimation error" and accounts for $21 billion for debt (4 per cent of actual debt) and $14 billion for debt service (13 per cent of actual debt service). The "estimation error" for debt

service was relatively large owing to the build-up of interest arrears in 1982 and delayed repayment of principal.

8.  The overall pattern for total non-oil LDCs (i.e. including OECD developing countries) is believed to be similar.

9.  Tables 13 and 14 do not include China, a large net creditor to the rest of the world. In recent years, the net external position of China has improved considerably. In particular, external reserves increased from $3 billion at end-1980 to an estimated $15 billion at end-1983, while long-term debt decreased from $4.2 billion to $3.4 billion during the same period.

10. For more detailed information, see Finance and Development, IMF and World Bank, Washington, DC, September 1983.

11. See also the information presented in the World Development Report 1983, World Bank, Washington, DC, July 1983.

List of Tables 1-22

53

Table 1

TOTAL DISBURSED LONG-TERM DEBT OF DEVELOPING COUNTRIES AT YEAR-END
1971-83, BY SOURCE AND TERMS OF LENDING
$ billion

| Source and terms of lending | 1971 | 1975 | 1976 | 1977 | 1978 | 1979 | 1980 | 1981 | 1982 | 1983 |
|---|---|---|---|---|---|---|---|---|---|---|
| 1. DAC countries and capital markets | 68 | 131 | 160 | 200 | 255 | 301 | 342 | 381 | 414 | 455 |
| ODA | 24 | 34 | 36 | 41 | 49 | 53 | 57 | 57 | 59 | 61 |
| Total export credits | 26 | 40 | 49 | 64 | 82 | 98 | 110 | 117 | 121 | 127 |
| Total private | 18 | 57 | 74 | 95 | 124 | 151 | 175 | 207 | 234 | 267 |
| of which: bank loans (a) | 10 | 46 | 59 | 75 | 98 | 123 | 145 | 175 | 200 | 234 |
| bonds | 4 | 5 | 6 | 9 | 13 | 13 | 15 | 16 | 16 | 15 |
| other | 3 | 6 | 9 | 11 | 13 | 14 | 15 | 17 | 18 | 18 |
| 2. Multilateral | 9 | 21 | 26 | 32 | 39 | 46 | 55 | 64 | 75 | 84 |
| of which: concessional | 6 | 10 | 12 | 14 | 17 | 20 | 24 | 27 | 30 | 33 |
| 3. CMEA countries | 6 | 9 | 9 | 11 | 12 | 15 | 15 | 16 | 17 | 18 |
| of which: concessional | 5 | 8 | 8 | 9 | 10 | 11 | 12 | 13 | 13 | 14 |
| 4. OPEC countries | x | 6 | 8 | 11 | 13 | 15 | 18 | 20 | 21 | 23 |
| of which: concessional | x | 5 | 6 | 8 | 9 | 11 | 12 | 14 | 15 | 16 |
| 5. Other LDCs | 2 | 3 | 3 | 4 | 5 | 6 | 7 | 7 | 7 | 8 |
| of which: concessional | 1 | 2 | 2 | 2 | 3 | 3 | 3 | 3 | 3 | 3 |
| 6. Other and adjustments | 1 | 3 | 5 | 5 | 7 | 8 | 8 | 13 | 18 | 18 |
| Total debt | 86 | 173 | 211 | 262 | 331 | 391 | 445 | 501 | 552 | 606 |
| of which: concessional | 33 | 59 | 65 | 76 | 89 | 99 | 109 | 114 | 121 | 130 |
| non-concessional | 53 | 114 | 146 | 186 | 243 | 292 | 336 | 387 | 431 | 476 |

a. Bank loans other than export credits.

54

Table 2

TOTAL ANNUAL LONG-TERM DEBT SERVICE OF DEVELOPING COUNTRIES DURING
1971-83, BY SOURCE AND TERMS OF LENDING
$ billion

| Source and terms of lending | 1971 | 1975 | 1976 | 1977 | 1978 | 1979 | 1980 | 1981 | 1982 | 1983 |
|---|---|---|---|---|---|---|---|---|---|---|
| 1. DAC countries and capital markets | 8.8 | 21.4 | 26.4 | 34.6 | 48.5 | 62.7 | 72.4 | 87.8 | 94.3 | 82.7 |
| ODA | 1.3 | 1.7 | 1.9 | 2.0 | 2.3 | 2.6 | 2.8 | 2.8 | 2.7 | 2.7 |
| Total export credits | 4.9 | 10.4 | 11.9 | 15.8 | 19.6 | 23.9 | 28.1 | 32.4 | 31.3 | 30.0 |
| Total private | 2.6 | 9.3 | 12.6 | 16.7 | 26.5 | 36.2 | 41.5 | 52.5 | 60.4 | 50.0 |
| of which: bank loans (a) | 1.9 | 7.8 | 10.2 | 13.6 | 22.5 | 31.3 | 36.3 | 46.8 | 53.4 | 44.4 |
| bonds | 0.4 | 0.7 | 0.5 | 0.8 | 1.3 | 1.9 | 1.6 | 2.1 | 3.0 | 2.6 |
| other | 0.4 | 0.9 | 1.8 | 2.4 | 2.8 | 3.1 | 3.6 | 3.7 | 3.9 | 3.0 |
| 2. Multilateral | 0.9 | 1.6 | 2.0 | 2.5 | 3.2 | 3.7 | 4.6 | 5.6 | 6.5 | 7.4 |
| of which: concessional | 0.2 | 0.6 | 0.6 | 0.7 | 0.8 | 0.7 | 0.8 | 0.9 | 1.2 | 1.4 |
| 3. CMEA countries | 0.6 | 0.8 | 0.9 | 1.1 | 1.3 | 1.6 | 1.8 | 1.9 | 1.9 | 1.8 |
| of which: concessional | 0.5 | 0.7 | 0.7 | 0.9 | 0.9 | 1.0 | 1.4 | 1.4 | 1.4 | 1.4 |
| 4. OPEC countries | x | 0.2 | 0.2 | 0.6 | 0.9 | 1.2 | 1.3 | 1.8 | 1.9 | 1.8 |
| of which: concessional | x | 0.1 | 0.1 | 0.4 | 0.4 | 0.5 | 0.6 | 0.8 | 0.9 | 0.9 |
| 5. Other LDCs | 0.1 | 0.3 | 0.4 | 0.4 | 0.4 | 0.6 | 0.7 | 0.9 | 1.0 | 0.9 |
| of which: concessional | x | x | x | x | x | 0.1 | 0.1 | 0.1 | 0.1 | 0.1 |
| 6. Other and adjustments | 0.2 | 0.7 | 1.0 | 0.9 | 1.0 | 1.3 | 1.5 | 1.7 | 1.9 | 1.5 |
| Total debt service | 10.5 | 25.1 | 30.9 | 40.1 | 55.3 | 71.2 | 82.3 | 99.7 | 107.6 | 96.1 |
| of which: interest | 3.2 | 8.8 | 10.2 | 12.7 | 17.4 | 25.5 | 35.2 | 43.2 | 50.3 | 48.1 |
| amortization | 7.3 | 16.3 | 20.6 | 27.4 | 37.9 | 45.7 | 47.1 | 56.5 | 57.3 | 48.0 |
| Total debt service | | | | | | | | | | |
| of which: concessional | 1.7 | 3.2 | 3.4 | 4.1 | 4.5 | 4.9 | 5.7 | 6.0 | 6.2 | 6.5 |
| non-concessional | 8.8 | 21.9 | 27.5 | 36.0 | 50.8 | 66.3 | 76.6 | 93.7 | 101.4 | 89.6 |

a. Bank loans other than export credits.

Table 3

TOTAL DISBURSED LONG-TERM DEBT OF LOW-INCOME DEVELOPING COUNTRIES AT YEAR-END
1971-83, BY SOURCE AND TERMS OF LENDING
$ billion

| Source and terms of lending | 1971 | 1975 | 1976 | 1977 | 1978 | 1979 | 1980 | 1981 | 1982 | 1983 |
|---|---|---|---|---|---|---|---|---|---|---|
| 1. DAC countries and capital markets | 16.3 | 30.1 | 34.4 | 40.4 | 48.2 | 53.7 | 58.8 | 62.3 | 66.9 | 72.7 |
| ODA | 12.6 | 19.1 | 20.6 | 24.0 | 28.3 | 30.5 | 32.8 | 33.4 | 34.8 | 35.5 |
| Total export credits | 3.0 | 6.8 | 8.5 | 10.7 | 13.3 | 16.1 | 18.6 | 19.9 | 21.4 | 24.0 |
| Total private | 0.7 | 4.2 | 5.2 | 5.7 | 6.6 | 7.1 | 7.4 | 9.0 | 10.8 | 13.2 |
| of which: bank loans (a) | 0.4 | 3.4 | 4.1 | 4.7 | 5.6 | 5.9 | 6.0 | 7.3 | 8.6 | 10.8 |
| bonds | 0.2 | 0.2 | 0.2 | 0.2 | 0.4 | 0.4 | 0.5 | 0.5 | 0.7 | 0.7 |
| other | 0.1 | 0.6 | 0.9 | 0.7 | 0.7 | 0.8 | 1.0 | 1.1 | 1.5 | 1.7 |
| 2. Multilateral | 3.2 | 7.6 | 9.7 | 13.2 | 16.7 | 19.8 | 24.6 | 28.2 | 32.2 | 35.4 |
| of which: concessional | 3.0 | 6.1 | 7.4 | 9.9 | 12.5 | 14.9 | 18.4 | 20.8 | 23.7 | .. |
| 3. CMEA countries | 1.6 | 4.2 | 4.2 | 4.3 | 4.8 | 5.4 | 5.8 | 6.1 | 6.4 | 7.0 |
| of which: concessional | 1.5 | 3.9 | 3.8 | 4.0 | 4.2 | 4.6 | 5.0 | 5.2 | 5.5 | .. |
| 4. OPEC countries | 0.2 | 4.8 | 6.3 | 7.4 | 8.3 | 9.3 | 10.3 | 11.0 | 11.6 | 13.0 |
| of which: concessional | x | 4.3 | 5.6 | 6.3 | 7.0 | 7.9 | 8.7 | 9.3 | 9.7 | .. |
| 5. Other LDCs | 0.6 | 2.0 | 2.2 | 2.5 | 3.0 | 3.4 | 3.8 | 3.9 | 3.8 | 4.2 |
| of which: concessional | 0.1 | 1.5 | 1.7 | 2.0 | 2.4 | 2.6 | 2.7 | 2.5 | 2.5 | .. |
| 6. Other and adjustments | 0.1 | 0.7 | 0.8 | 0.5 | 0.4 | 0.5 | 0.7 | 1.2 | 1.9 | 2.5 |
| Total debt | 22.0 | 49.4 | 57.5 | 68.3 | 81.4 | 92.1 | 104.0 | 112.6 | 122.8 | 134.8 |
| of which: concessional | 17.0 | 34.9 | 39.2 | 46.2 | 54.5 | 60.5 | 67.7 | 71.4 | 76.3 | 81.0 |
| non-concessional | 5.0 | 14.4 | 18.3 | 22.1 | 26.8 | 31.6 | 36.3 | 41.2 | 46.5 | 53.8 |

a. Bank loans other than export credits.

Table 4

TOTAL ANNUAL LONG-TERM DEBT SERVICE OF LOW-INCOME DEVELOPING COUNTRIES DURING
1971-83, BY SOURCE AND TERMS OF LENDING
$ billion

| Source and terms of lending | 1971 | 1975 | 1976 | 1977 | 1978 | 1979 | 1980 | 1981 | 1982 | 1983 |
|---|---|---|---|---|---|---|---|---|---|---|
| 1. DAC countries and capital markets | 1.1 | 3.0 | 3.3 | 4.3 | 5.8 | 6.4 | 7.2 | 7.7 | 8.2 | 8.6 |
| ODA | 0.5 | 0.8 | 0.9 | 1.0 | 1.2 | 1.3 | 1.4 | 1.4 | 1.4 | 1.4 |
| Total export credits | 0.5 | 1.6 | 1.7 | 2.1 | 2.6 | 3.2 | 4.1 | 4.4 | 4.3 | 4.6 |
| Total private | 0.1 | 0.6 | 0.7 | 1.2 | 2.0 | 2.0 | 1.7 | 1.9 | 2.5 | 2.6 |
| of which: bank loans (a) | 0.1 | 0.5 | 0.5 | 1.0 | 1.8 | 1.7 | 1.4 | 1.6 | 2.1 | 2.2 |
| bonds | x | x | x | x | 0.1 | x | x | x | 0.1 | 0.1 |
| other | x | x | 0.1 | 0.1 | 0.2 | 0.2 | 0.2 | 0.2 | 0.3 | 0.3 |
| 2. Multilateral | 0.2 | 0.3 | 0.4 | 0.5 | 0.7 | 0.8 | 0.9 | 1.1 | 1.7 | 2.2 |
| of which: concessional | x | 0.2 | 0.2 | 0.2 | 0.3 | 0.3 | 0.3 | 0.3 | 0.7 | 0.9 |
| 3. CMEA countries | 0.1 | 0.3 | 0.3 | 0.3 | 0.4 | 0.4 | 0.5 | 0.6 | 0.5 | 0.4 |
| of which: concessional | 0.1 | 0.3 | 0.2 | 0.3 | 0.3 | 0.3 | 0.4 | 0.4 | 0.4 | 0.4 |
| 4. OPEC countries | x | 0.1 | 0.1 | 0.4 | 0.4 | 0.4 | 0.5 | 0.7 | 0.7 | 0.7 |
| of which: concessional | .. | 0.1 | 0.1 | 0.4 | 0.3 | 0.3 | 0.4 | 0.6 | 0.7 | 0.7 |
| 5. Other LDCs | x | 0.2 | 0.2 | 0.1 | 0.1 | 0.2 | 0.2 | 0.2 | 0.3 | 0.3 |
| of which: concessional | .. | x | x | x | x | 0.1 | 0.1 | 0.1 | 0.1 | 0.1 |
| 6. Other and adjustments | - | 0.2 | 0.3 | 0.2 | 0.1 | 0.1 | 0.1 | 0.2 | 0.2 | 0.2 |
| Total debt service | 1.4 | 4.1 | 4.6 | 5.8 | 7.4 | 8.2 | 9.4 | 10.5 | 11.6 | 12.5 |
| of which: interest | 0.4 | 1.3 | 1.6 | 1.8 | 2.5 | 3.2 | 3.5 | 3.9 | 4.5 | 4.5 |
| amortization | 1.0 | 2.8 | 3.0 | 4.0 | 4.9 | 5.0 | 6.0 | 6.8 | 7.1 | 8.0 |
| Total debt service | | | | | | | | | | |
| of which: concessional | 0.6 | 1.3 | 1.4 | 1.9 | 2.1 | 2.2 | 2.6 | 2.8 | 3.2 | 3.5 |
| non-concessional | 0.8 | 2.8 | 3.2 | 3.9 | 5.3 | 6.0 | 6.8 | 7.7 | 8.4 | 9.0 |

a. Bank loans other than export credits.

Table 5

TOTAL DISBURSED LONG-TERM DEBT OF LOWER MIDDLE-INCOME DEVELOPING COUNTRIES AT YEAR-END
1971-83, BY SOURCE AND TERMS OF LENDING
$ billion

| Source and terms of lending | 1971 | 1975 | 1976 | 1977 | 1978 | 1979 | 1980 | 1981 | 1982 | 1983 |
|---|---|---|---|---|---|---|---|---|---|---|
| 1. DAC countries and capital markets | 7 | 15 | 18 | 23 | 29 | 36 | 43 | 48 | 54 | 59 |
| ODA | 2 | 4 | 4 | 5 | 6 | 6 | 7 | 7 | 8 | 9 |
| Total export credits | 2 | 5 | 6 | 8 | 10 | 13 | 16 | 17 | 19 | 20 |
| Total private | 3 | 6 | 8 | 10 | 13 | 17 | 20 | 23 | 27 | 30 |
| of which: bank loans (a) | 2 | 5 | 6 | 9 | 11 | 14 | 17 | 20 | 24 | 28 |
| bonds | x | x | 1 | 1 | 1 | 1 | 1 | 1 | 1 | 1 |
| other | x | 1 | 1 | 1 | 1 | 2 | 2 | 2 | 2 | 2 |
| 2. Multilateral | 2 | 4 | 4 | 5 | 7 | 8 | 10 | 12 | 14 | 16 |
| of which: concessional | : | 1 | 1 | 1 | 2 | 2 | 3 | 3 | 3 | : |
| 3. CMEA countries | 1 | 2 | 2 | 2 | 3 | 3 | 3 | 4 | 5 | 5 |
| of which: concessional | : | 2 | 2 | 2 | 3 | 3 | 3 | 4 | 4 | : |
| 4. OPEC countries | x | x | x | 1 | 2 | 2 | 3 | 4 | 4 | 5 |
| of which: concessional | : | x | x | 1 | 1 | 1 | 2 | 3 | 3 | : |
| 5. Other LDCs | x | x | x | 1 | 1 | 1 | 1 | 1 | 1 | 1 |
| of which: concessional | : | x | x | x | x | x | x | x | x | : |
| 6. Other and adjustments | x | x | 1 | 1 | 1 | 2 | 2 | 2 | 3 | 5 |
| Total debt | 10 | 21 | 26 | 34 | 43 | 52 | 61 | 71 | 81 | 91 |
| of which: concessional | 4 | 7 | 8 | 9 | 12 | 13 | 16 | 18 | 19 | 21 |
| non-concessional | 6 | 14 | 18 | 25 | 31 | 39 | 45 | 53 | 62 | 70 |

a. Bank loans other than export credits.

58

Table 6

TOTAL ANNUAL LONG-TERM DEBT SERVICE OF LOWER MIDDLE-INCOME DEVELOPING COUNTRIES DURING 1971-83, BY SOURCE AND TERMS OF LENDING

$ billion

| Source and terms of lending | 1971 | 1975 | 1976 | 1977 | 1978 | 1979 | 1980 | 1981 | 1982 | 1983 |
|---|---|---|---|---|---|---|---|---|---|---|
| 1. DAC countries and capital markets | 1.0 | 2.6 | 3.0 | 3.8 | 5.5 | 7.0 | 8.7 | 11.1 | 11.8 | 10.3 |
| ODA | 0.2 | 0.3 | 0.3 | 0.2 | 0.3 | 0.3 | 0.4 | 0.4 | 0.4 | 0.4 |
| Total export credits | 0.6 | 1.3 | 1.4 | 1.9 | 2.5 | 3.0 | 4.0 | 4.6 | 4.5 | 4.5 |
| Total private | 0.2 | 1.0 | 1.3 | 1.6 | 2.8 | 3.7 | 4.3 | 6.1 | 6.9 | 5.4 |
| of which: bank loans (a) | 0.2 | 0.7 | 0.8 | 1.2 | 2.2 | 2.9 | 3.6 | 5.3 | 6.1 | 4.8 |
| bonds | x | x | x | 0.1 | 0.1 | 0.1 | 0.1 | 0.1 | 0.2 | 0.1 |
| other | x | 0.2 | 0.5 | 0.4 | 0.5 | 0.6 | 0.6 | 0.6 | 0.6 | 0.5 |
| 2. Multilateral | 0.2 | 0.3 | 0.4 | 0.5 | 0.6 | 0.8 | 1.0 | 1.2 | 1.4 | 1.6 |
| of which: concessional | x | 0.1 | 0.1 | 0.1 | 0.1 | 0.1 | 0.2 | 0.2 | 0.2 | 0.2 |
| 3. CMEA countries | 0.1 | 0.1 | 0.2 | 0.2 | 0.2 | 0.3 | 0.4 | 0.3 | 0.4 | 0.4 |
| of which: concessional | x | 0.1 | 0.1 | 0.2 | 0.2 | 0.2 | 0.3 | 0.3 | 0.3 | 0.3 |
| 4. OPEC countries | x | x | x | x | 0.1 | 0.2 | 0.2 | 0.2 | 0.2 | 0.2 |
| of which: concessional | .. | x | x | x | 0.1 | 0.1 | 0.1 | 0.1 | 0.1 | 0.1 |
| 5. Other LDCs | x | x | x | 0.1 | 0.1 | 0.1 | 0.1 | 0.1 | 0.2 | 0.2 |
| of which: concessional | .. | x | x | x | x | x | x | x | x | x |
| 6. Other and adjustments | x | x | 0.1 | 0.1 | 0.1 | 0.1 | 0.2 | 0.3 | 0.3 | 0.2 |
| Total debt service | 1.4 | 3.1 | 3.7 | 4.7 | 6.7 | 8.5 | 10.6 | 13.2 | 14.4 | 12.9 |
| of which: interest | 0.5 | 0.9 | 1.0 | 1.3 | 1.8 | 3.1 | 4.5 | 5.5 | 7.0 | 6.7 |
| amortization | 0.9 | 2.2 | 2.7 | 3.4 | 4.9 | 5.4 | 6.1 | 7.7 | 7.5 | 6.2 |
| Total debt service |  |  |  |  |  |  |  |  |  |  |
| of which: concessional | 0.3 | 0.5 | 0.5 | 0.6 | 0.7 | 0.8 | 1.0 | 0.9 | 0.9 | 0.9 |
| non-concessional | 1.1 | 2.6 | 3.2 | 4.1 | 6.0 | 7.7 | 9.6 | 12.3 | 13.5 | 12.0 |

a. Bank loans other than export credits.

59

Table 7

TOTAL DISBURSED LONG-TERM DEBT OF UPPER MIDDLE-INCOME DEVELOPING COUNTRIES AT YEAR-END
1971-83, BY SOURCE AND TERMS OF LENDING
$ billion

| Source and terms of lending | 1971 | 1975 | 1976 | 1977 | 1978 | 1979 | 1980 | 1981 | 1982 | 1983 |
|---|---|---|---|---|---|---|---|---|---|---|
| 1. DAC countries and capital markets | 45 | 86 | 108 | 136 | 178 | 212 | 241 | 271 | 294 | 324 |
| ODA | 9 | 11 | 11 | 13 | 15 | 16 | 17 | 17 | 17 | 17 |
| Total export credits | 21 | 28 | 35 | 45 | 59 | 69 | 76 | 79 | 81 | 83 |
| Total private | 15 | 47 | 61 | 79 | 104 | 127 | 148 | 175 | 196 | 224 |
| of which: bank loans (a) | 8 | 38 | 49 | 62 | 82 | 103 | 123 | 147 | 168 | 196 |
| bonds | 3 | 4 | 5 | 8 | 11 | 12 | 13 | 14 | 14 | 13 |
| other | 3 | 4 | 7 | 9 | 11 | 12 | 13 | 14 | 14 | 14 |
| 2. Multilateral | 4 | 10 | 12 | 14 | 16 | 18 | 21 | 23 | 28 | 32 |
| of which: concessional | .. | 3 | 3 | 3 | 3 | 3 | 3 | 3 | 3 | .. |
| 3. CMEA countries | 3 | 3 | 3 | 4 | 5 | 6 | 6 | 6 | 6 | 6 |
| of which: concessional | .. | 3 | 3 | 3 | 4 | 4 | 4 | 3 | 3 | .. |
| 4. OPEC countries | x | 1 | 1 | 2 | 3 | 3 | 5 | 5 | 5 | 5 |
| of which: concessional | .. | x | 1 | 1 | 1 | 1 | 1 | 2 | 2 | .. |
| 5. Other LDCs | 1 | 1 | 1 | 1 | 1 | 2 | 2 | 2 | 2 | 3 |
| of which: concessional | .. | x | x | x | x | x | x | x | x | .. |
| 6. Other and adjustments | 1 | 2 | 3 | 3 | 5 | 6 | 6 | 10 | 13 | 11 |
| Total debt | 54 | 102 | 128 | 160 | 207 | 247 | 280 | 317 | 348 | 381 |
| of which: concessional | 12 | 17 | 18 | 20 | 23 | 25 | 25 | 25 | 25 | 25 |
| non-concessional | 42 | 85 | 109 | 140 | 184 | 222 | 255 | 292 | 223 | 356 |

a.  Bank loans other than export credits.

60

Table 8

TOTAL ANNUAL LONG-TERM DEBT SERVICE OF UPPER MIDDLE-INCOME DEVELOPING COUNTRIES DURING
1971-83, BY SOURCE AND TERMS OF LENDING
$ billion

| Source and terms of lending | 1971 | 1975 | 1976 | 1977 | 1978 | 1979 | 1980 | 1981 | 1982 | 1983 |
|---|---|---|---|---|---|---|---|---|---|---|
| 1. DAC countries and capital markets | 6.7 | 15.8 | 20.1 | 26.5 | 37.2 | 49.3 | 56.5 | 69.0 | 74.5 | 63.8 |
| ODA | 0.6 | 0.7 | 0.7 | 0.8 | 0.9 | 0.9 | 1.0 | 1.0 | 1.0 | 0.9 |
| Total export credits | 3.8 | 7.4 | 8.8 | 11.8 | 14.6 | 17.7 | 20.0 | 23.4 | 22.4 | 21.0 |
| Total private | 2.3 | 7.7 | 10.6 | 13.9 | 21.7 | 30.6 | 35.5 | 44.6 | 51.1 | 42.0 |
| of which: bank loans (a) | 1.6 | 6.5 | 8.9 | 11.4 | 18.5 | 26.6 | 31.2 | 39.9 | 45.3 | 37.4 |
| bonds | 0.3 | 0.6 | 0.4 | 0.7 | 1.1 | 1.7 | 1.4 | 1.9 | 2.7 | 2.4 |
| other | 0.3 | 0.6 | 1.2 | 1.9 | 2.1 | 2.3 | 2.8 | 2.8 | 3.1 | 2.2 |
| 2. Multilateral | 0.5 | 0.9 | 1.2 | 1.5 | 1.8 | 2.2 | 2.7 | 3.3 | 3.4 | 3.6 |
| of which: concessional | .. | 0.3 | 0.3 | 0.3 | 0.3 | 0.3 | 0.3 | 0.4 | 0.3 | 0.3 |
| 3. CMEA countries | 0.3 | 0.4 | 0.5 | 0.6 | 0.7 | 1.0 | 1.0 | 1.0 | 1.0 | 1.0 |
| of which: concessional | .. | 0.3 | 0.4 | 0.4 | 0.4 | 0.5 | 0.7 | 0.7 | 0.7 | 0.7 |
| 4. OPEC countries | x | 0.1 | 0.1 | 0.2 | 0.4 | 0.6 | 0.6 | 0.8 | 0.9 | 0.9 |
| of which: concessional | .. | x | x | 0.1 | 0.1 | 0.1 | 0.1 | 0.1 | 0.1 | 0.1 |
| 5. Other LDCs | x | 0.1 | 0.1 | 0.2 | 0.2 | 0.3 | 0.4 | 0.5 | 0.4 | 0.4 |
| of which: concessional | .. | x | x | x | x | x | x | x | x | x |
| 6. Other and adjustments | 0.2 | 0.5 | 0.6 | 0.6 | 0.8 | 1.1 | 1.2 | 1.3 | 1.3 | 1.0 |
| Total debt service | 7.7 | 17.9 | 22.5 | 29.5 | 41.2 | 54.6 | 62.3 | 76.0 | 81.6 | 70.7 |
| of which: interest | 2.4 | 6.6 | 7.6 | 9.6 | 13.1 | 19.2 | 27.2 | 33.9 | 38.8 | 36.9 |
| amortization | 5.3 | 11.3 | 14.9 | 20.0 | 28.1 | 35.3 | 35.1 | 42.1 | 42.8 | 33.8 |
| Total debt service | | | | | | | | | | |
| of which: concessional | 0.8 | 1.4 | 1.5 | 1.6 | 1.7 | 1.9 | 2.1 | 2.2 | 2.1 | 2.1 |
| non-concessional | 6.9 | 16.5 | 21.0 | 28.0 | 39.5 | 52.6 | 60.2 | 73.8 | 79.5 | 68.6 |

a. Bank loans other than export credits.

61

Table 9

TOTAL DISBURSED LONG-TERM DEBT OF NON-OPEC, NON-OECD DEVELOPING COUNTRIES AT YEAR-END
1971-83, BY SOURCE AND TERMS OF LENDING
$ billion

| Source and terms of lending | 1971 | 1975 | 1976 | 1977 | 1978 | 1979 | 1980 | 1981 | 1982 | 1983 |
|---|---|---|---|---|---|---|---|---|---|---|
| 1. DAC countries and capital markets | 49 | 95 | 115 | 141 | 177 | 207 | 238 | 276 | 306 | 337 |
| ODA | 21 | 27 | 29 | 33 | 38 | 41 | 44 | 45 | 46 | 47 |
| Total export credits | 15 | 23 | 28 | 36 | 47 | 55 | 64 | 72 | 77 | 82 |
| Total private | 13 | 45 | 58 | 72 | 92 | 111 | 130 | 160 | 183 | 208 |
| of which: bank loans (a) | 8 | 37 | 46 | 56 | 72 | 89 | 107 | 132 | 155 | 180 |
| bonds | 3 | 5 | 6 | 8 | 11 | 11 | 12 | 14 | 14 | 13 |
| other | 2 | 4 | 6 | 8 | 10 | 11 | 12 | 14 | 14 | 14 |
| 2. Multilateral | 7 | 17 | 21 | 26 | 32 | 38 | 46 | 53 | 62 | 69 |
| of which: concessional | .. | 8 | 10 | 12 | 15 | 18 | 22 | 25 | 28 | .. |
| 3. CMEA countries | 3 | 5 | 6 | 7 | 7 | 8 | 9 | 10 | 11 | 12 |
| of which: concessional | .. | 5 | 5 | 6 | 6 | 7 | 8 | 9 | 9 | .. |
| 4. OPEC countries | x | 5 | 7 | 9 | 11 | 13 | 15 | 17 | 18 | 20 |
| of which: concessional | x | 5 | 6 | 8 | 9 | 10 | 11 | 13 | 14 | .. |
| 5. Other LDCs | 2 | 3 | 3 | 4 | 4 | 5 | 6 | 6 | 6 | 7 |
| of which: concessional | x | 1 | 2 | 2 | 3 | 3 | 3 | 3 | 3 | .. |
| 6. Other and adjustments | 1 | 3 | 4 | 4 | 6 | 7 | 7 | 12 | 15 | 15 |
| Total debt | 63 | 129 | 156 | 191 | 238 | 278 | 321 | 374 | 418 | 460 |
| of which: concessional | 25 | 46 | 52 | 61 | 71 | 79 | 88 | 94 | 100 | 108 |
| non-concessional | 38 | 83 | 104 | 130 | 167 | 199 | 233 | 280 | 318 | 352 |

a. Bank loans other than export credits.

Table 10

TOTAL ANNUAL LONG-TERM DEBT SERVICE OF NON-OPEC, NON-OECD DEVELOPING COUNTRIES DURING
1971-83, BY SOURCE AND TERMS OF LENDING
$ billion

| Source and terms of lending | 1971 | 1975 | 1976 | 1977 | 1978 | 1979 | 1980 | 1981 | 1982 | 1983 |
|---|---|---|---|---|---|---|---|---|---|---|
| 1. DAC countries and capital markets | 5.8 | 14.5 | 17.5 | 22.7 | 33.3 | 42.0 | 46.4 | 55.5 | 62.7 | 52.7 |
| ODA | 1.0 | 1.4 | 1.5 | 1.6 | 1.8 | 2.1 | 2.2 | 2.2 | 2.0 | 2.0 |
| Total export credits | 2.8 | 5.9 | 6.4 | 7.9 | 10.1 | 12.0 | 14.2 | 15.3 | 16.2 | 16.0 |
| Total private | 1.9 | 7.2 | 9.6 | 13.3 | 21.4 | 28.0 | 30.0 | 38.0 | 44.5 | 34.7 |
| of which: bank loans (a) | 1.4 | 6.1 | 8.0 | 11.1 | 18.2 | 24.0 | 26.2 | 33.3 | 38.8 | 30.0 |
| bonds | 0.3 | 0.6 | 0.5 | 0.7 | 1.2 | 1.7 | 1.3 | 1.7 | 2.6 | 2.3 |
| other | 0.2 | 0.5 | 1.1 | 1.5 | 2.1 | 2.3 | 2.5 | 3.0 | 3.1 | 2.4 |
| 2. Multilateral | 0.7 | 1.3 | 1.6 | 2.0 | 2.5 | 2.9 | 3.5 | 4.0 | 5.0 | 5.9 |
| of which: concessional | .. | 0.5 | 0.5 | 0.5 | 0.7 | 0.6 | 0.6 | 0.7 | 1.0 | 1.3 |
| 3. CMEA countries | 0.4 | 0.5 | 0.5 | 0.7 | 0.8 | 0.9 | 1.1 | 1.1 | 1.1 | 1.0 |
| of which: concessional | .. | 0.4 | 0.4 | 0.5 | 0.5 | 0.6 | 0.9 | 0.8 | 0.8 | 0.8 |
| 4. OPEC countries | x | 0.2 | 0.2 | 0.5 | 0.6 | 0.8 | 0.9 | 1.3 | 1.3 | 1.2 |
| of which: concessional | x | 0.1 | 0.1 | 0.4 | 0.4 | 0.5 | 0.6 | 0.8 | 0.8 | 0.8 |
| 5. Other LDCs | 0.1 | 0.2 | 0.2 | 0.3 | 0.3 | 0.5 | 0.5 | 0.8 | 0.8 | 0.7 |
| of which: concessional | x | x | x | x | x | 0.1 | 0.1 | x | 0.1 | 0.1 |
| 6. Other and adjustments | 0.2 | 0.7 | 0.9 | 0.9 | 1.0 | 1.2 | 1.4 | 1.5 | 1.5 | 1.0 |
| Total debt service | 7.2 | 17.3 | 21.0 | 27.0 | 38.5 | 48.1 | 53.9 | 64.2 | 72.4 | 62.5 |
| of which: interest | 2.0 | 5.9 | 7.0 | 8.9 | 11.8 | 16.9 | 24.5 | 30.5 | 35.9 | 35.1 |
| amortization | 5.2 | 11.4 | 13.9 | 18.2 | 26.7 | 31.3 | 29.4 | 33.7 | 36.5 | 27.4 |
| Total debt service | | | | | | | | | | |
| of which: concessional | 1.3 | 2.4 | 2.5 | 3.0 | 3.4 | 3.8 | 4.4 | 4.5 | 4.8 | 5.1 |
| non-concessional | 5.9 | 14.9 | 18.4 | 24.0 | 35.1 | 44.3 | 49.5 | 59.7 | 67.6 | 57.4 |

a. Bank loans other than export credits.

Table 11

TOTAL DISBURSED LONG-TERM DEBT AT YEAR-END 1982 AND DEBT SERVICE DURING 1982
OF DEVELOPING COUNTRIES, BY SOURCE OF LENDING

| Source of lending | Debt outstanding | | Debt service | | Interest | | Principal | |
|---|---|---|---|---|---|---|---|---|
| | $ million | % of total | $ million | % of total | $ million | % of end-1981 debt | $ million | % of end-1981 debt |
| 1. DAC countries and capital markets | 414 234 | 75.1 | 94 326 | 87.7 | 43 588 | 11.4 | 50 738 | 13.3 |
| ODA | 59 297 | 10.7 | 2 682 | 2.5 | 1 230 | 2.1 | 1 452 | 2.5 |
| OOF | 25 905 | 4.7 | 3 402 | 3.2 | 1 361 | 5.6 | 2 041 | 8.3 |
| OGPEC | 94 755 | 17.2 | 27 855 | 25.9 | 8 220 | 8.9 | 19 635 | 21.3 |
| Banks (a) | 200 347 | 36.3 | 53 435 | 49.7 | 29 330 | 16.8 | 24 105 | 13.8 |
| Bonds | 16 422 | 3.0 | 3 035 | 2.8 | 1 285 | 8.1 | 1 750 | 11.1 |
| Other private | 17 508 | 3.2 | 3 917 | 3.6 | 2 162 | 13.1 | 1 755 | 10.6 |
| 2. Multilateral | 74 547 | 13.5 | 6 530 | 6.1 | 3 750 | 5.9 | 2 780 | 4.4 |
| 3. CMEA countries | 16 528 | 3.0 | 1 880 | 1.7 | 410 | 2.6 | 1 470 | 9.3 |
| 4. OPEC countries | 21 402 | 3.9 | 1 914 | 1.8 | 921 | 4.6 | 993 | 5.0 |
| 5. Other LDCs | 7 220 | 1.3 | 955 | 0.9 | 198 | 2.8 | 757 | 10.6 |
| 6. Other and adjustments | 17 790 | 3.2 | 1 946 | 1.8 | 1 400 | n.a. | 546 | n.a. |
| Total | 551 720 | 100.0 | 107 551 | 100.0 | 50 268 | 10.0 | 57 283 | 11.4 |

a. Total bank loans including loans through offshore centres, but excluding export credits and bonds (figures on debt service are provisional).

Table 12

INTEREST COST TO DEVELOPING COUNTRIES DURING 1972-83, BY TYPE OF
LONG-TERM CREDIT DISBURSED AND INCOME GROUP

Percentage

| Interest cost on disbursed debt (a) | 72/73 | 74/76 | 77/78 | 1979 | 1980 | 1981 | 1982 | 1983 |
|---|---|---|---|---|---|---|---|---|
| 1. Fixed-interest debt | 4.4 | 4.9 | 5.5 | 5.8 | 6.0 | 6.0 | 6.3 | 6.7 |
| DAC ODA loans | 2.5 | 2.4 | 2.3 | 2.2 | 2.3 | 2.2 | 2.1 | 2.2 |
| DAC export credits | 6.3 | 7.0 | 7.6 | 7.8 | 8.2 | 7.9 | 8.1 | 9.0 |
| Bonds | 5.2 | 4.9 | 6.1 | 7.0 | 7.5 | 7.6 | 8.1 | 8.1 |
| Other private credits | 8.4 | 8.5 | 8.5 | 9.2 | 11.5 | 13.4 | 13.1 | 12.6 |
| Multilateral loans: concessional | 3.5 | 3.2 | 2.8 | 2.2 | 1.9 | 1.9 | 1.9 | 1.9 |
| non-concessional | 8.9 | 9.0 | 9.8 | 10.0 | 9.6 | 8.6 | 8.9 | 9.5 |
| Non-DAC total bilateral loans | 2.2 | 2.3 | 3.4 | 3.2 | 3.6 | 3.6 | 4.5 | 4.5 |
| 2. Floating-interest debt | 8.3 | 9.9 | 8.4 | 12.3 | 15.5 | 17.4 | 17.1 | 12.7 |
| 3. Total LDC debt | 5.0 | 6.0 | 6.3 | 7.7 | 9.0 | 9.7 | 10.0 | 8.7 |
| of which: | | | | | | | | |
| LICs | 2.9 | 3.2 | 3.4 | 3.8 | 3.8 | 3.8 | 4.0 | 3.7 |
| LMICs | 4.6 | 5.0 | 5.2 | 7.3 | 8.7 | 9.0 | 9.8 | 8.3 |
| UMICs | 6.4 | 7.6 | 7.8 | 9.3 | 11.0 | 12.1 | 12.2 | 10.6 |
| PM: Total Non-OPEC, Non-OECD debt | 4.5 | 5.4 | 6.0 | 7.1 | 8.8 | 9.5 | 9.6 | 8.4 |

a. Annual interest payments and other charges (including spreads and fees on floating-interest debt) as a percentage of disbursed debt at the beginning of the year.

Table 13

ESTIMATED TOTAL LONG- AND SHORT-TERM EXTERNAL ASSETS AND LIABILITIES OF NON-OPEC,
NON-OECD DEVELOPING COUNTRIES, YEAR-END 1980-83 (a)
$ billion

| Type of liabilities and assets | Liabilities | | | | Assets | | | | Balance | | | |
|---|---|---|---|---|---|---|---|---|---|---|---|---|
| | 1980 | 1981 | 1982 | 1983 | 1980 | 1981 | 1982 | 1983 | 1980 | 1981 | 1982 | 1983 |
| 1. Long-term | -321 | -374 | -418 | -460 | 28 | 36 | 45 | 51 | -292 | -338 | -373 | -409 |
| Fixed-interest (b) | -204 | -232 | -250 | -265 | 25 | 31 | 38 | 41 | -179 | -201 | -212 | -224 |
| Floating-interest (c) | -116 | -142 | -168 | -195 | 3 | 5 | 7 | 10 | -113 | -137 | -161 | -185 |
| 2. Short-term (d) | -89 | -111 | -113 | -103 | 105 | 103 | 99 | 102 | 16 | -8 | -14 | -1 |
| of which: foreign exchange reserves (e) | - | - | - | - | (79) | (80) | (70) | (73) | - | - | - | - |
| 3. Total | -409 | -485 | -531 | -563 | 133 | 139 | 144 | 153 | -276 | -346 | -387 | -410 |
| Fixed-interest | -204 | -232 | -250 | -265 | 25 | 31 | 38 | 41 | -179 | -201 | -212 | -224 |
| Floating-interest | -205 | -253 | -281 | -298 | 108 | 108 | 106 | 112 | -97 | -145 | -175 | -186 |
| of which: 4 countries (f) | -117 | -153 | -171 | -179 | 30 | 26 | 26 | 27 | -87 | -127 | -145 | -152 |
| LICs | -17 | -20 | -21 | -24 | 20 | 18 | 18 | 20 | 3 | -2 | -3 | -4 |

a.  Excluding direct foreign investment, gold and IMF transactions, as well as interest payable and receivable.

b.  The bulk of which is not denominated in US dollars.

c.  The bulk of which is denominated in US dollars.

d.  Liabilities include arrears; assets exclude capital flight to foreign countries. All short-term transactions are assumed to be on floating interest, although a significant part of trade credits (for both imports and exports) and of arrears are below market rates.

e.  All foreign exchange reserves are assumed to be invested in short-term instruments.

f.  Argentina, Brazil, S. Korea and Mexico.

Table 14

ESTIMATED TOTAL NET LONG- AND SHORT-TERM FLOATING-INTEREST DEBT OF NON-OPEC, NON-OECD
DEVELOPING COUNTRIES AS PERCENTAGE OF (I) TOTAL NET LONG- AND
SHORT-TERM DEBT, AND OF (II) GNP, YEAR-END 1978-83

| Group/Country | 1978 | | | 1982 | | | 1983 | | |
|---|---|---|---|---|---|---|---|---|---|
| | Total $ bn. | I % | II % | Total $ bn. | I % | II % | Total $ bn. | I % | II % |
| 1. LICs | -3 | -5 | -1 | 3.1 | 3 | 1 | 4.1 | 4 | 1 |
| of which: | | | | | | | | | |
| Bolivia | 0.7 | 39 | 18 | 1.0 | 36 | 13 | 0.9 | 32 | 10 |
| India | -5.4 | -54 | -5 | -1.3 | -7 | x | -0.7 | -4 | x |
| Senegal | 0.2 | 25 | 10 | 0.3 | 20 | 13 | 0.3 | 18 | 11 |
| Sudan | 0.6 | 18 | 8 | 2.1 | 34 | 35 | 2.0 | 32 | 32 |
| Zaire | 1.4 | 33 | 22 | 1.0 | 21 | 16 | 1.2 | 24 | 19 |
| Zambia | 0.8 | 36 | 32 | 0.8 | 26 | 24 | 0.7 | 21 | 20 |
| Other LICs | -1.3 | -4 | -1 | -0.8 | -1 | x | -0.3 | x | x |
| 2. LMICs + UMICs | 60.2 | 42 | 8 | 171.9 | 59 | 12 | 181.9 | 59 | 12 |
| of which: | | | | | | | | | |
| Argentina | 1.5 | 26 | 2 | 20.3 | 71 | 10 | 20.2 | 70 | 9 |
| Brazil | 21.2 | 57 | 11 | 50.2 | 68 | 16 | 59.3 | 71 | 18 |
| Chile | 1.9 | 42 | 13 | 9.3 | 74 | 31 | 10.6 | 75 | 32 |
| Ivory Coast | 0.6 | 22 | 8 | 2.9 | 51 | 31 | 2.7 | 47 | 26 |
| Jamaica | 0.7 | 50 | 28 | 0.8 | 36 | 28 | 0.9 | 39 | 28 |
| Korea | 1.6 | 15 | 3 | 16.8 | 61 | 25 | 16.6 | 55 | 22 |
| Mexico | 23.5 | 71 | 23 | 57.0 | 78 | 25 | 55.4 | 78 | 22 |
| Morocco | 1.6 | 31 | 12 | 2.7 | 29 | 16 | 3.2 | 32 | 17 |
| Nicaragua | 0.7 | 54 | 37 | 1.2 | 46 | 43 | 1.3 | 45 | 42 |
| Peru | 2.3 | 37 | 20 | 2.8 | 29 | 12 | 2.9 | 33 | 11 |
| Philippines | 2.6 | 46 | 11 | 6.6 | 54 | 15 | 7.7 | 51 | 16 |
| Other LMICs + UMICs | 2.0 | 7 | 1.2 | 1.3 | 3 | x | 1.1 | 3 | x |
| 3. Total Non-OPEC, Non-OECD LDCs | 57.2 | 29 | 5 | 175.0 | 45 | 10 | 186.0 | 45 | 9 |

Notes: Total net floating-interest debt is defined as long-term plus short-term floating-interest debt
minus floating-interest assets.  For coverage, see notes to Table 13.

The sign "-" means that the country, or group of countries, has more assets than liabilities on
floating-interest rates.

GNP data are the World Bank's current GNP series for 1978 and the Secretariat's estimates for
1982-83.

Table 15

LONG- AND SHORT-TERM LENDING AND EXPOSURE OF BANKS (a) TO NON-OPEC, NON-OECD DEVELOPING COUNTRIES:  ESTIMATED OUTSTANDING DISBURSED AMOUNTS, YEAR-END 1977-83
$ billion

|  | 1977 | 1980 | 1981 | 1982 | 1983 |
|---|---|---|---|---|---|
| 1. Short-term credits | 31 | 77 | 95 | 104 | 96 (b) |
| 2. Medium- and long-term credits | 64 | 132 | 161 | 186 | 216 |
|     A. Officially guaranteed export credits | 8 | 25 | 29 | 32 | 36 |
|     B. Financial loans and credits | 56 | 107 | 132 | 155 | 180 (b) |
| 3. Total gross exposure (1 + 2) | 95 | 209 | 255 | 290 | 312 |
|     [of which 4 countries (c), in %] | (60) | (61) | (64) | (63) | (62) |
| 4. Deposits (banks' liabilities) | 70 | 100 | 116 | 118 | 120 |
|     [of which 4 countries (c), in %] | (29) | (24) | (24) | (22) | (25) |
| 5. Total net exposure (3 - 4) | 25 | 109 | 139 | 172 | 192 |
|     [of which 4 countries (c), in %] | (148) | (95) | (97) | (92) | (85) |
| 6. Net exposure excluding guaranteed export credits (5 - 2A) | 17 | 84 | 110 | 140 | 156 |
|     [of which 4 countries (c), in %] | (188) | (112) | (111) | (101) | (94) |

a.  International lending by commercial banks and other financial institutions, excluding Central Banks but including participation of non-OECD banks in international syndicates. Data exclude bonds and other bank assets which are not loans. They also exclude future interest payable but include interest arrears. Short-term debt covers credits with an original maturity of less than one year; an unknown amount of these short-term credits is guaranteed by governments in capital-exporting countries. Deposits are those with BIS banks.

b.  Assuming some consolidation of short-term debt into medium-term debt during 1983.

c.  Argentina, Brazil, South Korea and Mexico.

Table 16

TOTAL DISBURSED LONG-TERM DEBT AT YEAR-END 1971-83 AND DEBT SERVICE DURING 1983
OF DEVELOPING COUNTRIES, BY TERMS OF LENDING AND INCOME GROUP

| Group/Year | Total debt | ODA | Non-conc. multilat. | Total export credits | Private markets |
|---|---|---|---|---|---|
| | $ billion | % of total | | | |
| **1. LICs** | | | | | |
| 1971 | 22 | 77 | 7 | 14 | 3 |
| 1975 | 49 | 71 | 3 | 16 | 10 |
| 1980 | 104 | 65 | 6 | 21 | 8 |
| 1982 | 123 | 62 | 7 | 20 | 11 |
| 1983 | 135 | 60 | 10 | 19 | 11 |
| 1983 debt service | 12.5 | 28 | 10 | 40 | 22 |
| of which: | | | | | |
| LLDCs | | | | | |
| 1971 | .. | .. | .. | .. | .. |
| 1975 | 9 | 70 | 4 | 20 | 6 |
| 1980 | 22 | 67 | 4 | 22 | 6 |
| 1982 | 27 | 68 | 5 | 20 | 7 |
| 1983 | 30 | 67 | 5 | 21 | 7 |
| 1983 debt service | 1.5 | 36 | 9 | 39 | 16 |
| **2. LMICs** | | | | | |
| 1971 | 10 | 40 | 10 | 29 | 22 |
| 1975 | 21 | 34 | 12 | 26 | 28 |
| 1980 | 61 | 25 | 12 | 29 | 34 |
| 1982 | 81 | 24 | 13 | 27 | 36 |
| 1983 | 91 | 23 | 12 | 28 | 37 |
| 1983 debt service | 12.9 | 6 | 9 | 36 | 49 |
| **3. UMICs** | | | | | |
| 1971 | 54 | 26 | 3 | 40 | 32 |
| 1975 | 102 | 17 | 7 | 30 | 47 |
| 1980 | 280 | 9 | 6 | 30 | 54 |
| 1982 | 348 | 7 | 7 | 27 | 58 |
| 1983 | 381 | 7 | 6 | 26 | 61 |
| 1983 debt service | 70.7 | 3 | 5 | 30 | 62 |
| Total LDCs | | | | | |
| 1971 | 86 | 41 | 3 | 32 | 24 |
| 1975 | 173 | 34 | 6 | 25 | 34 |
| 1980 | 445 | 24 | 7 | 28 | 40 |
| 1982 | 552 | 22 | 8 | 25 | 44 |
| 1983 | 606 | 21 | 8 | 23 | 48 |
| 1983 debt service | 96.1 | 7 | 6 | 32 | 55 |

Table 17

TOTAL DISBURSED LONG-TERM DEBT AT YEAR-END 1976-83 AND OTHER ECONOMIC VARIABLES
OF DEVELOPING COUNTRIES, BY INCOME GROUP AND MAJOR BORROWER
Amounts

| Group/Borrower | 1976 | 1977 | 1978 | 1979 | 1980 | 1981 | 1982 | 1983 | 1981 Pop. | 1981 GNP | 1981 Exports (a) |
|---|---|---|---|---|---|---|---|---|---|---|---|
| | $ billion | | | | | | | | million | $ billion | $ billion |
| 1. LICs | 57.5 | 68.3 | 81.4 | 92.1 | 104.0 | 112.6 | 122.8 | 135.0 | 1 487 | 458 | 75 |
| of which: | | | | | | | | | | | |
| LLDCs | 10.5 | 12.8 | 15.8 | 18.8 | 21.7 | 24.6 | 26.5 | 29.0 | 290 | 64 | 10 |
| Indonesia | 10.7 | 12.3 | 14.5 | 15.1 | 16.6 | 17.5 | 20.4 | .. | 149 | 82 | 24 |
| Egypt | 5.9 | 8.3 | 10.4 | 12.2 | 13.8 | 15.2 | 16.6 | .. | 43 | 32 | 9 |
| India | 13.6 | 14.9 | 15.8 | 16.5 | 18.2 | 18.9 | 20.7 | .. | 690 | 162 | 14 |
| 2. LMICs | 25.8 | 33.6 | 42.6 | 51.9 | 61.4 | 70.7 | 81.2 | 91.0 | 313 | 279 | 68 |
| of which: | | | | | | | | | | | |
| Nigeria | 1.4 | 1.7 | 2.7 | 4.2 | 5.2 | 6.0 | 7.9 | .. | 88 | 71 | 18 |
| Peru | 3.9 | 5.2 | 6.0 | 6.5 | 7.1 | 7.4 | 8.4 | 9.2 | 17 | 21 | 4 |
| Philippines | 3.8 | 5.1 | 6.3 | 7.5 | 8.7 | 10.2 | 11.9 | 14.4 | 50 | 39 | 9 |
| 3. UMICs | 127.6 | 160.1 | 207.3 | 246.9 | 279.6 | 317.3 | 347.8 | 381.0 | 551 | 1 647 | 543 |
| of which: | | | | | | | | | | | |
| Brazil | 27.0 | 33.5 | 45.3 | 50.8 | 57.1 | 64.7 | 72.6 | 80.6 | 121 | 274 | 27 |
| Mexico | 21.6 | 26.7 | 32.5 | 37.7 | 43.5 | 53.5 | 60.4 | 70.0 | 71 | 231 | 30 |
| Argentina | 5.9 | 6.9 | 8.8 | 12.6 | 16.0 | 23.7 | 27.1 | 29.5 | 28 | 200 | 12 |
| 4. Total LDCs | 210.9 | 262.0 | 331.3 | 390.9 | 445.0 | 500.7 | 551.7 | 606.0 | 2 351 | 2 384 | 687 |

a.   Exports of goods, services and net private transfers.

Table 18

TOTAL ANNUAL LONG-TERM DEBT SERVICE DURING 1976-83 AND OTHER ECONOMIC VARIABLES
OF DEVELOPING COUNTRIES, BY INCOME GROUP AND MAJOR BORROWER
Amounts

| Group/Borrower | 1976 | 1977 | 1978 | 1979 | 1980 | 1981 | 1982 | 1983 | 1981 Pop. | 1981 GNP | 1981 Exports (a) |
|---|---|---|---|---|---|---|---|---|---|---|---|
| | $ billion | | | | | | | | million | $ billion | |
| 1. LICs | 4.6 | 5.8 | 7.4 | 8.2 | 9.4 | 10.5 | 11.6 | 12.5 | 1 487 | 458 | 75 |
| of which: | | | | | | | | | | | |
| LLDCs | 0.6 | 0.7 | 0.8 | 0.9 | 1.2 | 1.5 | 1.4 | 1.5 | 290 | 64 | 10 |
| Indonesia | 1.0 | 1.4 | 2.2 | 2.4 | 2.1 | 2.5 | 2.8 | 3.1 | 149 | 82 | 24 |
| Egypt | 0.7 | 1.1 | 1.3 | 1.3 | 1.5 | 2.1 | 2.5 | 2.3 | 43 | 32 | 9 |
| India | 0.9 | 0.9 | 1.1 | 1.2 | 1.4 | 1.4 | 1.7 | 1.9 | 690 | 162 | 14 |
| 2. LMICs | 3.7 | 4.7 | 6.7 | 8.5 | 10.6 | 13.2 | 14.4 | 12.9 | 313 | 279 | 68 |
| of which: | | | | | | | | | | | |
| Nigeria | 0.6 | 0.6 | 0.7 | 0.8 | 1.2 | 1.8 | 2.0 | 2.0 | 88 | 71 | 18 |
| Peru | 0.5 | 0.7 | 0.8 | 1.1 | 1.6 | 2.0 | 1.6 | 2.0 | 17 | 21 | 4 |
| Philippines | 0.5 | 0.6 | 1.2 | 1.3 | 1.2 | 1.7 | 1.8 | 1.9 | 50 | 39 | 9 |
| 3. UMICs | 22.5 | 29.5 | 41.2 | 54.6 | 62.3 | 76.0 | 81.6 | 70.7 | 551 | 1 647 | 543 |
| of which: | | | | | | | | | | | |
| Brazil | 5.0 | 6.4 | 8.4 | 11.4 | 13.3 | 15.3 | 18.1 | 13.1 | 121 | 274 | 27 |
| Mexico | 3.6 | 5.2 | 7.6 | 11.2 | 9.6 | 10.7 | 11.8 | 10.6 | 71 | 231 | 30 |
| Argentina | 1.5 | 1.6 | 2.6 | 2.1 | 2.8 | 4.4 | 6.3 | 7.0 | 28 | 200 | 12 |
| 4. Total LDCs | 30.9 | 40.1 | 55.3 | 71.2 | 82.3 | 99.7 | 107.6 | 96.1 | 2 351 | 2 384 | 687 |

a.    Exports of goods, services and net private transfers.

Table 19

TOTAL ANNUAL LONG-TERM INTEREST PAYMENTS OF DEVELOPING COUNTRIES DURING 1970-83
AS PERCENTAGE OF THEIR TOTAL EXPORTS (a) AND GNP, BY INCOME GROUP

| Income Group | 70/71 | 1973 | 1974 | 1975 | 1977 | 1979 | 1980 | 1981 | 1982 | 1983 |
|---|---|---|---|---|---|---|---|---|---|---|
| 1. Interest payments, $ billion | | | | | | | | | | |
| LICs | 0.4 | 0.8 | 1.0 | 1.3 | 1.8 | 3.2 | 3.5 | 3.9 | 4.5 | 4.5 |
| LMICs | 0.4 | 0.7 | 0.8 | 0.9 | 1.3 | 3.1 | 4.5 | 5.5 | 7.0 | 6.7 |
| UMICs | 2.4 | 3.5 | 5.1 | 6.6 | 9.6 | 19.2 | 27.2 | 33.9 | 38.8 | 36.9 |
| Total | 3.2 | 5.0 | 6.9 | 8.8 | 12.7 | 25.5 | 35.2 | 43.2 | 50.3 | 48.1 |
| 2. Interest payments, % of exports | | | | | | | | | | |
| LICs | 4 | 4 | 4 | 4 | 4 | 5 | 5 | 5 | 6 | 6 |
| LMICs | 4 | 4 | 3 | 3 | 3 | 5 | 6 | 8 | 12 | 12 |
| UMICs | 5 | 3 | 2 | 3 | 4 | 5 | 5 | 6 | 8 | 7 |
| Total | 4 | 3 | 3 | 3 | 4 | 5 | 5 | 6 | 8 | 8 |
| 3. Interest payments, % of GNP | | | | | | | | | | |
| LICs | 0.4 | 0.5 | 0.5 | 0.6 | 0.6 | 0.9 | 0.8 | 0.9 | 0.9 | 0.8 |
| LMICs | 0.7 | 0.8 | 0.7 | 0.7 | 0.8 | 1.3 | 1.6 | 2.0 | 2.3 | 2.0 |
| UMICs | 0.8 | 0.8 | 0.9 | 1.0 | 1.1 | 1.5 | 1.8 | 2.1 | 2.2 | 1.9 |
| Total | 0.7 | 0.8 | 0.8 | 0.9 | 1.0 | 1.4 | 1.6 | 1.8 | 1.9 | 1.6 |

a.  Exports of goods, services and net private transfers.

Table 20

MULTILATERAL OFFICIAL DEBT-RELIEF OPERATIONS
FOR DEVELOPING COUNTRIES, 1956-83

| Debtor country and date of agreement | Consolidation period | Estimated amount rescheduled ($ million) | Maturity (years) |
|---|---|---|---|
| 1. Argentina | | | |
| June 1956 | 1955 - June 1956 | 500 | 9 |
| Oct. 1962 | 1963 - 1964 | 270 | (8) |
| June 1965 | 1965 | 274 | 5 |
| 2. Brazil | | | |
| May 1961 | June 1961 - 1965 | 300 | 5 1/2 |
| July 1964 | 1964 - 1965 | 270 | 5 |
| Nov. 1983 | Aug. 1983 - Dec. 1984 | (3600) | 8 1/2 |
| 3. Central African Republic | | | |
| June 1981 | 1981 | 72 | 9 |
| 4. Chile | | | |
| Feb. 1965 | 1965 - 1966 | 90 | 5-6 |
| April 1972 | Nov. 1971 - 1972 | 258 | 8 |
| March 1974 | 1973 - 1974 | 460 | 8 1/2 |
| May 1975 | 1975 | 230 | 9 |
| 5. Costa Rica | | | |
| Jan. 1983 | July 1982 - Dec. 1983 | 215 | 9 |
| 6. Cuba | | | |
| Feb. 1983 | Sept. 1982 - Dec. 1983 | 415 | 8 1/2 |
| 7. Ecuador | | | |
| July 1983 | June 1983 - May 1984 | (165) | 8 |
| 8. Gabon | | | |
| June 1978 | .. | (630) | .. |
| 9. Ghana | | | |
| Dec. 1966 | June 1966 - 1968 | 170 | 10 |
| Oct. 1968 | 1969 - June 1972 | 100 | 9 |
| July 1970 | July 1970 - June 1972 | (18) | 10 |
| March 1974 | Feb. 1972 onwards | 190 | 29 |
| 10. India | | | |
| March 1968 | April 1968 - March 1971 | (100) | 25-30 |
| June 1971 | "    1971 -   "    1972 | 100 | 25-30 |

Table 20 (continued)

| Debtor country and date of agreement | Consolidation period | Estimated amount rescheduled ($ million) | Maturity (years) |
|---|---|---|---|
| 10. India (cont'd.) | | | |
| Feb. 1973 | April 1972 - March 1974 | 340 | 25-30 |
| Oct. 1974 | " 1974 - " 1975 | 194 | 25-30 |
| June 1975 | " 1975 - " 1976 | 228 | 25-30 |
| May 1976 | " 1976 - " 1977 | 200 | 25-30 |
| July 1977 | " 1977 - " 1978 | 110 | 25-30 |
| 11. Indonesia | | | |
| Dec. 1966 | July 1966 - 1967 | 310 | 10 |
| Oct. 1967 | 1968 | 110 | 10 |
| Oct. 1968 | 1969 | 180 | 10 |
| April 1970 | 1970 - 1983 | 2 090 | 30 |
| 12. Khmer Republic | | | |
| Jan. 1972 | 1972 | 2 | 8 |
| Oct. 1972 | 1973 | 2 | 10 |
| 13. Liberia | | | |
| Dec. 1980 | July 1980 - Dec. 1981 | 35 | 9 |
| Dec. 1981 | Jan. 1982 - June 1983 | 30 | 9 |
| Dec. 1983 | July 1983 - June 1984 | 25 | 9 |
| 14. Madagascar | | | |
| April 1981 | Jan. 1981 - June 1982 | 140 | 9 |
| July 1982 | July 1982 - June 1983 | 107 | 9 |
| 15. Malawi | | | |
| Sept. 1982 | July 1982 - June 1983 | 25 | 8 |
| Oct. 1983 | July 1983 - June 1984 | 36 | 8 |
| 16. Mexico | | | |
| June 1983 | July 1983 - Dec. 1983 | 1 520 | 6 |
| 17. Morocco | | | |
| Oct. 1983 | Sept. 1983 - Dec. 1984 | 610 | 8 |
| 18. Niger | | | |
| Nov. 1983 | Oct. 1983 - Sept. 1984 | 66 | 9 |
| 19. Pakistan | | | |
| May 1972 | May 1971 - June 1973 | 236 | 4 |
| July 1973 | July 1973 - June 1974 | 107 | 4 |
| June 1974 | July 1974 - June 1978 | 650 | 25-30 |
| Jan. 1981 | Jan. 1981 - July 1982 | 232 | (25-30) |

Table 20 (continued)

| Debtor country and date of agreement | Consolidation period | Estimated amount rescheduled ($ million) | Maturity (years) |
|---|---|---|---|
| **20. Peru** | | | |
| Sept. 1968 | July 1968 – 1969 | 120 | 4 |
| Nov. 1969 | 1970 – 1971 | (100) | 5 |
| Nov. 1978 | 1979 – 1980 | 420 | 6 1/2–7 1/2 |
| July 1983 | May 1983 – April 1984 | 560 | 8 |
| **21. Senegal** | | | |
| Oct. 1981 | July 1981 – June 1982 | 75 | 9 |
| Nov. 1982 | July 1982 – June 1983 | 80 | 9 |
| Dec. 1983 | July 1983 – June 1984 | 78 | 9 |
| **22. Sierra Leone** | | | |
| Sept. 1977 | July 1976 – June 1978 | 39 | 11 |
| Feb. 1980 | July 1979 – Dec. 1981 | 37 | 7 1/4–9 3/4 |
| **23. Sudan** | | | |
| Nov. 1979 | Oct. 1979 – June 1981 | 475 | 7–10 |
| March 1982 | July 1981 – Dec. 1982 | (145) | 10 |
| Feb. 1983 | 1983 | (540) | 16 |
| **24. Togo** | | | |
| June 1979 | 1979 – 1980 | 260 | 10 |
| Feb. 1981 | 1981 – 1982 | (232) | 9 |
| April 1983 | 1983 | (210) | 10 |
| **25. Turkey** | | | |
| May 1959 | Aug. 1958 – 1963 | 440 | 12 |
| March 1965 | 1965 – 1967 | 220 | 6–12 |
| May 1978 | Jan. 1977 – June 1979 | 1 300 | 6–8 |
| July 1979 | May 1978 – June 1980 | 1 200 | 7–8 |
| July 1980 | July 1980 – June 1983 | 3 000 | 8–10 |
| **26. Uganda** | | | |
| Nov. 1981 | July 1981 – June 1982 | 30 | 8–10 |
| Dec. 1982 | July 1982 – June 1983 | 20 | 10 |
| **27. Zaire** | | | |
| June 1976 | 1975 – 1976 | 270 | 9–10 |
| July 1977 | 1977 (except 2nd–half interest) | 170 | 9–10 |
| Dec. 1977 | July 1977 – Dec. 1977 | 40 | 9–10 |
| Dec. 1979 | 1978 – 1980 | 1 040 | 10 |
| July 1981 | 1981 – 1982 | 500 | 10 |
| Dec. 1983 | 1984 | 1 600 | 11 |
| **28. Zambia** | | | |
| May 1983 | 1983 | 310 | 10 |

Table 21

THE 20 LARGEST DEVELOPING COUNTRY BORROWERS (a): DISBURSED LONG-TERM DEBT, YEAR-END 1979-82

| Borrower | Year-end disbursed debt | | | | of which to banks (d) 1982 | Total reserves | | GNP annual growth rate 1975-81 | GNP per capita 1981 |
|---|---|---|---|---|---|---|---|---|---|
| | 1979 | 1980 | 1981 | 1982 | | 1981 | 1982 | | |
| | $ billion | | | | | $ billion | | % | $ |
| 1. Brazil | 50.8 | 57.1 | 64.7 | 72.6 | 43.9 | 7.5 | 4.0 | 4.7 | 2 222 |
| 2. Mexico (c) | 37.7 | 43.5 | 53.5 | 60.4 | 38.9 | 4.9 | 1.7 | 6.5 | 2 250 |
| 3. Argentina | 12.6 | 16.0 | 23.7 | 27.1 | 15.5 | 3.5 | 2.7 | 0.1 | 2 560 |
| 4. Venezuela (b) | 12.3 | 13.8 | 14.9 | 16.5 | 12.9 | 8.6 | 10.0 | 3.3 | 4 219 |
| 5. Algeria (b) | 17.0 | 17.3 | 16.9 | 16.8 | 3.2 | 3.9 | 2.6 | 6.6 | 2 143 |
| 6. Korea, Rep. | 15.5 | 17.6 | 20.0 | 22.0 | 8.7 | 2.7 | 2.8 | 7.0 | 1 700 |
| 7. Iran (b) | 10.1 | 10.0 | 6.9 | 5.0 | 0.2 | | | -3.7 | 1 843 |
| 8. Yugoslavia | 13.5 | 15.1 | 15.1 | 14.4 | 4.1 | 1.7 | 0.9 | 4.9 | 2 794 |
| 9. Chile | 7.1 | 8.9 | 11.9 | 13.4 | 8.5 | 3.9 | 2.5 | 7.0 | 2 559 |
| 10. Indonesia (b) | 15.1 | 16.6 | 17.5 | 20.4 | 3.8 | 6.1 | 4.2 | 7.7 | 527 |
| 11. Egypt (c) | 12.2 | 13.8 | 15.2 | 16.6 | 0.5 | 1.5 | 1.3 | 11.0 | 650 |
| 12. Saudi Arabia (b) | 2.7 | 2.9 | 2.4 | 2.7 | 0.8 | 32.4 | 29.7 | 9.8 | 14 062 |
| 13. Nigeria (b) | 4.2 | 5.2 | 6.0 | 7.9 | 3.5 | 3.9 | 1.6 | 2.0 | 870 |
| 14. Iraq (b) | 2.3 | 2.5 | 3.0 | 2.2 | 0.1 | | | 1.1 | 1 738 |
| 15. Peru (c) | 6.5 | 7.1 | 7.4 | 8.4 | 2.9 | 1.6 | 1.7 | 1.4 | 1 173 |
| 16. Philippines | 7.5 | 8.7 | 10.2 | 11.9 | 3.9 | 2.7 | 2.5 | 5.8 | 787 |
| 17. Greece | 5.6 | 7.0 | 8.2 | 8.8 | 5.4 | 1.2 | 1.0 | 3.4 | 4 418 |
| 18. Turkey | 11.8 | 13.9 | 14.5 | 15.0 | 3.6 | 1.4 | 1.1 | 2.8 | 1 533 |
| 19. Portugal | 5.2 | 6.0 | 7.1 | 9.1 | 5.2 | 6.2 | 6.1 | 3.8 | 2 502 |
| 20. India | 16.5 | 18.2 | 18.9 | 20.7 | 0.5 | 4.9 | 4.5 | 3.9 | 256 |
| Total 20 Countries | 266.2 | 301.2 | 338.1 | 372.0 | 165.6 | 98.7 | 81.0 | 4.3 | 1 038 |
| (% of Grand Total LDCs) | (68.1) | (67.7) | (67.5) | (67.4) | (82.6) | (58.4) | (52.9) | 4.8 | 931 |

a. Borrowers are ranked by average debt-service payments in 1981-82. Next-ranking countries include Israel (not including official military debt), Morocco, Thailand, Taiwan, Ivory Coast.

b. OPEC Member.

c. Net oil exporter.

d. Outstanding international bank loans from DAC countries and international capital markets (other than officially guaranteed export credits).

Table 22

THE 20 LARGEST DEVELOPING COUNTRY BORROWERS (a): ANNUAL DEBT-SERVICE AND INTEREST PAYMENTS ON LONG-TERM DEBT DURING 1980-83

| Borrower | Debt service paid ($ billion) | | | | Interest paid | | | | Interest payments as % of debt outstanding at previous year-end (%) | | | |
|---|---|---|---|---|---|---|---|---|---|---|---|---|
| | 1980 | 1981 | 1982 | 1983 | 1980 | 1981 | 1982 | 1983 (d) | 1980 | 1981 | 1982 | 1983 |
| 1. Brazil | 13.3 | 15.3 | 18.1 | 13.1 | 6.0 | 7.6 | 9.1 | 8.7 | 11.8 | 13.3 | 14.1 | 12.0 |
| 2. Mexico (c) | 9.6 | 10.7 | 11.8 | 10.6 | 5.0 | 6.3 | 6.1 | 8.3 | 13.3 | 14.5 | 11.4 | 13.7 |
| 3. Argentina | 2.8 | 4.4 | 6.3 | 7.0 | 1.3 | 1.8 | 3.4 | 3.1 | 10.3 | 11.3 | 14.3 | 11.4 |
| 4. Venezuela (b) | 4.7 | 5.0 | 5.2 | 4.0 | 1.5 | 2.0 | 2.2 | 2.0 | 12.2 | 14.5 | 14.8 | 12.1 |
| 5. Algeria (b) | 4.1 | 4.2 | 4.6 | 4.8 | 1.5 | 1.7 | 1.8 | 1.8 | 8.8 | 9.8 | 10.7 | 10.7 |
| 6. Korea, Rep. | 3.3 | 3.9 | 4.5 | 4.3 | 1.4 | 1.8 | 2.1 | 2.0 | 9.0 | 10.2 | 10.5 | 9.1 |
| 7. Iran (b) | 2.0 | 5.3 | 2.9 | 2.2 | 0.8 | 0.9 | 0.7 | 0.5 | 7.9 | 9.0 | 10.1 | 10.0 |
| 8. Yugoslavia | 3.3 | 3.4 | 3.6 | 2.4 | 1.2 | 1.6 | 1.5 | 1.3 | 8.9 | 10.6 | 9.9 | 9.0 |
| 9. Chile | 2.2 | 3.0 | 2.4 | 2.4 | 0.8 | 1.1 | 1.7 | 1.6 | 11.3 | 12.4 | 14.3 | 11.9 |
| 10. Indonesia (b) | 2.1 | 2.5 | 2.8 | 3.1 | 1.0 | 1.2 | 1.3 | 1.4 | 6.6 | 7.2 | 7.4 | 6.9 |
| 11. Egypt (c) | 1.5 | 2.1 | 2.5 | 2.3 | 0.3 | 0.6 | 0.6 | 0.7 | 2.5 | 4.0 | 3.9 | 4.2 |
| 12. Saudi Arabia (b) | 2.0 | 2.2 | 2.1 | 1.8 | 0.2 | 0.2 | 0.2 | 0.3 | 7.4 | 6.9 | 8.3 | 10.6 |
| 13. Nigeria (b) | 1.2 | 1.8 | 2.0 | 2.0 | 0.5 | 0.6 | 0.9 | 0.9 | 11.9 | 11.5 | 14.2 | 11.4 |
| 14. Iraq (b) | 1.1 | 1.8 | 1.9 | 0.4 | 0.2 | 0.2 | 0.2 | 0.2 | 8.7 | 8.0 | 8.3 | 9.1 |
| 15. Peru (c) | 1.6 | 2.0 | 1.6 | 2.0 | 0.6 | 0.7 | 0.9 | 1.0 | 9.4 | 10.4 | 12.2 | 11.3 |
| 16. Philippines | 1.2 | 1.7 | 1.8 | 1.9 | 0.6 | 0.7 | 1.0 | 1.1 | 8.0 | 8.0 | 9.8 | 9.2 |
| 17. Greece | 1.3 | 1.7 | 1.7 | 1.9 | 0.6 | 1.0 | 1.0 | 0.9 | 10.7 | 14.3 | 12.2 | 10.2 |
| 18. Turkey | 1.1 | 1.3 | 2.1 | 3.3 | 0.6 | 0.7 | 1.2 | 1.1 | 5.1 | 5.9 | 8.2 | 7.3 |
| 19. Portugal | 1.2 | 1.6 | 1.8 | 2.0 | 0.5 | 0.7 | 0.9 | 1.0 | 9.6 | 11.7 | 12.7 | 10.4 |
| 20. India | 1.4 | 1.4 | 1.7 | 1.9 | 0.3 | 0.4 | 0.6 | 0.7 | 1.8 | 2.2 | 3.2 | 3.3 |
| Total 20 Countries | 61.2 | 75.4 | 81.4 | 73.4 | 24.8 | 31.8 | 37.5 | 38.4 | 9.3 | 10.4 | 11.1 | 10.3 |
| (% of Grand Total LDCs) | (74.3) | (75.7) | (75.7) | (76.4) | (70.5) | (73.6) | (74.6) | (79.8) | 9.0 | 9.7 | 10.0 | 8.7 |

a.   Borrowers are ranked by average debt-service payments in 1981-82.  Next-ranking countries include Israel (not including official military debt), Morocco, Thailand, Taiwan, Ivory Coast.

b.   OPEC Member.

c.   Net oil exporter.

d.   Includes for some debtors payments of interest arrears accumulated in 1982.

Note:  Figures for 1983 are estimates of effective payments.

Technical Note

COVERAGE, SOURCES AND DEFINITIONS OF EXTERNAL DEBT STATISTICS

A. Coverage

The OECD presents external debt statistics for 157 individual developing countries and territories (LDCs). The statistics relate to amounts disbursed. They cover, in principle, all types of debt (public and private, bilateral and multilateral, concessional and non-concessional), with the exceptions of:

1. Debt with original maturities of less than one year. There is no comprehensive reporting of outstanding stocks of total short-term assets and of total liabilities of developing countries. It appears, however, that until 1981, for most developing countries, and for non-OPEC developing countries as a group, total short-term assets exceeded total short-term liabilities. Estimates of recent short-term data for non-OPEC, non-OECD developing countries and for selected debtors are contained in Tables 13 and 14. They are derived from IMF statistics, information provided by debtors' Central Banks and BIS data;

2. Military debt financed by official credits (military debt financed by private credits is indistinguishably included in private market debt). For a few debtors (e.g. Iraq, Israel), unreported official military debt can be as high as total reported non-military debt. However, for non-OPEC LDCs as a whole, official military debt is estimated to represent in 1982 only some 10 per cent of total reported long-term debt and well under 10 per cent of total reported debt service (a large part of military imports of LDCs is paid in cash or provided on a grant basis);

3. Debt to the IMF (other than to the IMF Trust Fund). The outstanding amount of Fund Credit to non-OPEC developing countries was some $9 billion at the end of 1980, $14 billion at the end of 1981, $19 billion at the end of 1982 and $26 billion at end-September 1983;

4. Debt in local currencies.

Due to presently incomplete data, the People's Republic of China is excluded as a debtor in all debt Tables (including Annex 1) and in Tables A and B. (External disbursed debt of China PR at end-1982 is estimated at some $3.9 billion and debt-service payments in 1982 at $1.5 billion.) As a creditor, China PR is included in "Other LDCs". However, the flow Tables of Chapter II (Tables C, D, E and F) include China as both a recipient and a source of external finance.

B. Sources

The OECD debt statistics are based on the following sources:

1. The OECD "Creditor Reporting System" (CRS). Under this system, DAC creditors report on officially extended or guaranteed debt of 157 developing countries and territories: debt arising from Official Development Assistance (ODA) loans, Other Official Flows (OOF, mainly official export credits), and Officially Guaranteed Private Export Credits (OGPEC) extended by suppliers and by banks of DAC countries. The amount of OGPEC reported debt which is effectively disbursed (principal only) is the Secretariat's estimate;

2. The World Bank's "Debtor Reporting System" (DRS). Under this system, 100 developing countries report on their external debt to all (DAC and non-DAC) creditors incurred or guaranteed by the public sector of the debtor countries, usually referred to as "External Public Debt";

3. In addition, other sources are used in order to present as complete a picture as possible of all developing countries' total debt and debt service including, in particular, private debt due to the private sector in the creditor country which is guaranteed in neither the debtor nor the creditor country's government. This is done by drawing on official data from Central Banks of debtor countries, the World Bank and other multilateral development lending institutions, the IMF and BIS. Some categories of debt (e.g. non-DAC credits to non-DRS countries) as well as interest payments effectively paid are estimated by the Secretariat.


C. Terms Used in Tables

DAC countries and capital markets: Total loans from DAC Member governments and from private lenders, including the participation of banks located in non-DAC countries in international syndication of Euro-loans and Euro-bonds.

ODA: Official Development Assistance (ODA) is defined as those resources to developing countries provided by official agencies, including state and local governments, or by their executive agencies, each transaction of which meets the following two tests: it is administered with the promotion of the economic development and welfare of developing countries as its main objective; and it is concessional in character, containing a grant element of at least 25 per cent. To calculate the grant element of an ODA transaction, a 10 per cent discount rate is used.

Total export credits: Official export credits and officially guaranteed private export credits (OGPEC) financed by suppliers and banks.

Bank loans: Total international bank loans, including loans through offshore centres but excluding bank-financed OGPEC and bonds.

Bonds: Foreign (bilateral) and international (multinational) bonds from DAC countries and international bonds from non-DAC countries.

Other private: Mainly intercorporate lending, private non-guaranteed credits, nationalisations.

Multilateral: Total official lending by international organisations other than the IMF.

CMEA countries: Total bilateral loans from official and private sources, excluding participation in syndications of Euro-loans and Euro-bonds.

OPEC countries: Total bilateral loans from official and private sources, excluding participation in syndications of Euro-loans and Euro-bonds.

Other LDCs: Total bilateral loans from official and private sources, excluding participation in syndications of Euro-loans and Euro-bonds.

Income groups: Individual countries and territories by income groups used in the Tables are listed in Annex 2. In all Tables except Tables 9, 10, 13, 14 and 15, non-OPEC LDCs include the Southern European LDCs (Greece, Portugal Turkey and Yugoslavia).

Floating- (variable-) interest debt: Loans whose interest rates float with the (principally six-month) LIBOR or the US prime rate. Regarding long-term loans at floating interest, trends in the annual interest cost shown in the Tables may differ substantially from trends in reported annual average LIBOR or US prime rates, due to time lags between the date of original contract or interest adjustment and the effective payments.


D. Impact of Exchange-Rate Fluctuations

All amounts are expressed in US dollars at current prices and exchange rates. Debt data are valued at year-end exchange rates, debt-service data at annual average exchange rates. All estimates for 1983 are based upon exchange rates prevailing in mid-October 1983. Large exchange-rate fluctuations of recent years have had a marked impact on annual changes in reported debt and debt service. The appreciation of the US dollar does not, of course, change the dollar value of the dollar-denominated indebtedness but it reduces the dollar value of the non-dollar-denominated indebtedness. Thus the increase in total indebtedness is understated. (This effect is reversed when the dollar depreciates.) The impact of exchange-rate fluctuations on debt depends directly on the composition of the debt by currencies and in particular on the share of debt denominated in US dollars: the higher the dollar share, the smaller the impact (see Section 2C of Chapter II and Section 3 of Chapter III).

Throughout the 1970s, roughly one-half of total debt and debt service was denominated in US dollars and the other half in other currencies. During 1980-83, the share of debt in US dollars has increased mainly as a result of massive increases in bank lending, and also as a result of the appreciation of the US dollar during this period. Regarding total debt service, the share denominated in US dollars also increased during 1980-82 but decreased sharply in 1983 as a combined result of the fall in LIBOR and of massive rescheduling of principal due on bank loans.

Other things being equal, the overall impact of exchange-rate fluctuations on total long-term indebtedness, as expressed in US dollars, including both dollar- and non-dollar-denominated debt, is estimated here (minus sign reflects the degree of underreporting due to the appreciation in the US dollar).

| Change in % | 1978 | 1979 | 1980 | 1981 | 1982 | 1983 |
|---|---|---|---|---|---|---|
| Debt | +6.0 | +0.3 | -0.4 | -6.5 | -4.1 | -3.6 |
| Debt service | +4.3 | +1.0 | -0.3 | -5.2 | -3.8 | -3.4 |

For individual debtor countries or groups of countries or categories of debt, the impact can be higher than the average impact indicated, e.g. for ODA and export-credit debt, of which some 70 per cent currently is not denominated in US dollars. Conversely, a very small impact falls on international bank debt, of which 90 per cent is denominated in US dollars. Regarding income groups, the impact is most pronounced for the LICs (higher share of ODA and export credits) and for OPEC countries (higher share of export credits). At the other extreme, the impact is minimal for the UMICs (higher share of bank lending). Consequently, the relative share of each income group in LDC total indebtedness is thus significantly affected by exchange-rate changes. During the last few years, the appreciation of the US dollar resulted in the relative reduction of the shares of LICs and OPEC, and in an increase in the share of non-OPEC UMICs. Also, the relative share of fixed- versus floating-interest debt in total debt was significantly affected during the 1981-83 period since the former is principally in non-US dollar denomination while over 80 per cent of the latter is denominated in US dollars.

Moreover, exchange-rate changes can affect the reconciliation, for a given period, of outstanding stocks, on the one hand, and net flows, on the other. Changes in stocks and net flows normally are equal at constant exchange rates (and, incidentally, also at changing exchange rates), provided that the average annual exchange rates (measuring flows) are identical to the end-year exchange rates (measuring stocks). In reality, however, the continuous rise in the US dollar exchange rates during the past three years vis-à-vis other currencies resulted in year-end values of the dollar higher than the average annual value. As a result, the year-end stocks are relatively more "underreported" than the annual net flows which, therefore, do not correspond to the changes in stocks. This divergence is particularly significant for ODA loans and export credits, where reported net flows are markedly higher than reported changes in stocks.

## E. Other

Estimates for 1983 were completed as of mid-November 1983, with particular uncertainty regarding the year-end exchange rate as well as the non-payment of debt-service obligations by a number of large debtors during the November-December period.

In all Tables, totals may not add up due to rounding.

INDIVIDUAL DEVELOPING COUNTRIES AND TERRITORIES:  TOTAL DISBURSED LONG-TERM
DEBT AT YEAR-END AND ANNUAL DEBT-SERVICE DURING 1975-82,
BY SOURCE AND TERMS OF LENDING

Notes

The People's Republic of China is not included as a debtor in this
Annex, but it is included as a creditor with "Other LDCs".

West Indies includes:  Anguilla, Antigua, Cayman Islands, Dominica,
Grenada, Montserrat, St. Kitts-Nevis, St. Lucia, St. Vincent, Turks and Caicos
Islands and the British Virgin Islands.

During 1975 to 1982, no data were reported for debt and debt service
for the following countries:  Bhutan, Kiribati, Mayotte, Niue Island,
St. Helena, Sao Tome and Principe, Tokelau Islands and Tuvalu.  These LDCs are
therefore not shown in this Annex.

# TOTAL LDC'S

US $ Million

| | 1975 | 1976 | 1977 | 1978 | 1979 | 1980 | 1981 | 1982 |
|---|---|---|---|---|---|---|---|---|
| **DEBT** | | | | | | | | |
| DAC countries and capital markets | 130687 | 159899 | 199829 | 255469 | 301388 | 342067 | 381020 | 414234 |
| ODA | 34152 | 36416 | 41221 | 48834 | 53036 | 56634 | 57405 | 59297 |
| Total export credits | 39691 | 49309 | 63588 | 82491 | 97617 | 110141 | 116739 | 120660 |
| Total private | 56844 | 74174 | 95020 | 124144 | 150735 | 175292 | 206876 | 234277 |
| *of which:* Bank loans | 46350 | 59058 | 74896 | 98083 | 123185 | 145464 | 174557 | 200347 |
| Bonds | 4864 | 5994 | 9144 | 12794 | 13375 | 14674 | 15815 | 16422 |
| Other | 5630 | 9122 | 10980 | 13267 | 14175 | 15154 | 16504 | 17508 |
| Multilateral | 21070 | 25720 | 31934 | 38927 | 46228 | 55336 | 63550 | 74547 |
| *of which:* Concessional | 10059 | 11555 | 14292 | 17419 | 20295 | 24337 | 26986 | 29992 |
| CMEA countries | 8717 | 9192 | 10884 | 12490 | 14745 | 15070 | 15740 | 16528 |
| *of which:* Concessional | 8033 | 8434 | 9438 | 10465 | 11396 | 11983 | 12548 | 13074 |
| OPEC countries | 5849 | 8180 | 10548 | 12904 | 14654 | 17555 | 19965 | 21402 |
| *of which:* Concessional | 4850 | 6418 | 7963 | 9187 | 10525 | 12125 | 13786 | 15046 |
| Other LDC'S | 2967 | 3393 | 4041 | 4843 | 5782 | 6699 | 7120 | 7220 |
| *of which:* Concessional | 1685 | 1948 | 2378 | 2844 | 3142 | 3292 | 3177 | 3180 |
| Other and adjustments | 3441 | 4547 | 4726 | 6655 | 8061 | 8316 | 13279 | 17790 |
| **Total Debt** | **172731** | **210932** | **261962** | **331288** | **390858** | **445042** | **500674** | **551720** |
| *of which:* Concessional | 59006 | 65023 | 75552 | 89033 | 98714 | 108710 | 114258 | 120964 |
| Non-concessional | 113724 | 145908 | 186410 | 242256 | 292144 | 336331 | 386416 | 430756 |
| | | | | | | | | |
| **DEBT SERVICE** | | | | | | | | |
| DAC countries and capital markets | 21445 | 26411 | 34576 | 48452 | 62723 | 72415 | 87761 | 94326 |
| ODA | 1745 | 1897 | 2002 | 2327 | 2594 | 2778 | 2831 | 2682 |
| Total export credits | 10377 | 11948 | 15824 | 19634 | 23890 | 28111 | 32405 | 31257 |
| Total private | 9323 | 12566 | 16750 | 26492 | 36238 | 41527 | 52525 | 60388 |
| *of which:* Bank loans | 7788 | 10242 | 13593 | 22466 | 31293 | 36290 | 46798 | 53435 |
| Bonds | 677 | 518 | 760 | 1262 | 1885 | 1589 | 2055 | 3035 |
| Other | 858 | 1805 | 2397 | 2763 | 3061 | 3648 | 3672 | 3917 |
| Multilateral | 1585 | 1958 | 2481 | 3172 | 3734 | 4589 | 5576 | 6530 |
| *of which:* Concessional | 586 | 610 | 673 | 778 | 723 | 770 | 865 | 1173 |
| CMEA countries | 832 | 895 | 1120 | 1333 | 1649 | 1818 | 1913 | 1880 |
| *of which:* Concessional | 714 | 732 | 872 | 920 | 963 | 1398 | 1387 | 1358 |
| OPEC countries | 232 | 241 | 644 | 889 | 1217 | 1338 | 1792 | 1914 |
| *of which:* Concessional | 128 | 128 | 429 | 390 | 491 | 647 | 824 | 880 |
| Other LDC'S | 288 | 388 | 352 | 387 | 565 | 689 | 921 | 955 |
| *of which:* Concessional | 40 | 33 | 48 | 33 | 62 | 75 | 66 | 85 |
| Other and adjustments | 712 | 962 | 901 | 1029 | 1321 | 1490 | 1732 | 1946 |
| **Total Debt Service** | **25095** | **30854** | **40075** | **55264** | **71209** | **82339** | **99696** | **107551** |
| *of which:* Concessional | 3229 | 3418 | 4051 | 4478 | 4870 | 5704 | 6005 | 6242 |
| Non-concessional | 21867 | 27436 | 36024 | 50785 | 66339 | 76635 | 93691 | 101309 |

*US $ Million*

| | 1975 | 1976 | 1977 | 1978 | 1979 | 1980 | 1981 | 1982 |
|---|---|---|---|---|---|---|---|---|
| **DEBT** | | | | | | | | |
| DAC countries and capital | | | | | | | | |
|   markets | 170 | 182 | 196 | 213 | 250 | 219 | 203 | 189 |
|   ODA | 158 | 172 | 180 | 197 | 206 | 190 | 169 | 159 |
|   Total export credits | 12 | 9 | 16 | 16 | 44 | 28 | 34 | 30 |
|   Total private | – | 1 | – | – | – | 1 | – | – |
|   *of which:* Bank loans | – | 1 | – | – | – | 1 | – | – |
|     Bonds | – | – | – | – | – | – | – | – |
|     Other | – | – | – | – | – | – | – | – |
| Multilateral | 22 | 42 | 63 | 89 | 107 | 121 | 132 | 159 |
|   *of which:* Concessional | 22 | 42 | 63 | 89 | 107 | 121 | 132 | 159 |
| CMEA countries | 609 | 659 | 732 | 811 | 818 | 722 | 667 | 631 |
|   *of which:* Concessional | 579 | 623 | 698 | 766 | 773 | 694 | 651 | 622 |
| OPEC countries | 2 | 33 | 67 | 91 | 92 | 105 | 112 | 113 |
|   *of which:* Concessional | 1 | 19 | 28 | 46 | 47 | 64 | 78 | 86 |
| Other LDC'S | 16 | 14 | 15 | 17 | 18 | 28 | 28 | 32 |
|   *of which:* Concessional | 16 | 14 | 15 | 17 | 18 | 28 | 28 | 32 |
| Other and adjustments | – | – | – | – | – | – | 100 | 200 |
| **Total Debt** | **819** | **930** | **1073** | **1221** | **1285** | **1195** | **1242** | **1324** |
|   *of which:* Concessional | 776 | 870 | 984 | 1115 | 1151 | 1097 | 1058 | 1058 |
|     Non-concessional | 43 | 60 | 89 | 106 | 134 | 98 | 184 | 266 |
| **DEBT SERVICE** | | | | | | | | |
| DAC countries and capital | | | | | | | | |
|   markets | 15 | 15 | 13 | 16 | 13 | 13 | 16 | 11 |
|   ODA | 9 | 9 | 10 | 11 | 8 | 11 | 14 | 10 |
|   Total export credits | 5 | 6 | 3 | 5 | 5 | 3 | 3 | 1 |
|   Total private | – | 0 | – | – | – | – | – | – |
|   *of which:* Bank loans | – | 0 | – | – | – | – | – | – |
|     Bonds | – | – | – | – | – | – | – | – |
|     Other | – | – | – | – | – | – | – | – |
| Multilateral | 0 | 0 | 0 | 1 | 1 | 1 | 2 | 3 |
|   *of which:* Concessional | 0 | 0 | 0 | 1 | 1 | 1 | 2 | 3 |
| CMEA countries | 11 | 10 | 22 | 31 | – | 154 | 109 | 86 |
|   *of which:* Concessional | 9 | 6 | 16 | 20 | – | 139 | 97 | 78 |
| OPEC countries | 2 | 1 | 2 | 7 | – | 11 | 12 | 13 |
|   *of which:* Concessional | – | – | 0 | 1 | – | 1 | 3 | 5 |
| Other LDC'S | 0 | 0 | – | 0 | – | 1 | 0 | 0 |
|   *of which:* Concessional | – | – | – | – | – | 0 | 0 | 0 |
| Other and adjustments | – | – | – | – | – | – | – | – |
| **Total Debt Service** | **27** | **26** | **38** | **55** | **13** | **180** | **140** | **112** |
|   *of which:* Concessional | 18 | 15 | 27 | 33 | 8 | 152 | 116 | 95 |
|     Non-concessional | 9 | 11 | 12 | 22 | 5 | 28 | 25 | 17 |

# ALGERIA

US $ Million

|  | 1975 | 1976 | 1977 | 1978 | 1979 | 1980 | 1981 | 1982 |
|---|---|---|---|---|---|---|---|---|
| **DEBT** | | | | | | | | |
| DAC countries and capital | | | | | | | | |
| markets | 5210 | 6603 | 8991 | 12813 | 15049 | 15298 | 14805 | 14068 |
| ODA | 291 | 307 | 344 | 429 | 435 | 408 | 337 | 297 |
| Total export credits | 3226 | 4146 | 6198 | 8324 | 9996 | 10440 | 10224 | 10318 |
| Total private | 1693 | 2150 | 2449 | 4060 | 4618 | 4450 | 4244 | 3453 |
| of which: Bank loans | 1673 | 2026 | 2256 | 3850 | 4260 | 4110 | 3913 | 3150 |
| Bonds | 20 | 20 | 93 | 100 | 258 | 240 | 216 | 153 |
| Other | – | 104 | 100 | 110 | 100 | 100 | 115 | 150 |
| Multilateral | 40 | 88 | 141 | 191 | 245 | 254 | 287 | 306 |
| of which: Concessional | 4 | 3 | 4 | 4 | 3 | 1 | 1 | 1 |
| CMEA countries | 347 | 338 | 382 | 416 | 507 | 511 | 483 | 438 |
| of which: Concessional | 346 | 338 | 375 | 396 | 467 | 452 | 396 | 339 |
| OPEC countries | 160 | 147 | 301 | 435 | 454 | 424 | 370 | 299 |
| of which: Concessional | 44 | 30 | 22 | 17 | 12 | 9 | 9 | 8 |
| Other LDC'S | 27 | 24 | 25 | 89 | 124 | 117 | 151 | 146 |
| of which: Concessional | 27 | 24 | 24 | 25 | 25 | 24 | 48 | 52 |
| Other and adjustments | 128 | 192 | 327 | 602 | 669 | 708 | 840 | 1536 |
| **Total Debt** | **5912** | **7393** | **10166** | **14546** | **17048** | **17313** | **16936** | **16794** |
| of which: Concessional | 727 | 731 | 788 | 890 | 965 | 910 | 801 | 704 |
| Non-concessional | 5185 | 6662 | 9378 | 13656 | 16083 | 16403 | 16135 | 16090 |
| **DEBT SERVICE** | | | | | | | | |
| DAC countries and capital | | | | | | | | |
| markets | 788 | 1119 | 1335 | 1887 | 2955 | 3834 | 3832 | 4087 |
| ODA | 16 | 17 | 14 | 26 | 24 | 28 | 21 | 18 |
| Total export credits | 589 | 928 | 1109 | 1435 | 1951 | 2491 | 2486 | 2747 |
| Total private | 182 | 174 | 212 | 427 | 980 | 1316 | 1325 | 1322 |
| of which: Bank loans | 180 | 164 | 199 | 407 | 948 | 1250 | 1250 | 1200 |
| Bonds | 2 | 2 | 1 | 5 | 12 | 41 | 45 | 82 |
| Other | – | 8 | 12 | 15 | 20 | 25 | 30 | 40 |
| Multilateral | 6 | 7 | 10 | 20 | 31 | 68 | 45 | 51 |
| of which: Concessional | 1 | 0 | 0 | 0 | 2 | 1 | 0 | 0 |
| CMEA countries | 38 | 36 | 37 | 44 | 61 | 61 | 112 | 102 |
| of which: Concessional | 37 | 35 | 37 | 40 | 55 | 54 | 90 | 73 |
| OPEC countries | 23 | 23 | 26 | 41 | 63 | 72 | 78 | 97 |
| of which: Concessional | 17 | 16 | 10 | 5 | 7 | 4 | 1 | 1 |
| Other LDC'S | 3 | 3 | 3 | 1 | 25 | 30 | 52 | 58 |
| of which: Concessional | 3 | 3 | 3 | – | – | – | 2 | 6 |
| Other and adjustments | 5 | 5 | 11 | 19 | 53 | 29 | 92 | 182 |
| **Total Debt Service** | **863** | **1192** | **1421** | **2012** | **3190** | **4096** | **4211** | **4578** |
| of which: Concessional | 74 | 71 | 68 | 76 | 93 | 92 | 118 | 101 |
| Non-concessional | 789 | 1121 | 1352 | 1935 | 3097 | 4003 | 4094 | 4477 |

*US $ Million*

| | 1975 | 1976 | 1977 | 1978 | 1979 | 1980 | 1981 | 1982 |
|---|---|---|---|---|---|---|---|---|
| **DEBT** | | | | | | | | |
| DAC countries and capital | | | | | | | | |
| markets | 193 | 146 | 120 | 124 | 186 | 287 | 423 | 515 |
| ODA | – | – | 3 | 5 | 9 | 12 | 16 | 23 |
| Total export credits | 193 | 146 | 117 | 119 | 177 | 275 | 382 | 467 |
| Total private | – | – | – | – | – | – | 25 | 25 |
| *of which:* Bank loans | – | – | – | – | – | – | 25 | 25 |
| Bonds | – | – | – | – | – | – | – | – |
| Other | – | – | – | – | – | – | – | – |
| Multilateral | – | – | – | – | – | – | – | – |
| *of which:* Concessional | – | – | – | – | – | – | – | – |
| CMEA countries | – | – | – | – | – | – | – | – |
| *of which:* Concessional | – | – | – | – | – | – | – | – |
| OPEC countries | – | – | – | – | – | – | – | – |
| *of which:* Concessional | – | – | – | – | – | – | – | – |
| Other LDC'S | – | – | – | – | – | – | – | – |
| *of which:* Concessional | – | – | – | – | – | – | – | – |
| Other and adjustments | – | – | – | 5 | 15 | 30 | 30 | 38 |
| **Total Debt** | **193** | **146** | **120** | **129** | **201** | **317** | **453** | **553** |
| *of which:* Concessional | – | – | 3 | 5 | 14 | 27 | 31 | 41 |
| Non-concessional | 193 | 146 | 117 | 124 | 187 | 290 | 422 | 512 |
| **DEBT SERVICE** | | | | | | | | |
| DAC countries and capital | | | | | | | | |
| markets | 19 | 25 | 28 | 37 | 48 | 100 | 120 | 137 |
| ODA | – | – | – | 0 | 0 | 1 | 1 | 1 |
| Total export credits | 19 | 25 | 28 | 37 | 48 | 99 | 116 | 133 |
| Total private | – | – | – | – | – | – | 3 | 4 |
| *of which:* Bank loans | – | – | – | – | – | – | 3 | 4 |
| Bonds | – | – | – | – | – | – | – | – |
| Other | – | – | – | – | – | – | – | – |
| Multilateral | – | – | – | – | – | – | – | – |
| *of which:* Concessional | – | – | – | – | – | – | – | – |
| CMEA countries | – | – | – | – | – | – | – | – |
| *of which:* Concessional | – | – | – | – | – | – | – | – |
| OPEC countries | – | – | – | – | – | – | – | – |
| *of which:* Concessional | – | – | – | – | – | – | – | – |
| Other LDC'S | – | – | – | – | – | – | – | – |
| *of which:* Concessional | – | – | – | – | – | – | – | – |
| Other and adjustments | – | – | – | – | – | 3 | 4 | 5 |
| **Total Debt Service** | **19** | **25** | **28** | **37** | **48** | **103** | **124** | **142** |
| *of which:* Concessional | – | – | – | 0 | 0 | 1 | 1 | 1 |
| Non-concessional | 19 | 25 | 28 | 37 | 48 | 102 | 123 | 141 |

*US $ Million*

| | 1975 | 1976 | 1977 | 1978 | 1979 | 1980 | 1981 | 1982 |
|---|---|---|---|---|---|---|---|---|
| **DEBT** | | | | | | | | |
| DAC countries and capital markets | 3356 | 4717 | 5687 | 7244 | 10695 | 13893 | 20370 | 22596 |
| ODA | 114 | 111 | 120 | 128 | 133 | 127 | 123 | 120 |
| Total export credits | 1630 | 1640 | 2044 | 2775 | 3000 | 4231 | 5033 | 4731 |
| Total private | 1612 | 2966 | 3523 | 4341 | 7562 | 9535 | 15214 | 17745 |
| of which: Bank loans | 832 | 1880 | 2328 | 2764 | 6046 | 7900 | 13100 | 15500 |
| Bonds | 550 | 734 | 683 | 966 | 907 | 828 | 734 | 645 |
| Other | 230 | 352 | 512 | 611 | 609 | 807 | 1380 | 1600 |
| Multilateral | 605 | 637 | 718 | 902 | 999 | 1087 | 1230 | 1321 |
| of which: Concessional | 155 | 152 | 148 | 147 | 155 | 153 | 152 | 148 |
| CMEA countries | 41 | 53 | 59 | 177 | 263 | 293 | 262 | 304 |
| of which: Concessional | 13 | 19 | 24 | 134 | 189 | 178 | 153 | 191 |
| OPEC countries | 50 | 50 | 10 | 1 | 0 | 0 | – | – |
| of which: Concessional | – | – | – | – | – | – | – | – |
| Other LDC'S | 3 | 2 | 1 | 14 | 32 | 40 | 29 | 24 |
| of which: Concessional | – | – | – | – | – | – | – | – |
| Other and adjustments | 259 | 392 | 436 | 452 | 634 | 681 | 1780 | 2857 |
| **Total Debt** | **4314** | **5852** | **6912** | **8789** | **12624** | **15994** | **23671** | **27101** |
| of which: Concessional | 282 | 282 | 291 | 408 | 477 | 458 | 428 | 458 |
| Non-concessional | 4031 | 5571 | 6621 | 8381 | 12148 | 15536 | 23244 | 26643 |
| **DEBT SERVICE** | | | | | | | | |
| DAC countries and capital markets | 888 | 1310 | 1282 | 2104 | 1661 | 2265 | 3989 | 5700 |
| ODA | 9 | 9 | 8 | 8 | 8 | 5 | 8 | 4 |
| Total export credits | 448 | 684 | 534 | 554 | 635 | 824 | 847 | 676 |
| Total private | 431 | 617 | 740 | 1543 | 1017 | 1436 | 3135 | 5019 |
| of which: Bank loans | 239 | 380 | 443 | 1214 | 578 | 1005 | 2530 | 4560 |
| Bonds | 167 | 181 | 195 | 215 | 287 | 258 | 200 | 109 |
| Other | 25 | 56 | 102 | 113 | 152 | 172 | 405 | 350 |
| Multilateral | 79 | 94 | 105 | 127 | 136 | 219 | 189 | 224 |
| of which: Concessional | 18 | 18 | 18 | 19 | 20 | 25 | 22 | 22 |
| CMEA countries | 4 | 14 | 17 | 18 | 37 | 46 | 51 | 52 |
| of which: Concessional | 1 | 2 | 3 | 4 | 24 | 26 | 27 | 26 |
| OPEC countries | 3 | – | 47 | 10 | 1 | 0 | 0 | – |
| of which: Concessional | – | – | – | – | – | – | – | – |
| Other LDC'S | 1 | 1 | 1 | 2 | 4 | 8 | 15 | 13 |
| of which: Concessional | – | – | – | – | – | – | – | – |
| Other and adjustments | 18 | 37 | 124 | 312 | 243 | 273 | 166 | 269 |
| **Total Debt Service** | **992** | **1456** | **1575** | **2572** | **2081** | **2811** | **4411** | **6258** |
| of which: Concessional | 28 | 29 | 29 | 31 | 53 | 56 | 57 | 53 |
| Non-concessional | 965 | 1427 | 1546 | 2541 | 2028 | 2754 | 4354 | 6205 |

*US $ Million*

| | 1975 | 1976 | 1977 | 1978 | 1979 | 1980 | 1981 | 1982 |
|---|---|---|---|---|---|---|---|---|
| **DEBT** | | | | | | | | |
| DAC countries and capital | | | | | | | | |
| markets | 119 | 116 | 88 | 81 | 76 | 105 | 149 | 162 |
| ODA | – | – | – | – | – | – | – | – |
| Total export credits | 94 | 96 | 67 | 70 | 66 | 75 | 103 | 92 |
| Total private | 25 | 20 | 21 | 11 | 10 | 30 | 46 | 70 |
| *of which:* Bank loans | 25 | 20 | 21 | 11 | 10 | 30 | 45 | 70 |
| Bonds | – | – | – | – | – | – | – | – |
| Other | – | – | – | – | – | – | 1 | – |
| Multilateral | – | – | 0 | 1 | 1 | 7 | 10 | 14 |
| *of which:* Concessional | – | – | – | – | – | – | – | – |
| CMEA countries | – | – | – | – | – | – | – | – |
| *of which:* Concessional | – | – | – | – | – | – | – | – |
| OPEC countries | – | – | – | – | – | – | – | – |
| *of which:* Concessional | – | – | – | – | – | – | – | – |
| Other LDC'S | – | – | – | – | – | – | – | – |
| *of which:* Concessional | – | – | – | – | – | – | – | – |
| Other and adjustments | – | – | – | – | – | – | – | – |
| **Total Debt** | **119** | **116** | **88** | **82** | **77** | **112** | **159** | **176** |
| *of which:* Concessional | – | – | – | – | – | – | – | – |
| Non-concessional | 119 | 116 | 88 | 82 | 77 | 112 | 159 | 176 |
| **DEBT SERVICE** | | | | | | | | |
| DAC countries and capital | | | | | | | | |
| markets | 53 | 46 | 50 | 39 | 33 | 42 | 45 | 41 |
| ODA | – | – | – | – | – | – | – | – |
| Total export credits | 44 | 40 | 49 | 27 | 31 | 38 | 38 | 31 |
| Total private | 9 | 6 | 2 | 12 | 2 | 5 | 7 | 11 |
| *of which:* Bank loans | 9 | 6 | 2 | 12 | 2 | 5 | 6 | 10 |
| Bonds | – | – | – | – | – | – | – | – |
| Other | – | – | – | – | – | – | 0 | 1 |
| Multilateral | – | – | 0 | 0 | 0 | 1 | 1 | 1 |
| *of which:* Concessional | – | – | – | – | – | – | – | – |
| CMEA countries | – | – | – | – | – | – | – | – |
| *of which:* Concessional | – | – | – | – | – | – | – | – |
| OPEC countries | – | – | – | – | – | – | – | – |
| *of which:* Concessional | – | – | – | – | – | – | – | – |
| Other LDC'S | – | – | – | – | – | – | – | – |
| *of which:* Concessional | – | – | – | – | – | – | – | – |
| Other and adjustments | – | – | – | – | – | – | – | – |
| **Total Debt Service** | **53** | **46** | **50** | **39** | **33** | **43** | **46** | **42** |
| *of which:* Concessional | – | – | – | – | – | – | – | – |
| Non-concessional | 53 | 46 | 50 | 39 | 33 | 43 | 46 | 42 |

## BAHRAIN

*US $ Million*

| | 1975 | 1976 | 1977 | 1978 | 1979 | 1980 | 1981 | 1982 |
|---|---|---|---|---|---|---|---|---|
| **DEBT** | | | | | | | | |
| DAC countries and capital markets | 71 | 70 | 152 | 180 | 157 | 327 | 261 | 450 |
| ODA | – | – | – | – | – | – | – | – |
| Total export credits | 71 | 70 | 152 | 180 | 157 | 147 | 141 | 300 |
| Total private | – | – | – | – | – | 180 | 120 | 150 |
| *of which:* Bank loans | – | – | – | – | – | 180 | 120 | 150 |
| Bonds | – | – | – | – | – | – | – | – |
| Other | – | – | – | – | – | – | – | – |
| Multilateral | – | – | – | – | – | – | – | – |
| *of which:* Concessional | – | – | – | – | – | – | – | – |
| CMEA countries | – | – | – | – | – | – | – | – |
| *of which:* Concessional | – | – | – | – | – | – | – | – |
| OPEC countries | 25 | 61 | 65 | 76 | 92 | 100 | 110 | 110 |
| *of which:* Concessional | – | – | – | – | – | – | – | – |
| Other LDC'S | – | – | – | – | – | – | – | – |
| *of which:* Concessional | – | – | – | – | – | – | – | – |
| Other and adjustments | – | – | – | – | – | – | – | – |
| **Total Debt** | **96** | **131** | **217** | **256** | **249** | **427** | **371** | **560** |
| *of which:* Concessional | – | – | – | – | – | – | – | – |
| Non-concessional | 96 | 131 | 217 | 256 | 249 | 427 | 371 | 560 |
| | | | | | | | | |
| **DEBT SERVICE** | | | | | | | | |
| DAC countries and capital markets | 36 | 31 | 32 | 62 | 59 | 74 | 129 | 132 |
| ODA | – | – | – | – | – | – | – | – |
| Total export credits | 36 | 31 | 32 | 62 | 59 | 74 | 69 | 96 |
| Total private | – | – | – | – | – | – | 60 | 36 |
| *of which:* Bank loans | – | – | – | – | – | – | 60 | 36 |
| Bonds | – | – | – | – | – | – | – | – |
| Other | – | – | – | – | – | – | – | – |
| Multilateral | – | – | – | – | – | – | – | – |
| *of which:* Concessional | – | – | – | – | – | – | – | – |
| CMEA countries | – | – | – | – | – | – | – | – |
| *of which:* Concessional | – | – | – | – | – | – | – | – |
| OPEC countries | 3 | 5 | 7 | 7 | 7 | 9 | 10 | 11 |
| *of which:* Concessional | – | – | – | – | – | – | – | – |
| Other LDC'S | – | – | – | – | – | – | – | – |
| *of which:* Concessional | – | – | – | – | – | – | – | – |
| Other and adjustments | – | – | – | – | – | – | – | – |
| **Total Debt Service** | **39** | **36** | **39** | **69** | **67** | **82** | **139** | **143** |
| *of which:* Concessional | – | – | – | – | – | – | – | – |
| Non-concessional | 39 | 36 | 39 | 69 | 67 | 82 | 139 | 143 |

*US $ Million*

| | 1975 | 1976 | 1977 | 1978 | 1979 | 1980 | 1981 | 1982 |
|---|---|---|---|---|---|---|---|---|
| **DEBT** | | | | | | | | |
| DAC countries and capital | | | | | | | | |
| markets | 936 | 1113 | 1340 | 1606 | 1853 | 1745 | 1817 | 1959 |
| ODA | 671 | 935 | 1290 | 1475 | 1731 | 1631 | 1689 | 1833 |
| Total export credits | 265 | 178 | 50 | 131 | 119 | 111 | 124 | 123 |
| Total private | – | – | – | – | 3 | 3 | 4 | 3 |
| *of which:* Bank loans | – | – | – | – | 3 | 3 | 4 | 3 |
| Bonds | – | – | – | – | – | – | – | – |
| Other | – | – | – | – | – | – | – | – |
| Multilateral | 373 | 498 | 627 | 818 | 1084 | 1385 | 1621 | 1878 |
| *of which:* Concessional | 366 | 491 | 621 | 812 | 1079 | 1379 | 1610 | 1847 |
| CMEA countries | 133 | 132 | 123 | 138 | 147 | 170 | 139 | 126 |
| *of which:* Concessional | 62 | 60 | 47 | 61 | 73 | 94 | 84 | 71 |
| OPEC countries | 75 | 82 | 97 | 109 | 136 | 183 | 237 | 307 |
| *of which:* Concessional | 75 | 82 | 97 | 109 | 136 | 183 | 237 | 307 |
| Other LDC'S | 84 | 109 | 120 | 122 | 128 | 131 | 124 | 147 |
| *of which:* Concessional | 42 | 60 | 75 | 75 | 78 | 74 | 63 | 84 |
| Other and adjustments | – | – | – | – | – | – | – | – |
| **Total Debt** | **1601** | **1934** | **2307** | **2793** | **3348** | **3614** | **3938** | **4417** |
| *of which:* Concessional | 1216 | 1628 | 2130 | 2532 | 3097 | 3361 | 3683 | 4142 |
| Non-concessional | 385 | 306 | 177 | 261 | 251 | 252 | 255 | 275 |
| **DEBT SERVICE** | | | | | | | | |
| DAC countries and capital | | | | | | | | |
| markets | 46 | 62 | 36 | 46 | 47 | 63 | 81 | 56 |
| ODA | 3 | 13 | 16 | 21 | 21 | 19 | 40 | 38 |
| Total export credits | 43 | 47 | 15 | 16 | 19 | 44 | 40 | 16 |
| Total private | 0 | 2 | 5 | 9 | 7 | 1 | 1 | 2 |
| *of which:* Bank loans | 0 | 2 | 5 | 9 | 7 | 1 | 1 | 2 |
| Bonds | – | – | – | – | – | – | – | – |
| Other | – | – | – | – | – | – | – | – |
| Multilateral | 2 | 7 | 8 | 10 | 14 | 13 | 15 | 28 |
| *of which:* Concessional | 2 | 6 | 7 | 9 | 13 | 12 | 14 | 18 |
| CMEA countries | 9 | 8 | 21 | 31 | 25 | 16 | 33 | 30 |
| *of which:* Concessional | 4 | 2 | 14 | 11 | 4 | 5 | 13 | 20 |
| OPEC countries | – | 0 | 0 | 1 | 1 | 6 | 8 | 13 |
| *of which:* Concessional | – | 0 | 0 | 1 | 1 | 6 | 8 | 13 |
| Other LDC'S | 4 | 9 | 18 | 14 | 12 | 11 | 15 | 12 |
| *of which:* Concessional | 1 | 1 | 4 | 5 | 7 | 8 | 9 | 7 |
| Other and adjustments | – | – | – | – | – | – | – | – |
| **Total Debt Service** | **61** | **86** | **84** | **102** | **99** | **109** | **151** | **138** |
| *of which:* Concessional | 9 | 23 | 42 | 47 | 46 | 50 | 84 | 95 |
| Non-concessional | 52 | 63 | 41 | 56 | 53 | 60 | 67 | 43 |

# BARBADOS

US $ Million

| | 1975 | 1976 | 1977 | 1978 | 1979 | 1980 | 1981 | 1982 |
|---|---|---|---|---|---|---|---|---|
| **DEBT** | | | | | | | | |
| DAC countries and capital | | | | | | | | |
|   markets | 30 | 35 | 43 | 53 | 58 | 68 | 92 | 146 |
| ODA | 12 | 12 | 13 | 19 | 22 | 23 | 24 | 22 |
| Total export credits | 14 | 17 | 13 | 13 | 23 | 35 | 30 | 32 |
| Total private | 4 | 6 | 17 | 21 | 13 | 10 | 38 | 92 |
|   of which: Bank loans | – | 2 | 17 | 21 | 13 | 10 | 38 | 92 |
|     Bonds | 4 | 4 | – | – | – | – | – | – |
|     Other | – | – | – | – | – | – | – | – |
| Multilateral | 0 | 3 | 10 | 15 | 24 | 40 | 63 | 81 |
|   of which: Concessional | 0 | 2 | 3 | 5 | 11 | 20 | 31 | 35 |
| CMEA countries | – | – | – | – | – | – | – | – |
|   of which: Concessional | – | – | – | – | – | – | – | – |
| OPEC countries | – | – | – | – | – | – | 0 | 2 |
|   of which: Concessional | – | – | – | – | – | – | – | 0 |
| Other LDC'S | – | – | 10 | 10 | 8 | 8 | 8 | – |
|   of which: Concessional | – | – | – | – | – | – | – | – |
| Other and adjustments | – | – | – | – | – | – | – | – |
| **Total Debt** | **30** | **37** | **63** | **78** | **90** | **116** | **164** | **229** |
|   of which: Concessional | 12 | 14 | 16 | 24 | 33 | 43 | 55 | 58 |
|     Non-concessional | 18 | 23 | 47 | 54 | 57 | 73 | 108 | 171 |
| **DEBT SERVICE** | | | | | | | | |
| DAC countries and capital | | | | | | | | |
|   markets | 3 | 4 | 10 | 9 | 10 | 12 | 16 | 28 |
| ODA | 1 | 1 | 1 | 1 | 1 | 1 | 2 | 2 |
| Total export credits | 2 | 3 | 3 | 3 | 3 | 6 | 11 | 18 |
| Total private | 0 | 0 | 7 | 5 | 6 | 5 | 4 | 8 |
|   of which: Bank loans | – | 0 | 4 | 5 | 6 | 5 | 4 | 8 |
|     Bonds | 0 | 0 | 3 | – | – | – | – | – |
|     Other | – | – | – | – | – | – | – | – |
| Multilateral | 0 | 0 | 0 | 1 | 1 | 2 | 6 | 5 |
|   of which: Concessional | 0 | 0 | 0 | 0 | 0 | 1 | 1 | 1 |
| CMEA countries | – | – | – | – | – | – | – | – |
|   of which: Concessional | – | – | – | – | – | – | – | – |
| OPEC countries | – | – | – | – | – | – | 0 | 0 |
|   of which: Concessional | – | – | – | – | – | – | – | 0 |
| Other LDC'S | – | – | 0 | 0 | 2 | – | – | 8 |
|   of which: Concessional | – | – | – | – | – | – | – | – |
| Other and adjustments | – | – | – | – | – | – | – | – |
| **Total Debt Service** | **3** | **4** | **11** | **10** | **14** | **14** | **22** | **42** |
|   of which: Concessional | 1 | 1 | 1 | 1 | 1 | 2 | 2 | 3 |
|     Non-concessional | 2 | 4 | 10 | 9 | 12 | 12 | 20 | 39 |

*US $ Million*

| | 1975 | 1976 | 1977 | 1978 | 1979 | 1980 | 1981 | 1982 |
|---|---|---|---|---|---|---|---|---|
| **DEBT** | | | | | | | | |
| DAC countries and capital | | | | | | | | |
|   markets | 9 | 10 | 9 | 14 | 23 | 32 | 33 | 29 |
|   ODA | 6 | 6 | 5 | 9 | 14 | 14 | 15 | 14 |
|   Total export credits | 3 | 4 | 4 | 5 | 9 | 18 | 18 | 15 |
|   Total private | – | – | – | – | – | – | – | – |
|     *of which:* Bank loans | – | – | – | – | – | – | – | – |
|     Bonds | – | – | – | – | – | – | – | – |
|     Other | – | – | – | – | – | – | – | – |
| Multilateral | 3 | 4 | 7 | 20 | 23 | 27 | 27 | 28 |
|   *of which:* Concessional | 2 | 3 | 7 | 19 | 22 | 24 | 24 | 24 |
| CMEA countries | – | – | – | – | – | – | – | – |
|   *of which:* Concessional | – | – | – | – | – | – | – | – |
| OPEC countries | – | – | – | – | – | – | – | 0 |
|   *of which:* Concessional | – | – | – | – | – | – | – | – |
| Other LDC'S | – | 0 | 0 | 0 | 0 | 0 | 0 | 0 |
|   *of which:* Concessional | – | 0 | 0 | 0 | 0 | 0 | 0 | 0 |
| Other and adjustments | – | – | – | – | – | – | – | – |
| **Total Debt** | **12** | **14** | **17** | **35** | **46** | **59** | **61** | **58** |
|   *of which:* Concessional | 8 | 10 | 12 | 29 | 36 | 38 | 39 | 39 |
|     Non-concessional | 4 | 5 | 5 | 6 | 10 | 21 | 21 | 19 |
| | | | | | | | | |
| **DEBT SERVICE** | | | | | | | | |
| DAC countries and capital | | | | | | | | |
|   markets | 1 | 2 | 2 | 2 | 5 | 8 | 2 | 4 |
|   ODA | 0 | 0 | 0 | 0 | 1 | 1 | 0 | 1 |
|   Total export credits | 1 | 1 | 2 | 1 | 4 | 8 | 1 | 3 |
|   Total private | – | – | – | – | – | – | – | – |
|     *of which:* Bank loans | – | – | – | – | – | – | – | – |
|     Bonds | – | – | – | – | – | – | – | – |
|     Other | – | – | – | – | – | – | – | – |
| Multilateral | 0 | 0 | 0 | 1 | 1 | 1 | 2 | 2 |
|   *of which:* Concessional | 0 | 0 | 0 | 1 | 1 | 1 | 1 | 2 |
| CMEA countries | – | – | – | – | – | – | – | – |
|   *of which:* Concessional | – | – | – | – | – | – | – | – |
| OPEC countries | – | – | – | – | – | – | – | 0 |
|   *of which:* Concessional | – | – | – | – | – | – | – | – |
| Other LDC'S | – | – | – | – | – | – | – | 0 |
|   *of which:* Concessional | – | – | – | – | – | – | – | 0 |
| Other and adjustments | – | – | – | – | – | – | – | – |
| **Total Debt Service** | **1** | **2** | **2** | **2** | **5** | **9** | **3** | **6** |
|   *of which:* Concessional | 0 | 0 | 1 | 1 | 1 | 1 | 2 | 2 |
|     Non-concessional | 1 | 1 | 2 | 1 | 4 | 8 | 1 | 4 |

## BENIN

US $ Million

| | 1975 | 1976 | 1977 | 1978 | 1979 | 1980 | 1981 | 1982 |
|---|---|---|---|---|---|---|---|---|
| **DEBT** | | | | | | | | |
| DAC countries and capital | | | | | | | | |
| markets | 59 | 72 | 84 | 88 | 118 | 331 | 410 | 370 |
| ODA | 28 | 38 | 50 | 44 | 55 | 46 | 44 | 45 |
| Total export credits | 18 | 22 | 24 | 29 | 50 | 205 | 291 | 240 |
| Total private | 13 | 12 | 10 | 15 | 13 | 80 | 75 | 85 |
| of which: Bank loans | 13 | 12 | 10 | 15 | 13 | 80 | 75 | 85 |
| Bonds | 0 | 0 | 0 | 0 | 0 | 0 | 0 | 0 |
| Other | – | – | – | – | – | – | – | – |
| Multilateral | 26 | 36 | 48 | 71 | 86 | 116 | 133 | 152 |
| of which: Concessional | 26 | 34 | 45 | 62 | 72 | 99 | 115 | 134 |
| CMEA countries | 2 | 2 | 2 | 1 | 2 | 2 | 2 | 3 |
| of which: Concessional | – | – | – | – | 1 | 1 | 1 | 3 |
| OPEC countries | – | – | 2 | 4 | 6 | 9 | 8 | 10 |
| of which: Concessional | – | – | 2 | 4 | 6 | 9 | 8 | 10 |
| Other LDC'S | 3 | 6 | 14 | 21 | 25 | 25 | 20 | 32 |
| of which: Concessional | 3 | 6 | 14 | 21 | 25 | 25 | 20 | 32 |
| Other and adjustments | 0 | – | – | – | – | – | – | – |
| **Total Debt** | **90** | **115** | **149** | **186** | **237** | **484** | **574** | **566** |
| of which: Concessional | 56 | 77 | 110 | 131 | 159 | 180 | 188 | 224 |
| Non-concessional | 33 | 38 | 39 | 55 | 78 | 304 | 385 | 343 |
| **DEBT SERVICE** | | | | | | | | |
| DAC countries and capital | | | | | | | | |
| markets | 9 | 6 | 10 | 13 | 14 | 22 | 43 | 45 |
| ODA | 1 | 2 | 3 | 1 | 1 | 1 | 1 | 1 |
| Total export credits | 7 | 4 | 6 | 11 | 11 | 18 | 26 | 22 |
| Total private | 1 | 1 | 1 | 1 | 2 | 3 | 16 | 22 |
| of which: Bank loans | 1 | 1 | 1 | 1 | 2 | 3 | 16 | 22 |
| Bonds | 0 | 0 | 0 | 0 | 0 | 0 | – | – |
| Other | – | – | – | – | – | – | – | – |
| Multilateral | 0 | 0 | 0 | 1 | 2 | 2 | 11 | 4 |
| of which: Concessional | 0 | 0 | 0 | 1 | 1 | 1 | 10 | 2 |
| CMEA countries | – | 0 | 0 | 0 | 0 | 0 | – | 1 |
| of which: Concessional | – | – | – | – | – | – | – | 1 |
| OPEC countries | – | – | 0 | 0 | 0 | 0 | 0 | 0 |
| of which: Concessional | – | – | 0 | 0 | 0 | 0 | 0 | 0 |
| Other LDC'S | 0 | 0 | 0 | – | – | – | – | 0 |
| of which: Concessional | 0 | 0 | 0 | – | – | – | – | 0 |
| Other and adjustments | 0 | 0 | – | – | – | – | – | 1 |
| **Total Debt Service** | **9** | **7** | **11** | **14** | **16** | **24** | **55** | **52** |
| of which: Concessional | 2 | 2 | 3 | 2 | 2 | 2 | 11 | 5 |
| Non-concessional | 8 | 5 | 7 | 12 | 14 | 22 | 44 | 47 |

# BERMUDA

| | 1975 | 1976 | 1977 | 1978 | 1979 | 1980 | 1981 | 1982 |
|---|---|---|---|---|---|---|---|---|
| **DEBT** | | | | | | | | |
| DAC countries and capital | | | | | | | | |
|   markets | 231 | 313 | 211 | 295 | 258 | 284 | 292 | 279 |
|   ODA | – | – | – | – | – | – | – | – |
|   Total export credits | 231 | 298 | 196 | 275 | 233 | 259 | 265 | 249 |
|   Total private | – | 15 | 15 | 20 | 25 | 25 | 27 | 30 |
|     *of which:* Bank loans | – | 15 | 15 | 20 | 25 | 25 | 27 | 30 |
|         Bonds | – | – | – | – | – | – | – | – |
|         Other | – | – | – | – | – | – | – | – |
| Multilateral | – | – | – | – | – | – | – | – |
|   *of which:* Concessional | – | – | – | – | – | – | – | – |
| CMEA countries | – | – | – | – | – | – | – | – |
|   *of which:* Concessional | – | – | – | – | – | – | – | – |
| OPEC countries | | | | | | | | |
|   *of which:* Concessional | – | – | – | – | – | – | – | – |
| Other LDC'S | – | – | – | – | – | – | – | – |
|   *of which:* Concessional | – | – | – | – | – | – | – | – |
| Other and adjustments | – | – | – | – | – | – | – | – |
| **Total Debt** | **231** | **313** | **211** | **295** | **258** | **284** | **292** | **279** |
|   *of which:* Concessional | – | – | – | – | – | – | – | – |
|         Non-concessional | 231 | 313 | 211 | 295 | 258 | 284 | 292 | 279 |
| | | | | | | | | |
| **DEBT SERVICE** | | | | | | | | |
| DAC countries and capital | | | | | | | | |
|   markets | 38 | 49 | 60 | 166 | 115 | 84 | 192 | 113 |
|   ODA | – | – | – | – | – | – | – | – |
|   Total export credits | 38 | 47 | 58 | 163 | 111 | 79 | 184 | 105 |
|   Total private | – | 2 | 2 | 3 | 4 | 5 | 8 | 8 |
|     *of which:* Bank loans | – | 2 | 2 | 3 | 4 | 5 | 8 | 8 |
|         Bonds | – | – | – | – | – | – | – | – |
|         Other | – | – | – | – | – | – | – | – |
| Multilateral | – | – | – | – | – | – | – | – |
|   *of which:* Concessional | – | – | – | – | – | – | – | – |
| CMEA countries | – | – | – | – | – | – | – | – |
|   *of which:* Concessional | – | – | – | – | – | – | – | – |
| OPEC countries | – | – | – | – | – | – | – | – |
|   *of which:* Concessional | – | – | – | – | – | – | – | – |
| Other LDC'S | – | – | – | – | – | – | – | – |
|   *of which:* Concessional | – | – | – | – | – | – | – | – |
| Other and adjustments | – | – | – | – | – | – | – | – |
| **Total Debt Service** | **38** | **49** | **60** | **166** | **115** | **84** | **192** | **113** |
|   *of which:* Concessional | – | – | – | – | – | – | – | – |
|         Non-concessional | 38 | 49 | 60 | 166 | 115 | 84 | 192 | 113 |

# BOLIVIA

*US $ Million*

| | 1975 | 1976 | 1977 | 1978 | 1979 | 1980 | 1981 | 1982 |
|---|---|---|---|---|---|---|---|---|
| **DEBT** | | | | | | | | |
| DAC countries and capital | | | | | | | | |
| markets | 568 | 715 | 1020 | 1237 | 1447 | 1435 | 1500 | 1348 |
| ODA | 216 | 238 | 276 | 312 | 348 | 362 | 389 | 408 |
| Total export credits | 142 | 144 | 198 | 292 | 415 | 355 | 338 | 290 |
| Total private | 210 | 333 | 546 | 633 | 684 | 718 | 773 | 650 |
| *of which:* Bank loans | 132 | 207 | 447 | 551 | 590 | 620 | 680 | 570 |
| Bonds | 63 | 62 | 76 | 75 | 74 | 73 | 73 | 58 |
| Other | 15 | 64 | 23 | 7 | 20 | 25 | 20 | 22 |
| Multilateral | 106 | 136 | 198 | 284 | 364 | 491 | 560 | 613 |
| *of which:* Concessional | 51 | 59 | 88 | 136 | 171 | 226 | 271 | 317 |
| CMEA countries | 20 | 24 | 29 | 33 | 30 | 35 | 35 | 29 |
| *of which:* Concessional | 12 | 14 | 15 | 15 | 13 | 20 | 17 | 13 |
| OPEC countries | 2 | 4 | 8 | 8 | 8 | 23 | 27 | 27 |
| *of which:* Concessional | 2 | 4 | 6 | 6 | 6 | 6 | 6 | 6 |
| Other LDC'S | 135 | 170 | 188 | 191 | 180 | 333 | 509 | 520 |
| *of which:* Concessional | 62 | 77 | 78 | 78 | 71 | 67 | 64 | 61 |
| Other and adjustments | 8 | 8 | 7 | 6 | 7 | 5 | 101 | 153 |
| **Total Debt** | **840** | **1058** | **1450** | **1758** | **2036** | **2323** | **2732** | **2690** |
| *of which:* Concessional | 343 | 393 | 463 | 547 | 610 | 681 | 747 | 805 |
| Non-concessional | 496 | 665 | 987 | 1211 | 1427 | 1642 | 1985 | 1885 |
| | | | | | | | | |
| **DEBT SERVICE** | | | | | | | | |
| DAC countries and capital | | | | | | | | |
| markets | 71 | 89 | 121 | 321 | 218 | 231 | 179 | 188 |
| ODA | 8 | 9 | 10 | 8 | 10 | 17 | 7 | 8 |
| Total export credits | 27 | 38 | 43 | 58 | 78 | 77 | 74 | 52 |
| Total private | 37 | 42 | 68 | 254 | 130 | 136 | 98 | 129 |
| *of which:* Bank loans | 34 | 25 | 48 | 234 | 120 | 130 | 88 | 110 |
| Bonds | 3 | 3 | 4 | 5 | 3 | 4 | 2 | 17 |
| Other | – | 15 | 17 | 15 | 7 | 2 | 8 | 2 |
| Multilateral | 5 | 10 | 12 | 17 | 21 | 28 | 36 | 40 |
| *of which:* Concessional | 1 | 1 | 1 | 2 | 2 | 3 | 4 | 4 |
| CMEA countries | 3 | 3 | 4 | 8 | 9 | 6 | 7 | 7 |
| *of which:* Concessional | 1 | 2 | 2 | 6 | 4 | 3 | 5 | 4 |
| OPEC countries | – | – | 0 | 0 | 1 | 1 | 2 | 2 |
| *of which:* Concessional | – | – | – | – | – | – | – | – |
| Other LDC'S | 13 | 21 | 21 | 17 | 26 | 26 | 51 | 70 |
| *of which:* Concessional | 5 | 7 | 5 | 1 | 9 | 6 | 4 | 4 |
| Other and adjustments | 1 | 1 | 2 | 2 | 1 | 3 | 1 | 1 |
| **Total Debt Service** | **93** | **124** | **160** | **364** | **276** | **294** | **277** | **308** |
| *of which:* Concessional | 15 | 19 | 18 | 17 | 25 | 29 | 20 | 19 |
| Non-concessional | 79 | 105 | 142 | 347 | 251 | 265 | 257 | 289 |

## BOTSWANA

US $ Million

| | 1975 | 1976 | 1977 | 1978 | 1979 | 1980 | 1981 | 1982 |
|---|---|---|---|---|---|---|---|---|
| **DEBT** | | | | | | | | |
| DAC countries and capital markets | 228 | 236 | 241 | 217 | 218 | 196 | 183 | 265 |
| ODA | 81 | 87 | 90 | 60 | 64 | 62 | 60 | 53 |
| Total export credits | 132 | 129 | 126 | 107 | 99 | 84 | 73 | 77 |
| Total private | 15 | 20 | 25 | 50 | 55 | 50 | 50 | 135 |
| *of which:* Bank loans | – | 10 | 15 | 35 | 40 | 30 | 20 | 25 |
| Bonds | – | – | – | – | – | – | – | – |
| Other | 15 | 10 | 10 | 15 | 15 | 20 | 30 | 110 |
| Multilateral | 50 | 56 | 61 | 67 | 75 | 84 | 100 | 115 |
| *of which:* Concessional | 16 | 20 | 22 | 25 | 28 | 34 | 38 | 40 |
| CMEA countries | – | – | – | – | – | – | – | – |
| *of which:* Concessional | – | – | – | – | – | – | – | – |
| OPEC countries | – | – | – | – | – | – | – | 6 |
| *of which:* Concessional | – | – | – | – | – | – | – | 6 |
| Other LDC'S | – | – | – | – | – | – | – | – |
| *of which:* Concessional | – | – | – | – | – | – | – | – |
| Other and adjustments | 0 | 2 | 2 | 2 | 2 | 3 | 2 | 2 |
| **Total Debt** | **278** | **294** | **304** | **286** | **295** | **283** | **285** | **388** |
| *of which:* Concessional | 97 | 107 | 112 | 85 | 92 | 96 | 98 | 99 |
| Non-concessional | 181 | 188 | 192 | 201 | 203 | 187 | 187 | 289 |
| **DEBT SERVICE** | | | | | | | | |
| DAC countries and capital markets | 16 | 15 | 37 | 59 | 38 | 29 | 29 | 21 |
| ODA | 1 | 0 | 0 | 1 | – | – | – | 1 |
| Total export credits | 14 | 13 | 33 | 54 | 32 | 25 | 14 | 14 |
| Total private | 2 | 2 | 4 | 4 | 7 | 5 | 15 | 6 |
| *of which:* Bank loans | – | – | 2 | 4 | 7 | 5 | 15 | 6 |
| Bonds | – | – | – | – | – | – | – | – |
| Other | 2 | 2 | 2 | – | – | – | – | – |
| Multilateral | 3 | 4 | 4 | 7 | 8 | 10 | 7 | 10 |
| *of which:* Concessional | 0 | 0 | 0 | 0 | 0 | 0 | 1 | 1 |
| CMEA countries | – | – | – | – | – | – | – | – |
| *of which:* Concessional | – | – | – | – | – | – | – | – |
| OPEC countries | – | – | – | – | – | – | – | 0 |
| *of which:* Concessional | – | – | – | – | – | – | – | 0 |
| Other LDC'S | – | – | – | – | – | – | – | – |
| *of which:* Concessional | – | – | – | – | – | – | – | – |
| Other and adjustments | 3 | 0 | 0 | 0 | 0 | 0 | 0 | 0 |
| **Total Debt Service** | **22** | **19** | **41** | **67** | **46** | **40** | **36** | **31** |
| *of which:* Concessional | 1 | 0 | 1 | 2 | 0 | 0 | 1 | 2 |
| Non-concessional | 22 | 19 | 41 | 65 | 46 | 39 | 35 | 29 |

US $ Million

| | 1975 | 1976 | 1977 | 1978 | 1979 | 1980 | 1981 | 1982 |
|---|---|---|---|---|---|---|---|---|
| **DEBT** | | | | | | | | |
| DAC countries and capital | | | | | | | | |
|   markets | 20221 | 24204 | 30297 | 41572 | 46651 | 51670 | 57493 | 64749 |
|   ODA | 1392 | 1430 | 1474 | 1533 | 1528 | 1483 | 1634 | 1595 |
|   Total export credits | 3753 | 5030 | 6688 | 8618 | 9847 | 11049 | 11740 | 12805 |
|   Total private | 15076 | 17744 | 22135 | 31421 | 35276 | 39138 | 44119 | 50349 |
|     *of which:* Bank loans | 13742 | 15952 | 19079 | 26001 | 29216 | 32390 | 37500 | 43900 |
|     Bonds | 134 | 330 | 1196 | 2320 | 2873 | 3148 | 2819 | 2549 |
|     Other | 1200 | 1462 | 1860 | 3100 | 3187 | 3600 | 3800 | 3900 |
| Multilateral | 1576 | 1775 | 2054 | 2385 | 2756 | 3106 | 3447 | 4018 |
|   *of which:* Concessional | 315 | 305 | 274 | 258 | 254 | 236 | 216 | 189 |
| CMEA countries | 99 | 107 | 159 | 145 | 165 | 142 | 145 | 176 |
|   *of which:* Concessional | – | – | – | – | – | – | – | – |
| OPEC countries | 25 | 25 | 21 | 83 | 127 | 599 | 858 | 849 |
|   *of which:* Concessional | – | – | – | 28 | 40 | 40 | 80 | 79 |
| Other LDC'S | 58 | 85 | 99 | 89 | 23 | 59 | 70 | 51 |
|   *of which:* Concessional | – | – | – | – | – | – | – | – |
| Other and adjustments | 775 | 827 | 854 | 1018 | 1081 | 1477 | 2723 | 2769 |
| **Total Debt** | **22755** | **27024** | **33484** | **45292** | **50803** | **57052** | **64737** | **72612** |
|   *of which:* Concessional | 1707 | 1735 | 1748 | 1819 | 1822 | 1759 | 1930 | 1863 |
|   Non-concessional | 21047 | 25289 | 31736 | 43473 | 48982 | 55293 | 62807 | 70749 |
| | | | | | | | | |
| **DEBT SERVICE** | | | | | | | | |
| DAC countries and capital | | | | | | | | |
|   markets | 3534 | 4371 | 5802 | 7787 | 10575 | 12466 | 14188 | 16827 |
|   ODA | 53 | 62 | 73 | 86 | 89 | 91 | 91 | 87 |
|   Total export credits | 796 | 780 | 1008 | 1602 | 1633 | 1816 | 1826 | 1915 |
|   Total private | 2685 | 3529 | 4722 | 6098 | 8854 | 10559 | 12271 | 14825 |
|     *of which:* Bank loans | 2490 | 3245 | 4234 | 5407 | 7949 | 9510 | 11100 | 13300 |
|     Bonds | 15 | 17 | 38 | 116 | 178 | 249 | 311 | 425 |
|     Other | 180 | 267 | 450 | 575 | 727 | 800 | 860 | 1100 |
| Multilateral | 162 | 215 | 314 | 345 | 367 | 421 | 467 | 566 |
|   *of which:* Concessional | 41 | 43 | 61 | 49 | 39 | 38 | 38 | 40 |
| CMEA countries | 29 | 46 | 60 | 60 | 57 | 42 | 41 | 38 |
|   *of which:* Concessional | – | – | – | – | – | – | – | – |
| OPEC countries | 3 | 3 | 7 | 5 | 10 | 34 | 149 | 146 |
|   *of which:* Concessional | – | – | – | – | 1 | 2 | 5 | 5 |
| Other LDC'S | 14 | 15 | 14 | 15 | 93 | 5 | 11 | 41 |
|   *of which:* Concessional | – | – | – | – | – | – | – | – |
| Other and adjustments | 248 | 361 | 162 | 164 | 316 | 331 | 445 | 443 |
| **Total Debt Service** | **3990** | **5010** | **6359** | **8377** | **11420** | **13299** | **15301** | **18059** |
|   *of which:* Concessional | 93 | 105 | 134 | 136 | 130 | 131 | 134 | 132 |
|   Non-concessional | 3896 | 4905 | 6225 | 8241 | 11290 | 13168 | 15167 | 17927 |

# BRUNEI

US $ Million

| | 1975 | 1976 | 1977 | 1978 | 1979 | 1980 | 1981 | 1982 |
|---|---|---|---|---|---|---|---|---|
| **DEBT** | | | | | | | | |
| DAC countries and capital | | | | | | | | |
| markets | 21 | 1 | 20 | 23 | 56 | 62 | 19 | 10 |
| ODA | – | – | – | – | – | – | – | – |
| Total export credits | 21 | 1 | 16 | 19 | 51 | 59 | 18 | 10 |
| Total private | – | – | 4 | 4 | 5 | 3 | 1 | – |
| of which: Bank loans | – | – | 4 | 4 | 5 | 3 | 1 | – |
| Bonds | – | – | – | – | – | – | – | – |
| Other | – | – | – | – | – | – | – | – |
| Multilateral | – | – | – | – | – | – | – | – |
| of which: Concessional | – | – | – | – | – | – | – | – |
| CMEA countries | – | – | – | – | – | – | – | – |
| of which: Concessional | – | – | – | – | – | – | – | – |
| OPEC countries | – | – | – | – | – | – | – | – |
| of which: Concessional | – | – | – | – | – | – | – | – |
| Other LDC'S | – | – | – | – | – | – | – | – |
| of which: Concessional | – | – | – | – | – | – | – | – |
| Other and adjustments | – | – | – | – | – | – | – | – |
| **Total Debt** | **21** | **1** | **20** | **23** | **56** | **62** | **19** | **10** |
| of which: Concessional | – | – | – | – | – | – | – | – |
| Non-concessional | 21 | 1 | 20 | 23 | 56 | 62 | 19 | 10 |
| | | | | | | | | |
| **DEBT SERVICE** | | | | | | | | |
| DAC countries and capital | | | | | | | | |
| markets | 6 | 21 | 3 | 5 | 6 | 7 | 70 | 16 |
| ODA | – | – | – | – | – | – | – | 0 |
| Total export credits | 6 | 21 | 1 | 2 | 4 | 4 | 68 | 15 |
| Total private | – | – | 2 | 2 | 2 | 3 | 2 | 1 |
| of which: Bank loans | – | – | 2 | 2 | 2 | 3 | 2 | 1 |
| Bonds | – | – | – | – | – | – | – | – |
| Other | – | – | – | – | – | – | – | – |
| Multilateral | – | – | – | – | – | – | – | – |
| of which: Concessional | – | – | – | – | – | – | – | – |
| CMEA countries | – | – | – | – | – | – | – | – |
| of which: Concessional | – | – | – | – | – | – | – | – |
| OPEC countries | – | – | – | – | – | – | – | – |
| of which: Concessional | – | – | – | – | – | – | – | – |
| Other LDC'S | – | – | – | – | – | – | – | – |
| of which: Concessional | – | – | – | – | – | – | – | – |
| Other and adjustments | – | – | – | – | – | – | – | – |
| **Total Debt Service** | **6** | **21** | **3** | **5** | **6** | **7** | **70** | **16** |
| of which: Concessional | – | – | – | – | – | – | – | 0 |
| Non-concessional | 6 | 21 | 3 | 5 | 6 | 7 | 70 | 16 |

US $ Million

| | 1975 | 1976 | 1977 | 1978 | 1979 | 1980 | 1981 | 1982 |
|---|---|---|---|---|---|---|---|---|
| **DEBT** | | | | | | | | |
| DAC countries and capital | | | | | | | | |
| markets | 186 | 226 | 360 | 574 | 806 | 1060 | 1156 | 1256 |
| ODA | 133 | 145 | 201 | 382 | 529 | 744 | 806 | 896 |
| Total export credits | 53 | 71 | 144 | 159 | 221 | 265 | 280 | 290 |
| Total private | – | 10 | 15 | 33 | 56 | 51 | 70 | 70 |
| of which: Bank loans | – | 10 | 15 | 33 | 56 | 51 | 70 | 70 |
| Bonds | – | – | – | – | – | – | – | – |
| Other | – | – | – | – | – | – | – | – |
| Multilateral | 28 | 53 | 106 | 217 | 292 | 342 | 409 | 497 |
| of which: Concessional | 26 | 52 | 103 | 212 | 286 | 336 | 403 | 492 |
| CMEA countries | 18 | 12 | 10 | 11 | 24 | 41 | 72 | 129 |
| of which: Concessional | 8 | 6 | 5 | 5 | 16 | 36 | 62 | 117 |
| OPEC countries | – | – | – | – | – | – | – | – |
| of which: Concessional | – | – | – | – | – | – | – | – |
| Other LDC'S | 49 | 44 | 64 | 75 | 80 | 82 | 100 | 99 |
| of which: Concessional | 47 | 44 | 52 | 61 | 59 | 59 | 45 | 46 |
| Other and adjustments | – | – | – | – | – | – | – | – |
| **Total Debt** | **281** | **336** | **540** | **876** | **1202** | **1525** | **1737** | **1981** |
| of which: Concessional | 213 | 246 | 362 | 659 | 891 | 1174 | 1316 | 1550 |
| Non-concessional | 67 | 90 | 178 | 217 | 311 | 350 | 421 | 431 |
| **DEBT SERVICE** | | | | | | | | |
| DAC countries and capital | | | | | | | | |
| markets | 25 | 26 | 29 | 47 | 88 | 95 | 135 | 128 |
| ODA | 6 | 5 | 8 | 11 | 23 | 28 | 30 | 29 |
| Total export credits | 19 | 19 | 21 | 34 | 46 | 44 | 82 | 75 |
| Total private | – | 2 | – | 2 | 19 | 23 | 22 | 24 |
| of which: Bank loans | – | 2 | – | 2 | 19 | 23 | 22 | 24 |
| Bonds | – | – | – | – | – | – | – | – |
| Other | – | – | – | – | – | – | – | – |
| Multilateral | 3 | 2 | 1 | 1 | 2 | 3 | 4 | 5 |
| of which: Concessional | 1 | 1 | 0 | 1 | 2 | 2 | 3 | 4 |
| CMEA countries | 4 | 7 | 4 | 5 | 5 | 5 | 5 | 7 |
| of which: Concessional | 2 | 2 | 1 | 1 | 2 | 2 | 3 | 4 |
| OPEC countries | – | – | – | – | – | – | – | – |
| of which: Concessional | – | – | – | – | – | – | – | – |
| Other LDC'S | 1 | 2 | 0 | 2 | 10 | 9 | 7 | 7 |
| of which: Concessional | – | – | – | – | 6 | 5 | 3 | 3 |
| Other and adjustments | – | – | – | – | – | 1 | – | – |
| **Total Debt Service** | **33** | **36** | **34** | **54** | **106** | **113** | **151** | **147** |
| of which: Concessional | 10 | 7 | 10 | 13 | 33 | 36 | 40 | 40 |
| Non-concessional | 23 | 29 | 24 | 41 | 73 | 76 | 111 | 107 |

# BURUNDI

*US $ Million*

| | 1975 | 1976 | 1977 | 1978 | 1979 | 1980 | 1981 | 1982 |
|---|---|---|---|---|---|---|---|---|
| **DEBT** | | | | | | | | |
| DAC countries and capital | | | | | | | | |
|   markets | 7 | 7 | 12 | 15 | 22 | 19 | 31 | 44 |
|   ODA | 2 | 2 | 3 | 6 | 7 | 7 | 6 | 20 |
|   Total export credits | 3 | 3 | 6 | 6 | 9 | 9 | 25 | 24 |
|   Total private | 2 | 2 | 3 | 3 | 6 | 3 | – | – |
|   *of which:* Bank loans | 2 | – | 1 | 3 | 6 | 3 | – | – |
|         Bonds | – | – | – | – | – | – | – | – |
|         Other | – | 2 | 2 | – | – | – | – | – |
| Multilateral | 7 | 9 | 17 | 34 | 57 | 83 | 99 | 122 |
|   *of which:* Concessional | 6 | 7 | 13 | 29 | 53 | 78 | 95 | 119 |
| CMEA countries | – | – | 1 | 1 | 3 | 4 | 6 | 8 |
|   *of which:* Concessional | – | – | 0 | 0 | 2 | 4 | 6 | 8 |
| OPEC countries | – | – | – | 2 | 4 | 7 | 9 | 15 |
|   *of which:* Concessional | – | – | – | 2 | 4 | 7 | 9 | 15 |
| Other LDC'S | 2 | 4 | 12 | 16 | 27 | 38 | 33 | 34 |
|   *of which:* Concessional | 2 | 4 | 12 | 16 | 27 | 38 | 33 | 34 |
| Other and adjustments | – | – | 1 | – | – | – | – | – |
| **Total Debt** | **17** | **20** | **44** | **68** | **112** | **151** | **178** | **223** |
|   *of which:* Concessional | 11 | 13 | 29 | 54 | 93 | 134 | 149 | 195 |
|         Non-concessional | 6 | 7 | 15 | 14 | 20 | 17 | 29 | 27 |
| | | | | | | | | |
| **DEBT SERVICE** | | | | | | | | |
| DAC countries and capital | | | | | | | | |
|   markets | 1 | 1 | 2 | 4 | 3 | 5 | 4 | 3 |
|   ODA | 0 | 0 | 0 | 0 | 0 | – | – | – |
|   Total export credits | 1 | 1 | 1 | 4 | 2 | 1 | 3 | 3 |
|   Total private | 0 | 0 | 1 | 1 | 1 | 4 | 2 | 1 |
|   *of which:* Bank loans | 0 | – | 1 | 1 | 1 | 4 | 2 | 1 |
|         Bonds | – | – | – | – | – | – | – | – |
|         Other | – | 0 | 0 | – | – | – | – | – |
| Multilateral | 0 | 0 | 1 | 0 | 1 | 1 | 1 | 1 |
|   *of which:* Concessional | 0 | 0 | 0 | 0 | 0 | 0 | 1 | 1 |
| CMEA countries | – | – | 0 | 0 | 1 | 1 | 1 | 1 |
|   *of which:* Concessional | – | – | 0 | 0 | 1 | 1 | 1 | 1 |
| OPEC countries | – | – | – | – | 0 | 0 | 0 | 0 |
|   *of which:* Concessional | – | – | – | – | 0 | 0 | 0 | 0 |
| Other LDC'S | – | – | – | – | – | – | – | – |
|   *of which:* Concessional | – | – | – | – | – | – | – | – |
| Other and adjustments | – | – | – | – | – | – | – | – |
| **Total Debt Service** | **2** | **2** | **3** | **5** | **4** | **7** | **7** | **5** |
|   *of which:* Concessional | 1 | 1 | 1 | 0 | 1 | 1 | 2 | 2 |
|         Non-concessional | 1 | 1 | 2 | 5 | 3 | 6 | 5 | 4 |

*US $ Million*

| | 1975 | 1976 | 1977 | 1978 | 1979 | 1980 | 1981 | 1982 |
|---|---|---|---|---|---|---|---|---|
| **DEBT** | | | | | | | | |
| DAC countries and capital | | | | | | | | |
| markets | 263 | 329 | 559 | 759 | 1186 | 1499 | 1546 | 1500 |
| ODA | 132 | 138 | 165 | 235 | 337 | 373 | 372 | 416 |
| Total export credits | 86 | 117 | 248 | 381 | 637 | 874 | 930 | 844 |
| Total private | 45 | 74 | 146 | 143 | 212 | 252 | 244 | 240 |
| *of which:* Bank loans | 45 | 67 | 136 | 131 | 200 | 240 | 230 | 220 |
| Bonds | 0 | 0 | 0 | 0 | – | – | – | – |
| Other | – | 7 | 10 | 12 | 12 | 12 | 14 | 20 |
| Multilateral | 141 | 166 | 215 | 316 | 400 | 463 | 516 | 553 |
| *of which:* Concessional | 89 | 108 | 142 | 193 | 244 | 276 | 314 | 339 |
| CMEA countries | 1 | 2 | 4 | 3 | 3 | 3 | – | – |
| *of which:* Concessional | 1 | 2 | 4 | 3 | 3 | 3 | – | – |
| OPEC countries | 6 | 11 | 25 | 31 | 51 | 72 | 71 | 67 |
| *of which:* Concessional | 6 | 9 | 23 | 29 | 49 | 71 | 70 | 66 |
| Other LDC'S | – | – | 40 | 74 | 101 | 99 | 88 | 80 |
| *of which:* Concessional | – | – | 40 | 74 | 100 | 98 | 86 | 78 |
| Other and adjustments | – | – | – | – | – | – | – | – |
| **Total Debt** | **411** | **508** | **843** | **1183** | **1741** | **2136** | **2221** | **2200** |
| *of which:* Concessional | 228 | 257 | 373 | 535 | 734 | 821 | 842 | 899 |
| Non-concessional | 183 | 251 | 469 | 649 | 1008 | 1315 | 1379 | 1301 |
| **DEBT SERVICE** | | | | | | | | |
| DAC countries and capital | | | | | | | | |
| markets | 39 | 48 | 69 | 104 | 158 | 220 | 206 | 316 |
| ODA | 15 | 13 | 8 | 15 | 15 | 19 | 19 | 14 |
| Total export credits | 18 | 27 | 46 | 66 | 102 | 132 | 136 | 250 |
| Total private | 5 | 9 | 16 | 23 | 41 | 70 | 52 | 52 |
| *of which:* Bank loans | 5 | 9 | 14 | 20 | 38 | 66 | 48 | 49 |
| Bonds | 0 | 0 | 0 | 0 | 0 | – | – | – |
| Other | – | 0 | 2 | 3 | 3 | 4 | 4 | 3 |
| Multilateral | 8 | 9 | 10 | 20 | 21 | 28 | 31 | 32 |
| *of which:* Concessional | 2 | 2 | 3 | 4 | 5 | 7 | 11 | 7 |
| CMEA countries | 0 | 0 | 0 | 0 | 0 | 0 | 3 | – |
| *of which:* Concessional | 0 | 0 | 0 | 0 | 0 | 0 | 3 | – |
| OPEC countries | – | – | 0 | 1 | 1 | 3 | 3 | 6 |
| *of which:* Concessional | – | – | 0 | 0 | 0 | 3 | 3 | 5 |
| Other LDC'S | – | – | – | 0 | – | 0 | 0 | 0 |
| *of which:* Concessional | – | – | – | – | – | – | – | – |
| Other and adjustments | – | – | – | – | – | – | – | – |
| **Total Debt Service** | **47** | **58** | **80** | **125** | **180** | **251** | **243** | **354** |
| *of which:* Concessional | 17 | 15 | 11 | 19 | 20 | 29 | 35 | 26 |
| Non-concessional | 30 | 43 | 69 | 106 | 160 | 222 | 207 | 328 |

# CAPE VERDE

| | 1975 | 1976 | 1977 | 1978 | 1979 | 1980 | 1981 | 1982 |
|---|---|---|---|---|---|---|---|---|
| **DEBT** | | | | | | | | |
| DAC countries and capital | | | | | | | | |
| markets | – | – | – | – | – | – | 1 | 1 |
| ODA | – | – | – | – | – | – | 1 | 1 |
| Total export credits | – | – | – | – | – | – | – | – |
| Total private | – | – | – | – | – | – | – | – |
| *of which:* Bank loans | – | – | – | – | – | – | – | – |
| Bonds | – | – | – | – | – | – | – | – |
| Other | – | – | – | – | – | – | – | – |
| Multilateral | 1 | 11 | 12 | 12 | 14 | 16 | 21 | 31 |
| *of which:* Concessional | 1 | 11 | 12 | 12 | 14 | 16 | 21 | 22 |
| CMEA countries | – | – | – | 0 | 1 | 1 | 1 | 3 |
| *of which:* Concessional | – | – | – | 0 | 1 | 1 | 1 | 3 |
| OPEC countries | – | – | – | – | – | – | – | – |
| *of which:* Concessional | – | – | – | – | – | – | – | – |
| Other LDC'S | – | 1 | 2 | 2 | 3 | 3 | 3 | 13 |
| *of which:* Concessional | – | – | 1 | 2 | 3 | 2 | 2 | 7 |
| Other and adjustments | – | – | – | – | – | – | 13 | 13 |
| **Total Debt** | **1** | **12** | **14** | **15** | **17** | **19** | **39** | **61** |
| *of which:* Concessional | 1 | 11 | 13 | 14 | 17 | 19 | 26 | 34 |
| Non-concessional | – | 1 | 1 | 1 | 1 | 0 | 13 | 27 |
| **DEBT SERVICE** | | | | | | | | |
| DAC countries and capital | | | | | | | | |
| markets | 0 | – | – | – | – | – | – | – |
| ODA | – | – | – | – | – | – | – | – |
| Total export credits | 0 | – | – | – | – | – | – | – |
| Total private | – | – | – | – | – | – | – | – |
| *of which:* Bank loans | – | – | – | – | – | – | – | – |
| Bonds | – | – | – | – | – | – | – | – |
| Other | – | – | – | – | – | – | – | – |
| Multilateral | – | – | – | 0 | 0 | 0 | 0 | 0 |
| *of which:* Concessional | – | – | – | 0 | 0 | 0 | 0 | 0 |
| CMEA countries | – | – | – | – | – | – | – | – |
| *of which:* Concessional | – | – | – | – | – | – | – | – |
| OPEC countries | – | – | – | – | – | – | – | – |
| *of which:* Concessional | – | – | – | – | – | – | – | – |
| Other LDC'S | – | 0 | 0 | 0 | 0 | 0 | 0 | 0 |
| *of which:* Concessional | – | – | – | – | – | – | – | – |
| Other and adjustments | – | – | – | – | – | – | – | 1 |
| **Total Debt Service** | **0** | **0** | **0** | **0** | **0** | **0** | **0** | **2** |
| *of which:* Concessional | – | – | – | 0 | 0 | 0 | 0 | 0 |
| Non-concessional | 0 | 0 | 0 | 0 | 0 | 0 | 0 | 1 |

*US $ Million*

| | 1975 | 1976 | 1977 | 1978 | 1979 | 1980 | 1981 | 1982 |
|---|---|---|---|---|---|---|---|---|
| **DEBT** | | | | | | | | |
| DAC countries and capital markets | 49 | 51 | 62 | 65 | 68 | 56 | 53 | 68 |
| ODA | 40 | 41 | 42 | 21 | 21 | 21 | 32 | 36 |
| Total export credits | 9 | 10 | 20 | 44 | 47 | 35 | 21 | 32 |
| Total private | – | – | – | – | – | – | – | – |
| of which: Bank loans | – | – | – | – | – | – | – | – |
| Bonds | – | – | – | – | – | – | – | – |
| Other | – | – | – | – | – | – | – | – |
| Multilateral | 10 | 11 | 13 | 22 | 33 | 62 | 64 | 71 |
| of which: Concessional | 10 | 10 | 13 | 21 | 32 | 61 | 63 | 69 |
| CMEA countries | 3 | 2 | 2 | 4 | 4 | 4 | 4 | 4 |
| of which: Concessional | 3 | 2 | 2 | 2 | 1 | 1 | 1 | 1 |
| OPEC countries | – | 1 | 5 | 5 | 6 | 8 | 8 | 9 |
| of which: Concessional | – | 1 | 5 | 5 | 6 | 8 | 8 | 9 |
| Other LDC'S | 18 | 17 | 17 | 16 | 17 | 16 | 28 | 27 |
| of which: Concessional | 2 | 2 | 2 | 2 | 2 | 2 | 2 | 1 |
| Other and adjustments | 1 | 6 | 12 | 12 | 15 | 32 | 32 | 36 |
| **Total Debt** | **82** | **89** | **112** | **125** | **142** | **178** | **189** | **215** |
| of which: Concessional | 56 | 57 | 64 | 52 | 64 | 95 | 105 | 116 |
| Non-concessional | 26 | 32 | 47 | 73 | 78 | 83 | 84 | 99 |
| **DEBT SERVICE** | | | | | | | | |
| DAC countries and capital markets | 6 | 4 | 6 | 4 | 3 | 1 | 2 | 1 |
| ODA | 2 | 1 | 2 | 0 | 2 | 0 | 0 | 0 |
| Total export credits | 4 | 3 | 4 | 4 | 1 | 1 | 2 | 1 |
| Total private | – | – | – | – | – | – | – | – |
| of which: Bank loans | – | – | – | – | – | – | – | – |
| Bonds | – | – | – | – | – | – | – | – |
| Other | – | – | – | – | – | – | – | – |
| Multilateral | 0 | 0 | 0 | 0 | 0 | 1 | 0 | 1 |
| of which: Concessional | 0 | 0 | 0 | – | 0 | 1 | 0 | 1 |
| CMEA countries | – | – | – | 0 | – | 0 | 1 | – |
| of which: Concessional | – | – | – | – | – | 0 | 0 | – |
| OPEC countries | – | – | – | – | 0 | – | 0 | 0 |
| of which: Concessional | – | – | – | – | 0 | – | 0 | 0 |
| Other LDC'S | 1 | 1 | 1 | 2 | – | – | 0 | 0 |
| of which: Concessional | – | – | – | – | – | – | – | – |
| Other and adjustments | – | – | 0 | 0 | 0 | – | – | 2 |
| **Total Debt Service** | **7** | **5** | **7** | **7** | **3** | **2** | **4** | **4** |
| of which: Concessional | 3 | 1 | 2 | 0 | 2 | 1 | 1 | 1 |
| Non-concessional | 5 | 4 | 5 | 6 | 1 | 1 | 3 | 3 |

## CHAD

US $ Million

| | 1975 | 1976 | 1977 | 1978 | 1979 | 1980 | 1981 | 1982 |
|---|---|---|---|---|---|---|---|---|
| **DEBT** | | | | | | | | |
| DAC countries and capital | | | | | | | | |
| markets | 31 | 52 | 52 | 72 | 73 | 57 | 32 | 32 |
| ODA | 14 | 11 | 15 | 23 | 20 | 17 | 6 | 5 |
| Total export credits | 16 | 35 | 35 | 47 | 52 | 39 | 26 | 27 |
| Total private | 1 | 6 | 2 | 2 | 1 | 1 | – | – |
| of which: Bank loans | 1 | 6 | 2 | 2 | 1 | 1 | – | – |
| Bonds | – | – | – | – | – | – | – | – |
| Other | – | – | – | – | – | – | – | – |
| Multilateral | 18 | 25 | 41 | 67 | 74 | 75 | 73 | 71 |
| of which: Concessional | 18 | 25 | 41 | 67 | 74 | 75 | 73 | 71 |
| CMEA countries | 3 | 3 | 2 | 2 | 1 | 1 | – | – |
| of which: Concessional | 3 | 3 | 2 | 2 | 1 | 1 | – | – |
| OPEC countries | 15 | 15 | 17 | 18 | 21 | 20 | 18 | 17 |
| of which: Concessional | 7 | 7 | 9 | 9 | 12 | 11 | 10 | 10 |
| Other LDC'S | 1 | 2 | 23 | 39 | 53 | 53 | 52 | 52 |
| of which: Concessional | 1 | 2 | 23 | 39 | 53 | 53 | 52 | 52 |
| Other and adjustments | – | – | – | – | – | – | – | 6 |
| **Total Debt** | **67** | **96** | **135** | **198** | **222** | **205** | **176** | **178** |
| of which: Concessional | 43 | 47 | 90 | 140 | 160 | 157 | 142 | 138 |
| Non-concessional | 25 | 49 | 45 | 58 | 62 | 48 | 34 | 40 |
| **DEBT SERVICE** | | | | | | | | |
| DAC countries and capital | | | | | | | | |
| markets | 5 | 6 | 9 | 13 | 12 | 10 | 5 | 1 |
| ODA | 1 | 2 | 1 | 2 | 4 | 1 | – | – |
| Total export credits | 4 | 4 | 7 | 10 | 7 | 7 | 5 | 1 |
| Total private | – | 0 | 0 | 0 | 2 | 2 | – | – |
| of which: Bank loans | – | 0 | 0 | 0 | 2 | 2 | – | – |
| Bonds | – | – | – | – | – | – | – | – |
| Other | – | – | – | – | – | – | – | – |
| Multilateral | 0 | 0 | 0 | 0 | 3 | 2 | 3 | 0 |
| of which: Concessional | 0 | 0 | 0 | 0 | 3 | 2 | 3 | 0 |
| CMEA countries | – | – | 1 | 1 | 1 | 1 | 1 | – |
| of which: Concessional | – | – | 1 | 1 | 1 | 1 | 1 | – |
| OPEC countries | 1 | – | – | – | – | – | – | – |
| of which: Concessional | – | – | – | – | – | – | – | – |
| Other LDC'S | – | – | 0 | 0 | 0 | – | – | – |
| of which: Concessional | – | – | 0 | 0 | 0 | – | – | – |
| Other and adjustments | – | – | – | – | – | – | – | – |
| **Total Debt Service** | **6** | **6** | **9** | **13** | **15** | **12** | **8** | **1** |
| of which: Concessional | 1 | 2 | 2 | 3 | 7 | 4 | 3 | 0 |
| Non-concessional | 5 | 4 | 8 | 11 | 8 | 8 | 5 | 1 |

US $ Million

| | 1975 | 1976 | 1977 | 1978 | 1979 | 1980 | 1981 | 1982 |
|---|---|---|---|---|---|---|---|---|
| **DEBT** | | | | | | | | |
| DAC countries and capital | | | | | | | | |
| markets | 2859 | 3062 | 3224 | 4459 | 5550 | 7336 | 9493 | 10563 |
| ODA | 907 | 865 | 888 | 843 | 776 | 709 | 642 | 586 |
| Total export credits | 1071 | 1138 | 953 | 916 | 646 | 621 | 609 | 531 |
| Total private | 881 | 1059 | 1383 | 2700 | 4128 | 6006 | 8242 | 9446 |
| of which: Bank loans | 556 | 657 | 972 | 2268 | 3496 | 5400 | 7400 | 8460 |
| Bonds | 25 | 18 | 13 | 12 | 51 | 106 | 92 | 86 |
| Other | 300 | 384 | 398 | 420 | 581 | 500 | 750 | 900 |
| Multilateral | 235 | 245 | 278 | 295 | 324 | 351 | 402 | 439 |
| of which: Concessional | 146 | 138 | 132 | 118 | 119 | 116 | 111 | 103 |
| CMEA countries | 157 | 135 | 115 | 103 | 40 | 13 | 8 | 4 |
| of which: Concessional | 22 | 20 | 16 | 43 | 35 | 7 | 4 | 2 |
| OPEC countries | – | – | – | 2 | 2 | 2 | 1 | 0 |
| of which: Concessional | – | – | – | – | – | – | – | – |
| Other LDC'S | 281 | 329 | 344 | 367 | 428 | 435 | 394 | 356 |
| of which: Concessional | 16 | 16 | 18 | 20 | 21 | 20 | 18 | 15 |
| Other and adjustments | 215 | 215 | 306 | 418 | 719 | 776 | 1573 | 2053 |
| **Total Debt** | **3746** | **3985** | **4267** | **5643** | **7063** | **8913** | **11871** | **13416** |
| of which: Concessional | 1091 | 1039 | 1054 | 1024 | 950 | 851 | 785 | 715 |
| Non-concessional | 2655 | 2946 | 3213 | 4619 | 6113 | 8062 | 11086 | 12701 |
| **DEBT SERVICE** | | | | | | | | |
| DAC countries and capital | | | | | | | | |
| markets | 530 | 642 | 775 | 1208 | 1369 | 1796 | 2611 | 2093 |
| ODA | 44 | 63 | 75 | 78 | 105 | 75 | 56 | 51 |
| Total export credits | 294 | 301 | 426 | 360 | 465 | 274 | 243 | 215 |
| Total private | 192 | 279 | 275 | 770 | 800 | 1447 | 2312 | 1827 |
| of which: Bank loans | 135 | 145 | 192 | 701 | 710 | 1289 | 2130 | 1660 |
| Bonds | 7 | 7 | 7 | 3 | 4 | 8 | 12 | 7 |
| Other | 50 | 127 | 76 | 66 | 86 | 150 | 170 | 160 |
| Multilateral | 33 | 33 | 38 | 56 | 37 | 41 | 45 | 54 |
| of which: Concessional | 20 | 17 | 13 | 27 | 13 | 13 | 11 | 13 |
| CMEA countries | 21 | 28 | 26 | 71 | 78 | 37 | 6 | 4 |
| of which: Concessional | – | 3 | 4 | 4 | 13 | 33 | 3 | 3 |
| OPEC countries | – | – | – | – | 1 | 0 | 1 | 1 |
| of which: Concessional | – | – | – | – | – | – | – | – |
| Other LDC'S | 41 | 50 | 72 | 93 | 78 | 95 | 93 | 90 |
| of which: Concessional | – | – | – | – | – | – | – | 2 |
| Other and adjustments | 10 | 27 | 30 | 30 | 165 | 240 | 246 | 122 |
| **Total Debt Service** | **636** | **780** | **941** | **1457** | **1729** | **2210** | **3003** | **2363** |
| of which: Concessional | 64 | 82 | 92 | 108 | 130 | 121 | 70 | 69 |
| Non-concessional | 571 | 697 | 849 | 1349 | 1598 | 2089 | 2933 | 2294 |

## COLOMBIA

US $ Million

| | 1975 | 1976 | 1977 | 1978 | 1979 | 1980 | 1981 | 1982 |
|---|---|---|---|---|---|---|---|---|
| **DEBT** | | | | | | | | |
| DAC countries and capital | | | | | | | | |
| markets | 1812 | 1846 | 2085 | 2273 | 2722 | 3572 | 4592 | 5285 |
| ODA | 856 | 875 | 889 | 908 | 908 | 884 | 868 | 867 |
| Total export credits | 271 | 234 | 286 | 434 | 630 | 792 | 844 | 990 |
| Total private | 685 | 737 | 910 | 931 | 1184 | 1896 | 2880 | 3428 |
| *of which:* Bank loans | 553 | 600 | 772 | 796 | 1060 | 1775 | 2750 | 3280 |
| Bonds | 52 | 50 | 48 | 45 | 34 | 31 | 30 | 23 |
| Other | 80 | 87 | 90 | 90 | 90 | 90 | 100 | 125 |
| Multilateral | 792 | 851 | 934 | 1016 | 1139 | 1345 | 1597 | 1864 |
| *of which:* Concessional | 264 | 246 | 230 | 215 | 205 | 223 | 236 | 244 |
| CMEA countries | 0 | 0 | 0 | 0 | 0 | – | – | 0 |
| *of which:* Concessional | – | – | 0 | 0 | 0 | – | – | – |
| OPEC countries | – | – | 0 | 2 | 2 | 2 | 1 | 1 |
| *of which:* Concessional | – | – | – | – | – | – | – | – |
| Other LDC'S | 12 | 11 | 17 | 18 | 22 | 25 | 41 | 64 |
| *of which:* Concessional | – | – | – | – | – | – | – | – |
| Other and adjustments | 52 | 47 | 45 | 39 | 35 | 27 | 22 | 15 |
| **Total Debt** | **2669** | **2756** | **3081** | **3349** | **3919** | **4970** | **6252** | **7229** |
| *of which:* Concessional | 1147 | 1145 | 1141 | 1143 | 1130 | 1122 | 1117 | 1120 |
| Non-concessional | 1522 | 1611 | 1940 | 2206 | 2790 | 3849 | 5136 | 6109 |
| **DEBT SERVICE** | | | | | | | | |
| DAC countries and capital | | | | | | | | |
| markets | 180 | 225 | 293 | 409 | 550 | 556 | 680 | 889 |
| ODA | 28 | 37 | 39 | 36 | 45 | 50 | 50 | 48 |
| Total export credits | 82 | 102 | 110 | 188 | 222 | 333 | 192 | 232 |
| Total private | 70 | 86 | 145 | 185 | 283 | 173 | 438 | 610 |
| *of which:* Bank loans | 41 | 63 | 120 | 160 | 240 | 150 | 395 | 560 |
| Bonds | 9 | 3 | 3 | 2 | 20 | 5 | 1 | 10 |
| Other | 20 | 20 | 22 | 23 | 23 | 18 | 42 | 40 |
| Multilateral | 96 | 103 | 121 | 146 | 160 | 180 | 204 | 256 |
| *of which:* Concessional | 38 | 37 | 38 | 37 | 34 | 32 | 31 | 32 |
| CMEA countries | 0 | 0 | 0 | 0 | 0 | 0 | – | 0 |
| *of which:* Concessional | – | – | 0 | 0 | 0 | 0 | – | – |
| OPEC countries | – | – | – | 0 | 0 | 0 | 0 | 0 |
| *of which:* Concessional | – | – | – | – | – | – | – | – |
| Other LDC'S | 2 | 4 | 3 | 3 | 5 | 5 | 9 | 10 |
| *of which:* Concessional | – | – | – | – | – | – | – | – |
| Other and adjustments | 6 | 8 | 7 | 7 | 6 | 9 | 6 | 8 |
| **Total Debt Service** | **284** | **339** | **426** | **565** | **721** | **750** | **900** | **1163** |
| *of which:* Concessional | 69 | 77 | 79 | 76 | 82 | 85 | 83 | 85 |
| Non-concessional | 215 | 262 | 346 | 490 | 638 | 665 | 817 | 1078 |

*US $ Million*

| | 1975 | 1976 | 1977 | 1978 | 1979 | 1980 | 1981 | 1982 |
|---|---|---|---|---|---|---|---|---|
| **DEBT** | | | | | | | | |
| DAC countries and capital markets | 5 | 4 | 6 | 8 | 9 | 7 | 1 | 2 |
| ODA | 5 | 4 | 6 | 7 | 6 | 5 | – | 2 |
| Total export credits | – | – | – | 1 | 3 | 2 | 1 | – |
| Total private | – | – | – | – | – | – | – | – |
| *of which:* Bank loans | – | – | – | – | – | – | – | – |
| Bonds | – | – | – | – | – | – | – | – |
| Other | – | – | – | – | – | – | – | – |
| Multilateral | – | 11 | 11 | 12 | 15 | 21 | 24 | 31 |
| *of which:* Concessional | – | 11 | 11 | 12 | 15 | 21 | 24 | 29 |
| CMEA countries | – | – | – | – | – | – | – | – |
| *of which:* Concessional | – | – | – | – | – | – | – | – |
| OPEC countries | – | 3 | 5 | 6 | 12 | 19 | 25 | 31 |
| *of which:* Concessional | – | 3 | 5 | 6 | 12 | 19 | 25 | 31 |
| Other LDC'S | – | – | 1 | 2 | 3 | 3 | 3 | 3 |
| *of which:* Concessional | – | – | 1 | 2 | 3 | 3 | 3 | 3 |
| Other and adjustments | – | – | – | – | – | – | – | – |
| **Total Debt** | **5** | **18** | **23** | **28** | **39** | **50** | **53** | **67** |
| *of which:* Concessional | 5 | 18 | 23 | 27 | 36 | 48 | 52 | 66 |
| Non-concessional | – | – | – | 1 | 3 | 2 | 1 | 1 |
| **DEBT SERVICE** | | | | | | | | |
| DAC countries and capital markets | 1 | 1 | 1 | 1 | 2 | 1 | 0 | 0 |
| ODA | 1 | 1 | 0 | 0 | 2 | 1 | – | – |
| Total export credits | – | – | 0 | 1 | 0 | 1 | 0 | 0 |
| Total private | – | – | – | – | – | – | – | – |
| *of which:* Bank loans | – | – | – | – | – | – | – | – |
| Bonds | – | – | – | – | – | – | – | – |
| Other | – | – | – | – | – | – | – | – |
| Multilateral | – | – | – | 0 | 0 | 0 | 0 | 0 |
| *of which:* Concessional | – | – | – | 0 | 0 | 0 | 0 | 0 |
| CMEA countries | – | – | – | – | – | – | – | – |
| *of which:* Concessional | – | – | – | – | – | – | – | – |
| OPEC countries | – | – | 0 | 0 | 0 | 0 | 0 | 0 |
| *of which:* Concessional | – | – | 0 | 0 | 0 | 0 | 0 | 0 |
| Other LDC'S | – | – | – | – | – | – | – | – |
| *of which:* Concessional | – | – | – | – | – | – | – | – |
| Other and adjustments | – | – | – | – | – | – | – | – |
| **Total Debt Service** | **1** | **1** | **1** | **1** | **2** | **2** | **1** | **1** |
| *of which:* Concessional | 1 | 1 | 0 | 0 | 2 | 1 | 0 | 1 |
| Non-concessional | – | – | 0 | 1 | 0 | 1 | 0 | 0 |

*US $ Million*

| | 1975 | 1976 | 1977 | 1978 | 1979 | 1980 | 1981 | 1982 |
|---|---|---|---|---|---|---|---|---|
| **DEBT** | | | | | | | | |
| DAC countries and capital | | | | | | | | |
| markets | 222 | 304 | 343 | 420 | 473 | 572 | 732 | 834 |
| ODA | 64 | 68 | 71 | 88 | 89 | 80 | 71 | 78 |
| Total export credits | 149 | 236 | 270 | 302 | 347 | 452 | 550 | 590 |
| Total private | 9 | – | 2 | 30 | 37 | 40 | 111 | 166 |
| *of which:* Bank loans | 9 | – | 2 | 30 | 37 | 40 | 106 | 160 |
| Bonds | – | – | – | – | – | – | – | – |
| Other | – | – | – | – | – | – | 5 | 6 |
| Multilateral | 41 | 53 | 62 | 92 | 111 | 119 | 141 | 206 |
| *of which:* Concessional | 15 | 21 | 25 | 34 | 51 | 59 | 78 | 92 |
| CMEA countries | 27 | 27 | 49 | 87 | 101 | 99 | 100 | 98 |
| *of which:* Concessional | 22 | 22 | 45 | 81 | 79 | 80 | 76 | 76 |
| OPEC countries | 22 | 24 | 36 | 65 | 77 | 85 | 83 | 77 |
| *of which:* Concessional | – | 4 | 10 | 16 | 28 | 38 | 40 | 42 |
| Other LDC'S | 62 | 67 | 86 | 123 | 160 | 129 | 138 | 155 |
| *of which:* Concessional | 62 | 67 | 84 | 120 | 153 | 117 | 121 | 122 |
| Other and adjustments | 1 | 1 | 1 | 1 | 1 | 6 | 13 | 23 |
| **Total Debt** | **375** | **477** | **577** | **788** | **924** | **1011** | **1207** | **1393** |
| *of which:* Concessional | 163 | 182 | 234 | 339 | 401 | 374 | 386 | 410 |
| Non-concessional | 212 | 295 | 343 | 449 | 523 | 637 | 821 | 983 |
| **DEBT SERVICE** | | | | | | | | |
| DAC countries and capital | | | | | | | | |
| markets | 40 | 61 | 66 | 96 | 102 | 144 | 116 | 216 |
| ODA | 4 | 3 | 3 | 3 | 9 | 5 | 7 | 3 |
| Total export credits | 35 | 51 | 62 | 90 | 88 | 134 | 96 | 144 |
| Total private | 1 | 7 | 1 | 3 | 5 | 5 | 14 | 70 |
| *of which:* Bank loans | 1 | 7 | 1 | 3 | 5 | 5 | 10 | 66 |
| Bonds | – | – | – | – | – | – | – | – |
| Other | – | – | – | – | – | – | 4 | 4 |
| Multilateral | 4 | 5 | 6 | 7 | 16 | 11 | 8 | 12 |
| *of which:* Concessional | 0 | 0 | 0 | 0 | 1 | 1 | 1 | 2 |
| CMEA countries | 1 | 1 | 2 | 0 | 3 | 2 | 10 | 16 |
| *of which:* Concessional | 0 | 1 | 0 | 0 | 1 | 0 | 6 | 10 |
| OPEC countries | – | 1 | – | 1 | 1 | 6 | 10 | 12 |
| *of which:* Concessional | – | – | – | 0 | 1 | 1 | 4 | 5 |
| Other LDC'S | – | – | 0 | 1 | 2 | 10 | 7 | 16 |
| *of which:* Concessional | – | – | – | 1 | 1 | 8 | 5 | 8 |
| Other and adjustments | 0 | – | – | – | 0 | 0 | 1 | 2 |
| **Total Debt Service** | **46** | **67** | **74** | **104** | **125** | **175** | **153** | **275** |
| *of which:* Concessional | 5 | 3 | 3 | 5 | 12 | 15 | 23 | 28 |
| Non-concessional | 41 | 64 | 71 | 99 | 113 | 159 | 130 | 247 |

*US $ Million*

| | 1975 | 1976 | 1977 | 1978 | 1979 | 1980 | 1981 | 1982 |
|---|---|---|---|---|---|---|---|---|
| **DEBT** | | | | | | | | |
| DAC countries and capital | | | | | | | | |
|   markets | – | – | – | – | – | 1 | 1 | 1 |
|   ODA | – | – | – | – | – | 1 | 1 | 1 |
|   Total export credits | – | – | – | – | – | – | – | – |
|   Total private | – | – | – | – | – | – | – | – |
|   *of which:* Bank loans | – | – | – | – | – | – | – | – |
|     Bonds | – | – | – | – | – | – | – | – |
|     Other | – | – | – | – | – | – | – | – |
| Multilateral | – | – | – | – | – | – | – | – |
|   *of which:* Concessional | – | – | – | – | – | – | – | – |
| CMEA countries | – | – | – | – | – | – | – | – |
|   *of which:* Concessional | – | – | – | – | – | – | – | – |
| OPEC countries | – | – | – | – | – | – | – | – |
|   *of which:* Concessional | – | – | – | – | – | – | – | – |
| Other LDC'S | – | – | – | – | – | – | – | – |
|   *of which:* Concessional | – | – | – | – | – | – | – | – |
| Other and adjustments | – | – | – | – | – | – | – | – |
| **Total Debt** | – | – | – | – | – | **1** | **1** | **1** |
|   *of which:* Concessional | – | – | – | – | – | 1 | 1 | 1 |
|     Non-concessional | – | – | – | – | – | – | – | – |
| **DEBT SERVICE** | | | | | | | | |
| DAC countries and capital | | | | | | | | |
|   markets | – | – | – | – | – | – | – | 0 |
|   ODA | – | – | – | – | – | – | – | 0 |
|   Total export credits | – | – | – | – | – | – | – | – |
|   Total private | – | – | – | – | – | – | – | – |
|   *of which:* Bank loans | – | – | – | – | – | – | – | – |
|     Bonds | – | – | – | – | – | – | – | – |
|     Other | – | – | – | – | – | – | – | – |
| Multilateral | – | – | – | – | – | – | – | – |
|   *of which:* Concessional | – | – | – | – | – | – | – | – |
| CMEA countries | – | – | – | – | – | – | – | – |
|   *of which:* Concessional | – | – | – | – | – | – | – | – |
| OPEC countries | – | – | – | – | – | – | – | – |
|   *of which:* Concessional | – | – | – | – | – | – | – | – |
| Other LDC'S | – | – | – | – | – | – | – | – |
|   *of which:* Concessional | – | – | – | – | – | – | – | – |
| Other and adjustments | – | – | – | – | – | – | – | – |
| **Total Debt Service** | – | – | – | – | – | – | – | **0** |
|   *of which:* Concessional | – | – | – | – | – | – | – | 0 |
|     Non-concessional | – | – | – | – | – | – | – | – |

*US $ Million*

| | 1975 | 1976 | 1977 | 1978 | 1979 | 1980 | 1981 | 1982 |
|---|---|---|---|---|---|---|---|---|
| **DEBT** | | | | | | | | |
| DAC countries and capital | | | | | | | | |
| markets | 264 | 377 | 435 | 616 | 868 | 1168 | 1518 | 1564 |
| ODA | 68 | 70 | 73 | 100 | 112 | 132 | 143 | 184 |
| Total export credits | 59 | 54 | 92 | 115 | 138 | 163 | 182 | 138 |
| Total private | 137 | 253 | 270 | 401 | 618 | 873 | 1193 | 1242 |
| *of which:* Bank loans | 137 | 244 | 264 | 376 | 593 | 702 | 705 | 705 |
| Bonds | 0 | 0 | 0 | 20 | 20 | 141 | 458 | 502 |
| Other | – | 9 | 6 | 5 | 5 | 30 | 30 | 35 |
| | | | | | | | | |
| Multilateral | 140 | 184 | 242 | 312 | 361 | 434 | 486 | 521 |
| *of which:* Concessional | 52 | 51 | 57 | 70 | 94 | 132 | 152 | 169 |
| | | | | | | | | |
| CMEA countries | 3 | 4 | 3 | 3 | 3 | 2 | 1 | 1 |
| *of which:* Concessional | 0 | 0 | 0 | 0 | – | – | – | – |
| | | | | | | | | |
| OPEC countries | 17 | 33 | 47 | 54 | 69 | 89 | 146 | 167 |
| *of which:* Concessional | – | – | – | – | – | – | – | – |
| | | | | | | | | |
| Other LDC'S | 3 | 3 | 4 | 19 | 18 | 69 | 144 | 210 |
| *of which:* Concessional | – | – | – | – | – | – | – | – |
| | | | | | | | | |
| Other and adjustments | 6 | 4 | 22 | 38 | 46 | 59 | 66 | 205 |
| | | | | | | | | |
| **Total Debt** | **432** | **605** | **754** | **1041** | **1364** | **1821** | **2362** | **2669** |
| *of which:* Concessional | 121 | 121 | 130 | 170 | 206 | 264 | 295 | 353 |
| Non-concessional | 311 | 483 | 624 | 871 | 1158 | 1558 | 2066 | 2316 |
| | | | | | | | | |
| **DEBT SERVICE** | | | | | | | | |
| DAC countries and capital | | | | | | | | |
| markets | 50 | 61 | 76 | 198 | 221 | 187 | 150 | 63 |
| ODA | 2 | 2 | 2 | 3 | 4 | 5 | 4 | 5 |
| Total export credits | 21 | 17 | 35 | 39 | 32 | 44 | 39 | 17 |
| Total private | 27 | 42 | 39 | 156 | 185 | 139 | 107 | 41 |
| *of which:* Bank loans | 24 | 41 | 38 | 153 | 174 | 131 | 86 | 26 |
| Bonds | 0 | 0 | 0 | 1 | 3 | 6 | 18 | 10 |
| Other | 3 | 1 | 1 | 2 | 8 | 2 | 4 | 5 |
| | | | | | | | | |
| Multilateral | 13 | 18 | 22 | 31 | 39 | 40 | 43 | 48 |
| *of which:* Concessional | 5 | 5 | 6 | 6 | 7 | 8 | 7 | 7 |
| | | | | | | | | |
| CMEA countries | 0 | 0 | 1 | 0 | 0 | 0 | 1 | 0 |
| *of which:* Concessional | 0 | 0 | 0 | 0 | 0 | – | – | – |
| | | | | | | | | |
| OPEC countries | – | 0 | 1 | 3 | 6 | 8 | 8 | 26 |
| *of which:* Concessional | – | – | – | – | – | – | – | – |
| | | | | | | | | |
| Other LDC'S | 1 | 1 | 1 | 1 | 3 | 5 | 5 | 6 |
| *of which:* Concessional | – | – | – | – | – | – | – | – |
| | | | | | | | | |
| Other and adjustments | 1 | 2 | 4 | 7 | 8 | 7 | 7 | 1 |
| | | | | | | | | |
| **Total Debt Service** | **66** | **82** | **105** | **240** | **279** | **247** | **214** | **144** |
| *of which:* Concessional | 7 | 7 | 8 | 9 | 11 | 12 | 11 | 13 |
| Non-concessional | 58 | 75 | 97 | 231 | 267 | 235 | 203 | 131 |

*US $ Million*

| | 1975 | 1976 | 1977 | 1978 | 1979 | 1980 | 1981 | 1982 |
|---|---|---|---|---|---|---|---|---|
| **DEBT** | | | | | | | | |
| DAC countries and capital | | | | | | | | |
|   markets | 515 | 819 | 936 | 1082 | 1313 | 1252 | 1198 | 1003 |
|   ODA | 2 | 13 | 25 | 33 | 49 | 48 | 42 | 37 |
|   Total export credits | 463 | 656 | 711 | 734 | 804 | 794 | 796 | 666 |
|   Total private | 50 | 150 | 200 | 315 | 460 | 410 | 360 | 300 |
|     *of which:* Bank loans | 50 | 150 | 200 | 315 | 460 | 410 | 360 | 300 |
|     Bonds | – | – | – | – | – | – | – | – |
|     Other | – | – | – | – | – | – | – | – |
| Multilateral | – | – | – | – | – | – | – | – |
|   *of which:* Concessional | – | – | – | – | – | – | – | – |
| CMEA countries | 1400 | 1600 | 1800 | 2000 | 2300 | 2500 | 3000 | 3500 |
|   *of which:* Concessional | 1400 | 1600 | 1800 | 2000 | 2300 | 2500 | 3000 | 3500 |
| OPEC countries | – | – | – | – | – | – | – | – |
|   *of which:* Concessional | – | – | – | – | – | – | – | – |
| Other LDC'S | – | – | – | – | – | – | – | – |
|   *of which:* Concessional | – | – | – | – | – | – | – | – |
| Other and adjustments | 110 | 200 | 250 | 350 | 460 | 580 | 585 | 600 |
| **Total Debt** | **2025** | **2619** | **2986** | **3432** | **4073** | **4332** | **4783** | **5103** |
|   *of which:* Concessional | 1402 | 1613 | 1825 | 2033 | 2349 | 2548 | 3042 | 3537 |
|     Non-concessional | 623 | 1006 | 1161 | 1399 | 1724 | 1784 | 1741 | 1566 |
| **DEBT SERVICE** | | | | | | | | |
| DAC countries and capital | | | | | | | | |
|   markets | 153 | 150 | 154 | 224 | 247 | 320 | 354 | 406 |
|   ODA | – | 0 | 0 | 0 | 1 | 2 | 1 | 1 |
|   Total export credits | 128 | 127 | 112 | 176 | 186 | 209 | 218 | 225 |
|   Total private | 25 | 23 | 42 | 48 | 60 | 110 | 135 | 180 |
|     *of which:* Bank loans | 25 | 23 | 42 | 48 | 60 | 110 | 135 | 180 |
|     Bonds | – | – | – | – | – | – | – | – |
|     Other | – | – | – | – | – | – | – | – |
| Multilateral | – | – | – | – | – | – | – | – |
|   *of which:* Concessional | – | – | – | – | – | – | – | – |
| CMEA countries | 120 | 130 | 150 | 175 | 200 | 280 | 150 | 150 |
|   *of which:* Concessional | 120 | 130 | 150 | 175 | 200 | 280 | 150 | 150 |
| OPEC countries | – | – | – | – | – | – | – | – |
|   *of which:* Concessional | – | – | – | – | – | – | – | – |
| Other LDC'S | – | – | – | – | – | – | – | – |
|   *of which:* Concessional | – | – | – | – | – | – | – | – |
| Other and adjustments | 10 | 25 | 40 | 45 | 60 | 100 | 160 | 180 |
| **Total Debt Service** | **283** | **305** | **344** | **444** | **507** | **700** | **664** | **736** |
|   *of which:* Concessional | 120 | 130 | 150 | 175 | 201 | 282 | 151 | 151 |
|     Non-concessional | 163 | 175 | 194 | 269 | 306 | 419 | 513 | 585 |

US $ Million

| | 1975 | 1976 | 1977 | 1978 | 1979 | 1980 | 1981 | 1982 |
|---|---|---|---|---|---|---|---|---|
| **DEBT** | | | | | | | | |
| DAC countries and capital | | | | | | | | |
| markets | 70 | 127 | 173 | 220 | 270 | 367 | 455 | 526 |
| ODA | 12 | 11 | 15 | 21 | 24 | 27 | 29 | 36 |
| Total export credits | 16 | 21 | 33 | 49 | 60 | 103 | 124 | 155 |
| Total private | 42 | 95 | 125 | 150 | 186 | 237 | 302 | 335 |
| *of which:* Bank loans | 2 | 45 | 65 | 70 | 106 | 157 | 217 | 250 |
| Bonds | – | – | – | – | – | – | – | – |
| Other | 40 | 50 | 60 | 80 | 80 | 80 | 85 | 85 |
| Multilateral | 45 | 70 | 81 | 101 | 112 | 124 | 137 | 174 |
| *of which:* Concessional | 10 | 9 | 8 | 16 | 16 | 14 | 14 | 12 |
| CMEA countries | – | – | – | – | – | 4 | 4 | 3 |
| *of which:* Concessional | – | – | – | – | – | 4 | 4 | 3 |
| OPEC countries | – | – | – | – | 1 | 2 | 2 | 3 |
| *of which:* Concessional | – | – | – | – | 1 | 2 | 2 | 3 |
| Other LDC'S | 7 | 6 | 7 | 5 | 5 | 4 | 3 | 3 |
| *of which:* Concessional | – | – | – | – | – | – | – | – |
| Other and adjustments | 1 | 0 | 0 | 0 | 0 | – | – | – |
| **Total Debt** | **123** | **204** | **262** | **326** | **388** | **501** | **601** | **709** |
| *of which:* Concessional | 22 | 20 | 23 | 37 | 41 | 47 | 48 | 54 |
| Non-concessional | 101 | 184 | 239 | 289 | 347 | 453 | 552 | 655 |
| | | | | | | | | |
| **DEBT SERVICE** | | | | | | | | |
| DAC countries and capital | | | | | | | | |
| markets | 19 | 24 | 35 | 49 | 54 | 72 | 93 | 128 |
| ODA | 1 | 1 | 1 | 1 | 1 | 1 | 2 | 2 |
| Total export credits | 15 | 7 | 10 | 17 | 19 | 26 | 38 | 24 |
| Total private | 3 | 16 | 24 | 31 | 34 | 45 | 53 | 102 |
| *of which:* Bank loans | – | 12 | 14 | 16 | 19 | 25 | 29 | 77 |
| Bonds | – | – | – | – | – | – | – | – |
| Other | 3 | 4 | 10 | 15 | 15 | 20 | 24 | 25 |
| Multilateral | 5 | 6 | 8 | 10 | 11 | 16 | 18 | 25 |
| *of which:* Concessional | 2 | 2 | 1 | 2 | 2 | 2 | 2 | 3 |
| CMEA countries | – | – | – | – | – | 0 | 1 | 1 |
| *of which:* Concessional | – | – | – | – | – | 0 | 1 | 1 |
| OPEC countries | – | – | – | – | 0 | 0 | 0 | 0 |
| *of which:* Concessional | – | – | – | – | 0 | 0 | 0 | 0 |
| Other LDC'S | 1 | 1 | 1 | 4 | 1 | 1 | 1 | 2 |
| *of which:* Concessional | – | – | – | – | – | – | – | – |
| Other and adjustments | 0 | 0 | 0 | 0 | 0 | 0 | – | – |
| **Total Debt Service** | **25** | **31** | **43** | **62** | **66** | **88** | **112** | **156** |
| *of which:* Concessional | 2 | 3 | 2 | 3 | 3 | 3 | 5 | 5 |
| Non-concessional | 23 | 29 | 41 | 60 | 63 | 85 | 108 | 150 |

# DJIBOUTI

| | 1975 | 1976 | 1977 | 1978 | 1979 | 1980 | 1981 | 1982 |
|---|---|---|---|---|---|---|---|---|
| **DEBT** | | | | | | | | |
| DAC countries and capital | | | | | | | | |
|   markets | 27 | 26 | 27 | 31 | 51 | 26 | 19 | 17 |
|   ODA | 24 | 23 | 26 | 28 | 28 | 18 | 13 | 11 |
|   Total export credits | 3 | 3 | 1 | 3 | 22 | 7 | 5 | 5 |
|   Total private | – | – | – | – | 1 | 1 | 1 | 1 |
|     *of which:* Bank loans | – | – | – | – | 1 | – | – | – |
|       Bonds | – | – | – | – | – | – | – | – |
|       Other | – | – | – | – | – | 1 | 1 | 1 |
| Multilateral | – | – | – | – | – | 2 | 3 | 6 |
|   *of which:* Concessional | – | – | – | – | – | 2 | 3 | 6 |
| CMEA countries | – | – | – | – | – | – | – | – |
|   *of which:* Concessional | – | – | – | – | – | – | – | – |
| OPEC countries | – | – | – | – | – | – | – | 16 |
|   *of which:* Concessional | – | – | – | – | – | – | – | 16 |
| Other LDC'S | – | – | – | – | – | – | – | – |
|   *of which:* Concessional | – | – | – | – | – | – | – | – |
| Other and adjustments | – | – | – | – | – | – | – | 4 |
| **Total Debt** | **27** | **26** | **27** | **31** | **51** | **28** | **22** | **43** |
|   *of which:* Concessional | 24 | 23 | 26 | 28 | 28 | 20 | 16 | 33 |
|       Non-concessional | 3 | 3 | 1 | 3 | 23 | 8 | 6 | 10 |
| **DEBT SERVICE** | | | | | | | | |
| DAC countries and capital | | | | | | | | |
|   markets | 4 | 4 | 4 | 3 | 11 | 6 | 4 | 3 |
|   ODA | 2 | 2 | 1 | 2 | 3 | 3 | 2 | 1 |
|   Total export credits | 3 | 2 | 3 | 1 | 9 | 3 | 2 | 1 |
|   Total private | – | – | – | – | – | – | 0 | 0 |
|     *of which:* Bank loans | – | – | – | – | – | – | – | – |
|       Bonds | – | – | – | – | – | – | – | – |
|       Other | – | – | – | – | – | – | 0 | 0 |
| Multilateral | – | – | – | – | – | – | 1 | 0 |
|   *of which:* Concessional | – | – | – | – | – | – | 1 | 0 |
| CMEA countries | – | – | – | – | – | – | – | – |
|   *of which:* Concessional | – | – | – | – | – | – | – | – |
| OPEC countries | – | – | – | – | – | – | – | 0 |
|   *of which:* Concessional | – | – | – | – | – | – | – | 0 |
| Other LDC'S | – | – | – | – | – | – | – | – |
|   *of which:* Concessional | – | – | – | – | – | – | – | – |
| Other and adjustments | – | – | – | – | – | – | – | 1 |
| **Total Debt Service** | **4** | **4** | **4** | **3** | **11** | **6** | **5** | **3** |
|   *of which:* Concessional | 2 | 2 | 1 | 2 | 3 | 3 | 3 | 2 |
|       Non-concessional | 3 | 2 | 3 | 1 | 9 | 3 | 2 | 2 |

# DOMINICAN REPUBLIC

*US $ Million*

|  | 1975 | 1976 | 1977 | 1978 | 1979 | 1980 | 1981 | 1982 |
|---|---|---|---|---|---|---|---|---|
| **DEBT** | | | | | | | | |
| DAC countries and capital | | | | | | | | |
| markets | 573 | 608 | 761 | 828 | 880 | 983 | 977 | 989 |
| ODA | 205 | 206 | 204 | 199 | 212 | 249 | 274 | 344 |
| Total export credits | 95 | 107 | 92 | 166 | 202 | 294 | 273 | 235 |
| Total private | 273 | 295 | 465 | 463 | 466 | 440 | 430 | 410 |
| *of which:* Bank loans | 223 | 205 | 350 | 343 | 356 | 400 | 390 | 330 |
| Bonds | – | – | – | – | – | – | – | – |
| Other | 50 | 90 | 115 | 120 | 110 | 40 | 40 | 80 |
| Multilateral | 29 | 35 | 54 | 87 | 117 | 205 | 277 | 348 |
| *of which:* Concessional | 9 | 15 | 33 | 65 | 94 | 146 | 193 | 230 |
| CMEA countries | – | – | – | – | – | – | – | – |
| *of which:* Concessional | – | – | – | – | – | – | – | – |
| OPEC countries | – | – | 46 | 60 | 60 | 155 | 197 | 246 |
| *of which:* Concessional | – | – | – | – | – | – | 22 | 51 |
| Other LDC'S | 1 | 9 | 12 | 15 | 15 | 13 | 58 | 83 |
| *of which:* Concessional | – | – | – | – | – | – | – | – |
| Other and adjustments | 10 | 10 | 16 | 20 | 20 | 41 | 58 | 115 |
| **Total Debt** | **613** | **662** | **888** | **1011** | **1091** | **1397** | **1567** | **1780** |
| *of which:* Concessional | 214 | 221 | 237 | 264 | 306 | 395 | 489 | 626 |
| Non-concessional | 398 | 442 | 651 | 746 | 786 | 1001 | 1078 | 1154 |
| **DEBT SERVICE** | | | | | | | | |
| DAC countries and capital | | | | | | | | |
| markets | 90 | 84 | 130 | 142 | 260 | 213 | 207 | 205 |
| ODA | 7 | 12 | 12 | 15 | 16 | 13 | 15 | 10 |
| Total export credits | 29 | 23 | 29 | 48 | 31 | 36 | 70 | 63 |
| Total private | 53 | 50 | 89 | 80 | 213 | 164 | 122 | 131 |
| *of which:* Bank loans | 48 | 45 | 49 | 70 | 195 | 162 | 115 | 126 |
| Bonds | – | – | – | – | – | – | – | – |
| Other | 5 | 5 | 40 | 10 | 18 | 2 | 7 | 5 |
| Multilateral | 5 | 4 | 5 | 5 | 6 | 7 | 12 | 14 |
| *of which:* Concessional | 0 | 0 | 1 | 1 | 1 | 2 | 3 | 4 |
| CMEA countries | – | – | – | – | – | – | – | – |
| *of which:* Concessional | – | – | – | – | – | – | – | – |
| OPEC countries | – | – | 0 | 4 | 5 | 7 | 32 | 24 |
| *of which:* Concessional | – | – | – | – | – | – | – | 1 |
| Other LDC'S | – | 0 | 0 | 1 | 4 | 3 | 6 | 11 |
| *of which:* Concessional | – | – | – | – | – | – | – | – |
| Other and adjustments | 1 | 1 | 1 | 2 | 1 | 2 | 9 | 12 |
| **Total Debt Service** | **96** | **90** | **137** | **155** | **276** | **232** | **266** | **266** |
| *of which:* Concessional | 7 | 12 | 13 | 16 | 17 | 15 | 18 | 15 |
| Non-concessional | 89 | 78 | 124 | 139 | 259 | 217 | 248 | 251 |

# ECUADOR

US $ Million

| | 1975 | 1976 | 1977 | 1978 | 1979 | 1980 | 1981 | 1982 |
|---|---|---|---|---|---|---|---|---|
| **DEBT** | | | | | | | | |
| DAC countries and capital | | | | | | | | |
| markets | 398 | 627 | 1202 | 1921 | 2352 | 2829 | 3229 | 2926 |
| ODA | 115 | 134 | 145 | 158 | 182 | 191 | 176 | 166 |
| Total export credits | 149 | 193 | 219 | 503 | 666 | 787 | 863 | 766 |
| Total private | 134 | 300 | 838 | 1260 | 1504 | 1851 | 2190 | 1994 |
| of which: Bank loans | 102 | 240 | 700 | 1073 | 1320 | 1680 | 2030 | 1810 |
| Bonds | 2 | 1 | 53 | 67 | 64 | 51 | 38 | 24 |
| Other | 30 | 59 | 85 | 120 | 120 | 120 | 122 | 160 |
| Multilateral | 131 | 165 | 191 | 224 | 282 | 354 | 458 | 548 |
| of which: Concessional | 91 | 106 | 120 | 129 | 138 | 145 | 169 | 178 |
| CMEA countries | 2 | 1 | 1 | 0 | 2 | 2 | 1 | 7 |
| of which: Concessional | – | – | – | – | – | – | – | – |
| OPEC countries | – | 7 | 13 | 24 | 31 | 31 | 34 | 32 |
| of which: Concessional | – | – | – | – | – | – | – | – |
| Other LDC'S | 1 | 1 | 8 | 27 | 31 | 63 | 275 | 270 |
| of which: Concessional | – | – | – | – | – | – | – | – |
| Other and adjustments | 6 | 7 | 6 | 106 | 104 | 102 | 153 | 159 |
| **Total Debt** | **539** | **809** | **1422** | **2302** | **2801** | **3382** | **4150** | **3943** |
| of which: Concessional | 206 | 240 | 265 | 287 | 320 | 336 | 345 | 344 |
| Non-concessional | 333 | 569 | 1157 | 2015 | 2482 | 3046 | 3805 | 3598 |
| **DEBT SERVICE** | | | | | | | | |
| DAC countries and capital | | | | | | | | |
| markets | 71 | 116 | 157 | 276 | 815 | 430 | 635 | 730 |
| ODA | 8 | 8 | 9 | 10 | 11 | 12 | 12 | 11 |
| Total export credits | 48 | 63 | 73 | 98 | 128 | 135 | 281 | 257 |
| Total private | 15 | 45 | 75 | 168 | 676 | 283 | 342 | 462 |
| of which: Bank loans | 11 | 30 | 50 | 138 | 635 | 232 | 290 | 425 |
| Bonds | 0 | 2 | 0 | 4 | 9 | 19 | 18 | 17 |
| Other | 4 | 13 | 25 | 26 | 32 | 32 | 34 | 20 |
| Multilateral | 12 | 15 | 20 | 23 | 28 | 37 | 50 | 63 |
| of which: Concessional | 8 | 8 | 7 | 6 | 6 | 6 | 7 | 7 |
| CMEA countries | 1 | 1 | 1 | 1 | 2 | 0 | 1 | 1 |
| of which: Concessional | – | – | – | – | – | – | – | – |
| OPEC countries | – | 0 | 1 | 2 | 1 | 4 | 6 | 6 |
| of which: Concessional | – | – | – | – | – | – | – | – |
| Other LDC'S | 1 | 1 | 3 | 2 | 5 | 4 | 14 | 42 |
| of which: Concessional | – | – | – | – | – | – | – | – |
| Other and adjustments | 1 | 2 | 3 | 1 | 82 | 82 | 102 | 150 |
| **Total Debt Service** | **86** | **135** | **183** | **304** | **934** | **556** | **808** | **993** |
| of which: Concessional | 16 | 16 | 16 | 15 | 17 | 18 | 19 | 19 |
| Non-concessional | 70 | 119 | 167 | 289 | 917 | 538 | 789 | 974 |

*US $ Million*

| | 1975 | 1976 | 1977 | 1978 | 1979 | 1980 | 1981 | 1982 |
|---|---|---|---|---|---|---|---|---|
| **DEBT** | | | | | | | | |
| DAC countries and capital markets | 1182 | 1581 | 2780 | 4301 | 5853 | 7273 | 8403 | 9985 |
| ODA | 571 | 936 | 1504 | 2438 | 3231 | 4144 | 4752 | 5388 |
| Total export credits | 362 | 382 | 825 | 1352 | 2081 | 2517 | 2948 | 3731 |
| Total private | 249 | 263 | 451 | 511 | 541 | 612 | 703 | 866 |
| *of which:* Bank loans | 203 | 224 | 317 | 310 | 324 | 400 | 450 | 490 |
| Bonds | 46 | 39 | 84 | 141 | 137 | 132 | 153 | 126 |
| Other | – | – | 50 | 60 | 80 | 80 | 100 | 250 |
| Multilateral | 104 | 183 | 1558 | 2306 | 2597 | 2872 | 3048 | 2921 |
| *of which:* Concessional | 84 | 127 | 1215 | 1893 | 2067 | 2183 | 2262 | 2132 |
| CMEA countries | 636 | 598 | 589 | 616 | 561 | 518 | 523 | 532 |
| *of which:* Concessional | 628 | 592 | 589 | 353 | 329 | 311 | 298 | 228 |
| OPEC countries | 2474 | 2845 | 2931 | 3012 | 3025 | 2988 | 2936 | 2772 |
| *of which:* Concessional | 2444 | 2815 | 2887 | 2968 | 2981 | 2945 | 2924 | 2761 |
| Other LDC'S | 68 | 70 | 73 | 84 | 80 | 70 | 67 | 60 |
| *of which:* Concessional | 47 | 53 | 59 | 74 | 74 | 68 | 67 | 60 |
| Other and adjustments | 626 | 635 | 330 | 125 | 120 | 115 | 260 | 356 |
| **Total Debt** | **5090** | **5912** | **8261** | **10443** | **12236** | **13837** | **15238** | **16625** |
| *of which:* Concessional | 3800 | 4558 | 6284 | 7751 | 8702 | 9666 | 10313 | 10575 |
| Non-concessional | 1290 | 1354 | 1976 | 2693 | 3534 | 4171 | 4925 | 6051 |
| **DEBT SERVICE** | | | | | | | | |
| DAC countries and capital markets | 247 | 310 | 477 | 869 | 1065 | 1225 | 1523 | 1616 |
| ODA | 34 | 43 | 63 | 84 | 105 | 123 | 190 | 139 |
| Total export credits | 166 | 202 | 339 | 660 | 830 | 918 | 1105 | 1157 |
| Total private | 47 | 66 | 75 | 125 | 131 | 185 | 228 | 321 |
| *of which:* Bank loans | 36 | 55 | 63 | 89 | 95 | 140 | 170 | 240 |
| Bonds | 11 | 11 | 12 | 16 | 16 | 15 | 23 | 41 |
| Other | – | – | – | 20 | 20 | 30 | 35 | 40 |
| Multilateral | 1 | 4 | 26 | 105 | 31 | 60 | 73 | 449 |
| *of which:* Concessional | 1 | 1 | 13 | 80 | 8 | 13 | 15 | 340 |
| CMEA countries | 99 | 58 | 76 | 97 | 94 | 95 | 116 | 79 |
| *of which:* Concessional | 91 | 56 | 70 | 60 | 58 | 64 | 62 | 35 |
| OPEC countries | 61 | 47 | 293 | 168 | 64 | 116 | 305 | 254 |
| *of which:* Concessional | 59 | 45 | 291 | 165 | 63 | 115 | 270 | 252 |
| Other LDC'S | 9 | 7 | 7 | 6 | 6 | 6 | 4 | 1 |
| *of which:* Concessional | 4 | 2 | 3 | 2 | 2 | 2 | 2 | 1 |
| Other and adjustments | 195 | 267 | 207 | 36 | 26 | 18 | 86 | 114 |
| **Total Debt Service** | **613** | **692** | **1087** | **1281** | **1287** | **1521** | **2108** | **2513** |
| *of which:* Concessional | 189 | 149 | 447 | 397 | 242 | 322 | 544 | 770 |
| Non-concessional | 424 | 544 | 640 | 884 | 1045 | 1199 | 1564 | 1743 |

# EL SALVADOR

| | 1975 | 1976 | 1977 | 1978 | 1979 | 1980 | 1981 | 1982 |
|---|---|---|---|---|---|---|---|---|
| **DEBT** | | | | | | | | |
| DAC countries and capital markets | 132 | 152 | 114 | 186 | 210 | 225 | 332 | 393 |
| ODA | 53 | 55 | 61 | 79 | 86 | 104 | 188 | 240 |
| Total export credits | 24 | 25 | 24 | 52 | 69 | 83 | 97 | 74 |
| Total private | 55 | 72 | 29 | 55 | 55 | 38 | 47 | 79 |
| of which: Bank loans | 50 | 70 | 29 | 50 | 50 | 30 | 40 | 35 |
| Bonds | 5 | 2 | – | – | – | – | – | 40 |
| Other | – | – | – | 5 | 5 | 8 | 7 | 4 |
| Multilateral | 78 | 95 | 128 | 181 | 229 | 286 | 351 | 401 |
| of which: Concessional | 51 | 59 | 78 | 108 | 138 | 178 | 229 | 259 |
| CMEA countries | – | – | – | – | – | – | – | – |
| of which: Concessional | – | – | – | – | – | – | – | – |
| OPEC countries | 23 | 44 | 61 | 74 | 88 | 96 | 113 | 109 |
| of which: Concessional | – | – | – | – | – | – | – | – |
| Other LDC'S | – | – | – | – | – | – | – | – |
| of which: Concessional | – | – | – | – | – | – | – | – |
| Other and adjustments | – | – | – | – | 1 | 5 | 5 | 8 |
| **Total Debt** | **233** | **291** | **303** | **442** | **528** | **612** | **801** | **911** |
| of which: Concessional | 104 | 114 | 139 | 187 | 224 | 282 | 417 | 499 |
| Non-concessional | 129 | 177 | 164 | 255 | 304 | 330 | 384 | 412 |
| **DEBT SERVICE** | | | | | | | | |
| DAC countries and capital markets | 56 | 30 | 62 | 37 | 37 | 46 | 38 | 46 |
| ODA | 3 | 3 | 3 | 3 | 4 | 4 | 6 | 5 |
| Total export credits | 13 | 10 | 21 | 29 | 18 | 24 | 18 | 28 |
| Total private | 40 | 18 | 38 | 5 | 15 | 18 | 14 | 13 |
| of which: Bank loans | 40 | 14 | 36 | 5 | 15 | 18 | 14 | 13 |
| Bonds | 0 | 4 | 2 | – | – | – | – | – |
| Other | – | – | – | – | – | – | – | – |
| Multilateral | 7 | 7 | 9 | 12 | 15 | 16 | 23 | 25 |
| of which: Concessional | 5 | 4 | 5 | 5 | 6 | 6 | 7 | 8 |
| CMEA countries | – | – | – | – | – | – | – | – |
| of which: Concessional | – | – | – | – | – | – | – | – |
| OPEC countries | – | 3 | 5 | 7 | 7 | 9 | 13 | 13 |
| of which: Concessional | – | – | – | – | – | – | – | – |
| Other LDC'S | – | – | – | – | – | – | – | 0 |
| of which: Concessional | – | – | – | – | – | – | – | – |
| Other and adjustments | – | – | – | – | 0 | 0 | – | – |
| **Total Debt Service** | **63** | **41** | **76** | **56** | **59** | **71** | **73** | **84** |
| of which: Concessional | 7 | 7 | 7 | 8 | 10 | 10 | 13 | 13 |
| Non-concessional | 55 | 35 | 69 | 47 | 49 | 61 | 61 | 72 |

*US $ Million*

| | 1975 | 1976 | 1977 | 1978 | 1979 | 1980 | 1981 | 1982 |
|---|---|---|---|---|---|---|---|---|
| **DEBT** | | | | | | | | |
| DAC countries and capital | | | | | | | | |
| markets | 2 | 1 | – | – | – | – | – | – |
| ODA | – | – | – | – | – | – | – | – |
| Total export credits | 2 | 1 | – | – | – | – | – | – |
| Total private | – | – | – | – | – | – | – | – |
| of which: Bank loans | – | – | – | – | – | – | – | – |
| Bonds | – | – | – | – | – | – | – | – |
| Other | – | – | – | – | – | – | – | – |
| Multilateral | – | – | – | – | – | – | – | – |
| of which: Concessional | – | – | – | – | – | – | – | – |
| CMEA countries | – | – | – | – | – | – | – | – |
| of which: Concessional | – | – | – | – | – | – | – | – |
| OPEC countries | – | – | – | – | – | – | – | – |
| of which: Concessional | – | – | – | – | – | – | – | – |
| Other LDC'S | – | – | – | – | – | – | – | – |
| of which: Concessional | – | – | – | – | – | – | – | – |
| Other and adjustments | – | – | – | – | – | – | – | – |
| **Total Debt** | **2** | **1** | – | – | – | – | – | – |
| of which: Concessional | – | – | – | – | – | – | – | – |
| Non-concessional | 2 | 1 | – | – | – | – | – | – |
| | | | | | | | | |
| **DEBT SERVICE** | | | | | | | | |
| DAC countries and capital | | | | | | | | |
| markets | 2 | 2 | 1 | – | – | – | – | – |
| ODA | – | – | – | – | – | – | – | – |
| Total export credits | 2 | 2 | 1 | – | – | – | – | – |
| Total private | – | – | – | – | – | – | – | – |
| of which: Bank loans | – | – | – | – | – | – | – | – |
| Bonds | – | – | – | – | – | – | – | – |
| Other | – | – | – | – | – | – | – | – |
| Multilateral | – | – | – | – | – | – | – | – |
| of which: Concessional | – | – | – | – | – | – | – | – |
| CMEA countries | – | – | – | – | – | – | – | – |
| of which: Concessional | – | – | – | – | – | – | – | – |
| OPEC countries | – | – | – | – | – | – | – | – |
| of which: Concessional | – | – | – | – | – | – | – | – |
| Other LDC'S | – | – | – | – | – | – | – | – |
| of which: Concessional | – | – | – | – | – | – | – | – |
| Other and adjustments | – | – | – | – | – | – | – | – |
| **Total Debt Service** | **2** | **2** | **1** | – | – | – | – | – |
| of which: Concessional | – | – | – | – | – | – | – | – |
| Non-concessional | 2 | 2 | 1 | – | – | – | – | – |

# ETHIOPIA

*US $ Million*

| | 1975 | 1976 | 1977 | 1978 | 1979 | 1980 | 1981 | 1982 |
|---|---|---|---|---|---|---|---|---|
| **DEBT** | | | | | | | | |
| DAC countries and capital | | | | | | | | |
| markets | 215 | 222 | 227 | 243 | 234 | 237 | 276 | 300 |
| ODA | 156 | 176 | 187 | 191 | 197 | 196 | 184 | 183 |
| Total export credits | 34 | 34 | 28 | 46 | 28 | 30 | 79 | 104 |
| Total private | 25 | 12 | 12 | 6 | 9 | 11 | 13 | 13 |
| *of which:* Bank loans | 25 | 12 | 12 | 6 | 9 | 11 | 13 | 13 |
| Bonds | – | – | – | – | – | – | – | – |
| Other | – | – | – | – | – | – | – | – |
| Multilateral | 157 | 192 | 227 | 275 | 334 | 373 | 410 | 441 |
| *of which:* Concessional | 125 | 158 | 193 | 242 | 301 | 340 | 375 | 407 |
| CMEA countries | 13 | 10 | 9 | 7 | 13 | 38 | 67 | 104 |
| *of which:* Concessional | 12 | 10 | 8 | 7 | 12 | 31 | 54 | 91 |
| OPEC countries | – | – | – | – | 15 | 15 | 15 | 15 |
| *of which:* Concessional | – | – | – | – | 15 | 15 | 15 | 15 |
| Other LDC'S | 1 | 5 | 10 | 17 | 21 | 40 | 36 | 38 |
| *of which:* Concessional | 1 | 5 | 10 | 16 | 20 | 25 | 23 | 23 |
| Other and adjustments | – | – | – | – | – | – | – | – |
| **Total Debt** | **386** | **430** | **473** | **543** | **616** | **703** | **804** | **898** |
| *of which:* Concessional | 294 | 349 | 397 | 456 | 546 | 607 | 652 | 718 |
| Non-concessional | 92 | 81 | 76 | 87 | 71 | 96 | 152 | 179 |
| | | | | | | | | |
| **DEBT SERVICE** | | | | | | | | |
| DAC countries and capital | | | | | | | | |
| markets | 19 | 13 | 18 | 19 | 15 | 20 | 37 | 40 |
| ODA | 5 | 7 | 8 | 7 | 6 | 8 | 11 | 9 |
| Total export credits | 8 | 4 | 9 | 9 | 7 | 10 | 18 | 20 |
| Total private | 6 | 2 | 2 | 3 | 2 | 2 | 8 | 12 |
| *of which:* Bank loans | 6 | 2 | 2 | 3 | 2 | 2 | 8 | 12 |
| Bonds | – | – | – | – | – | – | – | – |
| Other | – | – | – | – | – | – | – | – |
| Multilateral | 10 | 10 | 11 | 10 | 11 | 13 | 11 | 13 |
| *of which:* Concessional | 6 | 7 | 7 | 6 | 7 | 7 | 8 | 8 |
| CMEA countries | 3 | 2 | 3 | 2 | 2 | 1 | 4 | 6 |
| *of which:* Concessional | 3 | 2 | 2 | 2 | 2 | 1 | 3 | 4 |
| OPEC countries | – | – | – | – | – | 0 | 0 | 0 |
| *of which:* Concessional | – | – | – | – | – | 0 | 0 | 0 |
| Other LDC'S | 0 | 0 | 0 | 0 | 0 | 1 | 3 | 1 |
| *of which:* Concessional | 0 | 0 | 0 | 0 | 0 | 0 | 0 | – |
| Other and adjustments | – | – | – | – | – | – | – | – |
| **Total Debt Service** | **31** | **26** | **32** | **32** | **28** | **35** | **55** | **62** |
| *of which:* Concessional | 15 | 16 | 17 | 16 | 15 | 17 | 23 | 22 |
| Non-concessional | 17 | 10 | 15 | 16 | 13 | 18 | 32 | 40 |

# FALKLAND ISLANDS

| | 1975 | 1976 | 1977 | 1978 | 1979 | 1980 | 1981 | 1982 |
|---|---|---|---|---|---|---|---|---|
| **DEBT** | | | | | | | | |
| DAC countries and capital markets | – | – | – | – | 1 | 1 | 1 | – |
| ODA | – | – | – | – | 1 | 1 | 1 | – |
| Total export credits | – | – | – | – | – | – | – | – |
| Total private | – | – | – | – | – | – | – | – |
| *of which:* Bank loans | – | – | – | – | – | – | – | – |
| Bonds | – | – | – | – | – | – | – | – |
| Other | – | – | – | – | – | – | – | – |
| Multilateral | – | – | – | – | – | – | – | – |
| *of which:* Concessional | – | – | – | – | – | – | – | – |
| CMEA countries | – | – | – | – | – | – | – | – |
| *of which:* Concessional | – | – | – | – | – | – | – | – |
| OPEC countries | – | – | – | – | – | – | – | – |
| *of which:* Concessional | – | – | – | – | – | – | – | – |
| Other LDC'S | – | – | – | – | – | – | – | – |
| *of which:* Concessional | – | – | – | – | – | – | – | – |
| Other and adjustments | – | – | – | – | – | – | – | – |
| **Total Debt** | – | – | – | – | 1 | 1 | 1 | – |
| *of which:* Concessional | – | – | – | – | 1 | 1 | 1 | – |
| Non-concessional | – | – | – | – | – | – | – | – |
| **DEBT SERVICE** | | | | | | | | |
| DAC countries and capital markets | – | – | – | – | – | – | – | 0 |
| ODA | – | – | – | – | – | – | – | – |
| Total export credits | – | – | – | – | – | – | – | 0 |
| Total private | – | – | – | – | – | – | – | – |
| *of which:* Bank loans | – | – | – | – | – | – | – | – |
| Bonds | – | – | – | – | – | – | – | – |
| Other | – | – | – | – | – | – | – | – |
| Multilateral | – | – | – | – | – | – | – | – |
| *of which:* Concessional | – | – | – | – | – | – | – | – |
| CMEA countries | – | – | – | – | – | – | – | – |
| *of which:* Concessional | – | – | – | – | – | – | – | – |
| OPEC countries | – | – | – | – | – | – | – | – |
| *of which:* Concessional | – | – | – | – | – | – | – | – |
| Other LDC'S | – | – | – | – | – | – | – | – |
| *of which:* Concessional | – | – | – | – | – | – | – | – |
| Other and adjustments | – | – | – | – | – | – | – | – |
| **Total Debt Service** | – | – | – | – | – | – | – | 0 |
| *of which:* Concessional | – | – | – | – | – | – | – | – |
| Non-concessional | – | – | – | – | – | – | – | 0 |

US $ Million

| | 1975 | 1976 | 1977 | 1978 | 1979 | 1980 | 1981 | 1982 |
|---|---|---|---|---|---|---|---|---|
| **DEBT** | | | | | | | | |
| DAC countries and capital | | | | | | | | |
| markets | 34 | 40 | 52 | 61 | 71 | 132 | 146 | 139 |
| ODA | 11 | 14 | 19 | 25 | 28 | 32 | 29 | 23 |
| Total export credits | 11 | 13 | 14 | 15 | 20 | 69 | 88 | 95 |
| Total private | 12 | 13 | 19 | 21 | 23 | 31 | 29 | 21 |
| of which: Bank loans | 6 | 8 | 15 | 17 | 19 | 28 | 28 | 20 |
| Bonds | 6 | 5 | 4 | 4 | 4 | 3 | 1 | 1 |
| Other | – | – | – | – | – | – | – | – |
| Multilateral | 19 | 25 | 32 | 32 | 44 | 66 | 88 | 106 |
| of which: Concessional | – | 1 | 3 | 0 | 4 | 11 | 20 | 23 |
| CMEA countries | – | – | – | – | – | – | – | – |
| of which: Concessional | – | – | – | – | – | – | – | – |
| OPEC countries | – | – | – | – | – | – | – | – |
| of which: Concessional | – | – | – | – | – | – | – | – |
| Other LDC'S | 4 | 4 | 4 | 4 | 4 | 4 | 3 | – |
| of which: Concessional | – | – | – | – | – | – | – | – |
| Other and adjustments | – | – | – | – | – | – | – | – |
| **Total Debt** | **57** | **69** | **88** | **97** | **119** | **202** | **236** | **244** |
| of which: Concessional | 11 | 15 | 22 | 25 | 32 | 43 | 49 | 46 |
| Non-concessional | 46 | 54 | 66 | 71 | 87 | 159 | 188 | 198 |
| **DEBT SERVICE** | | | | | | | | |
| DAC countries and capital | | | | | | | | |
| markets | 6 | 6 | 7 | 11 | 11 | 18 | 25 | 22 |
| ODA | 1 | 1 | 2 | 2 | 2 | 3 | 3 | 4 |
| Total export credits | 4 | 3 | 4 | 3 | 6 | 8 | 13 | 14 |
| Total private | 1 | 1 | 2 | 6 | 3 | 7 | 9 | 4 |
| of which: Bank loans | 1 | 1 | 1 | 6 | 3 | 5 | 7 | 4 |
| Bonds | 0 | 0 | 1 | 1 | 0 | 2 | 2 | 0 |
| Other | – | – | – | – | – | – | – | – |
| Multilateral | 1 | 2 | 3 | 6 | 4 | 4 | 7 | 9 |
| of which: Concessional | – | – | – | 2 | 0 | 0 | 1 | 1 |
| CMEA countries | – | – | – | – | – | – | – | – |
| of which: Concessional | – | – | – | – | – | – | – | – |
| OPEC countries | – | – | – | – | – | – | – | – |
| of which: Concessional | – | – | – | – | – | – | – | – |
| Other LDC'S | 0 | 0 | 0 | 0 | 0 | 0 | 1 | 2 |
| of which: Concessional | – | – | – | – | – | – | – | – |
| Other and adjustments | – | – | – | – | – | – | – | – |
| **Total Debt Service** | **7** | **8** | **10** | **17** | **15** | **23** | **33** | **33** |
| of which: Concessional | 1 | 1 | 2 | 5 | 2 | 3 | 4 | 4 |
| Non-concessional | 6 | 7 | 9 | 13 | 13 | 20 | 29 | 29 |

# GABON

|  | 1975 | 1976 | 1977 | 1978 | 1979 | 1980 | 1981 | 1982 |
|---|---|---|---|---|---|---|---|---|
| **DEBT** | | | | | | | | |
| DAC countries and capital | | | | | | | | |
|   markets | 675 | 1057 | 1404 | 1435 | 1392 | 1227 | 925 | 936 |
|   ODA | 70 | 54 | 55 | 74 | 72 | 74 | 66 | 71 |
|   Total export credits | 342 | 707 | 670 | 907 | 883 | 731 | 573 | 698 |
|   Total private | 263 | 296 | 679 | 454 | 437 | 422 | 286 | 167 |
|     *of which:* Bank loans | 257 | 264 | 650 | 430 | 420 | 417 | 280 | 160 |
|       Bonds | 6 | 5 | 4 | 4 | 3 | 2 | 1 | 1 |
|       Other | – | 27 | 25 | 20 | 14 | 3 | 5 | 6 |
| Multilateral | 28 | 29 | 29 | 38 | 40 | 39 | 53 | 52 |
|   *of which:* Concessional | 17 | 16 | 16 | 24 | 23 | 21 | 19 | 16 |
| CMEA countries | – | – | – | 1 | 1 | 1 | 1 | 1 |
|   *of which:* Concessional | – | – | – | – | – | – | – | – |
| OPEC countries | 2 | 32 | 33 | 33 | 30 | 29 | 26 | 26 |
|   *of which:* Concessional | – | – | – | 1 | 1 | 4 | 4 | 4 |
| Other LDC'S | 79 | 91 | 90 | 97 | 96 | 101 | 82 | 63 |
|   *of which:* Concessional | 25 | 27 | 29 | 33 | 33 | 33 | 29 | 26 |
| Other and adjustments | 3 | 3 | 6 | 5 | 5 | 5 | 3 | 3 |
| **Total Debt** | **787** | **1212** | **1561** | **1609** | **1565** | **1403** | **1090** | **1080** |
|   *of which:* Concessional | 116 | 100 | 103 | 136 | 133 | 136 | 120 | 120 |
|     Non-concessional | 671 | 1112 | 1458 | 1473 | 1431 | 1267 | 970 | 960 |
| **DEBT SERVICE** | | | | | | | | |
| DAC countries and capital | | | | | | | | |
|   markets | 107 | 148 | 244 | 354 | 471 | 448 | 423 | 415 |
|   ODA | 10 | 8 | 8 | 10 | 11 | 8 | 6 | 4 |
|   Total export credits | 64 | 102 | 178 | 205 | 318 | 287 | 312 | 241 |
|   Total private | 33 | 39 | 59 | 139 | 143 | 153 | 105 | 171 |
|     *of which:* Bank loans | 32 | 27 | 43 | 124 | 126 | 150 | 102 | 168 |
|       Bonds | 1 | 1 | 1 | 1 | 1 | 1 | 1 | 0 |
|       Other | – | 10 | 15 | 15 | 16 | 2 | 2 | 3 |
| Multilateral | 3 | 3 | 4 | 4 | 4 | 4 | 5 | 6 |
|   *of which:* Concessional | 2 | 2 | 2 | 2 | 2 | 2 | 2 | 2 |
| CMEA countries | – | – | – | – | 0 | 0 | 0 | 0 |
|   *of which:* Concessional | – | – | – | – | – | – | – | – |
| OPEC countries | – | – | 2 | 6 | 6 | 5 | 5 | 0 |
|   *of which:* Concessional | – | – | – | – | – | – | 0 | 0 |
| Other LDC'S | 3 | 2 | 7 | 16 | 16 | 21 | 23 | 20 |
|   *of which:* Concessional | – | – | – | – | – | – | – | – |
| Other and adjustments | – | – | 0 | 1 | 1 | 1 | 1 | 1 |
| **Total Debt Service** | **113** | **154** | **257** | **380** | **498** | **479** | **457** | **443** |
|   *of which:* Concessional | 12 | 10 | 10 | 12 | 13 | 10 | 9 | 6 |
|     Non-concessional | 101 | 144 | 247 | 368 | 485 | 469 | 448 | 437 |

US $ Million

| | 1975 | 1976 | 1977 | 1978 | 1979 | 1980 | 1981 | 1982 |
|---|---|---|---|---|---|---|---|---|
| **DEBT** | | | | | | | | |
| DAC countries and capital markets | 9 | 9 | 18 | 22 | 32 | 39 | 42 | 39 |
| ODA | 9 | 9 | 11 | 17 | 20 | 13 | 12 | 14 |
| Total export credits | – | – | 7 | 5 | 12 | 26 | 30 | 25 |
| Total private | – | – | – | – | – | – | – | – |
| of which: Bank loans | – | – | – | – | – | – | – | – |
| Bonds | – | – | – | – | – | – | – | – |
| Other | – | – | – | – | – | – | – | – |
| Multilateral | 5 | 5 | 10 | 16 | 27 | 45 | 54 | 60 |
| of which: Concessional | 5 | 5 | 10 | 16 | 25 | 42 | 48 | 53 |
| CMEA countries | – | – | – | – | – | – | – | – |
| of which: Concessional | – | – | – | – | – | – | – | – |
| OPEC countries | – | – | 1 | 8 | 14 | 19 | 26 | 40 |
| of which: Concessional | – | – | 1 | 8 | 14 | 19 | 26 | 40 |
| Other LDC'S | – | – | – | – | 5 | 9 | 11 | 12 |
| of which: Concessional | – | – | – | – | 5 | 9 | 11 | 12 |
| Other and adjustments | – | – | – | – | – | – | – | – |
| **Total Debt** | **14** | **14** | **29** | **47** | **78** | **112** | **133** | **151** |
| of which: Concessional | 14 | 14 | 22 | 42 | 65 | 84 | 96 | 119 |
| Non-concessional | – | – | 7 | 5 | 13 | 29 | 37 | 33 |
| | | | | | | | | |
| **DEBT SERVICE** | | | | | | | | |
| DAC countries and capital markets | 0 | 0 | 1 | 1 | 1 | 1 | 6 | 4 |
| ODA | 0 | 0 | 0 | 0 | 0 | 0 | 0 | 0 |
| Total export credits | – | – | 0 | 1 | 0 | 1 | 6 | 4 |
| Total private | – | – | – | – | – | – | – | – |
| of which: Bank loans | – | – | – | – | – | – | – | – |
| Bonds | – | – | – | – | – | – | – | – |
| Other | – | – | – | – | – | – | – | – |
| Multilateral | 0 | 0 | 0 | 0 | 0 | 0 | 1 | 2 |
| of which: Concessional | 0 | 0 | 0 | 0 | 0 | 0 | 1 | 2 |
| CMEA countries | – | – | – | – | – | – | – | – |
| of which: Concessional | – | – | – | – | – | – | – | – |
| OPEC countries | – | – | – | 0 | 0 | 0 | 0 | 1 |
| of which: Concessional | – | – | – | 0 | 0 | 0 | 0 | 1 |
| Other LDC'S | – | – | – | – | – | – | – | – |
| of which: Concessional | – | – | – | – | – | – | – | – |
| Other and adjustments | – | – | – | – | – | – | – | – |
| **Total Debt Service** | **0** | **0** | **1** | **1** | **1** | **2** | **7** | **7** |
| of which: Concessional | 0 | 0 | 0 | 0 | 0 | 0 | 1 | 3 |
| Non-concessional | – | – | 0 | 1 | 0 | 1 | 6 | 5 |

# GHANA

US $ Million

| | 1975 | 1976 | 1977 | 1978 | 1979 | 1980 | 1981 | 1982 |
|---|---|---|---|---|---|---|---|---|
| **DEBT** | | | | | | | | |
| DAC countries and capital | | | | | | | | |
| markets | 560 | 561 | 596 | 677 | 733 | 761 | 752 | 688 |
| ODA | 361 | 369 | 395 | 434 | 485 | 519 | 510 | 506 |
| Total export credits | 199 | 192 | 201 | 243 | 248 | 242 | 242 | 182 |
| Total private | – | – | – | – | – | – | – | – |
| of which: Bank loans | – | – | – | – | – | – | – | – |
| Bonds | – | – | – | – | – | – | – | – |
| Other | – | – | – | – | – | – | – | – |
| Multilateral | 83 | 96 | 137 | 190 | 264 | 336 | 374 | 402 |
| of which: Concessional | 83 | 94 | 121 | 147 | 190 | 235 | 243 | 261 |
| CMEA countries | 75 | 62 | 58 | 25 | 24 | 57 | 52 | 47 |
| of which: Concessional | 68 | 56 | 52 | 22 | 22 | 53 | 48 | 44 |
| OPEC countries | – | – | – | 16 | 27 | 61 | 69 | 75 |
| of which: Concessional | – | – | – | 16 | 27 | 61 | 69 | 75 |
| Other LDC'S | 23 | 8 | 22 | 16 | 15 | 16 | 15 | 10 |
| of which: Concessional | 8 | 8 | 8 | 3 | 3 | 3 | 3 | – |
| Other and adjustments | 2 | 2 | 1 | – | – | – | – | 10 |
| **Total Debt** | **743** | **728** | **814** | **924** | **1063** | **1231** | **1261** | **1233** |
| of which: Concessional | 520 | 526 | 576 | 622 | 726 | 871 | 873 | 885 |
| Non-concessional | 222 | 202 | 238 | 302 | 337 | 361 | 388 | 347 |
| | | | | | | | | |
| **DEBT SERVICE** | | | | | | | | |
| DAC countries and capital | | | | | | | | |
| markets | 47 | 35 | 28 | 48 | 52 | 66 | 71 | 47 |
| ODA | 25 | 21 | 18 | 15 | 23 | 24 | 23 | 26 |
| Total export credits | 22 | 15 | 10 | 33 | 28 | 43 | 49 | 21 |
| Total private | – | – | – | – | – | – | – | – |
| of which: Bank loans | – | – | – | – | – | – | – | – |
| Bonds | – | – | – | – | – | – | – | – |
| Other | – | – | – | – | – | – | – | – |
| Multilateral | 5 | 5 | 6 | 9 | 13 | 14 | 16 | 22 |
| of which: Concessional | 5 | 5 | 5 | 6 | 7 | 7 | 8 | 7 |
| CMEA countries | – | 14 | 4 | – | 1 | – | 6 | 5 |
| of which: Concessional | – | 14 | 4 | – | 1 | – | 6 | 4 |
| OPEC countries | – | – | – | – | – | 1 | 1 | 7 |
| of which: Concessional | – | – | – | – | – | 1 | 1 | 7 |
| Other LDC'S | – | – | 1 | 2 | 2 | – | – | 1 |
| of which: Concessional | – | – | – | – | – | – | – | – |
| Other and adjustments | 1 | 1 | 1 | 1 | – | – | – | – |
| **Total Debt Service** | **53** | **55** | **40** | **60** | **68** | **81** | **95** | **82** |
| of which: Concessional | 30 | 39 | 27 | 22 | 31 | 31 | 37 | 45 |
| Non-concessional | 23 | 16 | 13 | 38 | 37 | 50 | 58 | 37 |

## GIBRALTAR

US $ Million

| | 1975 | 1976 | 1977 | 1978 | 1979 | 1980 | 1981 | 1982 |
|---|---|---|---|---|---|---|---|---|
| **DEBT** | | | | | | | | |
| DAC countries and capital | | | | | | | | |
| markets | 5 | 5 | 8 | 12 | 9 | 25 | 24 | 40 |
| ODA | 5 | 4 | 4 | 5 | 5 | 5 | 3 | 3 |
| Total export credits | – | 1 | 4 | 7 | 4 | 20 | 21 | 22 |
| Total private | – | – | – | – | – | – | – | 15 |
| of which: Bank loans | – | – | – | – | – | – | – | – |
| Bonds | – | – | – | – | – | – | – | – |
| Other | – | – | – | – | – | – | – | 15 |
| Multilateral | – | – | – | – | – | – | – | – |
| of which: Concessional | – | – | – | – | – | – | – | – |
| CMEA countries | – | – | – | – | – | – | – | – |
| of which: Concessional | – | – | – | – | – | – | – | – |
| OPEC countries | – | – | – | – | – | – | – | – |
| of which: Concessional | – | – | – | – | – | – | – | – |
| Other LDC'S | – | – | – | – | – | – | – | – |
| of which: Concessional | – | – | – | – | – | – | – | – |
| Other and adjustments | – | – | – | – | – | – | – | – |
| **Total Debt** | **5** | **5** | **8** | **12** | **9** | **25** | **24** | **40** |
| of which: Concessional | 5 | 4 | 4 | 5 | 5 | 5 | 3 | 3 |
| Non-concessional | – | 1 | 4 | 7 | 4 | 20 | 21 | 37 |
| **DEBT SERVICE** | | | | | | | | |
| DAC countries and capital | | | | | | | | |
| markets | 1 | 0 | 1 | 2 | 2 | 3 | 7 | 9 |
| ODA | 0 | 0 | 0 | 1 | 1 | 1 | 1 | 0 |
| Total export credits | 0 | – | 1 | 1 | 2 | 2 | 6 | 9 |
| Total private | – | – | – | – | – | – | – | – |
| of which: Bank loans | – | – | – | – | – | – | – | – |
| Bonds | – | – | – | – | – | – | – | – |
| Other | – | – | – | – | – | – | – | – |
| Multilateral | – | – | – | – | – | – | – | – |
| of which: Concessional | – | – | – | – | – | – | – | – |
| CMEA countries | – | – | – | – | – | – | – | – |
| of which: Concessional | – | – | – | – | – | – | – | – |
| OPEC countries | – | – | – | – | – | – | – | – |
| of which: Concessional | – | – | – | – | – | – | – | – |
| Other LDC'S | – | – | – | – | – | – | – | – |
| of which: Concessional | – | – | – | – | – | – | – | – |
| Other and adjustments | – | – | – | – | – | – | – | – |
| **Total Debt Service** | **1** | **0** | **1** | **2** | **2** | **3** | **7** | **9** |
| of which: Concessional | 0 | 0 | 0 | 1 | 1 | 1 | 1 | 0 |
| Non-concessional | 0 | – | 1 | 1 | 2 | 2 | 6 | 9 |

*US $ Million*

| | 1975 | 1976 | 1977 | 1978 | 1979 | 1980 | 1981 | 1982 |
|---|---|---|---|---|---|---|---|---|
| **DEBT** | | | | | | | | |
| DAC countries and capital | | | | | | | | |
| markets | 3201 | 3547 | 4208 | 4580 | 5219 | 6627 | 7627 | 7878 |
| ODA | 167 | 145 | 159 | 234 | 238 | 222 | 198 | 183 |
| Total export credits | 1134 | 1535 | 1607 | 1449 | 1590 | 1729 | 2187 | 1969 |
| Total private | 1900 | 1867 | 2442 | 2897 | 3391 | 4676 | 5242 | 5726 |
| *of which:* Bank loans | 1657 | 1593 | 2113 | 2567 | 3058 | 4320 | 4850 | 5350 |
| Bonds | 143 | 124 | 129 | 130 | 133 | 136 | 142 | 126 |
| Other | 100 | 150 | 200 | 200 | 200 | 220 | 250 | 250 |
| Multilateral | 168 | 206 | 233 | 255 | 317 | 352 | 472 | 893 |
| *of which:* Concessional | 12 | 11 | 10 | 15 | 14 | 12 | 14 | 27 |
| CMEA countries | 27 | 27 | 22 | 22 | 44 | 52 | 76 | 70 |
| *of which:* Concessional | 1 | 1 | 0 | – | – | – | – | – |
| OPEC countries | – | – | – | – | – | – | – | – |
| *of which:* Concessional | – | – | – | – | – | – | – | – |
| Other LDC'S | 10 | 6 | 3 | 1 | 2 | 2 | 3 | 1 |
| *of which:* Concessional | – | – | – | – | – | – | – | – |
| Other and adjustments | 2 | 2 | 1 | 1 | 1 | 0 | 0 | 0 |
| **Total Debt** | **3408** | **3788** | **4467** | **4858** | **5582** | **7034** | **8177** | **8842** |
| *of which:* Concessional | 180 | 156 | 169 | 249 | 252 | 234 | 212 | 210 |
| Non-concessional | 3229 | 3631 | 4298 | 4610 | 5330 | 6800 | 7966 | 8632 |
| **DEBT SERVICE** | | | | | | | | |
| DAC countries and capital | | | | | | | | |
| markets | 633 | 764 | 842 | 907 | 1050 | 1223 | 1670 | 1634 |
| ODA | 25 | 23 | 23 | 26 | 29 | 25 | 18 | 17 |
| Total export credits | 304 | 347 | 517 | 448 | 549 | 544 | 598 | 475 |
| Total private | 305 | 394 | 301 | 433 | 472 | 654 | 1054 | 1142 |
| *of which:* Bank loans | 297 | 357 | 270 | 401 | 440 | 622 | 1010 | 1080 |
| Bonds | 8 | 7 | 6 | 7 | 7 | 7 | 9 | 12 |
| Other | – | 30 | 25 | 25 | 25 | 25 | 35 | 50 |
| Multilateral | 23 | 33 | 35 | 43 | 49 | 56 | 62 | 70 |
| *of which:* Concessional | 2 | 2 | 2 | 2 | 2 | 2 | 2 | 1 |
| CMEA countries | 4 | 7 | 10 | 9 | 9 | 13 | 17 | 15 |
| *of which:* Concessional | 0 | 0 | 1 | 0 | – | – | – | – |
| OPEC countries | – | – | – | – | – | – | – | – |
| *of which:* Concessional | – | – | – | – | – | – | – | – |
| Other LDC'S | 0 | 3 | 3 | 3 | 4 | 0 | 0 | 1 |
| *of which:* Concessional | – | – | – | – | – | – | – | – |
| Other and adjustments | 1 | 0 | 0 | 0 | 0 | 0 | 0 | 0 |
| **Total Debt Service** | **661** | **807** | **891** | **962** | **1112** | **1293** | **1750** | **1721** |
| *of which:* Concessional | 27 | 25 | 25 | 28 | 31 | 27 | 20 | 18 |
| Non-concessional | 634 | 782 | 865 | 933 | 1082 | 1266 | 1729 | 1703 |

# GUADELOUPE

US $ Million

| | 1975 | 1976 | 1977 | 1978 | 1979 | 1980 | 1981 | 1982 |
|---|---|---|---|---|---|---|---|---|
| **DEBT** | | | | | | | | |
| DAC countries and capital | | | | | | | | |
| markets | 128 | 125 | 127 | 144 | 142 | 119 | 87 | 68 |
| ODA | 128 | 121 | 122 | 138 | 136 | 113 | 83 | 65 |
| Total export credits | – | 4 | 5 | 6 | 6 | 6 | 4 | 3 |
| Total private | – | – | – | – | – | – | – | – |
| of which: Bank loans | – | – | – | – | – | – | – | – |
| Bonds | – | – | – | – | – | – | – | – |
| Other | – | – | – | – | – | – | – | – |
| Multilateral | – | – | – | – | – | – | – | – |
| of which: Concessional | – | – | – | – | – | – | – | – |
| CMEA countries | – | – | – | – | – | – | – | – |
| of which: Concessional | – | – | – | – | – | – | – | – |
| OPEC countries | – | – | – | – | – | – | – | – |
| of which: Concessional | – | – | – | – | – | – | – | – |
| Other LDC'S | – | – | – | – | – | – | – | – |
| of which: Concessional | – | – | – | – | – | – | – | – |
| Other and adjustments | – | – | – | – | – | – | – | – |
| **Total Debt** | **128** | **125** | **127** | **144** | **142** | **119** | **87** | **68** |
| of which: Concessional | 128 | 121 | 122 | 138 | 136 | 113 | 83 | 65 |
| Non-concessional | – | 4 | 5 | 6 | 6 | 6 | 4 | 3 |
| **DEBT SERVICE** | | | | | | | | |
| DAC countries and capital | | | | | | | | |
| markets | 10 | 12 | 11 | 14 | 13 | 16 | 9 | 8 |
| ODA | 10 | 11 | 11 | 13 | 13 | 14 | 9 | 7 |
| Total export credits | – | 1 | 1 | 1 | 0 | 2 | 1 | 1 |
| Total private | – | – | – | – | – | – | – | – |
| of which: Bank loans | – | – | – | – | – | – | – | – |
| Bonds | – | – | – | – | – | – | – | – |
| Other | – | – | – | – | – | – | – | – |
| Multilateral | – | – | – | – | – | – | – | – |
| of which: Concessional | – | – | – | – | – | – | – | – |
| CMEA countries | – | – | – | – | – | – | – | – |
| of which: Concessional | – | – | – | – | – | – | – | – |
| OPEC countries | – | – | – | – | – | – | – | – |
| of which: Concessional | – | – | – | – | – | – | – | – |
| Other LDC'S | – | – | – | – | – | – | – | – |
| of which: Concessional | – | – | – | – | – | – | – | – |
| Other and adjustments | – | – | – | – | – | – | – | – |
| **Total Debt Service** | **10** | **12** | **11** | **14** | **13** | **16** | **9** | **8** |
| of which: Concessional | 10 | 11 | 11 | 13 | 13 | 14 | 9 | 7 |
| Non-concessional | – | 1 | 1 | 1 | 0 | 2 | 1 | 1 |

# GUATEMALA

US $ Million

| | 1975 | 1976 | 1977 | 1978 | 1979 | 1980 | 1981 | 1982 |
|---|---|---|---|---|---|---|---|---|
| **DEBT** | | | | | | | | |
| DAC countries and capital | | | | | | | | |
|   markets | 94 | 147 | 186 | 286 | 299 | 316 | 358 | 355 |
|   ODA | 60 | 66 | 69 | 68 | 71 | 77 | 84 | 94 |
|   Total export credits | 34 | 49 | 82 | 168 | 158 | 149 | 179 | 136 |
|   Total private | 0 | 32 | 35 | 50 | 70 | 90 | 95 | 125 |
|     *of which:* Bank loans | – | 32 | 30 | 40 | 55 | 75 | 85 | 110 |
|     Bonds | 0 | 0 | – | – | – | – | – | – |
|     Other | – | – | 5 | 10 | 15 | 15 | 10 | 15 |
| Multilateral | 75 | 92 | 133 | 200 | 285 | 350 | 435 | 524 |
|   *of which:* Concessional | 43 | 48 | 63 | 102 | 130 | 163 | 201 | 225 |
| CMEA countries | – | – | – | – | – | – | – | – |
|   *of which:* Concessional | – | – | – | – | – | – | – | – |
| OPEC countries | – | – | 16 | 35 | 72 | 114 | 174 | 211 |
|   *of which:* Concessional | – | – | – | – | 9 | 27 | 27 | 27 |
| Other LDC'S | – | 1 | 1 | 1 | 1 | 1 | 21 | 31 |
|   *of which:* Concessional | – | 1 | 1 | 1 | 1 | 1 | 1 | 1 |
| Other and adjustments | 5 | 4 | 3 | 2 | 1 | 1 | 44 | 188 |
| **Total Debt** | **174** | **244** | **339** | **524** | **659** | **782** | **1032** | **1309** |
|   *of which:* Concessional | 103 | 115 | 133 | 170 | 211 | 267 | 313 | 346 |
|   Non-concessional | 71 | 129 | 206 | 354 | 448 | 515 | 719 | 963 |
| | | | | | | | | |
| **DEBT SERVICE** | | | | | | | | |
| DAC countries and capital | | | | | | | | |
|   markets | 14 | 25 | 38 | 46 | 74 | 98 | 108 | 111 |
|   ODA | 2 | 2 | 3 | 2 | 3 | 3 | 3 | 4 |
|   Total export credits | 12 | 18 | 29 | 38 | 61 | 74 | 74 | 89 |
|   Total private | 0 | 5 | 6 | 6 | 10 | 21 | 31 | 18 |
|     *of which:* Bank loans | – | 5 | 6 | 6 | 6 | 16 | 25 | 18 |
|     Bonds | 0 | 0 | 0 | – | – | – | – | – |
|     Other | – | – | – | – | 4 | 5 | 6 | – |
| Multilateral | 7 | 8 | 10 | 19 | 27 | 32 | 35 | 47 |
|   *of which:* Concessional | 4 | 4 | 4 | 6 | 7 | 7 | 7 | 8 |
| CMEA countries | – | – | – | – | – | – | – | – |
|   *of which:* Concessional | – | – | – | – | – | – | – | – |
| OPEC countries | – | – | 1 | 2 | 4 | 8 | 13 | 22 |
|   *of which:* Concessional | – | – | – | – | 0 | 2 | 3 | 3 |
| Other LDC'S | – | 0 | 0 | 0 | 0 | 0 | 1 | 5 |
|   *of which:* Concessional | – | 0 | 0 | 0 | 0 | 0 | 0 | 0 |
| Other and adjustments | 1 | 1 | 1 | 1 | 1 | 1 | 1 | – |
| **Total Debt Service** | **22** | **35** | **50** | **68** | **105** | **138** | **157** | **185** |
|   *of which:* Concessional | 6 | 6 | 7 | 8 | 10 | 12 | 13 | 15 |
|   Non-concessional | 16 | 28 | 43 | 60 | 95 | 126 | 145 | 170 |

*US $ Million*

| | 1975 | 1976 | 1977 | 1978 | 1979 | 1980 | 1981 | 1982 |
|---|---|---|---|---|---|---|---|---|
| **DEBT** | | | | | | | | |
| DAC countries and capital markets | 28 | 25 | 29 | 29 | 28 | 26 | 20 | 18 |
| ODA | 28 | 25 | 26 | 28 | 27 | 24 | 18 | 15 |
| Total export credits | – | – | 3 | 1 | 1 | 2 | 2 | 3 |
| Total private | – | – | – | – | – | – | – | – |
| *of which:* Bank loans | – | – | – | – | – | – | – | – |
| Bonds | – | – | – | – | – | – | – | – |
| Other | – | – | – | – | – | – | – | – |
| Multilateral | – | – | – | – | – | – | – | – |
| *of which:* Concessional | – | – | – | – | – | – | – | – |
| CMEA countries | – | – | – | – | – | – | – | – |
| *of which:* Concessional | – | – | – | – | – | – | – | – |
| OPEC countries | – | – | – | – | – | – | – | – |
| *of which:* Concessional | – | – | – | – | – | – | – | – |
| Other LDC'S | – | – | – | – | – | – | – | – |
| *of which:* Concessional | – | – | – | – | – | – | – | – |
| Other and adjustments | – | – | – | – | – | – | – | – |
| **Total Debt** | **28** | **25** | **29** | **29** | **28** | **26** | **20** | **18** |
| *of which:* Concessional | 28 | 25 | 26 | 28 | 27 | 24 | 18 | 15 |
| Non-concessional | – | – | 3 | 1 | 1 | 2 | 2 | 3 |
| **DEBT SERVICE** | | | | | | | | |
| DAC countries and capital markets | 3 | 2 | 3 | 3 | 3 | 3 | 2 | 4 |
| ODA | 3 | 2 | 2 | 3 | 3 | 3 | 2 | 1 |
| Total export credits | – | – | 1 | 0 | 0 | 1 | 0 | 3 |
| Total private | – | – | – | – | – | – | – | – |
| *of which:* Bank loans | – | – | – | – | – | – | – | – |
| Bonds | – | – | – | – | – | – | – | – |
| Other | – | – | – | – | – | – | – | – |
| Multilateral | – | – | – | – | – | – | – | – |
| *of which:* Concessional | – | – | – | – | – | – | – | – |
| CMEA countries | – | – | – | – | – | – | – | – |
| *of which:* Concessional | – | – | – | – | – | – | – | – |
| OPEC countries | – | – | – | – | – | – | – | – |
| *of which:* Concessional | – | – | – | – | – | – | – | – |
| Other LDC'S | – | – | – | – | – | – | – | – |
| *of which:* Concessional | – | – | – | – | – | – | – | – |
| Other and adjustments | – | – | – | – | – | – | – | – |
| **Total Debt Service** | **3** | **2** | **3** | **3** | **3** | **3** | **2** | **4** |
| *of which:* Concessional | 3 | 2 | 2 | 3 | 3 | 3 | 2 | 1 |
| Non-concessional | – | – | 1 | 0 | 0 | 1 | 0 | 3 |

*US $ Million*

| | 1975 | 1976 | 1977 | 1978 | 1979 | 1980 | 1981 | 1982 |
|---|---|---|---|---|---|---|---|---|
| **DEBT** | | | | | | | | |
| DAC countries and capital | | | | | | | | |
| markets | 240 | 267 | 253 | 317 | 379 | 421 | 373 | 345 |
| ODA | 123 | 107 | 113 | 125 | 123 | 132 | 132 | 134 |
| Total export credits | 95 | 142 | 126 | 177 | 231 | 259 | 223 | 198 |
| Total private | 22 | 18 | 14 | 15 | 25 | 30 | 18 | 13 |
| *of which:* Bank loans | 22 | 18 | 14 | 15 | 25 | 30 | 18 | 13 |
| Bonds | – | – | – | – | – | – | – | – |
| Other | – | – | – | – | – | – | – | – |
| Multilateral | 72 | 72 | 83 | 106 | 134 | 156 | 179 | 194 |
| *of which:* Concessional | – | 1 | 13 | 35 | 55 | 90 | 118 | 136 |
| CMEA countries | 354 | 362 | 331 | 307 | 277 | 238 | 426 | 401 |
| *of which:* Concessional | 324 | 335 | 303 | 275 | 245 | 210 | 400 | 379 |
| OPEC countries | 18 | 18 | 23 | 29 | 41 | 40 | 64 | 90 |
| *of which:* Concessional | 6 | 6 | 11 | 18 | 20 | 20 | 44 | 70 |
| Other LDC'S | 140 | 153 | 171 | 203 | 210 | 226 | 216 | 197 |
| *of which:* Concessional | 131 | 150 | 167 | 198 | 208 | 226 | 216 | 197 |
| Other and adjustments | 24 | 24 | 24 | 24 | 24 | 27 | 41 | 56 |
| **Total Debt** | **848** | **897** | **885** | **987** | **1065** | **1108** | **1301** | **1284** |
| *of which:* Concessional | 584 | 600 | 607 | 650 | 651 | 678 | 910 | 916 |
| Non-concessional | 264 | 297 | 278 | 337 | 415 | 431 | 391 | 368 |
| **DEBT SERVICE** | | | | | | | | |
| DAC countries and capital | | | | | | | | |
| markets | 24 | 23 | 39 | 40 | 42 | 50 | 57 | 26 |
| ODA | 9 | 4 | 6 | 7 | 4 | 5 | 8 | 9 |
| Total export credits | 15 | 16 | 32 | 31 | 35 | 39 | 46 | 15 |
| Total private | – | 3 | 2 | 3 | 3 | 6 | 3 | 2 |
| *of which:* Bank loans | – | 3 | 2 | 3 | 3 | 6 | 3 | 2 |
| Bonds | – | – | – | – | – | – | – | – |
| Other | – | – | – | – | – | – | – | – |
| Multilateral | 8 | 8 | 9 | 10 | 9 | 22 | 11 | 12 |
| *of which:* Concessional | – | 0 | 0 | 0 | 0 | 0 | 0 | 2 |
| CMEA countries | 20 | 23 | 47 | 43 | 57 | 49 | 46 | 36 |
| *of which:* Concessional | 19 | 21 | 45 | 43 | 57 | 46 | 44 | 31 |
| OPEC countries | 0 | 0 | 1 | 0 | 2 | 3 | 1 | 1 |
| *of which:* Concessional | – | 0 | 0 | 0 | 2 | 1 | 1 | 1 |
| Other LDC'S | 2 | 1 | 1 | 3 | 6 | 4 | 3 | 4 |
| *of which:* Concessional | – | – | 1 | 1 | 2 | 2 | 3 | 4 |
| Other and adjustments | – | 0 | 0 | 0 | 0 | 1 | 0 | 1 |
| **Total Debt Service** | **54** | **56** | **98** | **97** | **117** | **128** | **118** | **79** |
| *of which:* Concessional | 27 | 25 | 52 | 51 | 65 | 54 | 57 | 47 |
| Non-concessional | 26 | 31 | 46 | 46 | 52 | 74 | 61 | 32 |

# GUINEA-BISSAU

US $ Million

|  | 1975 | 1976 | 1977 | 1978 | 1979 | 1980 | 1981 | 1982 |
|---|---|---|---|---|---|---|---|---|
| **DEBT** | | | | | | | | |
| DAC countries and capital markets | – | 2 | 3 | 8 | 19 | 29 | 27 | 25 |
| ODA | – | – | 1 | 3 | 4 | 6 | 7 | 7 |
| Total export credits | – | 2 | 2 | 5 | 15 | 16 | 13 | 12 |
| Total private | – | – | – | – | – | 7 | 7 | 6 |
| of which: Bank loans | – | – | – | – | – | 7 | 7 | 6 |
| Bonds | – | – | – | – | – | – | – | – |
| Other | – | – | – | – | – | – | – | – |
| Multilateral | – | – | 2 | 2 | 5 | 26 | 37 | 48 |
| of which: Concessional | – | – | 2 | 2 | 5 | 11 | 23 | 33 |
| CMEA countries | – | 1 | 5 | 13 | 15 | 19 | 20 | 25 |
| of which: Concessional | – | 1 | 2 | 10 | 13 | 17 | 17 | 17 |
| OPEC countries | 2 | 5 | 5 | 7 | 9 | 10 | 10 | 12 |
| of which: Concessional | 2 | 5 | 5 | 7 | 9 | 10 | 10 | 12 |
| Other LDC'S | 5 | 11 | 10 | 13 | 18 | 17 | 15 | 17 |
| of which: Concessional | 5 | 11 | 10 | 12 | 11 | 11 | 9 | 6 |
| Other and adjustments | – | – | – | – | – | – | – | – |
| **Total Debt** | 7 | 19 | 24 | 42 | 66 | 101 | 109 | 127 |
| of which: Concessional | 7 | 17 | 20 | 34 | 42 | 55 | 67 | 75 |
| Non-concessional | – | 2 | 5 | 9 | 24 | 46 | 42 | 51 |
| **DEBT SERVICE** | | | | | | | | |
| DAC countries and capital markets | – | 0 | 0 | 1 | 4 | 4 | 4 | 3 |
| ODA | – | – | – | – | 0 | – | – | – |
| Total export credits | – | 0 | 0 | 1 | 3 | 4 | 3 | 2 |
| Total private | – | – | – | – | – | – | 1 | 1 |
| of which: Bank loans | – | – | – | – | – | – | 1 | 1 |
| Bonds | – | – | – | – | – | – | – | – |
| Other | – | – | – | – | – | – | – | – |
| Multilateral | – | – | 0 | 0 | 0 | 0 | 0 | 0 |
| of which: Concessional | – | – | 0 | 0 | 0 | 0 | 0 | 0 |
| CMEA countries | – | – | – | 0 | – | 0 | – | – |
| of which: Concessional | – | – | – | 0 | – | – | – | – |
| OPEC countries | – | 0 | 0 | 0 | 0 | 0 | 0 | 0 |
| of which: Concessional | – | 0 | 0 | 0 | 0 | 0 | 0 | 0 |
| Other LDC'S | – | – | – | – | – | 0 | – | – |
| of which: Concessional | – | – | – | – | – | – | – | – |
| Other and adjustments | – | – | – | – | – | – | – | – |
| **Total Debt Service** | – | 0 | 0 | 1 | 4 | 4 | 4 | 4 |
| of which: Concessional | – | 0 | 0 | 0 | 0 | 0 | 0 | 0 |
| Non-concessional | – | 0 | 0 | 1 | 3 | 4 | 4 | 3 |

*US $ Million*

| DEBT | 1975 | 1976 | 1977 | 1978 | 1979 | 1980 | 1981 | 1982 |
|---|---|---|---|---|---|---|---|---|
| **DEBT** | | | | | | | | |
| DAC countries and capital | | | | | | | | |
| markets | 237 | 287 | 313 | 336 | 359 | 408 | 374 | 333 |
| ODA | 107 | 106 | 109 | 127 | 139 | 150 | 146 | 146 |
| Total export credits | 18 | 38 | 60 | 72 | 79 | 114 | 97 | 61 |
| Total private | 112 | 143 | 144 | 137 | 141 | 144 | 131 | 126 |
| *of which:* Bank loans | 70 | 80 | 59 | 55 | 58 | 60 | 62 | 60 |
| Bonds | 12 | 10 | 12 | 12 | 13 | 14 | 7 | 6 |
| Other | 30 | 53 | 73 | 70 | 70 | 70 | 62 | 60 |
| Multilateral | 20 | 24 | 29 | 42 | 71 | 107 | 170 | 202 |
| *of which:* Concessional | 7 | 8 | 12 | 19 | 36 | 65 | 117 | 131 |
| CMEA countries | 6 | 13 | 14 | 17 | 16 | 16 | 13 | 22 |
| *of which:* Concessional | – | – | – | – | – | – | – | – |
| OPEC countries | 15 | 20 | 22 | 22 | 26 | 24 | 24 | 26 |
| *of which:* Concessional | 15 | 20 | 20 | 19 | 18 | 17 | 15 | 15 |
| Other LDC'S | 22 | 22 | 29 | 34 | 35 | 40 | 108 | 90 |
| *of which:* Concessional | 2 | 2 | 4 | 7 | 9 | 10 | 79 | 78 |
| Other and adjustments | – | – | – | – | – | – | – | – |
| **Total Debt** | **300** | **366** | **407** | **451** | **507** | **596** | **689** | **672** |
| *of which:* Concessional | 130 | 136 | 144 | 173 | 203 | 242 | 357 | 371 |
| Non-concessional | 169 | 230 | 263 | 278 | 304 | 354 | 331 | 302 |
| **DEBT SERVICE** | | | | | | | | |
| DAC countries and capital | | | | | | | | |
| markets | 24 | 37 | 43 | 47 | 85 | 65 | 71 | 39 |
| ODA | 7 | 6 | 6 | 7 | 9 | 10 | 8 | 2 |
| Total export credits | 9 | 6 | 9 | 12 | 19 | 23 | 32 | 24 |
| Total private | 8 | 26 | 29 | 28 | 57 | 32 | 31 | 13 |
| *of which:* Bank loans | 8 | 12 | 21 | 19 | 48 | 21 | 15 | 11 |
| Bonds | 1 | 0 | 0 | 0 | 1 | 1 | 6 | 0 |
| Other | – | 13 | 8 | 8 | 9 | 10 | 11 | 2 |
| Multilateral | 1 | 1 | 2 | 2 | 3 | 5 | 6 | 6 |
| *of which:* Concessional | 0 | 0 | 0 | 0 | 1 | 1 | 2 | 2 |
| CMEA countries | 0 | 1 | 0 | 1 | 5 | 6 | 6 | 5 |
| *of which:* Concessional | – | – | – | – | – | – | – | – |
| OPEC countries | – | – | 0 | 1 | 1 | 2 | 2 | 0 |
| *of which:* Concessional | – | – | – | 1 | 1 | 2 | 2 | – |
| Other LDC'S | 1 | 1 | – | 2 | 1 | 2 | 2 | 1 |
| *of which:* Concessional | – | – | – | – | – | – | – | – |
| Other and adjustments | – | – | – | – | – | – | – | – |
| **Total Debt Service** | **26** | **41** | **46** | **53** | **96** | **80** | **86** | **51** |
| *of which:* Concessional | 7 | 6 | 6 | 9 | 11 | 13 | 11 | 3 |
| Non-concessional | 20 | 35 | 40 | 44 | 85 | 67 | 75 | 47 |

# HAITI

*US $ Million*

| | 1975 | 1976 | 1977 | 1978 | 1979 | 1980 | 1981 | 1982 |
|---|---|---|---|---|---|---|---|---|
| **DEBT** | | | | | | | | |
| DAC countries and capital | | | | | | | | |
| markets | 42 | 55 | 66 | 81 | 99 | 110 | 163 | 173 |
| ODA | 3 | 10 | 24 | 42 | 55 | 65 | 75 | 89 |
| Total export credits | 39 | 36 | 26 | 21 | 32 | 33 | 35 | 30 |
| Total private | – | 9 | 16 | 18 | 12 | 12 | 53 | 54 |
| *of which:* Bank loans | – | 2 | 4 | 7 | 4 | 6 | 47 | 48 |
| Bonds | – | – | – | – | – | – | – | – |
| Other | – | 7 | 12 | 11 | 8 | 6 | 6 | 6 |
| Multilateral | 11 | 31 | 70 | 104 | 128 | 157 | 179 | 203 |
| *of which:* Concessional | 11 | 31 | 70 | 104 | 128 | 157 | 179 | 203 |
| CMEA countries | – | – | – | – | – | 1 | 1 | 0 |
| *of which:* Concessional | – | – | – | – | – | – | – | – |
| OPEC countries | – | – | – | – | – | – | 6 | 9 |
| *of which:* Concessional | – | – | – | – | – | – | – | – |
| Other LDC'S | 4 | – | – | – | – | 1 | 2 | 3 |
| *of which:* Concessional | – | – | – | – | – | – | – | – |
| Other and adjustments | – | – | – | – | – | 11 | 12 | 10 |
| **Total Debt** | **57** | **86** | **136** | **185** | **227** | **280** | **363** | **398** |
| *of which:* Concessional | 14 | 41 | 94 | 146 | 183 | 222 | 254 | 292 |
| Non-concessional | 43 | 45 | 42 | 39 | 44 | 58 | 109 | 106 |
| **DEBT SERVICE** | | | | | | | | |
| DAC countries and capital | | | | | | | | |
| markets | 7 | 10 | 18 | 18 | 11 | 20 | 14 | 12 |
| ODA | – | – | – | 1 | 1 | 1 | 1 | 2 |
| Total export credits | 7 | 10 | 9 | 10 | 5 | 13 | 5 | 3 |
| Total private | – | 0 | 9 | 7 | 5 | 7 | 8 | 7 |
| *of which:* Bank loans | – | 0 | 0 | 1 | 1 | 3 | 6 | 5 |
| Bonds | – | – | – | – | – | – | – | – |
| Other | – | – | 9 | 6 | 3 | 4 | 2 | 2 |
| Multilateral | 0 | 0 | 1 | 1 | 1 | 1 | 1 | 2 |
| *of which:* Concessional | 0 | 0 | 1 | 1 | 1 | 1 | 1 | 2 |
| CMEA countries | – | – | – | – | – | 0 | 1 | 1 |
| *of which:* Concessional | – | – | – | – | – | – | – | – |
| OPEC countries | – | – | – | – | – | – | 0 | 1 |
| *of which:* Concessional | – | – | – | – | – | – | – | – |
| Other LDC'S | – | – | – | – | – | – | – | – |
| *of which:* Concessional | – | – | – | – | – | – | – | – |
| Other and adjustments | – | – | – | – | – | 3 | 4 | 3 |
| **Total Debt Service** | **8** | **10** | **19** | **19** | **12** | **25** | **20** | **19** |
| *of which:* Concessional | 0 | 0 | 1 | 2 | 2 | 2 | 3 | 4 |
| Non-concessional | 7 | 10 | 18 | 17 | 10 | 22 | 17 | 15 |

133

# HONDURAS

US $ Million

| | 1975 | 1976 | 1977 | 1978 | 1979 | 1980 | 1981 | 1982 |
|---|---|---|---|---|---|---|---|---|
| **DEBT** | | | | | | | | |
| DAC countries and capital | | | | | | | | |
| markets | 138 | 179 | 254 | 388 | 464 | 491 | 572 | 601 |
| ODA | 51 | 60 | 67 | 83 | 99 | 123 | 148 | 206 |
| Total export credits | 12 | 22 | 22 | 105 | 123 | 148 | 164 | 170 |
| Total private | 75 | 97 | 165 | 200 | 242 | 220 | 260 | 225 |
| of which: Bank loans | 55 | 72 | 140 | 170 | 217 | 200 | 240 | 205 |
| Bonds | – | – | – | – | – | – | – | – |
| Other | 20 | 25 | 25 | 30 | 25 | 20 | 20 | 20 |
| Multilateral | 163 | 191 | 238 | 313 | 378 | 483 | 564 | 638 |
| of which: Concessional | 79 | 83 | 104 | 153 | 197 | 239 | 275 | 313 |
| CMEA countries | – | – | – | – | – | – | – | – |
| of which: Concessional | – | – | – | – | – | – | – | – |
| OPEC countries | 27 | 43 | 57 | 78 | 98 | 109 | 126 | 132 |
| of which: Concessional | 5 | 10 | 10 | 10 | 10 | 10 | 10 | 10 |
| Other LDC'S | 6 | 7 | 7 | 6 | 5 | 6 | 9 | 7 |
| of which: Concessional | – | – | – | – | – | – | – | – |
| Other and adjustments | – | – | – | – | – | 1 | 4 | 4 |
| **Total Debt** | **334** | **420** | **556** | **785** | **945** | **1091** | **1275** | **1383** |
| of which: Concessional | 135 | 153 | 181 | 246 | 306 | 372 | 433 | 529 |
| Non-concessional | 199 | 267 | 376 | 539 | 638 | 718 | 842 | 854 |
| **DEBT SERVICE** | | | | | | | | |
| DAC countries and capital | | | | | | | | |
| markets | 9 | 17 | 28 | 31 | 81 | 76 | 97 | 100 |
| ODA | 1 | 2 | 2 | 2 | 3 | 3 | 3 | 6 |
| Total export credits | 6 | 4 | 9 | 9 | 27 | 30 | 50 | 33 |
| Total private | 2 | 11 | 17 | 20 | 52 | 44 | 44 | 61 |
| of which: Bank loans | 2 | 7 | 13 | 15 | 46 | 38 | 38 | 55 |
| Bonds | – | – | – | – | – | – | – | – |
| Other | – | 4 | 4 | 5 | 6 | 6 | 6 | 6 |
| Multilateral | 11 | 20 | 25 | 31 | 39 | 45 | 47 | 63 |
| of which: Concessional | 6 | 6 | 7 | 8 | 8 | 9 | 10 | 10 |
| CMEA countries | – | – | – | – | – | – | – | – |
| of which: Concessional | – | – | – | – | – | – | – | – |
| OPEC countries | 1 | 2 | 3 | 5 | 6 | 5 | 8 | 5 |
| of which: Concessional | – | 0 | – | – | – | – | – | – |
| Other LDC'S | 0 | 1 | 1 | 1 | 1 | 1 | 2 | 2 |
| of which: Concessional | – | – | – | – | – | – | – | – |
| Other and adjustments | – | – | – | – | – | 0 | 0 | 1 |
| **Total Debt Service** | **21** | **40** | **57** | **69** | **128** | **127** | **154** | **171** |
| of which: Concessional | 7 | 8 | 9 | 10 | 11 | 12 | 13 | 16 |
| Non-concessional | 14 | 32 | 48 | 59 | 117 | 115 | 141 | 155 |

*US $ Million*

| | 1975 | 1976 | 1977 | 1978 | 1979 | 1980 | 1981 | 1982 |
|---|---|---|---|---|---|---|---|---|
| **DEBT** | | | | | | | | |
| DAC countries and capital | | | | | | | | |
| markets | 424 | 572 | 764 | 1238 | 1848 | 2471 | 2904 | 3765 |
| ODA | 4 | 3 | 3 | 3 | 3 | 3 | 3 | 2 |
| Total export credits | 140 | 254 | 446 | 870 | 1321 | 1938 | 2402 | 3233 |
| Total private | 280 | 315 | 315 | 365 | 524 | 530 | 499 | 530 |
| *of which:* Bank loans | 200 | 215 | 205 | 250 | 404 | 410 | 369 | 380 |
| Bonds | – | – | – | – | – | – | – | – |
| Other | 80 | 100 | 110 | 115 | 120 | 120 | 130 | 150 |
| Multilateral | 18 | 19 | 17 | 18 | 28 | 42 | 47 | 53 |
| *of which:* Concessional | – | – | – | – | – | – | – | – |
| CMEA countries | – | – | – | – | – | – | – | – |
| *of which:* Concessional | – | – | – | – | – | – | – | – |
| OPEC countries | – | – | – | – | – | – | – | – |
| *of which:* Concessional | – | – | – | – | – | – | – | – |
| Other LDC'S | – | – | – | – | – | – | – | – |
| *of which:* Concessional | – | – | – | – | – | – | – | – |
| Other and adjustments | – | – | – | – | – | – | – | – |
| **Total Debt** | **442** | **591** | **781** | **1256** | **1876** | **2513** | **2951** | **3818** |
| *of which:* Concessional | 4 | 3 | 3 | 3 | 3 | 3 | 3 | 2 |
| Non-concessional | 438 | 588 | 778 | 1253 | 1873 | 2510 | 2948 | 3816 |
| | | | | | | | | |
| **DEBT SERVICE** | | | | | | | | |
| DAC countries and capital | | | | | | | | |
| markets | 224 | 95 | 94 | 197 | 308 | 337 | 621 | 626 |
| ODA | 1 | 0 | 0 | 1 | 1 | 1 | 1 | 1 |
| Total export credits | 208 | 47 | 38 | 146 | 232 | 256 | 460 | 507 |
| Total private | 15 | 48 | 55 | 50 | 76 | 80 | 160 | 118 |
| *of which:* Bank loans | 15 | 39 | 45 | 35 | 56 | 58 | 135 | 88 |
| Bonds | – | – | – | – | – | – | – | – |
| Other | – | 9 | 10 | 15 | 20 | 22 | 25 | 30 |
| Multilateral | 2 | 3 | 4 | 4 | 4 | 7 | 15 | 7 |
| *of which:* Concessional | – | – | – | – | – | – | – | – |
| CMEA countries | – | – | – | – | – | – | – | – |
| *of which:* Concessional | – | – | – | – | – | – | – | – |
| OPEC countries | – | – | – | – | – | – | – | – |
| *of which:* Concessional | – | – | – | – | – | – | – | – |
| Other LDC'S | – | – | – | – | – | – | – | – |
| *of which:* Concessional | – | – | – | – | – | – | – | – |
| Other and adjustments | – | – | – | – | – | – | – | – |
| **Total Debt Service** | **226** | **98** | **98** | **201** | **312** | **343** | **636** | **632** |
| *of which:* Concessional | 1 | 0 | 0 | 1 | 1 | 1 | 1 | 1 |
| Non-concessional | 225 | 98 | 98 | 201 | 312 | 343 | 635 | 631 |

*US $ Million*

| | 1975 | 1976 | 1977 | 1978 | 1979 | 1980 | 1981 | 1982 |
|---|---|---|---|---|---|---|---|---|
| **DEBT** | | | | | | | | |
| DAC countries and capital | | | | | | | | |
| markets | 8126 | 8390 | 9049 | 9430 | 9572 | 9858 | 9630 | 10127 |
| ODA | 7274 | 7216 | 8105 | 8770 | 8831 | 8751 | 8249 | 7940 |
| Total export credits | 841 | 1137 | 892 | 603 | 664 | 955 | 1144 | 1635 |
| Total private | 11 | 37 | 52 | 57 | 77 | 152 | 237 | 552 |
| *of which:* Bank loans | 9 | 35 | 50 | 50 | 65 | 100 | 150 | 450 |
| Bonds | 2 | 2 | 2 | 2 | 2 | 32 | 62 | 62 |
| Other | – | – | – | 5 | 10 | 20 | 25 | 40 |
| Multilateral | 3245 | 3789 | 4218 | 4654 | 5297 | 6720 | 7801 | 9126 |
| *of which:* Concessional | 3063 | 3563 | 3873 | 4180 | 4732 | 6050 | 6790 | 7909 |
| CMEA countries | 364 | 356 | 346 | 323 | 316 | 311 | 261 | 283 |
| *of which:* Concessional | 314 | 303 | 297 | 279 | 279 | 279 | 238 | 241 |
| OPEC countries | 706 | 981 | 1206 | 1297 | 1304 | 1252 | 1151 | 1130 |
| *of which:* Concessional | 703 | 979 | 1205 | 1297 | 1304 | 1252 | 1151 | 1027 |
| Other LDC'S | 30 | 55 | 62 | 68 | 55 | 41 | 31 | 21 |
| *of which:* Concessional | 3 | 2 | 2 | 2 | 2 | – | – | – |
| Other and adjustments | – | – | – | – | – | – | – | – |
| **Total Debt** | **12471** | **13571** | **14881** | **15773** | **16545** | **18183** | **18874** | **20687** |
| *of which:* Concessional | 11356 | 12064 | 13483 | 14528 | 15149 | 16332 | 16428 | 17117 |
| Non-concessional | 1114 | 1507 | 1398 | 1244 | 1396 | 1851 | 2446 | 3570 |
| | | | | | | | | |
| **DEBT SERVICE** | | | | | | | | |
| DAC countries and capital | | | | | | | | |
| markets | 656 | 636 | 695 | 756 | 813 | 1003 | 969 | 1162 |
| ODA | 283 | 321 | 366 | 466 | 550 | 520 | 513 | 458 |
| Total export credits | 371 | 309 | 323 | 269 | 225 | 450 | 420 | 644 |
| Total private | 2 | 6 | 6 | 21 | 38 | 33 | 36 | 60 |
| *of which:* Bank loans | 2 | 6 | 6 | 20 | 36 | 30 | 31 | 50 |
| Bonds | 0 | 0 | 0 | 0 | 0 | 0 | 0 | 0 |
| Other | – | – | – | 1 | 2 | 3 | 5 | 10 |
| Multilateral | 113 | 118 | 142 | 165 | 174 | 193 | 202 | 252 |
| *of which:* Concessional | 70 | 72 | 90 | 93 | 89 | 92 | 83 | 98 |
| CMEA countries | 80 | 74 | 74 | 67 | 62 | 58 | 45 | 36 |
| *of which:* Concessional | 74 | 66 | 65 | 58 | 54 | 50 | 38 | 29 |
| OPEC countries | 3 | 12 | 19 | 63 | 129 | 126 | 152 | 195 |
| *of which:* Concessional | 2 | 11 | 18 | 62 | 129 | 126 | 152 | 188 |
| Other LDC'S | 9 | 12 | 14 | 17 | 16 | 14 | 12 | 11 |
| *of which:* Concessional | 5 | 1 | 0 | 0 | 0 | 0 | – | – |
| Other and adjustments | – | – | – | – | – | – | – | – |
| **Total Debt Service** | **861** | **851** | **944** | **1067** | **1195** | **1394** | **1380** | **1656** |
| *of which:* Concessional | 433 | 471 | 539 | 679 | 821 | 788 | 786 | 773 |
| Non-concessional | 428 | 380 | 405 | 388 | 373 | 606 | 593 | 882 |

US $ Million

| | 1975 | 1976 | 1977 | 1978 | 1979 | 1980 | 1981 | 1982 |
|---|---|---|---|---|---|---|---|---|
| **DEBT** | | | | | | | | |
| DAC countries and capital | | | | | | | | |
| markets | 6936 | 8749 | 9998 | 11896 | 12156 | 13335 | 13872 | 15896 |
| ODA | 3207 | 3537 | 4173 | 5294 | 5291 | 6086 | 6191 | 6345 |
| Total export credits | 1608 | 2463 | 3335 | 3773 | 4239 | 4604 | 4270 | 4975 |
| Total private | 2121 | 2749 | 2490 | 2829 | 2626 | 2645 | 3411 | 4576 |
| *of which:* Bank loans | 1641 | 2080 | 2080 | 2394 | 2160 | 2100 | 2850 | 3750 |
| Bonds | – | – | – | 106 | 139 | 175 | 201 | 426 |
| Other | 480 | 669 | 410 | 329 | 327 | 370 | 360 | 400 |
| Multilateral | 427 | 718 | 984 | 1191 | 1440 | 1834 | 2250 | 2863 |
| *of which:* Concessional | 367 | 490 | 551 | 585 | 617 | 661 | 730 | 806 |
| CMEA countries | 1060 | 1041 | 1026 | 985 | 944 | 904 | 864 | 822 |
| *of which:* Concessional | 1060 | 1041 | 1026 | 985 | 944 | 904 | 864 | 822 |
| OPEC countries | – | 15 | 132 | 205 | 246 | 223 | 206 | 258 |
| *of which:* Concessional | – | – | 27 | 58 | 63 | 62 | 68 | 68 |
| Other LDC'S | 279 | 188 | 201 | 247 | 308 | 340 | 337 | 322 |
| *of which:* Concessional | 138 | 135 | 132 | 127 | 122 | 128 | 120 | 111 |
| Other and adjustments | – | – | – | – | – | – | – | 209 |
| **Total Debt** | **8702** | **10710** | **12341** | **14524** | **15093** | **16635** | **17529** | **20371** |
| *of which:* Concessional | 4772 | 5203 | 5909 | 7050 | 7037 | 7841 | 7972 | 8152 |
| Non-concessional | 3930 | 5507 | 6432 | 7474 | 8056 | 8794 | 9557 | 12219 |
| | | | | | | | | |
| **DEBT SERVICE** | | | | | | | | |
| DAC countries and capital | | | | | | | | |
| markets | 591 | 856 | 1357 | 1995 | 2185 | 1809 | 2168 | 2414 |
| ODA | 90 | 97 | 149 | 198 | 231 | 279 | 296 | 310 |
| Total export credits | 218 | 396 | 503 | 616 | 910 | 973 | 1197 | 1062 |
| Total private | 283 | 363 | 705 | 1181 | 1044 | 558 | 675 | 1043 |
| *of which:* Bank loans | 263 | 310 | 625 | 1090 | 960 | 455 | 565 | 855 |
| Bonds | – | – | – | 1 | 4 | 18 | 15 | 38 |
| Other | 20 | 53 | 80 | 90 | 80 | 85 | 95 | 150 |
| Multilateral | 4 | 9 | 38 | 72 | 112 | 145 | 185 | 257 |
| *of which:* Concessional | 2 | 4 | 5 | 7 | 9 | 11 | 14 | 14 |
| CMEA countries | 26 | 30 | 32 | 42 | 42 | 42 | 42 | 48 |
| *of which:* Concessional | 26 | 30 | 32 | 42 | 42 | 42 | 42 | 48 |
| OPEC countries | – | 1 | 6 | 34 | 35 | 42 | 42 | 56 |
| *of which:* Concessional | – | – | 1 | 2 | 3 | 7 | 4 | 23 |
| Other LDC'S | 65 | 122 | 4 | 10 | 17 | 44 | 38 | 47 |
| *of which:* Concessional | 6 | 3 | 4 | 5 | 6 | 13 | 9 | 9 |
| Other and adjustments | – | – | – | – | – | – | 4 | 15 |
| **Total Debt Service** | **686** | **1018** | **1438** | **2153** | **2391** | **2081** | **2479** | **2838** |
| *of which:* Concessional | 124 | 135 | 191 | 255 | 291 | 351 | 365 | 404 |
| Non-concessional | 562 | 884 | 1247 | 1898 | 2101 | 1730 | 2114 | 2433 |

# IRAN

| | 1975 | 1976 | 1977 | 1978 | 1979 | 1980 | 1981 | 1982 |
|---|---|---|---|---|---|---|---|---|
| **DEBT** | | | | | | | | |
| DAC countries and capital | | | | | | | | |
| markets | 3740 | 3799 | 6453 | 8853 | 8372 | 8145 | 5552 | 3747 |
| ODA | 191 | 160 | 187 | 304 | 258 | 282 | 245 | 215 |
| Total export credits | 2693 | 2482 | 3742 | 5415 | 5344 | 5209 | 3940 | 3262 |
| Total private | 856 | 1157 | 2524 | 3134 | 2770 | 2654 | 1367 | 270 |
| *of which:* Bank loans | 844 | 1100 | 2400 | 2960 | 2600 | 2520 | 1280 | 200 |
| Bonds | 12 | 38 | 94 | 124 | 120 | 94 | 67 | 50 |
| Other | – | 19 | 30 | 50 | 50 | 40 | 20 | 20 |
| | | | | | | | | |
| Multilateral | 589 | 627 | 655 | 635 | 587 | 539 | 489 | 396 |
| *of which:* Concessional | 69 | 64 | 59 | 54 | 48 | 42 | 35 | 22 |
| | | | | | | | | |
| CMEA countries | 1053 | 1141 | 1203 | 1187 | 1108 | 952 | 763 | 558 |
| *of which:* Concessional | 1027 | 1104 | 1116 | 1101 | 1032 | 886 | 711 | 521 |
| | | | | | | | | |
| OPEC countries | – | – | – | – | – | – | – | – |
| *of which:* Concessional | – | – | – | – | – | – | – | – |
| | | | | | | | | |
| Other LDC'S | 24 | 18 | 17 | 12 | 18 | 20 | 23 | 25 |
| *of which:* Concessional | – | – | – | – | – | – | – | – |
| | | | | | | | | |
| Other and adjustments | 4 | 4 | 12 | 25 | 24 | 313 | 30 | 275 |
| | | | | | | | | |
| **Total Debt** | **5410** | **5589** | **8340** | **10712** | **10109** | **9969** | **6857** | **5001** |
| *of which:* Concessional | 1287 | 1328 | 1362 | 1459 | 1338 | 1210 | 991 | 758 |
| Non-concessional | 4123 | 4261 | 6978 | 9253 | 8771 | 8759 | 5866 | 4243 |
| | | | | | | | | |
| **DEBT SERVICE** | | | | | | | | |
| DAC countries and capital | | | | | | | | |
| markets | 1133 | 1255 | 1726 | 1922 | 1656 | 1655 | 4534 | 2507 |
| ODA | 35 | 32 | 25 | 23 | 32 | 21 | 22 | 22 |
| Total export credits | 934 | 891 | 1523 | 1607 | 1439 | 1338 | 2210 | 1131 |
| Total private | 163 | 332 | 178 | 292 | 185 | 296 | 2302 | 1354 |
| *of which:* Bank loans | 156 | 327 | 160 | 260 | 175 | 250 | 2250 | 1321 |
| Bonds | 7 | 1 | 8 | 7 | – | 34 | 27 | 23 |
| Other | – | 5 | 10 | 25 | 10 | 12 | 25 | 10 |
| | | | | | | | | |
| Multilateral | 62 | 72 | 87 | 98 | 109 | 101 | 486 | 126 |
| *of which:* Concessional | 10 | 10 | 10 | 10 | 11 | 11 | 74 | 16 |
| | | | | | | | | |
| CMEA countries | 161 | 171 | 177 | 170 | 104 | 255 | 256 | 249 |
| *of which:* Concessional | 156 | 164 | 165 | 156 | 83 | 235 | 237 | 231 |
| | | | | | | | | |
| OPEC countries | – | – | – | – | – | – | – | – |
| *of which:* Concessional | – | – | – | – | – | – | – | – |
| | | | | | | | | |
| Other LDC'S | 11 | 9 | 7 | 6 | 5 | 26 | 24 | 23 |
| *of which:* Concessional | – | – | – | – | – | – | – | – |
| | | | | | | | | |
| Other and adjustments | 1 | 1 | 1 | 2 | 1 | 3 | 11 | 11 |
| | | | | | | | | |
| **Total Debt Service** | **1368** | **1508** | **1997** | **2197** | **1875** | **2040** | **5311** | **2916** |
| *of which:* Concessional | 201 | 206 | 200 | 190 | 126 | 267 | 332 | 269 |
| Non-concessional | 1167 | 1302 | 1797 | 2008 | 1749 | 1773 | 4979 | 2648 |

US $ Million

| | 1975 | 1976 | 1977 | 1978 | 1979 | 1980 | 1981 | 1982 |
|---|---|---|---|---|---|---|---|---|
| **DEBT** | | | | | | | | |
| DAC countries and capital | | | | | | | | |
| markets | 790 | 926 | 1155 | 1243 | 1759 | 2041 | 2651 | 1745 |
| ODA | 34 | 38 | 110 | 189 | 153 | 181 | 166 | 155 |
| Total export credits | 656 | 758 | 765 | 824 | 1376 | 1720 | 2420 | 1520 |
| Total private | 100 | 130 | 280 | 230 | 230 | 140 | 65 | 70 |
| of which: Bank loans | 100 | 130 | 280 | 230 | 210 | 120 | 50 | 50 |
| Bonds | – | – | – | – | – | – | – | – |
| Other | – | – | – | – | 20 | 20 | 15 | 20 |
| Multilateral | 29 | 45 | 70 | 81 | 87 | 83 | 79 | 74 |
| of which: Concessional | 15 | 14 | 13 | 11 | 10 | 9 | 8 | 6 |
| CMEA countries | 253 | 249 | 296 | 335 | 329 | 269 | 230 | 167 |
| of which: Concessional | 250 | 248 | 296 | 335 | 329 | 269 | 230 | 167 |
| OPEC countries | 89 | 76 | 53 | 51 | 48 | 44 | 31 | 26 |
| of which: Concessional | 89 | 76 | 53 | 51 | 48 | 44 | 31 | 26 |
| Other LDC'S | – | – | 17 | 35 | 47 | 54 | 52 | 56 |
| of which: Concessional | – | – | 17 | 35 | 47 | 54 | 52 | 56 |
| Other and adjustments | 9 | 4 | – | – | – | – | – | 120 |
| **Total Debt** | **1170** | **1300** | **1591** | **1745** | **2270** | **2491** | **3043** | **2188** |
| of which: Concessional | 388 | 376 | 489 | 621 | 587 | 557 | 487 | 410 |
| Non-concessional | 782 | 924 | 1102 | 1124 | 1683 | 1934 | 2556 | 1778 |
| **DEBT SERVICE** | | | | | | | | |
| DAC countries and capital | | | | | | | | |
| markets | 167 | 427 | 588 | 559 | 631 | 1010 | 1742 | 1822 |
| ODA | 1 | 2 | 4 | 7 | 8 | 7 | 8 | 7 |
| Total export credits | 151 | 412 | 545 | 431 | 544 | 906 | 1642 | 1800 |
| Total private | 15 | 13 | 40 | 121 | 80 | 96 | 93 | 15 |
| of which: Bank loans | 15 | 13 | 40 | 121 | 80 | 90 | 85 | 10 |
| Bonds | – | – | – | – | – | – | – | – |
| Other | – | – | – | – | – | 6 | 8 | 5 |
| Multilateral | 6 | 5 | 8 | 9 | 11 | 11 | 10 | 10 |
| of which: Concessional | 2 | 2 | 2 | 2 | 2 | 2 | 2 | 2 |
| CMEA countries | 40 | 39 | 71 | 72 | 90 | 88 | 81 | 70 |
| of which: Concessional | 37 | 37 | 70 | 72 | 90 | 88 | 81 | 70 |
| OPEC countries | 3 | 3 | 28 | 6 | 6 | 7 | 6 | 6 |
| of which: Concessional | 3 | 3 | 28 | 6 | 6 | 7 | 6 | 6 |
| Other LDC'S | – | – | – | – | – | – | – | – |
| of which: Concessional | – | – | – | – | – | – | – | – |
| Other and adjustments | 6 | 6 | 5 | – | – | – | – | – |
| **Total Debt Service** | **221** | **479** | **700** | **646** | **738** | **1116** | **1839** | **1908** |
| of which: Concessional | 43 | 43 | 104 | 87 | 106 | 105 | 97 | 85 |
| Non-concessional | 179 | 435 | 596 | 559 | 632 | 1011 | 1743 | 1823 |

# ISREAL

|  | 1975 | 1976 | 1977 | 1978 | 1979 | 1980 | 1981 | 1982 |
|---|---|---|---|---|---|---|---|---|
| **DEBT** | | | | | | | | |
| DAC countries and capital | | | | | | | | |
| markets | 4012 | 4848 | 5341 | 6008 | 6640 | 7584 | 8381 | 8864 |
| ODA | 925 | 1098 | 1382 | 1872 | 2445 | 2472 | 2307 | 2306 |
| Total export credits | 378 | 501 | 647 | 767 | 998 | 1195 | 1313 | 1552 |
| Total private | 2709 | 3249 | 3312 | 3369 | 3197 | 3917 | 4761 | 5006 |
| of which: Bank loans | 547 | 1005 | 1089 | 1310 | 1360 | 1500 | 1920 | 2150 |
| Bonds | 2062 | 2062 | 2063 | 1999 | 1767 | 2318 | 2791 | 2806 |
| Other | 100 | 182 | 160 | 60 | 70 | 99 | 50 | 50 |
| Multilateral | 112 | 113 | 110 | 114 | 113 | 111 | 128 | 118 |
| of which: Concessional | 26 | 23 | 20 | 16 | 13 | 10 | 8 | 6 |
| CMEA countries | 3 | 3 | 2 | 1 | 1 | – | – | – |
| of which: Concessional | – | – | – | – | – | – | – | – |
| OPEC countries | – | – | – | – | – | – | – | – |
| of which: Concessional | – | – | – | – | – | – | – | – |
| Other LDC'S | – | – | – | – | – | – | – | – |
| of which: Concessional | – | – | – | – | – | – | – | – |
| Other and adjustments | 1 | 0 | 0 | 0 | 20 | 41 | 13 | – |
| **Total Debt** | **4128** | **4964** | **5454** | **6124** | **6774** | **7737** | **8522** | **8982** |
| of which: Concessional | 951 | 1121 | 1402 | 1888 | 2458 | 2482 | 2315 | 2312 |
| Non-concessional | 3177 | 3843 | 4052 | 4235 | 4316 | 5255 | 6207 | 6669 |
| **DEBT SERVICE** | | | | | | | | |
| DAC countries and capital | | | | | | | | |
| markets | 498 | 320 | 565 | 630 | 1079 | 940 | 1393 | 1506 |
| ODA | 57 | 37 | 68 | 63 | 87 | 110 | 111 | 111 |
| Total export credits | 92 | 120 | 158 | 145 | 212 | 253 | 268 | 287 |
| Total private | 349 | 163 | 339 | 422 | 781 | 577 | 1015 | 1108 |
| of which: Bank loans | 110 | 96 | 140 | 225 | 305 | 380 | 505 | 540 |
| Bonds | 224 | – | 134 | 88 | 441 | 171 | 500 | 543 |
| Other | 15 | 67 | 65 | 109 | 35 | 26 | 10 | 25 |
| Multilateral | 20 | 26 | 22 | 22 | 31 | 25 | 25 | 24 |
| of which: Concessional | 5 | 5 | 5 | 5 | 5 | 3 | 2 | 2 |
| CMEA countries | 1 | 1 | 1 | 1 | 1 | 1 | – | – |
| of which: Concessional | – | – | – | – | – | – | – | – |
| OPEC countries | – | – | – | – | – | – | – | – |
| of which: Concessional | – | – | – | – | – | – | – | – |
| Other LDC'S | – | – | – | – | – | – | – | – |
| of which: Concessional | – | – | – | – | – | – | – | – |
| Other and adjustments | 0 | 0 | 0 | 0 | 0 | 2 | 28 | 14 |
| **Total Debt Service** | **519** | **347** | **587** | **652** | **1111** | **968** | **1446** | **1545** |
| of which: Concessional | 61 | 41 | 73 | 67 | 91 | 114 | 113 | 114 |
| Non-concessional | 458 | 306 | 515 | 585 | 1020 | 855 | 1333 | 1431 |

*US $ Million*

| | 1975 | 1976 | 1977 | 1978 | 1979 | 1980 | 1981 | 1982 |
|---|---|---|---|---|---|---|---|---|
| **DEBT** | | | | | | | | |
| DAC countries and capital | | | | | | | | |
| markets | 788 | 942 | 1713 | 2721 | 3384 | 4000 | 4142 | 4274 |
| ODA | 168 | 165 | 194 | 235 | 281 | 270 | 243 | 261 |
| Total export credits | 295 | 402 | 850 | 1438 | 1785 | 1947 | 1702 | 1515 |
| Total private | 325 | 375 | 669 | 1048 | 1318 | 1783 | 2197 | 2498 |
| *of which:* Bank loans | 301 | 320 | 610 | 983 | 1250 | 1700 | 2120 | 2420 |
| Bonds | 24 | 20 | 19 | 20 | 18 | 28 | 22 | 18 |
| Other | – | 35 | 40 | 45 | 50 | 55 | 55 | 60 |
| Multilateral | 146 | 167 | 236 | 366 | 437 | 580 | 589 | 784 |
| *of which:* Concessional | 29 | 35 | 57 | 99 | 104 | 156 | 147 | 154 |
| CMEA countries | – | – | – | – | – | – | – | – |
| *of which:* Concessional | – | – | – | – | – | – | – | – |
| OPEC countries | – | – | – | – | – | – | – | – |
| *of which:* Concessional | – | – | – | – | – | – | – | – |
| Other LDC'S | 13 | 15 | 13 | 12 | 11 | 23 | 25 | 27 |
| *of which:* Concessional | – | – | – | – | – | – | – | – |
| Other and adjustments | – | 47 | 22 | – | – | 4 | 4 | 127 |
| **Total Debt** | **947** | **1171** | **1985** | **3099** | **3832** | **4607** | **4761** | **5212** |
| *of which:* Concessional | 197 | 200 | 251 | 334 | 385 | 426 | 390 | 415 |
| Non-concessional | 750 | 971 | 1734 | 2766 | 3446 | 4181 | 4371 | 4796 |
| **DEBT SERVICE** | | | | | | | | |
| DAC countries and capital | | | | | | | | |
| markets | 122 | 150 | 257 | 488 | 627 | 842 | 978 | 1005 |
| ODA | 17 | 16 | 11 | 34 | 22 | 25 | 20 | 11 |
| Total export credits | 53 | 50 | 124 | 215 | 272 | 386 | 365 | 352 |
| Total private | 52 | 84 | 122 | 239 | 333 | 432 | 593 | 642 |
| *of which:* Bank loans | 49 | 75 | 113 | 230 | 320 | 420 | 580 | 628 |
| Bonds | 3 | 3 | 3 | 3 | 4 | 2 | 4 | 3 |
| Other | – | 6 | 6 | 6 | 9 | 10 | 9 | 11 |
| Multilateral | 12 | 16 | 20 | 29 | 40 | 49 | 62 | 77 |
| *of which:* Concessional | 2 | 2 | 3 | 4 | 5 | 5 | 5 | 7 |
| CMEA countries | – | – | – | – | – | – | – | – |
| *of which:* Concessional | – | – | – | – | – | – | – | – |
| OPEC countries | – | – | – | – | – | – | – | – |
| *of which:* Concessional | – | – | – | – | – | – | – | – |
| Other LDC'S | 1 | 3 | 2 | 2 | 2 | 3 | 3 | 9 |
| *of which:* Concessional | – | – | – | – | – | – | – | – |
| Other and adjustments | – | 7 | 25 | 22 | – | – | – | 39 |
| **Total Debt Service** | **136** | **176** | **304** | **540** | **669** | **894** | **1043** | **1130** |
| *of which:* Concessional | 19 | 18 | 14 | 38 | 26 | 30 | 26 | 18 |
| Non-concessional | 116 | 158 | 290 | 502 | 643 | 864 | 1017 | 1112 |

# JAMAICA

US $ Million

|  | 1975 | 1976 | 1977 | 1978 | 1979 | 1980 | 1981 | 1982 |
|---|---|---|---|---|---|---|---|---|
| **DEBT** | | | | | | | | |
| DAC countries and capital | | | | | | | | |
| markets | 608 | 749 | 786 | 857 | 861 | 932 | 1009 | 1070 |
| ODA | 73 | 70 | 83 | 164 | 231 | 293 | 352 | 464 |
| Total export credits | 129 | 127 | 150 | 160 | 158 | 168 | 185 | 286 |
| Total private | 406 | 552 | 553 | 533 | 472 | 471 | 472 | 320 |
| *of which:* Bank loans | 293 | 440 | 440 | 440 | 360 | 348 | 360 | 255 |
| Bonds | 63 | 47 | 48 | 33 | 26 | 19 | 14 | 5 |
| Other | 50 | 65 | 65 | 60 | 86 | 104 | 98 | 60 |
| Multilateral | 53 | 73 | 99 | 157 | 194 | 277 | 350 | 486 |
| *of which:* Concessional | 16 | 19 | 25 | 35 | 56 | 89 | 112 | 130 |
| CMEA countries | – | – | – | – | – | – | – | – |
| *of which:* Concessional | – | – | – | – | – | – | – | – |
| OPEC countries | – | 20 | 28 | 29 | 52 | 118 | 128 | 148 |
| *of which:* Concessional | – | – | – | – | 25 | 35 | 35 | 44 |
| Other LDC'S | – | 58 | 60 | 59 | 49 | 45 | 51 | 18 |
| *of which:* Concessional | – | – | 1 | 1 | 1 | 1 | 11 | 8 |
| Other and adjustments | 10 | 10 | 10 | 20 | 20 | 75 | 80 | 50 |
| **Total Debt** | **671** | **910** | **983** | **1122** | **1176** | **1446** | **1619** | **1773** |
| *of which:* Concessional | 89 | 89 | 109 | 201 | 314 | 418 | 509 | 646 |
| Non-concessional | 582 | 821 | 874 | 921 | 862 | 1028 | 1110 | 1127 |
| | | | | | | | | |
| **DEBT SERVICE** | | | | | | | | |
| DAC countries and capital | | | | | | | | |
| markets | 94 | 122 | 133 | 172 | 183 | 149 | 306 | 176 |
| ODA | 6 | 4 | 5 | 6 | 9 | 12 | 17 | 20 |
| Total export credits | 28 | 26 | 37 | 38 | 49 | 54 | 62 | 55 |
| Total private | 60 | 92 | 92 | 128 | 126 | 83 | 227 | 101 |
| *of which:* Bank loans | 47 | 67 | 79 | 101 | 95 | 63 | 212 | 76 |
| Bonds | 9 | 13 | 6 | 19 | 12 | 10 | 2 | 8 |
| Other | 5 | 12 | 6 | 9 | 19 | 9 | 13 | 17 |
| Multilateral | 6 | 7 | 10 | 14 | 19 | 25 | 28 | 38 |
| *of which:* Concessional | 2 | 2 | 2 | 2 | 3 | 3 | 4 | 5 |
| CMEA countries | – | – | – | – | – | – | – | – |
| *of which:* Concessional | – | – | – | – | – | – | – | – |
| OPEC countries | – | – | 1 | 4 | 8 | 11 | 20 | 24 |
| *of which:* Concessional | – | – | – | – | – | – | 1 | 3 |
| Other LDC'S | – | – | 5 | 6 | 15 | 8 | 6 | 17 |
| *of which:* Concessional | – | – | – | – | – | – | – | 1 |
| Other and adjustments | – | – | – | – | – | 0 | 0 | 0 |
| **Total Debt Service** | **100** | **129** | **149** | **196** | **225** | **193** | **360** | **255** |
| *of which:* Concessional | 7 | 6 | 7 | 8 | 11 | 15 | 22 | 29 |
| Non-concessional | 93 | 123 | 142 | 189 | 214 | 178 | 338 | 225 |

*US $ Million*

| | 1975 | 1976 | 1977 | 1978 | 1979 | 1980 | 1981 | 1982 |
|---|---|---|---|---|---|---|---|---|
| **DEBT** | | | | | | | | |
| DAC countries and capital | | | | | | | | |
|   markets | 236 | 315 | 558 | 835 | 900 | 1255 | 1428 | 1509 |
|   ODA | 169 | 198 | 262 | 342 | 425 | 457 | 471 | 488 |
|   Total export credits | 58 | 114 | 194 | 365 | 370 | 738 | 847 | 871 |
|   Total private | 9 | 3 | 102 | 128 | 105 | 60 | 110 | 150 |
|   *of which:* Bank loans | 9 | 3 | 102 | 128 | 105 | 60 | 110 | 150 |
|     Bonds | – | – | – | – | – | – | – | – |
|     Other | – | – | – | – | – | – | – | – |
| Multilateral | 33 | 45 | 56 | 73 | 106 | 159 | 207 | 263 |
|   *of which:* Concessional | 33 | 45 | 56 | 73 | 96 | 113 | 137 | 155 |
| CMEA countries | – | – | – | – | – | 0 | 0 | 1 |
|   *of which:* Concessional | – | – | – | – | – | 0 | 0 | 1 |
| OPEC countries | 73 | 91 | 124 | 192 | 270 | 319 | 363 | 425 |
|   *of which:* Concessional | 70 | 88 | 122 | 183 | 262 | 297 | 340 | 403 |
| Other LDC'S | 2 | 5 | 8 | 8 | 8 | 8 | 8 | 7 |
|   *of which:* Concessional | – | – | – | – | – | – | – | – |
| Other and adjustments | 2 | 1 | 1 | 1 | 0 | 0 | – | – |
| **Total Debt** | **345** | **456** | **747** | **1109** | **1285** | **1741** | **2007** | **2205** |
|   *of which:* Concessional | 271 | 331 | 440 | 597 | 783 | 866 | 948 | 1047 |
|     Non-concessional | 74 | 126 | 307 | 511 | 502 | 875 | 1058 | 1158 |
| **DEBT SERVICE** | | | | | | | | |
| DAC countries and capital | | | | | | | | |
|   markets | 42 | 33 | 45 | 62 | 132 | 416 | 568 | 409 |
|   ODA | 7 | 7 | 8 | 14 | 19 | 17 | 21 | 23 |
|   Total export credits | 33 | 26 | 23 | 19 | 76 | 345 | 523 | 354 |
|   Total private | 2 | 1 | 14 | 28 | 37 | 54 | 25 | 32 |
|   *of which:* Bank loans | 2 | 1 | 14 | 28 | 37 | 54 | 25 | 32 |
|     Bonds | – | – | – | – | – | – | – | – |
|     Other | – | – | – | – | – | – | – | – |
| Multilateral | 0 | 0 | 1 | 2 | 3 | 7 | 9 | 13 |
|   *of which:* Concessional | 0 | 0 | 1 | 2 | 2 | 5 | 5 | 6 |
| CMEA countries | – | – | – | – | – | – | 0 | 0 |
|   *of which:* Concessional | – | – | – | – | – | – | 0 | 0 |
| OPEC countries | 2 | 5 | 6 | 9 | 15 | 19 | 26 | 25 |
|   *of which:* Concessional | 1 | 4 | 6 | 8 | 11 | 15 | 22 | 21 |
| Other LDC'S | – | 0 | 0 | 1 | 1 | – | 1 | 1 |
|   *of which:* Concessional | – | – | – | – | – | – | – | – |
| Other and adjustments | 0 | 0 | 0 | 0 | 0 | 0 | 0 | – |
| **Total Debt Service** | **44** | **39** | **53** | **73** | **151** | **441** | **604** | **448** |
|   *of which:* Concessional | 9 | 11 | 14 | 24 | 32 | 36 | 48 | 50 |
|     Non-concessional | 35 | 28 | 39 | 49 | 119 | 405 | 556 | 398 |

# KAMPUCHEA

US $ Million

| | 1975 | 1976 | 1977 | 1978 | 1979 | 1980 | 1981 | 1982 |
|---|---|---|---|---|---|---|---|---|
| **DEBT** | | | | | | | | |
| DAC countries and capital | | | | | | | | |
| markets | 31 | 28 | 36 | 249 | 251 | 251 | 244 | 240 |
| ODA | 25 | 23 | 31 | 243 | 245 | 245 | 239 | 236 |
| Total export credits | 6 | 5 | 5 | 6 | 6 | 6 | 5 | 4 |
| Total private | – | – | – | – | – | – | – | – |
| of which: Bank loans | – | – | – | – | – | – | – | – |
| Bonds | – | – | – | – | – | – | – | – |
| Other | – | – | – | – | – | – | – | – |
| Multilateral | – | – | – | – | – | – | – | – |
| of which: Concessional | – | – | – | – | – | – | – | – |
| CMEA countries | – | – | – | – | – | – | – | – |
| of which: Concessional | – | – | – | – | – | – | – | – |
| OPEC countries | – | – | – | – | – | – | – | – |
| of which: Concessional | – | – | – | – | – | – | – | – |
| Other LDC'S | – | – | – | – | – | – | – | – |
| of which: Concessional | – | – | – | – | – | – | – | – |
| Other and adjustments | – | – | – | – | – | – | – | 1 |
| **Total Debt** | **31** | **28** | **36** | **249** | **251** | **251** | **244** | **241** |
| of which: Concessional | 25 | 23 | 31 | 243 | 245 | 245 | 239 | 236 |
| Non-concessional | 6 | 5 | 5 | 6 | 6 | 6 | 5 | 5 |
| **DEBT SERVICE** | | | | | | | | |
| DAC countries and capital | | | | | | | | |
| markets | 2 | – | 0 | 0 | – | 1 | 0 | – |
| ODA | 0 | – | – | – | – | – | – | – |
| Total export credits | 2 | – | 0 | 0 | – | 1 | 0 | – |
| Total private | – | – | – | – | – | – | – | – |
| of which: Bank loans | – | – | – | – | – | – | – | – |
| Bonds | – | – | – | – | – | – | – | – |
| Other | – | – | – | – | – | – | – | – |
| Multilateral | – | – | – | – | – | – | – | – |
| of which: Concessional | – | – | – | – | – | – | – | – |
| CMEA countries | – | – | – | – | – | – | – | – |
| of which: Concessional | – | – | – | – | – | – | – | – |
| OPEC countries | – | – | – | – | – | – | – | – |
| of which: Concessional | – | – | – | – | – | – | – | – |
| Other LDC'S | – | – | – | – | – | – | – | – |
| of which: Concessional | – | – | – | – | – | – | – | – |
| Other and adjustments | – | – | – | – | – | – | – | – |
| **Total Debt Service** | **2** | **–** | **0** | **0** | **–** | **1** | **0** | **–** |
| of which: Concessional | 0 | – | – | – | – | – | – | – |
| Non-concessional | 2 | – | 0 | 0 | – | 1 | 0 | – |

# KENYA

| | 1975 | 1976 | 1977 | 1978 | 1979 | 1980 | 1981 | 1982 |
|---|---|---|---|---|---|---|---|---|
| **DEBT** | | | | | | | | |
| DAC countries and capital | | | | | | | | |
| markets | 481 | 622 | 808 | 887 | 1248 | 1459 | 1555 | 1496 |
| ODA | 287 | 295 | 325 | 394 | 489 | 536 | 573 | 639 |
| Total export credits | 137 | 278 | 429 | 474 | 620 | 730 | 654 | 592 |
| Total private | 57 | 49 | 54 | 19 | 139 | 193 | 328 | 265 |
| of which: Bank loans | 6 | 10 | 10 | 10 | 129 | 182 | 320 | 265 |
| Bonds | 51 | 39 | 44 | 9 | 10 | 11 | 8 | 0 |
| Other | – | – | – | – | – | – | – | – |
| Multilateral | 190 | 273 | 344 | 457 | 551 | 699 | 766 | 937 |
| of which: Concessional | 85 | 102 | 132 | 185 | 241 | 349 | 370 | 460 |
| CMEA countries | 0 | 0 | 0 | 0 | 0 | 0 | 0 | 0 |
| of which: Concessional | 0 | 0 | 0 | 0 | 0 | 0 | 0 | 0 |
| OPEC countries | – | – | – | – | – | – | 8 | 13 |
| of which: Concessional | – | – | – | – | – | – | 8 | 13 |
| Other LDC'S | 3 | 15 | 28 | 35 | 32 | 26 | 24 | 23 |
| of which: Concessional | – | – | – | – | – | – | – | – |
| Other and adjustments | – | – | – | – | – | – | – | 40 |
| **Total Debt** | **675** | **911** | **1180** | **1379** | **1831** | **2184** | **2353** | **2509** |
| of which: Concessional | 372 | 397 | 458 | 579 | 730 | 885 | 951 | 1113 |
| Non-concessional | 302 | 514 | 722 | 800 | 1101 | 1300 | 1402 | 1397 |
| **DEBT SERVICE** | | | | | | | | |
| DAC countries and capital | | | | | | | | |
| markets | 86 | 71 | 82 | 140 | 143 | 270 | 326 | 295 |
| ODA | 20 | 19 | 20 | 18 | 19 | 19 | 17 | 20 |
| Total export credits | 59 | 47 | 58 | 82 | 115 | 230 | 234 | 143 |
| Total private | 7 | 5 | 5 | 40 | 8 | 21 | 75 | 132 |
| of which: Bank loans | 4 | – | 3 | 4 | 7 | 19 | 75 | 125 |
| Bonds | 2 | 5 | 2 | 36 | 1 | 1 | 0 | 7 |
| Other | – | – | – | – | – | – | – | – |
| Multilateral | 7 | 16 | 20 | 28 | 38 | 48 | 50 | 59 |
| of which: Concessional | 1 | 1 | 2 | 2 | 3 | 4 | 5 | 6 |
| CMEA countries | 0 | 0 | 0 | 0 | 0 | 0 | 0 | 0 |
| of which: Concessional | 0 | 0 | 0 | 0 | 0 | 0 | 0 | 0 |
| OPEC countries | – | – | – | – | – | – | 0 | 0 |
| of which: Concessional | – | – | – | – | – | – | 0 | 0 |
| Other LDC'S | 0 | 0 | 1 | 2 | 5 | 6 | 3 | 3 |
| of which: Concessional | – | – | – | – | – | – | – | – |
| Other and adjustments | – | – | – | – | – | – | – | – |
| **Total Debt Service** | **93** | **87** | **103** | **170** | **185** | **324** | **379** | **357** |
| of which: Concessional | 21 | 20 | 21 | 20 | 23 | 23 | 22 | 26 |
| Non-concessional | 73 | 67 | 82 | 150 | 162 | 301 | 357 | 331 |

US $ Million

| | 1975 | 1976 | 1977 | 1978 | 1979 | 1980 | 1981 | 1982 |
|---|---|---|---|---|---|---|---|---|
| **DEBT** | | | | | | | | |
| DAC countries and capital | | | | | | | | |
| markets | 5017 | 5928 | 7992 | 10911 | 13192 | 15050 | 17169 | 18505 |
| ODA | 1716 | 1885 | 2185 | 2612 | 2441 | 2709 | 2873 | 2755 |
| Total export credits | 1943 | 2449 | 3733 | 5147 | 6015 | 6034 | 5953 | 6548 |
| Total private | 1358 | 1594 | 2074 | 3152 | 4736 | 6307 | 8343 | 9202 |
| of which: Bank loans | 1258 | 1345 | 1752 | 2770 | 4337 | 5712 | 7800 | 8650 |
| Bonds | – | 49 | 122 | 182 | 149 | 200 | 193 | 202 |
| Other | 100 | 200 | 200 | 200 | 250 | 395 | 350 | 350 |
| Multilateral | 690 | 1046 | 1295 | 1660 | 2109 | 2347 | 2711 | 3340 |
| of which: Concessional | 135 | 162 | 190 | 196 | 198 | 196 | 194 | 192 |
| CMEA countries | – | – | – | – | – | – | – | – |
| of which: Concessional | – | – | – | – | – | – | – | – |
| OPEC countries | 19 | 44 | 65 | 120 | 150 | 155 | 135 | 127 |
| of which: Concessional | – | – | 21 | 36 | 55 | 64 | 65 | 60 |
| Other LDC'S | 20 | 22 | 23 | 24 | 21 | 17 | 14 | 10 |
| of which: Concessional | – | – | – | – | – | – | – | – |
| Other and adjustments | 17 | 214 | 116 | 14 | 12 | 11 | 7 | 3 |
| **Total Debt** | **5762** | **7255** | **9492** | **12729** | **15484** | **17579** | **20036** | **21985** |
| of which: Concessional | 1851 | 2047 | 2396 | 2843 | 2694 | 2970 | 3132 | 3006 |
| Non-concessional | 3911 | 5208 | 7096 | 9886 | 12790 | 14610 | 16904 | 18979 |
| | | | | | | | | |
| **DEBT SERVICE** | | | | | | | | |
| DAC countries and capital | | | | | | | | |
| markets | 634 | 833 | 1150 | 1809 | 2683 | 2994 | 3555 | 4087 |
| ODA | 71 | 76 | 106 | 130 | 150 | 156 | 175 | 179 |
| Total export credits | 429 | 545 | 650 | 1073 | 1613 | 1658 | 1738 | 1696 |
| Total private | 134 | 212 | 395 | 605 | 919 | 1180 | 1643 | 2211 |
| of which: Bank loans | 134 | 150 | 362 | 563 | 850 | 1110 | 1542 | 2085 |
| Bonds | – | 2 | 2 | 12 | 39 | 12 | 41 | 36 |
| Other | – | 60 | 30 | 30 | 30 | 59 | 60 | 90 |
| Multilateral | 49 | 79 | 120 | 168 | 227 | 298 | 341 | 414 |
| of which: Concessional | 3 | 5 | 6 | 8 | 8 | 8 | 8 | 8 |
| CMEA countries | – | – | – | – | – | – | – | – |
| of which: Concessional | – | – | – | – | – | – | – | – |
| OPEC countries | 2 | 4 | 4 | 6 | 17 | 15 | 33 | 15 |
| of which: Concessional | – | – | 0 | 1 | 1 | 5 | 8 | 7 |
| Other LDC'S | 2 | 2 | 4 | 5 | 5 | 5 | 5 | 4 |
| of which: Concessional | – | – | – | – | – | – | – | – |
| Other and adjustments | 1 | 4 | 4 | 3 | 4 | 5 | 4 | 3 |
| **Total Debt Service** | **689** | **922** | **1282** | **1991** | **2936** | **3317** | **3938** | **4523** |
| of which: Concessional | 74 | 80 | 112 | 138 | 159 | 168 | 190 | 195 |
| Non-concessional | 615 | 842 | 1170 | 1852 | 2776 | 3149 | 3748 | 4329 |

# KUWAIT

US $ Million

| | 1975 | 1976 | 1977 | 1978 | 1979 | 1980 | 1981 | 1982 |
|---|---|---|---|---|---|---|---|---|
| **DEBT** | | | | | | | | |
| DAC countries and capital markets | 253 | 240 | 234 | 377 | 532 | 653 | 850 | 1310 |
| ODA | – | – | – | – | – | – | – | – |
| Total export credits | 233 | 210 | 194 | 277 | 382 | 493 | 675 | 980 |
| Total private | 20 | 30 | 40 | 100 | 150 | 160 | 175 | 330 |
| of which: Bank loans | 20 | 30 | 40 | 100 | 150 | 160 | 175 | 330 |
| Bonds | – | – | – | – | – | – | – | – |
| Other | – | – | – | – | – | – | – | – |
| Multilateral | – | – | – | – | – | – | – | – |
| of which: Concessional | – | – | – | – | – | – | – | – |
| CMEA countries | – | – | – | – | – | – | – | – |
| of which: Concessional | – | – | – | – | – | – | – | – |
| OPEC countries | – | – | – | – | – | – | – | – |
| of which: Concessional | – | – | – | – | – | – | – | – |
| Other LDC'S | – | – | – | – | – | – | – | – |
| of which: Concessional | – | – | – | – | – | – | – | – |
| Other and adjustments | – | – | – | – | – | – | – | – |
| **Total Debt** | **253** | **240** | **234** | **377** | **532** | **653** | **850** | **1310** |
| of which: Concessional | – | – | – | – | – | – | – | – |
| Non-concessional | 253 | 240 | 234 | 377 | 532 | 653 | 850 | 1310 |
| **DEBT SERVICE** | | | | | | | | |
| DAC countries and capital markets | 111 | 83 | 115 | 154 | 177 | 263 | 376 | 484 |
| ODA | – | – | – | – | – | – | – | – |
| Total export credits | 109 | 78 | 109 | 142 | 157 | 239 | 319 | 424 |
| Total private | 2 | 5 | 6 | 12 | 20 | 24 | 57 | 60 |
| of which: Bank loans | 2 | 5 | 6 | 12 | 20 | 24 | 57 | 60 |
| Bonds | – | – | – | – | – | – | – | – |
| Other | – | – | – | – | – | – | – | – |
| Multilateral | – | – | – | – | – | – | – | – |
| of which: Concessional | – | – | – | – | – | – | – | – |
| CMEA countries | – | – | – | – | – | – | – | – |
| of which: Concessional | – | – | – | – | – | – | – | – |
| OPEC countries | – | – | – | – | – | – | – | – |
| of which: Concessional | – | – | – | – | – | – | – | – |
| Other LDC'S | – | – | – | – | – | – | – | – |
| of which: Concessional | – | – | – | – | – | – | – | – |
| Other and adjustments | – | – | – | – | – | – | – | – |
| **Total Debt Service** | **111** | **83** | **115** | **154** | **177** | **263** | **376** | **484** |
| of which: Concessional | – | – | – | – | – | – | – | – |
| Non-concessional | 111 | 83 | 115 | 154 | 177 | 263 | 376 | 484 |

# LAO PDR

| | 1975 | 1976 | 1977 | 1978 | 1979 | 1980 | 1981 | 1982 |
|---|---|---|---|---|---|---|---|---|
| **DEBT** | | | | | | | | |
| DAC countries and capital | | | | | | | | |
| markets | 25 | 35 | 48 | 77 | 77 | 75 | 65 | 59 |
| ODA | 20 | 29 | 44 | 72 | 72 | 70 | 61 | 56 |
| Total export credits | 5 | 6 | 4 | 5 | 5 | 5 | 4 | 3 |
| Total private | – | – | – | – | – | – | – | – |
| of which: Bank loans | – | – | – | – | – | – | – | – |
| Bonds | – | – | – | – | – | – | – | – |
| Other | – | – | – | – | – | – | – | – |
| Multilateral | – | – | – | – | – | – | – | – |
| of which: Concessional | – | – | – | – | – | – | – | – |
| CMEA countries | – | – | – | – | – | – | – | – |
| of which: Concessional | – | – | – | – | – | – | – | – |
| OPEC countries | – | – | – | – | – | – | – | – |
| of which: Concessional | – | – | – | – | – | – | – | – |
| Other LDC'S | – | – | – | – | – | – | – | – |
| of which: Concessional | – | – | – | – | – | – | – | – |
| Other and adjustments | – | – | – | – | – | – | – | 1 |
| **Total Debt** | **25** | **35** | **48** | **77** | **77** | **75** | **65** | **60** |
| of which: Concessional | 20 | 29 | 44 | 72 | 72 | 70 | 61 | 56 |
| Non-concessional | 5 | 6 | 4 | 5 | 5 | 5 | 4 | 4 |
| **DEBT SERVICE** | | | | | | | | |
| DAC countries and capital | | | | | | | | |
| markets | 2 | 2 | 3 | 2 | 3 | 2 | 2 | 2 |
| ODA | 1 | 1 | 1 | 2 | 1 | 2 | 2 | 2 |
| Total export credits | 2 | 1 | 2 | 0 | 2 | 1 | 0 | – |
| Total private | – | – | – | – | – | – | – | – |
| of which: Bank loans | – | – | – | – | – | – | – | – |
| Bonds | – | – | – | – | – | – | – | – |
| Other | – | – | – | – | – | – | – | – |
| Multilateral | – | – | – | – | – | – | – | – |
| of which: Concessional | – | – | – | – | – | – | – | – |
| CMEA countries | – | – | – | – | – | – | – | – |
| of which: Concessional | – | – | – | – | – | – | – | – |
| OPEC countries | – | – | – | – | – | – | – | – |
| of which: Concessional | – | – | – | – | – | – | – | – |
| Other LDC'S | – | – | – | – | – | – | – | – |
| of which: Concessional | – | – | – | – | – | – | – | – |
| Other and adjustments | – | – | – | – | – | – | – | – |
| **Total Debt Service** | **2** | **2** | **3** | **2** | **3** | **2** | **2** | **2** |
| of which: Concessional | 1 | 1 | 1 | 2 | 1 | 2 | 2 | 2 |
| Non-concessional | 2 | 1 | 2 | 0 | 2 | 1 | 0 | – |

# LEBANON

US $ Million

| | 1975 | 1976 | 1977 | 1978 | 1979 | 1980 | 1981 | 1982 |
|---|---|---|---|---|---|---|---|---|
| **DEBT** | | | | | | | | |
| DAC countries and capital | | | | | | | | |
| markets | 95 | 98 | 72 | 100 | 107 | 194 | 308 | 271 |
| ODA | 13 | 13 | 16 | 20 | 22 | 32 | 39 | 35 |
| Total export credits | 82 | 85 | 56 | 72 | 74 | 91 | 177 | 166 |
| Total private | – | – | – | 8 | 11 | 71 | 92 | 70 |
| of which: Bank loans | – | – | – | 8 | 11 | 71 | 92 | 70 |
| Bonds | – | – | – | – | – | – | – | – |
| Other | – | – | – | – | – | – | – | – |
| Multilateral | 16 | 14 | 12 | 17 | 61 | 75 | 85 | 87 |
| of which: Concessional | 10 | 8 | 6 | 12 | 42 | 43 | 43 | 40 |
| CMEA countries | – | – | – | – | – | – | – | – |
| of which: Concessional | – | – | – | – | – | – | – | – |
| OPEC countries | 14 | 12 | 9 | 7 | 10 | 11 | 12 | 11 |
| of which: Concessional | 14 | 12 | 9 | 7 | 10 | 11 | 12 | 11 |
| Other LDC'S | – | – | – | – | – | – | – | – |
| of which: Concessional | – | – | – | – | – | – | – | – |
| Other and adjustments | – | – | – | – | – | – | – | – |
| **Total Debt** | **125** | **123** | **93** | **124** | **177** | **280** | **404** | **369** |
| of which: Concessional | 38 | 33 | 32 | 39 | 74 | 86 | 94 | 86 |
| Non-concessional | 87 | 90 | 61 | 85 | 103 | 194 | 310 | 283 |
| **DEBT SERVICE** | | | | | | | | |
| DAC countries and capital | | | | | | | | |
| markets | 38 | 23 | 41 | 38 | 14 | 17 | 74 | 73 |
| ODA | 1 | 0 | 3 | 4 | 1 | 3 | 3 | 1 |
| Total export credits | 38 | 22 | 37 | 34 | 13 | 14 | 39 | 33 |
| Total private | – | – | – | 0 | 0 | 1 | 33 | 39 |
| of which: Bank loans | – | – | – | 0 | 0 | 1 | 33 | 39 |
| Bonds | – | – | – | – | – | – | – | – |
| Other | – | – | – | – | – | – | – | – |
| Multilateral | 3 | 3 | 3 | 3 | 5 | 7 | 9 | 15 |
| of which: Concessional | 2 | 2 | 2 | 2 | 3 | 4 | 2 | 6 |
| CMEA countries | – | – | – | – | – | – | – | – |
| of which: Concessional | – | – | – | – | – | – | – | – |
| OPEC countries | 3 | 3 | 3 | 3 | 3 | 2 | 2 | 2 |
| of which: Concessional | 3 | 3 | 3 | 3 | 3 | 2 | 2 | 2 |
| Other LDC'S | – | – | – | – | – | – | – | – |
| of which: Concessional | – | – | – | – | – | – | – | – |
| Other and adjustments | – | – | – | – | – | – | – | – |
| **Total Debt Service** | **44** | **29** | **47** | **44** | **21** | **26** | **86** | **89** |
| of which: Concessional | 6 | 6 | 9 | 9 | 7 | 9 | 7 | 9 |
| Non-concessional | 38 | 23 | 38 | 35 | 14 | 17 | 79 | 81 |

*US $ Million*

| | 1975 | 1976 | 1977 | 1978 | 1979 | 1980 | 1981 | 1982 |
|---|---|---|---|---|---|---|---|---|
| **DEBT** | | | | | | | | |
| DAC countries and capital | | | | | | | | |
| markets | 1 | 1 | 2 | 2 | 9 | 21 | 27 | 24 |
| ODA | 1 | 1 | 1 | 1 | 4 | 3 | 3 | 3 |
| Total export credits | – | – | 1 | 1 | 3 | 4 | 9 | 11 |
| Total private | – | – | – | – | 2 | 14 | 15 | 10 |
| *of which:* Bank loans | – | – | – | – | 2 | 14 | 15 | 10 |
| Bonds | – | – | – | – | – | – | – | – |
| Other | – | – | – | – | – | – | – | – |
| Multilateral | 11 | 14 | 21 | 29 | 38 | 46 | 79 | 108 |
| *of which:* Concessional | 11 | 14 | 21 | 29 | 38 | 46 | 68 | 90 |
| CMEA countries | – | – | – | – | – | – | – | – |
| *of which:* Concessional | – | – | – | – | – | – | – | – |
| OPEC countries | – | – | 1 | 1 | 1 | 1 | 1 | 3 |
| *of which:* Concessional | – | – | – | 0 | 0 | 0 | 1 | 3 |
| Other LDC'S | – | – | – | – | – | 1 | 2 | 1 |
| *of which:* Concessional | – | – | – | – | – | – | – | – |
| Other and adjustments | 1 | 1 | 1 | 1 | 5 | 5 | 3 | 16 |
| **Total Debt** | **13** | **16** | **24** | **32** | **54** | **73** | **112** | **152** |
| *of which:* Concessional | 13 | 15 | 22 | 30 | 43 | 50 | 72 | 96 |
| Non-concessional | 0 | 0 | 2 | 2 | 11 | 23 | 40 | 56 |
| **DEBT SERVICE** | | | | | | | | |
| DAC countries and capital | | | | | | | | |
| markets | 0 | 0 | 0 | 1 | 1 | 3 | 4 | 8 |
| ODA | 0 | 0 | 0 | – | – | – | – | – |
| Total export credits | 0 | – | – | 1 | 1 | 1 | 1 | 1 |
| Total private | 0 | – | 0 | – | 0 | 2 | 4 | 7 |
| *of which:* Bank loans | 0 | – | 0 | – | 0 | 2 | 4 | 7 |
| Bonds | – | – | – | – | – | – | – | – |
| Other | – | – | – | – | – | – | – | – |
| Multilateral | 0 | 0 | 0 | 0 | 0 | 1 | 1 | 1 |
| *of which:* Concessional | 0 | 0 | 0 | 0 | 0 | 0 | 1 | 1 |
| CMEA countries | – | – | – | – | – | – | – | – |
| *of which:* Concessional | – | – | – | – | – | – | – | – |
| OPEC countries | – | – | – | 0 | 0 | 0 | 0 | 0 |
| *of which:* Concessional | – | – | – | – | 0 | 0 | 0 | 0 |
| Other LDC'S | – | – | – | – | – | – | 3 | 1 |
| *of which:* Concessional | – | – | – | – | – | – | – | – |
| Other and adjustments | 0 | 0 | 0 | 0 | 0 | 2 | 1 | 2 |
| **Total Debt Service** | **0** | **0** | **0** | **1** | **2** | **6** | **10** | **11** |
| *of which:* Concessional | 0 | 0 | 0 | 0 | 0 | 1 | 1 | 1 |
| Non-concessional | 0 | 0 | 0 | 1 | 1 | 5 | 9 | 10 |

# LIBERIA

*US $ Million*

| | 1975 | 1976 | 1977 | 1978 | 1979 | 1980 | 1981 | 1982 |
|---|---|---|---|---|---|---|---|---|
| **DEBT** | | | | | | | | |
| DAC countries and capital | | | | | | | | |
| markets | 137 | 157 | 197 | 244 | 310 | 345 | 377 | 402 |
| ODA | 83 | 91 | 105 | 119 | 132 | 155 | 180 | 201 |
| Total export credits | 44 | 56 | 49 | 44 | 50 | 49 | 42 | 59 |
| Total private | 10 | 10 | 43 | 81 | 128 | 141 | 155 | 142 |
| *of which:* Bank loans | 10 | 10 | 43 | 81 | 128 | 131 | 135 | 122 |
| Bonds | – | – | – | – | – | – | – | – |
| Other | – | – | – | – | – | 10 | 20 | 20 |
| Multilateral | 34 | 43 | 59 | 85 | 128 | 166 | 190 | 203 |
| *of which:* Concessional | 11 | 13 | 21 | 37 | 57 | 76 | 81 | 87 |
| CMEA countries | – | – | – | – | – | – | – | – |
| *of which:* Concessional | – | – | – | – | – | – | – | – |
| OPEC countries | – | – | – | – | 12 | 22 | 25 | 26 |
| *of which:* Concessional | – | – | – | – | 12 | 22 | 25 | 26 |
| Other LDC'S | 4 | 10 | 9 | 9 | 9 | 9 | 9 | 9 |
| *of which:* Concessional | – | – | – | – | – | – | – | – |
| Other and adjustments | – | – | – | – | – | – | – | – |
| **Total Debt** | **175** | **210** | **266** | **338** | **459** | **542** | **601** | **641** |
| *of which:* Concessional | 94 | 104 | 126 | 156 | 201 | 253 | 286 | 314 |
| Non-concessional | 81 | 106 | 139 | 182 | 258 | 289 | 315 | 326 |
| | | | | | | | | |
| **DEBT SERVICE** | | | | | | | | |
| DAC countries and capital | | | | | | | | |
| markets | 28 | 16 | 23 | 21 | 69 | 34 | 25 | 24 |
| ODA | 5 | 6 | 5 | 5 | 6 | 5 | 6 | 4 |
| Total export credits | 20 | 8 | 13 | 8 | 6 | 6 | 3 | 5 |
| Total private | 3 | 2 | 5 | 8 | 57 | 22 | 17 | 15 |
| *of which:* Bank loans | 3 | 2 | 5 | 8 | 57 | 22 | 17 | 12 |
| Bonds | – | – | – | – | – | – | – | – |
| Other | – | – | – | – | – | – | – | 3 |
| Multilateral | 4 | 4 | 5 | 7 | 9 | 8 | 9 | 13 |
| *of which:* Concessional | 1 | 1 | 1 | 1 | 1 | 1 | 1 | 2 |
| CMEA countries | – | – | – | – | – | – | – | – |
| *of which:* Concessional | – | – | – | – | – | – | – | – |
| OPEC countries | – | – | – | – | 0 | 0 | 0 | 1 |
| *of which:* Concessional | – | – | – | – | 0 | 0 | 0 | 1 |
| Other LDC'S | 0 | 0 | 0 | – | – | – | – | – |
| *of which:* Concessional | – | – | – | – | – | – | – | – |
| Other and adjustments | – | – | – | – | – | – | – | – |
| **Total Debt Service** | **32** | **21** | **28** | **28** | **79** | **42** | **34** | **38** |
| *of which:* Concessional | 6 | 7 | 6 | 6 | 8 | 7 | 7 | 7 |
| Non-concessional | 26 | 14 | 22 | 22 | 71 | 35 | 27 | 31 |

US $ Million

| | 1975 | 1976 | 1977 | 1978 | 1979 | 1980 | 1981 | 1982 |
|---|---|---|---|---|---|---|---|---|
| **DEBT** | | | | | | | | |
| DAC countries and capital | | | | | | | | |
|   markets | 264 | 555 | 744 | 1048 | 1046 | 1139 | 1308 | 824 |
|   ODA | – | – | – | – | – | – | – | – |
|   Total export credits | 264 | 525 | 694 | 988 | 966 | 1079 | 1258 | 754 |
|   Total private | – | 30 | 50 | 60 | 80 | 60 | 50 | 70 |
|     *of which:* Bank loans | – | – | – | – | – | – | – | – |
|     Bonds | – | – | – | – | – | – | – | – |
|     Other | – | 30 | 50 | 60 | 80 | 60 | 50 | 70 |
| Multilateral | – | – | – | – | – | – | – | – |
|   *of which:* Concessional | – | – | – | – | – | – | – | – |
| CMEA countries | – | – | – | – | – | – | – | – |
|   *of which:* Concessional | – | – | – | – | – | – | – | – |
| OPEC countries | – | – | – | – | – | – | – | – |
|   *of which:* Concessional | – | – | – | – | – | – | – | – |
| Other LDC'S | – | – | – | – | – | – | – | – |
|   *of which:* Concessional | – | – | – | – | – | – | – | – |
| Other and adjustments | – | – | – | – | – | – | – | 20 |
| **Total Debt** | **264** | **555** | **744** | **1048** | **1046** | **1139** | **1308** | **844** |
|   *of which:* Concessional | – | – | – | – | – | – | – | – |
|   Non-concessional | 264 | 555 | 744 | 1048 | 1046 | 1139 | 1308 | 844 |
| | | | | | | | | |
| **DEBT SERVICE** | | | | | | | | |
| DAC countries and capital | | | | | | | | |
|   markets | 278 | 239 | 473 | 614 | 824 | 925 | 1074 | 1060 |
|   ODA | – | – | – | – | – | – | – | – |
|   Total export credits | 278 | 229 | 458 | 596 | 804 | 900 | 1044 | 1040 |
|   Total private | – | 10 | 15 | 18 | 20 | 25 | 30 | 20 |
|     *of which:* Bank loans | – | – | – | – | – | – | – | – |
|     Bonds | – | – | – | – | – | – | – | – |
|     Other | – | 10 | 15 | 18 | 20 | 25 | 30 | 20 |
| Multilateral | – | – | – | – | – | – | – | – |
|   *of which:* Concessional | – | – | – | – | – | – | – | – |
| CMEA countries | – | – | – | – | – | – | – | – |
|   *of which:* Concessional | – | – | – | – | – | – | – | – |
| OPEC countries | – | – | – | – | – | – | – | – |
|   *of which:* Concessional | – | – | – | – | – | – | – | – |
| Other LDC'S | – | – | – | – | – | – | – | – |
|   *of which:* Concessional | – | – | – | – | – | – | – | – |
| Other and adjustments | – | – | – | – | – | – | – | – |
| **Total Debt Service** | **278** | **239** | **473** | **614** | **824** | **925** | **1074** | **1060** |
|   *of which:* Concessional | – | – | – | – | – | – | – | – |
|   Non-concessional | 278 | 239 | 473 | 614 | 824 | 925 | 1074 | 1060 |

# MACAO

| | 1975 | 1976 | 1977 | 1978 | 1979 | 1980 | 1981 | 1982 |
|---|---|---|---|---|---|---|---|---|
| **DEBT** | | | | | | | | |
| DAC countries and capital markets | 9 | 7 | 5 | 5 | 3 | 3 | 12 | 46 |
| ODA | – | – | – | – | – | – | – | – |
| Total export credits | 9 | 7 | 5 | 5 | 3 | 3 | 2 | 1 |
| Total private | – | – | – | – | – | – | 10 | 45 |
| *of which:* Bank loans | – | – | – | – | – | – | 10 | 45 |
| Bonds | – | – | – | – | – | – | – | – |
| Other | – | – | – | – | – | – | – | – |
| Multilateral | – | – | – | – | – | – | – | – |
| *of which:* Concessional | – | – | – | – | – | – | – | – |
| CMEA countries | – | – | – | – | – | – | – | – |
| *of which:* Concessional | – | – | – | – | – | – | – | – |
| OPEC countries | – | – | – | – | – | – | – | – |
| *of which:* Concessional | – | – | – | – | – | – | – | – |
| Other LDC'S | – | – | – | – | – | – | – | – |
| *of which:* Concessional | – | – | – | – | – | – | – | – |
| Other and adjustments | – | – | – | – | – | – | – | – |
| **Total Debt** | **9** | **7** | **5** | **5** | **3** | **3** | **12** | **46** |
| *of which:* Concessional | – | – | – | – | – | – | – | – |
| Non-concessional | 9 | 7 | 5 | 5 | 3 | 3 | 12 | 46 |
| **DEBT SERVICE** | | | | | | | | |
| DAC countries and capital markets | 0 | 3 | 3 | 2 | 3 | 2 | 2 | 3 |
| ODA | – | – | – | – | – | – | – | – |
| Total export credits | 0 | 3 | 3 | 2 | 3 | 2 | 1 | 1 |
| Total private | – | – | – | – | – | – | 2 | 3 |
| *of which:* Bank loans | – | – | – | – | – | – | 2 | 3 |
| Bonds | – | – | – | – | – | – | – | – |
| Other | – | – | – | – | – | – | – | – |
| Multilateral | – | – | – | – | – | – | – | – |
| *of which:* Concessional | – | – | – | – | – | – | – | – |
| CMEA countries | – | – | – | – | – | – | – | – |
| *of which:* Concessional | – | – | – | – | – | – | – | – |
| OPEC countries | – | – | – | – | – | – | – | – |
| *of which:* Concessional | – | – | – | – | – | – | – | – |
| Other LDC'S | – | – | – | – | – | – | – | – |
| *of which:* Concessional | – | – | – | – | – | – | – | – |
| Other and adjustments | – | – | – | – | – | – | – | – |
| **Total Debt Service** | **0** | **3** | **3** | **2** | **3** | **2** | **2** | **3** |
| *of which:* Concessional | – | – | – | – | – | – | – | – |
| Non-concessional | 0 | 3 | 3 | 2 | 3 | 2 | 2 | 3 |

# MADAGASCAR

| | 1975 | 1976 | 1977 | 1978 | 1979 | 1980 | 1981 | 1982 |
|---|---|---|---|---|---|---|---|---|
| **DEBT** | | | | | | | | |
| DAC countries and capital | | | | | | | | |
|   markets | 88 | 86 | 105 | 188 | 366 | 499 | 595 | 691 |
|   ODA | 74 | 65 | 71 | 83 | 105 | 138 | 147 | 221 |
|   Total export credits | 10 | 11 | 24 | 78 | 203 | 288 | 361 | 345 |
|   Total private | 4 | 10 | 10 | 27 | 58 | 73 | 87 | 125 |
|   *of which:* Bank loans | 4 | 10 | 10 | 17 | 38 | 58 | 75 | 65 |
|     Bonds | – | – | – | – | – | – | – | – |
|     Other | – | – | – | 10 | 20 | 15 | 12 | 60 |
| Multilateral | 80 | 96 | 108 | 132 | 157 | 221 | 260 | 309 |
|   *of which:* Concessional | 67 | 81 | 93 | 116 | 139 | 195 | 232 | 281 |
| CMEA countries | – | 0 | 11 | 12 | 20 | 79 | 163 | 177 |
|   *of which:* Concessional | – | 0 | 2 | 4 | 8 | 29 | 88 | 97 |
| OPEC countries | 1 | 0 | 0 | 0 | 87 | 135 | 191 | 194 |
|   *of which:* Concessional | – | – | – | – | 84 | 132 | 188 | 190 |
| Other LDC'S | 8 | 10 | 11 | 18 | 20 | 30 | 38 | 47 |
|   *of which:* Concessional | 7 | 9 | 11 | 17 | 19 | 29 | 34 | 41 |
| Other and adjustments | – | – | – | – | 66 | 87 | 113 | 131 |
| **Total Debt** | **176** | **193** | **235** | **350** | **716** | **1051** | **1360** | **1550** |
|   *of which:* Concessional | 148 | 155 | 176 | 220 | 361 | 533 | 693 | 830 |
|     Non-concessional | 28 | 37 | 59 | 131 | 355 | 518 | 667 | 719 |
| | | | | | | | | |
| **DEBT SERVICE** | | | | | | | | |
| DAC countries and capital | | | | | | | | |
|   markets | 18 | 18 | 21 | 22 | 34 | 51 | 63 | 87 |
|   ODA | 10 | 9 | 4 | 12 | 7 | 9 | 5 | 6 |
|   Total export credits | 7 | 8 | 15 | 9 | 21 | 36 | 35 | 49 |
|   Total private | 1 | – | 2 | 2 | 5 | 6 | 23 | 33 |
|   *of which:* Bank loans | 1 | – | 2 | 2 | 4 | 6 | 22 | 30 |
|     Bonds | – | – | – | – | – | – | – | – |
|     Other | – | – | – | – | 2 | – | 1 | 3 |
| Multilateral | 1 | 2 | 3 | 3 | 4 | 4 | 9 | 5 |
|   *of which:* Concessional | 1 | 1 | 2 | 2 | 2 | 3 | 8 | 3 |
| CMEA countries | – | – | 1 | 2 | 3 | 5 | 3 | 2 |
|   *of which:* Concessional | – | – | 0 | 0 | 0 | 0 | 1 | 0 |
| OPEC countries | 0 | 0 | 0 | 0 | 0 | 1 | 1 | 4 |
|   *of which:* Concessional | – | – | – | – | 0 | 1 | 1 | 4 |
| Other LDC'S | – | – | 1 | 1 | 0 | 2 | – | – |
|   *of which:* Concessional | – | – | 1 | 1 | 0 | 2 | – | – |
| Other and adjustments | – | – | – | – | 1 | 5 | 0 | 4 |
| **Total Debt Service** | **20** | **20** | **25** | **29** | **42** | **68** | **77** | **103** |
|   *of which:* Concessional | 12 | 11 | 7 | 16 | 11 | 15 | 15 | 14 |
|     Non-concessional | 8 | 9 | 18 | 14 | 32 | 53 | 62 | 89 |

*US $ Million*

| | 1975 | 1976 | 1977 | 1978 | 1979 | 1980 | 1981 | 1982 |
|---|---|---|---|---|---|---|---|---|
| **DEBT** | | | | | | | | |
| DAC countries and capital | | | | | | | | |
| markets | 186 | 206 | 275 | 307 | 330 | 429 | 404 | 364 |
| ODA | 144 | 145 | 178 | 169 | 141 | 165 | 148 | 133 |
| Total export credits | 9 | 15 | 28 | 55 | 85 | 115 | 91 | 77 |
| Total private | 33 | 46 | 69 | 83 | 104 | 149 | 165 | 154 |
| *of which:* Bank loans | 25 | 40 | 62 | 80 | 102 | 148 | 160 | 150 |
| Bonds | 8 | 6 | 7 | 3 | 2 | 1 | – | – |
| Other | – | – | – | – | – | – | 5 | 4 |
| Multilateral | 66 | 78 | 107 | 144 | 188 | 240 | 291 | 340 |
| *of which:* Concessional | 62 | 74 | 90 | 120 | 153 | 196 | 224 | 255 |
| CMEA countries | – | – | – | – | – | – | – | – |
| *of which:* Concessional | – | – | – | – | – | – | – | – |
| OPEC countries | – | – | – | – | – | – | – | – |
| *of which:* Concessional | – | – | – | – | – | – | – | – |
| Other LDC'S | – | – | – | – | – | – | 2 | 3 |
| *of which:* Concessional | – | – | – | – | – | – | – | – |
| Other and adjustments | 27 | 26 | 25 | 40 | 48 | 76 | 67 | 73 |
| **Total Debt** | **279** | **310** | **407** | **492** | **566** | **745** | **764** | **779** |
| *of which:* Concessional | 225 | 238 | 287 | 310 | 316 | 384 | 389 | 404 |
| Non-concessional | 55 | 72 | 120 | 182 | 251 | 361 | 375 | 376 |
| **DEBT SERVICE** | | | | | | | | |
| DAC countries and capital | | | | | | | | |
| markets | 15 | 21 | 25 | 32 | 37 | 60 | 76 | 59 |
| ODA | 5 | 5 | 6 | 6 | 4 | 5 | 6 | 4 |
| Total export credits | 5 | 4 | 6 | 9 | 12 | 24 | 24 | 23 |
| Total private | 5 | 13 | 13 | 17 | 21 | 32 | 46 | 33 |
| *of which:* Bank loans | 3 | 12 | 12 | 14 | 20 | 31 | 45 | 31 |
| Bonds | 2 | 1 | 1 | 3 | 1 | 1 | 1 | – |
| Other | – | – | – | – | – | – | – | 2 |
| Multilateral | 1 | 1 | 1 | 3 | 4 | 5 | 10 | 10 |
| *of which:* Concessional | 0 | 1 | 1 | 1 | 2 | 3 | 3 | 4 |
| CMEA countries | – | – | – | – | – | – | – | – |
| *of which:* Concessional | – | – | – | – | – | – | – | – |
| OPEC countries | – | – | – | – | – | – | – | – |
| *of which:* Concessional | – | – | – | – | – | – | – | – |
| Other LDC'S | – | – | – | – | – | – | – | 0 |
| *of which:* Concessional | – | – | – | – | – | – | – | – |
| Other and adjustments | 5 | 4 | 2 | 3 | 5 | 5 | 6 | 8 |
| **Total Debt Service** | **20** | **26** | **28** | **37** | **46** | **70** | **91** | **77** |
| *of which:* Concessional | 8 | 8 | 7 | 9 | 8 | 9 | 10 | 8 |
| Non-concessional | 12 | 19 | 21 | 29 | 38 | 61 | 81 | 70 |

# MALAYSIA

| | 1975 | 1976 | 1977 | 1978 | 1979 | 1980 | 1981 | 1982 |
|---|---|---|---|---|---|---|---|---|
| **DEBT** | | | | | | | | |
| DAC countries and capital | | | | | | | | |
| markets | 1415 | 1879 | 2090 | 2440 | 2747 | 3059 | 4527 | 7102 |
| ODA | 235 | 256 | 332 | 455 | 453 | 594 | 581 | 598 |
| Total export credits | 410 | 739 | 859 | 982 | 1086 | 1088 | 1442 | 1666 |
| Total private | 770 | 884 | 899 | 1003 | 1208 | 1377 | 2504 | 4838 |
| of which: Bank loans | 664 | 800 | 802 | 822 | 936 | 1080 | 2220 | 3960 |
| Bonds | 86 | 64 | 57 | 131 | 222 | 227 | 206 | 788 |
| Other | 20 | 20 | 40 | 50 | 50 | 70 | 78 | 90 |
| Multilateral | 319 | 396 | 492 | 573 | 658 | 745 | 849 | 982 |
| of which: Concessional | 122 | 117 | 110 | 105 | 97 | 88 | 79 | 69 |
| CMEA countries | – | – | – | – | – | – | – | – |
| of which: Concessional | – | – | – | – | – | – | – | – |
| OPEC countries | – | – | 2 | 7 | 12 | 20 | 29 | 43 |
| of which: Concessional | – | – | 2 | 7 | 12 | 20 | 29 | 43 |
| Other LDC'S | 41 | 28 | 30 | 34 | 35 | 48 | 45 | 39 |
| of which: Concessional | 24 | 20 | 22 | 24 | 26 | 28 | 22 | 19 |
| Other and adjustments | – | – | – | – | – | – | – | – |
| **Total Debt** | **1775** | **2303** | **2614** | **3055** | **3453** | **3873** | **5450** | **8167** |
| of which: Concessional | 380 | 392 | 466 | 591 | 588 | 730 | 711 | 730 |
| Non-concessional | 1395 | 1911 | 2147 | 2464 | 2865 | 3142 | 4739 | 7437 |
| | | | | | | | | |
| **DEBT SERVICE** | | | | | | | | |
| DAC countries and capital | | | | | | | | |
| markets | 179 | 235 | 452 | 738 | 541 | 403 | 589 | 924 |
| ODA | 14 | 14 | 18 | 27 | 34 | 42 | 45 | 43 |
| Total export credits | 68 | 80 | 115 | 152 | 169 | 156 | 232 | 341 |
| Total private | 96 | 140 | 318 | 559 | 338 | 205 | 313 | 540 |
| of which: Bank loans | 84 | 110 | 296 | 536 | 307 | 165 | 280 | 470 |
| Bonds | 9 | 26 | 17 | 17 | 21 | 25 | 15 | 43 |
| Other | 4 | 4 | 5 | 6 | 10 | 15 | 18 | 27 |
| Multilateral | 33 | 42 | 52 | 70 | 81 | 92 | 108 | 121 |
| of which: Concessional | 14 | 15 | 15 | 17 | 17 | 17 | 16 | 15 |
| CMEA countries | – | – | – | – | – | – | – | – |
| of which: Concessional | – | – | – | – | – | – | – | – |
| OPEC countries | – | 2 | 0 | 0 | 0 | 1 | 2 | 4 |
| of which: Concessional | – | 2 | 0 | 0 | 0 | 1 | 2 | 4 |
| Other LDC'S | 3 | 11 | 2 | 2 | 3 | 6 | 6 | 6 |
| of which: Concessional | 1 | 1 | 1 | 1 | 1 | 1 | 1 | 1 |
| Other and adjustments | – | – | – | – | – | – | – | – |
| **Total Debt Service** | **214** | **289** | **505** | **810** | **625** | **502** | **706** | **1055** |
| of which: Concessional | 30 | 32 | 35 | 45 | 53 | 61 | 64 | 64 |
| Non-concessional | 185 | 257 | 471 | 765 | 572 | 441 | 642 | 992 |

# MALDIVES

| | 1975 | 1976 | 1977 | 1978 | 1979 | 1980 | 1981 | 1982 |
|---|---|---|---|---|---|---|---|---|
| **DEBT** | | | | | | | | |
| DAC countries and capital markets | 1 | 1 | 1 | 3 | 3 | 3 | 5 | 4 |
| ODA | 1 | 1 | 1 | 3 | 3 | 3 | 3 | 2 |
| Total export credits | – | – | – | – | – | – | 1 | 1 |
| Total private | – | – | – | – | – | – | 1 | 1 |
| of which: Bank loans | – | – | – | – | – | – | – | – |
| Bonds | – | – | – | – | – | – | – | – |
| Other | – | – | – | – | – | – | 1 | 1 |
| Multilateral | – | – | 1 | 1 | 1 | 4 | 9 | 16 |
| of which: Concessional | – | – | 1 | 1 | 1 | 4 | 6 | 6 |
| CMEA countries | – | – | – | – | – | – | – | – |
| of which: Concessional | – | – | – | – | – | – | – | – |
| OPEC countries | – | 0 | 1 | 3 | 6 | 21 | 25 | 27 |
| of which: Concessional | – | 0 | 1 | 3 | 6 | 21 | 25 | 27 |
| Other LDC'S | – | – | – | – | – | – | – | – |
| of which: Concessional | – | – | – | – | – | – | – | – |
| Other and adjustments | – | – | – | – | – | – | – | – |
| **Total Debt** | 1 | 1 | 3 | 7 | 10 | 28 | 39 | 47 |
| of which: Concessional | 1 | 1 | 3 | 7 | 10 | 28 | 34 | 35 |
| Non-concessional | – | – | – | – | – | – | 6 | 12 |
| **DEBT SERVICE** | | | | | | | | |
| DAC countries and capital markets | – | – | 0 | 0 | 0 | 0 | 1 | 2 |
| ODA | – | – | 0 | 0 | 0 | 0 | 0 | 1 |
| Total export credits | – | – | – | – | – | – | – | 1 |
| Total private | – | – | – | – | – | – | 0 | 0 |
| of which: Bank loans | – | – | – | – | – | – | – | – |
| Bonds | – | – | – | – | – | – | – | – |
| Other | – | – | – | – | – | – | 0 | 0 |
| Multilateral | – | – | 0 | 0 | 0 | 0 | 0 | 0 |
| of which: Concessional | – | – | 0 | 0 | 0 | 0 | 0 | 0 |
| CMEA countries | – | – | – | – | – | – | – | – |
| of which: Concessional | – | – | – | – | – | – | – | – |
| OPEC countries | – | – | 0 | 0 | 0 | 0 | 0 | 1 |
| of which: Concessional | – | – | 0 | 0 | 0 | 0 | 0 | 1 |
| Other LDC'S | – | – | – | – | – | – | – | – |
| of which: Concessional | – | – | – | – | – | – | – | – |
| Other and adjustments | – | – | – | – | – | – | – | – |
| **Total Debt Service** | – | – | 0 | 0 | 0 | 0 | 1 | 3 |
| of which: Concessional | – | – | 0 | 0 | 0 | 0 | 1 | 2 |
| Non-concessional | – | – | – | – | – | – | 0 | 1 |

*US $ Million*

| | 1975 | 1976 | 1977 | 1978 | 1979 | 1980 | 1981 | 1982 |
|---|---|---|---|---|---|---|---|---|
| **DEBT** | | | | | | | | |
| DAC countries and capital | | | | | | | | |
| markets | 66 | 72 | 96 | 128 | 76 | 82 | 70 | 62 |
| ODA | 30 | 39 | 54 | 81 | 22 | 26 | 26 | 28 |
| Total export credits | 35 | 33 | 42 | 47 | 54 | 55 | 43 | 34 |
| Total private | 1 | – | – | – | – | 1 | 1 | – |
| of which: Bank loans | 1 | – | – | – | – | 1 | 1 | – |
| Bonds | – | – | – | – | – | – | – | – |
| Other | – | – | – | – | – | – | – | – |
| Multilateral | 43 | 57 | 82 | 114 | 156 | 198 | 247 | 288 |
| of which: Concessional | 43 | 57 | 81 | 111 | 151 | 192 | 242 | 283 |
| CMEA countries | 105 | 111 | 112 | 112 | 111 | 177 | 191 | 214 |
| of which: Concessional | 104 | 110 | 112 | 111 | 111 | 177 | 191 | 214 |
| OPEC countries | 8 | 8 | 14 | 15 | 24 | 47 | 61 | 100 |
| of which: Concessional | 8 | 8 | 14 | 15 | 24 | 47 | 61 | 100 |
| Other LDC'S | 115 | 104 | 129 | 149 | 166 | 189 | 174 | 164 |
| of which: Concessional | 114 | 103 | 129 | 148 | 166 | 188 | 174 | 164 |
| Other and adjustments | – | – | – | – | – | – | – | – |
| **Total Debt** | **337** | **351** | **433** | **518** | **533** | **692** | **744** | **829** |
| of which: Concessional | 299 | 317 | 390 | 467 | 474 | 630 | 694 | 789 |
| Non-concessional | 37 | 34 | 44 | 51 | 59 | 62 | 49 | 40 |
| **DEBT SERVICE** | | | | | | | | |
| DAC countries and capital | | | | | | | | |
| markets | 5 | 5 | 9 | 12 | 16 | 12 | 9 | 7 |
| ODA | 2 | 2 | 2 | 2 | 2 | 1 | 1 | 0 |
| Total export credits | 3 | 3 | 7 | 10 | 13 | 11 | 8 | 6 |
| Total private | – | – | – | 1 | 1 | 1 | 0 | 1 |
| of which: Bank loans | – | – | – | 1 | 1 | 1 | 0 | 1 |
| Bonds | – | – | – | – | – | – | – | – |
| Other | – | – | – | – | – | – | – | – |
| Multilateral | 0 | 0 | 1 | 3 | 2 | 2 | 2 | 4 |
| of which: Concessional | 0 | 0 | 1 | 3 | 2 | 1 | 2 | 3 |
| CMEA countries | 0 | 0 | 1 | 0 | 0 | 1 | 1 | – |
| of which: Concessional | 0 | 0 | 1 | 0 | 0 | 0 | 1 | – |
| OPEC countries | 0 | 0 | 1 | 1 | 1 | 1 | 1 | 1 |
| of which: Concessional | 0 | 0 | 1 | 1 | 1 | 1 | 1 | 1 |
| Other LDC'S | 1 | 1 | 1 | 1 | 1 | 1 | 0 | – |
| of which: Concessional | 0 | 1 | 1 | 1 | 1 | 0 | 0 | – |
| Other and adjustments | – | – | – | – | – | – | – | – |
| **Total Debt Service** | **6** | **7** | **13** | **18** | **21** | **17** | **13** | **12** |
| of which: Concessional | 3 | 4 | 5 | 7 | 7 | 5 | 4 | 5 |
| Non-concessional | 3 | 4 | 8 | 11 | 14 | 12 | 9 | 7 |

*US $ Million*

| | 1975 | 1976 | 1977 | 1978 | 1979 | 1980 | 1981 | 1982 |
|---|---|---|---|---|---|---|---|---|
| **DEBT** | | | | | | | | |
| DAC countries and capital | | | | | | | | |
| markets | 20 | 27 | 30 | 47 | 50 | 49 | 56 | 54 |
| ODA | 18 | 22 | 21 | 34 | 36 | 36 | 31 | 38 |
| Total export credits | – | 1 | – | 3 | 4 | 5 | 16 | 11 |
| Total private | 2 | 4 | 9 | 10 | 10 | 8 | 9 | 5 |
| of which: Bank loans | 2 | 4 | 5 | 6 | 6 | 4 | 4 | 2 |
| Bonds | – | – | – | – | – | – | – | – |
| Other | – | – | 4 | 4 | 4 | 4 | 5 | 3 |
| Multilateral | 3 | 2 | 2 | 1 | 5 | 6 | 9 | 8 |
| of which: Concessional | 3 | 2 | 2 | 1 | 5 | 6 | 9 | 8 |
| CMEA countries | – | – | – | – | – | – | – | – |
| of which: Concessional | – | – | – | – | – | – | – | – |
| OPEC countries | 8 | 8 | 8 | 9 | 9 | 9 | 13 | 26 |
| of which: Concessional | 8 | 8 | 8 | 9 | 9 | 9 | 13 | 26 |
| Other LDC'S | 5 | 16 | 20 | 23 | 24 | 54 | 47 | 43 |
| of which: Concessional | 5 | 16 | 20 | 23 | 24 | 54 | 47 | 43 |
| Other and adjustments | – | – | – | – | – | – | – | – |
| **Total Debt** | **35** | **53** | **61** | **80** | **87** | **118** | **126** | **131** |
| of which: Concessional | 33 | 48 | 52 | 67 | 73 | 105 | 101 | 115 |
| Non-concessional | 2 | 5 | 9 | 13 | 14 | 13 | 25 | 16 |
| **DEBT SERVICE** | | | | | | | | |
| DAC countries and capital | | | | | | | | |
| markets | 3 | 3 | 5 | 4 | 4 | 4 | 8 | 18 |
| ODA | 2 | 1 | 2 | 2 | 2 | 2 | 2 | 1 |
| Total export credits | 0 | 0 | 0 | 0 | 0 | 1 | 5 | 12 |
| Total private | 0 | 1 | 3 | 3 | 2 | 1 | 2 | 5 |
| of which: Bank loans | 0 | 1 | 2 | 2 | 1 | 1 | 1 | 3 |
| Bonds | – | – | – | – | – | – | – | – |
| Other | – | – | 0 | 0 | 0 | 1 | 1 | 3 |
| Multilateral | 1 | 1 | 0 | 1 | 1 | 1 | 0 | 0 |
| of which: Concessional | 1 | 1 | 0 | 1 | 1 | 1 | 0 | 0 |
| CMEA countries | – | – | – | – | – | – | – | – |
| of which: Concessional | – | – | – | – | – | – | – | – |
| OPEC countries | – | 0 | 0 | 0 | 0 | 0 | 2 | 2 |
| of which: Concessional | – | 0 | 0 | 0 | 0 | 0 | 2 | 2 |
| Other LDC'S | – | – | – | – | – | – | – | – |
| of which: Concessional | – | – | – | – | – | – | – | – |
| Other and adjustments | – | – | – | – | – | – | – | – |
| **Total Debt Service** | **3** | **3** | **5** | **5** | **5** | **5** | **10** | **21** |
| of which: Concessional | 3 | 2 | 2 | 2 | 4 | 3 | 4 | 4 |
| Non-concessional | 1 | 1 | 3 | 3 | 2 | 2 | 6 | 17 |

# MARTINIQUE

| | 1975 | 1976 | 1977 | 1978 | 1979 | 1980 | 1981 | 1982 |
|---|---|---|---|---|---|---|---|---|
| **DEBT** | | | | | | | | |
| DAC countries and capital | | | | | | | | |
| markets | 104 | 98 | 95 | 110 | 106 | 86 | 62 | 48 |
| ODA | 104 | 95 | 92 | 107 | 102 | 82 | 59 | 46 |
| Total export credits | – | 3 | 3 | 3 | 4 | 4 | 3 | 2 |
| Total private | – | – | – | – | – | – | – | – |
| of which: Bank loans | – | – | – | – | – | – | – | – |
| Bonds | – | – | – | – | – | – | – | – |
| Other | – | – | – | – | – | – | – | – |
| Multilateral | – | – | – | – | – | – | – | – |
| of which: Concessional | – | – | – | – | – | – | – | – |
| CMEA countries | – | – | – | – | – | – | – | – |
| of which: Concessional | – | – | – | – | – | – | – | – |
| OPEC countries | – | – | – | – | – | – | – | – |
| of which: Concessional | – | – | – | – | – | – | – | – |
| Other LDC'S | – | – | – | – | – | – | – | – |
| of which: Concessional | – | – | – | – | – | – | – | – |
| Other and adjustments | – | – | – | – | – | – | – | – |
| **Total Debt** | **104** | **98** | **95** | **110** | **106** | **86** | **62** | **48** |
| of which: Concessional | 104 | 95 | 92 | 107 | 102 | 82 | 59 | 46 |
| Non-concessional | – | 3 | 3 | 3 | 4 | 4 | 3 | 2 |
| **DEBT SERVICE** | | | | | | | | |
| DAC countries and capital | | | | | | | | |
| markets | 10 | 10 | 10 | 12 | 15 | 14 | 8 | 6 |
| ODA | 10 | 10 | 10 | 12 | 15 | 13 | 8 | 6 |
| Total export credits | – | 0 | 0 | 1 | 1 | 1 | 1 | 1 |
| Total private | – | – | – | – | – | – | – | – |
| of which: Bank loans | – | – | – | – | – | – | – | – |
| Bonds | – | – | – | – | – | – | – | – |
| Other | – | – | – | – | – | – | – | – |
| Multilateral | – | – | – | – | – | – | – | – |
| of which: Concessional | – | – | – | – | – | – | – | – |
| CMEA countries | – | – | – | – | – | – | – | – |
| of which: Concessional | – | – | – | – | – | – | – | – |
| OPEC countries | – | – | – | – | – | – | – | – |
| of which: Concessional | – | – | – | – | – | – | – | – |
| Other LDC'S | – | – | – | – | – | – | – | – |
| of which: Concessional | – | – | – | – | – | – | – | – |
| Other and adjustments | – | – | – | – | – | – | – | – |
| **Total Debt Service** | **10** | **10** | **10** | **12** | **15** | **14** | **8** | **6** |
| of which: Concessional | 10 | 10 | 10 | 12 | 15 | 13 | 8 | 6 |
| Non-concessional | – | 0 | 0 | 1 | 1 | 1 | 1 | 1 |

# MAURITANIA

US $ Million

|  | 1975 | 1976 | 1977 | 1978 | 1979 | 1980 | 1981 | 1982 |
|---|---|---|---|---|---|---|---|---|
| **DEBT** | | | | | | | | |
| DAC countries and capital | | | | | | | | |
| markets | 61 | 151 | 178 | 218 | 179 | 184 | 181 | 161 |
| ODA | 30 | 24 | 26 | 42 | 44 | 39 | 36 | 43 |
| Total export credits | 19 | 59 | 95 | 116 | 105 | 127 | 143 | 117 |
| Total private | 12 | 68 | 57 | 60 | 30 | 18 | 2 | 1 |
| of which: Bank loans | 12 | 25 | 27 | 30 | 20 | 8 | – | – |
| Bonds | 0 | 0 | 0 | 0 | 0 | 0 | 0 | – |
| Other | – | 43 | 30 | 30 | 10 | 10 | 2 | 1 |
| Multilateral | 22 | 43 | 63 | 99 | 112 | 142 | 171 | 253 |
| of which: Concessional | 21 | 42 | 61 | 97 | 107 | 124 | 135 | 159 |
| CMEA countries | – | – | – | – | – | – | – | – |
| of which: Concessional | – | – | – | – | – | – | – | – |
| OPEC countries | 76 | 166 | 185 | 210 | 250 | 326 | 427 | 492 |
| of which: Concessional | 76 | 126 | 141 | 154 | 193 | 267 | 335 | 397 |
| Other LDC'S | 31 | 32 | 33 | 49 | 71 | 81 | 79 | 76 |
| of which: Concessional | 31 | 32 | 33 | 49 | 61 | 65 | 61 | 59 |
| Other and adjustments | – | – | – | 7 | 8 | 13 | 13 | 22 |
| **Total Debt** | **190** | **392** | **458** | **583** | **620** | **746** | **871** | **1005** |
| of which: Concessional | 159 | 224 | 260 | 349 | 413 | 508 | 581 | 680 |
| Non-concessional | 32 | 168 | 198 | 234 | 208 | 238 | 291 | 325 |
| **DEBT SERVICE** | | | | | | | | |
| DAC countries and capital | | | | | | | | |
| markets | 20 | 33 | 40 | 43 | 42 | 31 | 41 | 23 |
| ODA | 5 | 8 | 5 | 4 | 3 | 4 | 2 | 2 |
| Total export credits | 15 | 14 | 12 | 16 | 22 | 19 | 19 | 19 |
| Total private | – | 12 | 23 | 23 | 18 | 8 | 19 | 2 |
| of which: Bank loans | – | 4 | 13 | 13 | 8 | 5 | 9 | – |
| Bonds | – | 0 | – | – | – | 0 | – | – |
| Other | – | 8 | 10 | 10 | 10 | 3 | 10 | 2 |
| Multilateral | 10 | 1 | 1 | 2 | 4 | 5 | 6 | 10 |
| of which: Concessional | 1 | 1 | 1 | 1 | 3 | 3 | 2 | 5 |
| CMEA countries | – | – | – | – | – | – | – | – |
| of which: Concessional | – | – | – | – | – | – | – | – |
| OPEC countries | 12 | 4 | 11 | 6 | 5 | 5 | 11 | 16 |
| of which: Concessional | 1 | 2 | 2 | 2 | 3 | 3 | 7 | 11 |
| Other LDC'S | – | 0 | 0 | – | – | – | 1 | 1 |
| of which: Concessional | – | 0 | 0 | – | – | – | – | – |
| Other and adjustments | – | – | – | – | 0 | 0 | 0 | 0 |
| **Total Debt Service** | **42** | **38** | **52** | **51** | **51** | **41** | **59** | **50** |
| of which: Concessional | 6 | 10 | 7 | 7 | 8 | 10 | 11 | 19 |
| Non-concessional | 35 | 28 | 45 | 44 | 42 | 31 | 48 | 31 |

US $ Million

| | 1975 | 1976 | 1977 | 1978 | 1979 | 1980 | 1981 | 1982 |
|---|---|---|---|---|---|---|---|---|
| **DEBT** | | | | | | | | |
| DAC countries and capital | | | | | | | | |
|   markets | 39 | 43 | 45 | 102 | 167 | 209 | 208 | 233 |
|   ODA | 26 | 21 | 21 | 24 | 34 | 46 | 54 | 56 |
|   Total export credits | 10 | 18 | 19 | 36 | 39 | 44 | 35 | 29 |
|   Total private | 3 | 4 | 5 | 42 | 94 | 119 | 119 | 148 |
|     *of which:* Bank loans | – | 1 | 5 | 37 | 88 | 112 | 112 | 140 |
|       Bonds | 3 | 3 | – | – | – | – | – | – |
|       Other | – | – | – | 5 | 6 | 7 | 7 | 8 |
| Multilateral | 19 | 26 | 38 | 65 | 74 | 89 | 115 | 129 |
|   *of which:* Concessional | 15 | 17 | 22 | 40 | 41 | 45 | 48 | 56 |
| CMEA countries | – | – | – | – | – | – | – | – |
|   *of which:* Concessional | – | – | – | – | – | – | – | – |
| OPEC countries | – | – | – | – | – | – | 1 | 3 |
|   *of which:* Concessional | – | – | – | – | – | – | 1 | 3 |
| Other LDC'S | 0 | 0 | 0 | 3 | 6 | 9 | 15 | 14 |
|   *of which:* Concessional | 0 | 0 | 0 | 2 | 2 | 2 | 4 | 4 |
| Other and adjustments | – | – | – | – | – | – | 3 | 2 |
| **Total Debt** | **58** | **69** | **84** | **170** | **247** | **307** | **341** | **382** |
|   *of which:* Concessional | 41 | 39 | 43 | 66 | 77 | 93 | 110 | 121 |
|     Non-concessional | 17 | 30 | 41 | 104 | 170 | 214 | 231 | 261 |
| **DEBT SERVICE** | | | | | | | | |
| DAC countries and capital | | | | | | | | |
|   markets | 12 | 9 | 14 | 11 | 19 | 34 | 51 | 53 |
|   ODA | 2 | 2 | 2 | 3 | 4 | 3 | 3 | 3 |
|   Total export credits | 7 | 7 | 9 | 4 | 8 | 10 | 12 | 8 |
|   Total private | 3 | 1 | 4 | 4 | 8 | 21 | 36 | 42 |
|     *of which:* Bank loans | – | 1 | 1 | 4 | 7 | 20 | 35 | 41 |
|       Bonds | 3 | 0 | 3 | – | – | – | – | – |
|       Other | – | – | – | 0 | 1 | 1 | 1 | 1 |
| Multilateral | 1 | 1 | 2 | 3 | 5 | 6 | 8 | 12 |
|   *of which:* Concessional | 1 | 1 | 1 | 1 | 1 | 1 | 2 | 2 |
| CMEA countries | – | – | – | – | – | – | – | – |
|   *of which:* Concessional | – | – | – | – | – | – | – | – |
| OPEC countries | – | – | – | – | – | – | 0 | 0 |
|   *of which:* Concessional | – | – | – | – | – | – | 0 | 0 |
| Other LDC'S | – | – | – | 1 | 1 | 1 | 2 | 3 |
|   *of which:* Concessional | – | – | – | 0 | 1 | 0 | 0 | 1 |
| Other and adjustments | – | – | – | – | – | – | – | – |
| **Total Debt Service** | **13** | **11** | **16** | **14** | **25** | **41** | **60** | **67** |
|   *of which:* Concessional | 3 | 3 | 2 | 4 | 5 | 5 | 5 | 5 |
|     Non-concessional | 10 | 8 | 14 | 10 | 20 | 36 | 56 | 61 |

US $ Million

| | 1975 | 1976 | 1977 | 1978 | 1979 | 1980 | 1981 | 1982 |
|---|---|---|---|---|---|---|---|---|
| **DEBT** | | | | | | | | |
| DAC countries and capital markets | 14667 | 19172 | 23970 | 28367 | 32720 | 38737 | 46972 | 52544 |
| ODA | 123 | 115 | 108 | 106 | 120 | 113 | 152 | 173 |
| Total export credits | 1840 | 1982 | 2677 | 3103 | 3635 | 4155 | 4641 | 5614 |
| Total private | 12704 | 17075 | 21185 | 25158 | 28965 | 34469 | 42179 | 46757 |
| of which: Bank loans | 11140 | 14400 | 16049 | 18893 | 23059 | 28600 | 34450 | 38900 |
| Bonds | 664 | 919 | 2136 | 2765 | 2687 | 2669 | 3829 | 4257 |
| Other | 900 | 1756 | 3000 | 3500 | 3219 | 3200 | 3900 | 3600 |
| Multilateral | 1624 | 1825 | 2095 | 2365 | 2726 | 3196 | 3666 | 4967 |
| of which: Concessional | 528 | 517 | 496 | 459 | 419 | 375 | 326 | 276 |
| CMEA countries | 2 | 4 | 4 | 4 | 4 | 6 | 11 | 17 |
| of which: Concessional | 2 | 4 | 4 | 4 | 4 | 4 | 4 | 4 |
| OPEC countries | 24 | 119 | 146 | 210 | 206 | 201 | 166 | 128 |
| of which: Concessional | – | – | – | – | – | – | – | – |
| Other LDC'S | 28 | 28 | 28 | 30 | 369 | 411 | 244 | 240 |
| of which: Concessional | – | – | – | – | – | – | – | – |
| Other and adjustments | 216 | 420 | 485 | 1553 | 1649 | 955 | 2436 | 2491 |
| **Total Debt** | **16562** | **21568** | **26729** | **32529** | **37674** | **43506** | **53496** | **60386** |
| of which: Concessional | 653 | 636 | 608 | 570 | 544 | 493 | 496 | 483 |
| Non-concessional | 15908 | 20932 | 26121 | 31960 | 37131 | 43014 | 53000 | 59903 |
| | | | | | | | | |
| **DEBT SERVICE** | | | | | | | | |
| DAC countries and capital markets | 2211 | 3325 | 4823 | 7056 | 10707 | 8898 | 9850 | 11241 |
| ODA | 17 | 11 | 13 | 15 | 13 | 13 | 14 | 10 |
| Total export credits | 402 | 495 | 1027 | 758 | 1120 | 1196 | 1182 | 1581 |
| Total private | 1792 | 2820 | 3783 | 6283 | 9575 | 7690 | 8654 | 9650 |
| of which: Bank loans | 1608 | 2467 | 3312 | 5490 | 8661 | 6920 | 7760 | 8220 |
| Bonds | 84 | 100 | 131 | 243 | 476 | 320 | 344 | 960 |
| Other | 100 | 253 | 340 | 550 | 439 | 450 | 550 | 470 |
| Multilateral | 165 | 196 | 234 | 295 | 333 | 378 | 423 | 483 |
| of which: Concessional | 66 | 67 | 69 | 71 | 71 | 68 | 66 | 65 |
| CMEA countries | – | 0 | 1 | 0 | – | – | 2 | 1 |
| of which: Concessional | – | 0 | 1 | 0 | – | – | – | – |
| OPEC countries | 1 | 3 | 12 | 15 | 19 | 22 | 43 | 50 |
| of which: Concessional | – | – | – | – | – | – | – | – |
| Other LDC'S | 3 | 2 | 2 | 2 | 3 | 134 | 214 | 19 |
| of which: Concessional | – | – | – | – | – | – | – | – |
| Other and adjustments | 105 | 103 | 138 | 196 | 175 | 144 | 139 | 42 |
| **Total Debt Service** | **2484** | **3630** | **5210** | **7565** | **11237** | **9577** | **10670** | **11836** |
| of which: Concessional | 82 | 78 | 83 | 86 | 84 | 81 | 81 | 77 |
| Non-concessional | 2402 | 3552 | 5127 | 7479 | 11153 | 9496 | 10590 | 11759 |

# MOROCCO

| | 1975 | 1976 | 1977 | 1978 | 1979 | 1980 | 1981 | 1982 |
|---|---|---|---|---|---|---|---|---|
| **DEBT** | | | | | | | | |
| DAC countries and capital | | | | | | | | |
| markets | 1359 | 1990 | 3107 | 4087 | 4864 | 5023 | 4975 | 5586 |
| ODA | 619 | 651 | 749 | 923 | 1009 | 978 | 911 | 958 |
| Total export credits | 322 | 463 | 874 | 1016 | 1260 | 1350 | 1533 | 1662 |
| Total private | 418 | 876 | 1484 | 2148 | 2595 | 2695 | 2531 | 2966 |
| *of which:* Bank loans | 374 | 820 | 1386 | 1956 | 2210 | 2320 | 2190 | 2680 |
| Bonds | 44 | 41 | 68 | 132 | 185 | 175 | 161 | 106 |
| Other | – | 15 | 30 | 60 | 200 | 200 | 180 | 180 |
| Multilateral | 295 | 348 | 425 | 578 | 736 | 846 | 1012 | 1169 |
| *of which:* Concessional | 58 | 63 | 81 | 128 | 177 | 241 | 247 | 263 |
| CMEA countries | 27 | 25 | 24 | 20 | 16 | 13 | 21 | 17 |
| *of which:* Concessional | 23 | 23 | 22 | 18 | 14 | 12 | 9 | 8 |
| OPEC countries | 102 | 161 | 677 | 869 | 1034 | 1618 | 2334 | 2747 |
| *of which:* Concessional | 100 | 136 | 640 | 822 | 984 | 1554 | 2278 | 2665 |
| Other LDC'S | 0 | 0 | – | – | – | 1 | 1 | 1 |
| *of which:* Concessional | – | – | – | – | – | – | – | – |
| Other and adjustments | 34 | 30 | 25 | 36 | 50 | 47 | 39 | 123 |
| **Total Debt** | **1818** | **2553** | **4258** | **5589** | **6699** | **7548** | **8382** | **9643** |
| *of which:* Concessional | 824 | 894 | 1509 | 1911 | 2204 | 2801 | 3459 | 3904 |
| Non-concessional | 994 | 1659 | 2749 | 3678 | 4495 | 4747 | 4923 | 5739 |
| | | | | | | | | |
| **DEBT SERVICE** | | | | | | | | |
| DAC countries and capital | | | | | | | | |
| markets | 129 | 178 | 252 | 543 | 791 | 1127 | 1230 | 1339 |
| ODA | 31 | 37 | 32 | 28 | 48 | 65 | 91 | 27 |
| Total export credits | 74 | 101 | 146 | 207 | 282 | 315 | 322 | 423 |
| Total private | 23 | 40 | 73 | 307 | 462 | 747 | 817 | 889 |
| *of which:* Bank loans | 20 | 33 | 65 | 286 | 425 | 686 | 730 | 765 |
| Bonds | 3 | 5 | 5 | 13 | 17 | 26 | 22 | 64 |
| Other | – | 2 | 3 | 8 | 20 | 35 | 65 | 60 |
| Multilateral | 33 | 36 | 43 | 56 | 82 | 100 | 132 | 126 |
| *of which:* Concessional | 3 | 3 | 4 | 4 | 5 | 5 | 8 | 10 |
| CMEA countries | 1 | 2 | 2 | 4 | 5 | 3 | 8 | 5 |
| *of which:* Concessional | 1 | 1 | 2 | 4 | 4 | 3 | 8 | 2 |
| OPEC countries | 9 | 10 | 21 | 45 | 79 | 99 | 60 | 57 |
| *of which:* Concessional | 8 | 9 | 19 | 42 | 73 | 75 | 41 | 48 |
| Other LDC'S | 0 | 0 | 0 | – | – | – | – | 0 |
| *of which:* Concessional | – | – | – | – | – | – | – | – |
| Other and adjustments | 2 | 1 | 1 | 2 | 2 | 5 | 6 | 7 |
| **Total Debt Service** | **174** | **227** | **319** | **650** | **958** | **1334** | **1435** | **1533** |
| *of which:* Concessional | 45 | 51 | 58 | 79 | 131 | 149 | 148 | 87 |
| Non-concessional | 129 | 177 | 261 | 571 | 827 | 1185 | 1287 | 1446 |

US $ Million

| | 1975 | 1976 | 1977 | 1978 | 1979 | 1980 | 1981 | 1982 |
|---|---|---|---|---|---|---|---|---|
| **DEBT** | | | | | | | | |
| DAC countries and capital | | | | | | | | |
| markets | 38 | 93 | 87 | 158 | 271 | 417 | 474 | 545 |
| ODA | – | – | 4 | 12 | 40 | 73 | 70 | 108 |
| Total export credits | 38 | 93 | 83 | 143 | 228 | 321 | 378 | 416 |
| Total private | – | – | – | 3 | 3 | 23 | 26 | 21 |
| of which: Bank loans | – | – | – | – | – | 20 | 20 | 15 |
| Bonds | – | – | – | – | – | – | – | – |
| Other | – | – | – | 3 | 3 | 3 | 6 | 6 |
| Multilateral | – | – | – | – | – | – | – | – |
| of which: Concessional | – | – | – | – | – | – | – | – |
| CMEA countries | – | – | – | – | – | – | – | – |
| of which: Concessional | – | – | – | – | – | – | – | – |
| OPEC countries | – | – | – | – | – | – | – | – |
| of which: Concessional | – | – | – | – | – | – | – | – |
| Other LDC'S | – | – | – | – | – | – | – | – |
| of which: Concessional | – | – | – | – | – | – | – | – |
| Other and adjustments | – | – | – | – | – | 15 | 35 | 40 |
| **Total Debt** | **38** | **93** | **87** | **158** | **271** | **432** | **509** | **585** |
| of which: Concessional | – | – | 4 | 12 | 40 | 83 | 85 | 128 |
| Non-concessional | 38 | 93 | 83 | 146 | 231 | 349 | 424 | 457 |
| | | | | | | | | |
| **DEBT SERVICE** | | | | | | | | |
| DAC countries and capital | | | | | | | | |
| markets | 20 | 16 | 17 | 13 | 21 | 48 | 57 | 91 |
| ODA | – | – | – | – | – | – | 0 | 0 |
| Total export credits | 20 | 16 | 17 | 13 | 20 | 46 | 53 | 82 |
| Total private | – | – | – | – | 1 | 2 | 5 | 10 |
| of which: Bank loans | – | – | – | – | – | 2 | 4 | 9 |
| Bonds | – | – | – | – | – | – | – | – |
| Other | – | – | – | – | 1 | 1 | 1 | 1 |
| Multilateral | – | – | – | – | – | – | – | – |
| of which: Concessional | – | – | – | – | – | – | – | – |
| CMEA countries | – | – | – | – | – | – | – | – |
| of which: Concessional | – | – | – | – | – | – | – | – |
| OPEC countries | – | – | – | – | – | – | – | – |
| of which: Concessional | – | – | – | – | – | – | – | – |
| Other LDC'S | – | – | – | – | – | – | – | – |
| of which: Concessional | – | – | – | – | – | – | – | – |
| Other and adjustments | – | – | – | – | – | 1 | 4 | 5 |
| **Total Debt Service** | **20** | **16** | **17** | **13** | **21** | **49** | **61** | **96** |
| of which: Concessional | – | – | – | – | – | – | 0 | 0 |
| Non-concessional | 20 | 16 | 17 | 13 | 21 | 49 | 61 | 96 |

# NAURU

US $ Million

| | 1975 | 1976 | 1977 | 1978 | 1979 | 1980 | 1981 | 1982 |
|---|---|---|---|---|---|---|---|---|
| **DEBT** | | | | | | | | |
| DAC countries and capital | | | | | | | | |
|   markets | – | – | – | 20 | 25 | 29 | 26 | 25 |
|   ODA | – | – | – | – | – | – | – | – |
|   Total export credits | – | – | – | – | 5 | 4 | 6 | 5 |
|   Total private | – | – | – | 20 | 20 | 25 | 20 | 20 |
|     *of which:* Bank loans | – | – | – | 20 | 20 | 25 | 20 | 20 |
|       Bonds | – | – | – | – | – | – | – | – |
|       Other | – | – | – | – | – | – | – | – |
| Multilateral | – | – | – | – | – | – | – | – |
|   *of which:* Concessional | – | – | – | – | – | – | – | – |
| CMEA countries | – | – | – | – | – | – | – | – |
|   *of which:* Concessional | – | – | – | – | – | – | – | – |
| OPEC countries | – | – | – | – | – | – | – | – |
|   *of which:* Concessional | – | – | – | – | – | – | – | – |
| Other LDC'S | – | – | – | – | – | – | – | – |
|   *of which:* Concessional | – | – | – | – | – | – | – | – |
| Other and adjustments | – | – | – | – | – | – | – | – |
| **Total Debt** | – | – | – | **20** | **25** | **29** | **26** | **25** |
|   *of which:* Concessional | – | – | – | – | – | – | – | – |
|     Non-concessional | – | – | – | 20 | 25 | 29 | 26 | 25 |
| | | | | | | | | |
| **DEBT SERVICE** | | | | | | | | |
| DAC countries and capital | | | | | | | | |
|   markets | – | – | – | – | 5 | 6 | 10 | 8 |
|   ODA | – | – | – | – | – | – | – | – |
|   Total export credits | – | – | – | – | 3 | 3 | 2 | 2 |
|   Total private | – | – | – | – | 2 | 3 | 8 | 6 |
|     *of which:* Bank loans | – | – | – | – | 2 | 3 | 8 | 6 |
|       Bonds | – | – | – | – | – | – | – | – |
|       Other | – | – | – | – | – | – | – | – |
| Multilateral | – | – | – | – | – | – | – | – |
|   *of which:* Concessional | – | – | – | – | – | – | – | – |
| CMEA countries | – | – | – | – | – | – | – | – |
|   *of which:* Concessional | – | – | – | – | – | – | – | – |
| OPEC countries | – | – | – | – | – | – | – | – |
|   *of which:* Concessional | – | – | – | – | – | – | – | – |
| Other LDC'S | – | – | – | – | – | – | – | – |
|   *of which:* Concessional | – | – | – | – | – | – | – | – |
| Other and adjustments | – | – | – | – | – | – | – | – |
| **Total Debt Service** | – | – | – | – | **5** | **6** | **10** | **8** |
|   *of which:* Concessional | – | – | – | – | – | – | – | – |
|     Non-concessional | – | – | – | – | 5 | 6 | 10 | 8 |

*US $ Million*

| | 1975 | 1976 | 1977 | 1978 | 1979 | 1980 | 1981 | 1982 |
|---|---|---|---|---|---|---|---|---|
| **DEBT** | | | | | | | | |
| DAC countries and capital markets | 18 | 15 | 15 | 24 | 39 | 23 | 26 | 27 |
| ODA | 15 | 15 | 14 | 16 | 29 | 19 | 20 | 21 |
| Total export credits | 3 | – | 1 | 8 | 10 | 4 | 6 | 6 |
| Total private | – | – | – | – | – | – | – | – |
| *of which:* Bank loans | – | – | – | – | – | – | – | – |
| Bonds | – | – | – | – | – | – | – | – |
| Other | – | – | – | – | – | – | – | – |
| Multilateral | 19 | 30 | 53 | 75 | 106 | 144 | 192 | 251 |
| *of which:* Concessional | 18 | 28 | 51 | 74 | 105 | 144 | 192 | 251 |
| CMEA countries | – | – | – | – | – | – | – | 3 |
| *of which:* Concessional | – | – | – | – | – | – | – | 3 |
| OPEC countries | – | – | 5 | 6 | 9 | 17 | 24 | 23 |
| *of which:* Concessional | – | – | 5 | 6 | 9 | 17 | 24 | 23 |
| Other LDC'S | 0 | 1 | 1 | 1 | 1 | 1 | 0 | 0 |
| *of which:* Concessional | 0 | 1 | 1 | 1 | 1 | 1 | 0 | 0 |
| Other and adjustments | – | – | – | – | – | – | – | – |
| **Total Debt** | **38** | **45** | **73** | **106** | **155** | **185** | **243** | **305** |
| *of which:* Concessional | 33 | 44 | 71 | 97 | 144 | 180 | 236 | 299 |
| Non-concessional | 5 | 1 | 2 | 9 | 11 | 5 | 6 | 6 |
| **DEBT SERVICE** | | | | | | | | |
| DAC countries and capital markets | 3 | 1 | 1 | 1 | 2 | 10 | 4 | 5 |
| ODA | 1 | 1 | 1 | 1 | 0 | 0 | 1 | 1 |
| Total export credits | 3 | 0 | 0 | – | 2 | 9 | 3 | 4 |
| Total private | – | – | – | – | – | – | – | – |
| *of which:* Bank loans | – | – | – | – | – | – | – | – |
| Bonds | – | – | – | – | – | – | – | – |
| Other | – | – | – | – | – | – | – | – |
| Multilateral | 1 | 1 | 1 | 2 | 3 | 3 | 4 | 4 |
| *of which:* Concessional | 1 | 1 | 1 | 2 | 3 | 3 | 3 | 4 |
| CMEA countries | – | – | – | – | – | – | – | 0 |
| *of which:* Concessional | – | – | – | – | – | – | – | 0 |
| OPEC countries | – | – | – | 0 | 0 | 0 | 1 | 1 |
| *of which:* Concessional | – | – | – | 0 | 0 | 0 | 1 | 1 |
| Other LDC'S | 0 | 0 | 0 | 0 | 0 | 0 | 0 | 0 |
| *of which:* Concessional | 0 | 0 | 0 | 0 | 0 | 0 | 0 | 0 |
| Other and adjustments | – | – | – | – | – | – | – | – |
| **Total Debt Service** | **5** | **2** | **2** | **3** | **5** | **13** | **8** | **10** |
| *of which:* Concessional | 1 | 1 | 2 | 3 | 3 | 4 | 5 | 5 |
| Non-concessional | 3 | 0 | 1 | 0 | 2 | 9 | 4 | 4 |

# NETHERLANDS ANTILLES

US $ Million

| | 1975 | 1976 | 1977 | 1978 | 1979 | 1980 | 1981 | 1982 |
|---|---|---|---|---|---|---|---|---|
| **DEBT** | | | | | | | | |
| DAC countries and capital | | | | | | | | |
| markets | 213 | 226 | 275 | 343 | 354 | 473 | 478 | 623 |
| ODA | 116 | 130 | 150 | 202 | 226 | 228 | 218 | 227 |
| Total export credits | 97 | 86 | 109 | 120 | 106 | 200 | 210 | 320 |
| Total private | – | 10 | 16 | 21 | 22 | 45 | 50 | 76 |
| *of which:* Bank loans | – | 10 | 11 | 11 | 10 | 30 | 35 | 60 |
| Bonds | – | – | – | – | – | – | – | – |
| Other | – | – | 5 | 10 | 12 | 15 | 15 | 16 |
| Multilateral | – | – | – | – | – | – | – | – |
| *of which:* Concessional | – | – | – | – | – | – | – | – |
| CMEA countries | – | – | – | – | – | – | – | – |
| *of which:* Concessional | – | – | – | – | – | – | – | – |
| OPEC countries | – | – | – | – | – | – | – | – |
| *of which:* Concessional | – | – | – | – | – | – | – | – |
| Other LDC'S | – | – | – | – | – | – | – | – |
| *of which:* Concessional | – | – | – | – | – | – | – | – |
| Other and adjustments | – | – | – | – | – | – | – | – |
| **Total Debt** | **213** | **226** | **275** | **343** | **354** | **473** | **478** | **623** |
| *of which:* Concessional | 116 | 130 | 150 | 202 | 226 | 228 | 218 | 227 |
| Non-concessional | 97 | 96 | 125 | 141 | 128 | 245 | 260 | 396 |
| **DEBT SERVICE** | | | | | | | | |
| DAC countries and capital | | | | | | | | |
| markets | 13 | 13 | 28 | 36 | 58 | 81 | 89 | 64 |
| ODA | 4 | 4 | 6 | 9 | 10 | 13 | 10 | 9 |
| Total export credits | 9 | 8 | 20 | 25 | 45 | 63 | 68 | 42 |
| Total private | – | 1 | 2 | 2 | 3 | 6 | 11 | 13 |
| *of which:* Bank loans | – | 1 | 2 | 2 | 2 | 4 | 8 | 10 |
| Bonds | – | – | – | – | – | – | – | – |
| Other | – | – | – | 1 | 1 | 2 | 4 | 4 |
| Multilateral | – | – | – | – | – | – | – | – |
| *of which:* Concessional | – | – | – | – | – | – | – | – |
| CMEA countries | – | – | – | – | – | – | – | – |
| *of which:* Concessional | – | – | – | – | – | – | – | – |
| OPEC countries | – | – | – | – | – | – | – | – |
| *of which:* Concessional | – | – | – | – | – | – | – | – |
| Other LDC'S | – | – | – | – | – | – | – | – |
| *of which:* Concessional | – | – | – | – | – | – | – | – |
| Other and adjustments | – | – | – | – | – | – | – | – |
| **Total Debt Service** | **13** | **13** | **28** | **36** | **58** | **81** | **89** | **64** |
| *of which:* Concessional | 4 | 4 | 6 | 9 | 10 | 13 | 10 | 9 |
| Non-concessional | 9 | 9 | 22 | 27 | 48 | 69 | 79 | 55 |

US $ Million

| | 1975 | 1976 | 1977 | 1978 | 1979 | 1980 | 1981 | 1982 |
|---|---|---|---|---|---|---|---|---|
| **DEBT** | | | | | | | | |
| DAC countries and capital markets | 153 | 145 | 152 | 184 | 213 | 221 | 193 | 184 |
| ODA | 153 | 138 | 140 | 153 | 159 | 143 | 116 | 118 |
| Total export credits | – | 7 | 12 | 31 | 53 | 76 | 72 | 66 |
| Total private | – | – | – | – | 1 | 2 | 5 | – |
| of which: Bank loans | – | – | – | – | 1 | 2 | 5 | – |
| Bonds | – | – | – | – | – | – | – | – |
| Other | – | – | – | – | – | – | – | – |
| Multilateral | – | – | – | – | – | – | – | – |
| of which: Concessional | – | – | – | – | – | – | – | – |
| CMEA countries | – | – | – | – | – | – | – | – |
| of which: Concessional | – | – | – | – | – | – | – | – |
| OPEC countries | – | – | – | – | – | – | – | – |
| of which: Concessional | – | – | – | – | – | – | – | – |
| Other LDC'S | – | – | – | – | – | – | – | – |
| of which: Concessional | – | – | – | – | – | – | – | – |
| Other and adjustments | – | – | – | – | – | – | – | – |
| **Total Debt** | **153** | **145** | **152** | **184** | **213** | **221** | **193** | **184** |
| of which: Concessional | 153 | 138 | 140 | 153 | 159 | 143 | 116 | 118 |
| Non-concessional | – | 7 | 12 | 31 | 54 | 78 | 77 | 66 |
| **DEBT SERVICE** | | | | | | | | |
| DAC countries and capital markets | 19 | 17 | 18 | 18 | 17 | 23 | 22 | 25 |
| ODA | 18 | 16 | 10 | 15 | 13 | 17 | 12 | 10 |
| Total export credits | 1 | 1 | 8 | 2 | 4 | 6 | 10 | 9 |
| Total private | – | – | – | – | – | 0 | 1 | 6 |
| of which: Bank loans | – | – | – | – | – | 0 | 1 | 6 |
| Bonds | – | – | – | – | – | – | – | – |
| Other | – | – | – | – | – | – | – | – |
| Multilateral | – | – | – | – | – | – | – | – |
| of which: Concessional | – | – | – | – | – | – | – | – |
| CMEA countries | – | – | – | – | – | – | – | – |
| of which: Concessional | – | – | – | – | – | – | – | – |
| OPEC countries | – | – | – | – | – | – | – | – |
| of which: Concessional | – | – | – | – | – | – | – | – |
| Other LDC'S | – | – | – | – | – | – | – | – |
| of which: Concessional | – | – | – | – | – | – | – | – |
| Other and adjustments | – | – | – | – | – | – | – | – |
| **Total Debt Service** | **19** | **17** | **18** | **18** | **17** | **23** | **22** | **25** |
| of which: Concessional | 18 | 16 | 10 | 15 | 13 | 17 | 12 | 10 |
| Non-concessional | 1 | 1 | 8 | 2 | 4 | 6 | 10 | 14 |

*US $ Million*

| | 1975 | 1976 | 1977 | 1978 | 1979 | 1980 | 1981 | 1982 |
|---|---|---|---|---|---|---|---|---|
| **DEBT** | | | | | | | | |
| DAC countries and capital | | | | | | | | |
| markets | 476 | 547 | 650 | 696 | 802 | 989 | 1109 | 1184 |
| ODA | 109 | 119 | 134 | 158 | 187 | 262 | 283 | 305 |
| Total export credits | 30 | 38 | 36 | 64 | 40 | 37 | 36 | 69 |
| Total private | 337 | 390 | 480 | 474 | 575 | 690 | 790 | 810 |
| *of which:* Bank loans | 327 | 290 | 401 | 406 | 527 | 660 | 760 | 780 |
| Bonds | 10 | 10 | 9 | 8 | 8 | – | – | – |
| Other | – | 90 | 70 | 60 | 40 | 30 | 30 | 30 |
| | | | | | | | | |
| Multilateral | 135 | 165 | 212 | 241 | 350 | 426 | 563 | 583 |
| *of which:* Concessional | 69 | 82 | 102 | 116 | 140 | 210 | 281 | 308 |
| | | | | | | | | |
| CMEA countries | – | – | – | – | – | 9 | 23 | 72 |
| *of which:* Concessional | – | – | – | – | – | 4 | 8 | 18 |
| | | | | | | | | |
| OPEC countries | – | 19 | 28 | 51 | 71 | 104 | 238 | 250 |
| *of which:* Concessional | – | – | – | – | – | – | – | 30 |
| | | | | | | | | |
| Other LDC'S | 3 | 4 | 7 | 9 | 9 | 56 | 93 | 117 |
| *of which:* Concessional | – | – | – | – | – | – | – | – |
| | | | | | | | | |
| Other and adjustments | – | – | 57 | 74 | 74 | 93 | 91 | 156 |
| | | | | | | | | |
| **Total Debt** | **613** | **735** | **953** | **1072** | **1306** | **1677** | **2117** | **2363** |
| *of which:* Concessional | 178 | 201 | 236 | 274 | 327 | 476 | 572 | 661 |
| Non-concessional | 435 | 533 | 717 | 798 | 980 | 1201 | 1545 | 1702 |
| | | | | | | | | |
| **DEBT SERVICE** | | | | | | | | |
| DAC countries and capital | | | | | | | | |
| markets | 50 | 73 | 101 | 82 | 36 | 42 | 75 | 91 |
| ODA | 3 | 3 | 4 | 4 | 4 | 4 | 11 | 1 |
| Total export credits | 14 | 14 | 21 | 27 | 13 | 9 | 4 | 6 |
| Total private | 34 | 55 | 77 | 50 | 20 | 29 | 60 | 84 |
| *of which:* Bank loans | 34 | 42 | 55 | 47 | 15 | 14 | 50 | 79 |
| Bonds | 0 | 1 | 2 | 2 | 0 | – | – | – |
| Other | – | 13 | 20 | 2 | 5 | 15 | 10 | 5 |
| | | | | | | | | |
| Multilateral | 12 | 14 | 17 | 17 | 22 | 44 | 60 | 62 |
| *of which:* Concessional | 5 | 5 | 6 | 5 | 8 | 11 | 9 | 8 |
| | | | | | | | | |
| CMEA countries | – | – | – | – | – | – | 1 | 16 |
| *of which:* Concessional | – | – | – | – | – | – | 1 | 1 |
| | | | | | | | | |
| OPEC countries | – | 0 | 1 | 1 | 2 | 5 | 9 | 41 |
| *of which:* Concessional | – | – | – | – | – | – | – | 0 |
| | | | | | | | | |
| Other LDC'S | 1 | 1 | 1 | 1 | 1 | 2 | 27 | 58 |
| *of which:* Concessional | – | – | – | – | – | – | – | – |
| | | | | | | | | |
| Other and adjustments | – | – | 4 | 7 | 4 | – | 1 | 32 |
| | | | | | | | | |
| **Total Debt Service** | **63** | **88** | **124** | **108** | **65** | **94** | **173** | **300** |
| *of which:* Concessional | 7 | 8 | 10 | 9 | 11 | 15 | 21 | 10 |
| Non-concessional | 55 | 80 | 114 | 99 | 54 | 79 | 152 | 290 |

*US $ Million*

| | 1975 | 1976 | 1977 | 1978 | 1979 | 1980 | 1981 | 1982 |
|---|---|---|---|---|---|---|---|---|
| **DEBT** | | | | | | | | |
| DAC countries and capital | | | | | | | | |
|   markets | 93 | 125 | 158 | 229 | 281 | 427 | 457 | 430 |
|   ODA | 76 | 86 | 102 | 82 | 51 | 67 | 84 | 82 |
|   Total export credits | 16 | 38 | 55 | 134 | 215 | 255 | 253 | 238 |
|   Total private | 1 | 1 | 1 | 13 | 15 | 105 | 120 | 110 |
|     *of which:* Bank loans | 1 | 1 | 1 | 13 | 15 | 105 | 120 | 110 |
|     Bonds | 0 | 0 | 0 | 0 | 0 | 0 | 0 | – |
|     Other | – | – | – | – | – | – | – | – |
| Multilateral | 22 | 29 | 39 | 66 | 109 | 161 | 203 | 197 |
|   *of which:* Concessional | 20 | 27 | 38 | 63 | 91 | 132 | 151 | 166 |
| CMEA countries | – | – | – | – | – | – | – | – |
|   *of which:* Concessional | – | – | – | – | – | – | – | – |
| OPEC countries | 1 | 1 | 4 | 4 | 6 | 9 | 27 | 47 |
|   *of which:* Concessional | 1 | 1 | 4 | 4 | 4 | 4 | 23 | 42 |
| Other LDC'S | 2 | 3 | 6 | 10 | 10 | 11 | 11 | 12 |
|   *of which:* Concessional | 2 | 3 | 6 | 10 | 10 | 11 | 11 | 12 |
| Other and adjustments | – | – | – | – | – | – | 5 | 6 |
| **Total Debt** | **117** | **158** | **207** | **310** | **406** | **608** | **703** | **692** |
|   *of which:* Concessional | 98 | 117 | 150 | 159 | 156 | 214 | 268 | 302 |
|     Non-concessional | 19 | 41 | 57 | 151 | 250 | 394 | 435 | 390 |
| **DEBT SERVICE** | | | | | | | | |
| DAC countries and capital | | | | | | | | |
|   markets | 9 | 11 | 17 | 27 | 44 | 70 | 90 | 119 |
|   ODA | 4 | 4 | 3 | 6 | 5 | 5 | 5 | 5 |
|   Total export credits | 5 | 6 | 14 | 21 | 37 | 56 | 46 | 73 |
|   Total private | 0 | 0 | 0 | 0 | 2 | 9 | 40 | 42 |
|     *of which:* Bank loans | 0 | 0 | 0 | 0 | 2 | 9 | 40 | 42 |
|     Bonds | 0 | 0 | – | – | 0 | – | 0 | – |
|     Other | – | – | – | – | – | – | – | – |
| Multilateral | 0 | 0 | 1 | 1 | 2 | 17 | 25 | 30 |
|   *of which:* Concessional | 0 | 0 | 0 | 0 | 1 | 16 | 7 | 4 |
| CMEA countries | – | – | – | – | – | – | – | – |
|   *of which:* Concessional | – | – | – | – | – | – | – | – |
| OPEC countries | – | 0 | 0 | 0 | 0 | 0 | 0 | 1 |
|   *of which:* Concessional | – | 0 | 0 | 0 | 0 | 0 | 0 | 1 |
| Other LDC'S | – | – | – | – | – | – | – | – |
|   *of which:* Concessional | – | – | – | – | – | – | – | – |
| Other and adjustments | – | – | – | – | – | – | – | 0 |
| **Total Debt Service** | **9** | **11** | **18** | **28** | **46** | **87** | **116** | **150** |
|   *of which:* Concessional | 4 | 5 | 3 | 6 | 6 | 21 | 12 | 9 |
|     Non-concessional | 6 | 7 | 14 | 22 | 40 | 66 | 103 | 140 |

# NIGERIA

| | 1975 | 1976 | 1977 | 1978 | 1979 | 1980 | 1981 | 1982 |
|---|---|---|---|---|---|---|---|---|
| **DEBT** | | | | | | | | |
| DAC countries and capital markets | 1022 | 1013 | 1270 | 2244 | 3639 | 4660 | 5409 | 7120 |
| ODA | 360 | 357 | 384 | 427 | 402 | 389 | 337 | 307 |
| Total export credits | 365 | 521 | 711 | 967 | 1527 | 2101 | 2342 | 3183 |
| Total private | 297 | 135 | 175 | 850 | 1710 | 2170 | 2730 | 3630 |
| *of which:* Bank loans | 14 | 110 | 145 | 820 | 1650 | 2100 | 2650 | 3480 |
| Bonds | 6 | 5 | – | – | – | – | – | – |
| Other | 277 | 20 | 30 | 30 | 60 | 70 | 80 | 150 |
| Multilateral | 365 | 406 | 451 | 490 | 524 | 571 | 620 | 739 |
| *of which:* Concessional | 167 | 159 | 152 | 144 | 138 | 131 | 123 | 116 |
| CMEA countries | 3 | 3 | 3 | 2 | 19 | 17 | 14 | 11 |
| *of which:* Concessional | 3 | 3 | 3 | 2 | 19 | 17 | 14 | 11 |
| OPEC countries | – | – | – | – | – | – | – | – |
| *of which:* Concessional | – | – | – | – | – | – | – | – |
| Other LDC'S | 6 | 5 | – | – | – | – | – | – |
| *of which:* Concessional | – | – | – | – | – | – | – | – |
| Other and adjustments | 3 | 3 | 3 | – | – | – | – | 18 |
| **Total Debt** | **1399** | **1430** | **1726** | **2737** | **4182** | **5248** | **6043** | **7889** |
| *of which:* Concessional | 530 | 519 | 538 | 574 | 559 | 537 | 475 | 434 |
| Non-concessional | 869 | 911 | 1188 | 2163 | 3623 | 4711 | 5568 | 7455 |
| **DEBT SERVICE** | | | | | | | | |
| DAC countries and capital markets | 364 | 533 | 549 | 609 | 776 | 1115 | 1730 | 1880 |
| ODA | 23 | 22 | 22 | 22 | 35 | 28 | 29 | 26 |
| Total export credits | 180 | 223 | 446 | 502 | 526 | 782 | 1101 | 794 |
| Total private | 160 | 288 | 82 | 85 | 215 | 305 | 600 | 1060 |
| *of which:* Bank loans | 6 | 11 | 27 | 55 | 185 | 260 | 580 | 1060 |
| Bonds | 0 | 0 | 5 | – | – | – | – | – |
| Other | 154 | 277 | 50 | 30 | 30 | 45 | 20 | – |
| Multilateral | 37 | 41 | 50 | 54 | 67 | 71 | 74 | 88 |
| *of which:* Concessional | 17 | 16 | 18 | 16 | 14 | 15 | 14 | 13 |
| CMEA countries | 0 | 1 | 0 | 1 | 2 | 3 | 3 | 6 |
| *of which:* Concessional | 0 | 1 | 0 | 1 | 2 | 3 | 3 | 4 |
| OPEC countries | – | – | – | – | – | – | – | – |
| *of which:* Concessional | – | – | – | – | – | – | – | – |
| Other LDC'S | 1 | 1 | 5 | – | – | – | – | – |
| *of which:* Concessional | – | – | – | – | – | – | – | – |
| Other and adjustments | – | – | – | 3 | – | – | – | 0 |
| **Total Debt Service** | **402** | **576** | **605** | **666** | **846** | **1188** | **1807** | **1973** |
| *of which:* Concessional | 40 | 39 | 40 | 39 | 52 | 45 | 45 | 43 |
| Non-concessional | 362 | 537 | 565 | 627 | 794 | 1143 | 1762 | 1930 |

*US $ Million*

| | 1975 | 1976 | 1977 | 1978 | 1979 | 1980 | 1981 | 1982 |
|---|---|---|---|---|---|---|---|---|
| **DEBT** | | | | | | | | |
| DAC countries and capital markets | 365 | 460 | 401 | 407 | 331 | 489 | 539 | 834 |
| ODA | – | – | – | – | – | – | – | – |
| Total export credits | 330 | 440 | 375 | 375 | 287 | 479 | 504 | 764 |
| Total private | 35 | 20 | 26 | 32 | 44 | 10 | 35 | 70 |
| *of which:* Bank loans | 35 | 20 | 26 | 32 | 44 | 10 | 35 | 70 |
| Bonds | – | – | – | – | – | – | – | – |
| Other | – | – | – | – | – | – | – | – |
| Multilateral | 0 | 1 | 8 | 25 | 31 | 40 | 52 | 42 |
| *of which:* Concessional | – | – | – | – | 1 | 6 | 6 | 5 |
| CMEA countries | – | – | – | – | – | – | – | – |
| *of which:* Concessional | – | – | – | – | – | – | – | – |
| OPEC countries | 72 | 154 | 169 | 196 | 369 | 270 | 280 | 298 |
| *of which:* Concessional | 50 | 136 | 149 | 175 | 193 | 90 | 136 | 189 |
| Other LDC'S | – | – | – | – | – | – | – | – |
| *of which:* Concessional | – | – | – | – | – | – | – | – |
| Other and adjustments | – | – | – | – | – | – | – | – |
| **Total Debt** | **437** | **615** | **578** | **628** | **732** | **800** | **871** | **1174** |
| *of which:* Concessional | 50 | 136 | 149 | 175 | 194 | 96 | 142 | 194 |
| Non-concessional | 387 | 479 | 429 | 453 | 538 | 704 | 729 | 980 |
| **DEBT SERVICE** | | | | | | | | |
| DAC countries and capital markets | 94 | 121 | 127 | 115 | 156 | 251 | 357 | 204 |
| ODA | – | – | – | – | – | – | – | – |
| Total export credits | 89 | 119 | 121 | 96 | 101 | 203 | 331 | 188 |
| Total private | 5 | 2 | 7 | 19 | 55 | 48 | 26 | 16 |
| *of which:* Bank loans | 5 | 2 | 7 | 19 | 55 | 48 | 26 | 16 |
| Bonds | – | – | – | – | – | – | – | – |
| Other | – | – | – | – | – | – | – | – |
| Multilateral | – | – | 0 | 1 | 2 | 5 | 11 | 6 |
| *of which:* Concessional | – | – | – | – | – | 0 | – | 0 |
| CMEA countries | – | – | – | – | – | – | – | – |
| *of which:* Concessional | – | – | – | – | – | – | – | – |
| OPEC countries | 20 | 7 | 0 | 0 | 30 | 10 | 57 | 55 |
| *of which:* Concessional | 10 | – | 0 | 0 | 7 | 10 | 15 | 13 |
| Other LDC'S | – | – | – | – | – | – | – | – |
| *of which:* Concessional | – | – | – | – | – | – | – | – |
| Other and adjustments | – | – | – | – | – | – | – | – |
| **Total Debt Service** | **114** | **127** | **128** | **116** | **189** | **265** | **425** | **265** |
| *of which:* Concessional | 10 | – | 0 | 0 | 7 | 10 | 15 | 14 |
| Non-concessional | 104 | 127 | 128 | 116 | 182 | 255 | 409 | 251 |

*US $ Million*

| | 1975 | 1976 | 1977 | 1978 | 1979 | 1980 | 1981 | 1982 |
|---|---|---|---|---|---|---|---|---|
| **DEBT** | | | | | | | | |
| DAC countries and capital | | | | | | | | |
| markets | – | – | – | – | – | 2 | 2 | 24 |
| ODA | – | – | – | – | – | – | 1 | 2 |
| Total export credits | – | – | – | – | – | 2 | 1 | 22 |
| Total private | – | – | – | – | – | – | – | – |
| *of which:* Bank loans | – | – | – | – | – | – | – | – |
| Bonds | – | – | – | – | – | – | – | – |
| Other | – | – | – | – | – | – | – | – |
| Multilateral | – | – | – | – | – | – | – | – |
| *of which:* Concessional | – | – | – | – | – | – | – | – |
| CMEA countries | – | – | – | – | – | – | – | – |
| *of which:* Concessional | – | – | – | – | – | – | – | – |
| OPEC countries | – | – | – | – | – | – | – | – |
| *of which:* Concessional | – | – | – | – | – | – | – | – |
| Other LDC'S | – | – | – | – | – | – | – | – |
| *of which:* Concessional | – | – | – | – | – | – | – | – |
| Other and adjustments | – | – | – | – | – | – | – | – |
| **Total Debt** | – | – | – | – | – | 2 | 2 | 24 |
| *of which:* Concessional | – | – | – | – | – | – | 1 | 2 |
| Non-concessional | – | – | – | – | – | 2 | 1 | 22 |
| | | | | | | | | |
| **DEBT SERVICE** | | | | | | | | |
| DAC countries and capital | | | | | | | | |
| markets | – | – | – | – | – | – | 1 | 1 |
| ODA | – | – | – | – | – | – | – | 0 |
| Total export credits | – | – | – | – | – | – | 1 | 1 |
| Total private | – | – | – | – | – | – | – | – |
| *of which:* Bank loans | – | – | – | – | – | – | – | – |
| Bonds | – | – | – | – | – | – | – | – |
| Other | – | – | – | – | – | – | – | – |
| Multilateral | – | – | – | – | – | – | – | – |
| *of which:* Concessional | – | – | – | – | – | – | – | – |
| CMEA countries | – | – | – | – | – | – | – | – |
| *of which:* Concessional | – | – | – | – | – | – | – | – |
| OPEC countries | – | – | – | – | – | – | – | – |
| *of which:* Concessional | – | – | – | – | – | – | – | – |
| Other LDC'S | – | – | – | – | – | – | – | – |
| *of which:* Concessional | – | – | – | – | – | – | – | – |
| Other and adjustments | – | – | – | – | – | – | – | – |
| **Total Debt Service** | – | – | – | – | – | – | 1 | 1 |
| *of which:* Concessional | – | – | – | – | – | – | – | 0 |
| Non-concessional | – | – | – | – | – | – | 1 | 1 |

*US $ Million*

| | 1975 | 1976 | 1977 | 1978 | 1979 | 1980 | 1981 | 1982 |
|---|---|---|---|---|---|---|---|---|
| **DEBT** | | | | | | | | |
| DAC countries and capital | | | | | | | | |
| markets | 3703 | 3905 | 4359 | 4868 | 5160 | 5616 | 5545 | 5594 |
| ODA | 3268 | 3512 | 3816 | 4233 | 4490 | 4722 | 4716 | 4741 |
| Total export credits | 415 | 323 | 433 | 475 | 420 | 524 | 529 | 473 |
| Total private | 20 | 70 | 110 | 160 | 250 | 370 | 300 | 380 |
| *of which:* Bank loans | 20 | 70 | 100 | 140 | 220 | 330 | 260 | 320 |
| Bonds | – | – | – | – | – | – | – | – |
| Other | – | – | 10 | 20 | 30 | 40 | 40 | 60 |
| Multilateral | 868 | 991 | 1175 | 1405 | 1540 | 1819 | 1902 | 2158 |
| *of which:* Concessional | 644 | 721 | 861 | 1028 | 1124 | 1376 | 1457 | 1639 |
| CMEA countries | 103 | 111 | 155 | 232 | 304 | 352 | 367 | 394 |
| *of which:* Concessional | 101 | 98 | 139 | 220 | 294 | 344 | 361 | 385 |
| OPEC countries | 641 | 1003 | 1095 | 1117 | 1198 | 1259 | 1232 | 1244 |
| *of which:* Concessional | 640 | 980 | 1043 | 1064 | 1153 | 1208 | 1175 | 1190 |
| Other LDC'S | 85 | 104 | 113 | 137 | 146 | 158 | 148 | 187 |
| *of which:* Concessional | 74 | 91 | 100 | 125 | 133 | 143 | 137 | 179 |
| Other and adjustments | – | – | – | – | – | – | – | – |
| **Total Debt** | **5400** | **6113** | **6897** | **7759** | **8348** | **9204** | **9194** | **9576** |
| *of which:* Concessional | 4728 | 5402 | 5959 | 6670 | 7195 | 7793 | 7847 | 8133 |
| Non-concessional | 672 | 711 | 939 | 1089 | 1154 | 1412 | 1347 | 1443 |
| **DEBT SERVICE** | | | | | | | | |
| DAC countries and capital | | | | | | | | |
| markets | 209 | 210 | 283 | 312 | 355 | 466 | 407 | 575 |
| ODA | 52 | 123 | 160 | 156 | 155 | 214 | 99 | 175 |
| Total export credits | 147 | 84 | 102 | 129 | 117 | 150 | 137 | 136 |
| Total private | 10 | 4 | 21 | 27 | 83 | 103 | 171 | 263 |
| *of which:* Bank loans | 10 | 4 | 20 | 23 | 75 | 95 | 155 | 245 |
| Bonds | – | – | – | – | – | – | – | – |
| Other | – | 0 | 1 | 4 | 8 | 8 | 16 | 18 |
| Multilateral | 48 | 77 | 65 | 81 | 109 | 103 | 115 | 108 |
| *of which:* Concessional | 25 | 39 | 30 | 34 | 36 | 37 | 41 | 36 |
| CMEA countries | 11 | 23 | 20 | 25 | 25 | 31 | 59 | 46 |
| *of which:* Concessional | 11 | 18 | 16 | 21 | 20 | 28 | 56 | 44 |
| OPEC countries | 10 | 18 | 24 | 26 | 60 | 98 | 95 | 104 |
| *of which:* Concessional | 10 | 18 | 22 | 23 | 50 | 96 | 92 | 100 |
| Other LDC'S | 1 | 1 | 1 | 2 | 3 | 3 | 4 | 4 |
| *of which:* Concessional | – | – | – | 0 | 0 | – | – | 0 |
| Other and adjustments | – | – | – | – | – | – | – | – |
| **Total Debt Service** | **280** | **330** | **392** | **446** | **553** | **701** | **679** | **836** |
| *of which:* Concessional | 98 | 198 | 228 | 234 | 261 | 375 | 289 | 355 |
| Non-concessional | 182 | 132 | 164 | 213 | 292 | 327 | 390 | 480 |

# PANAMA

| | 1975 | 1976 | 1977 | 1978 | 1979 | 1980 | 1981 | 1982 |
|---|---|---|---|---|---|---|---|---|
| **DEBT** | | | | | | | | |
| DAC countries and capital | | | | | | | | |
| markets | 606 | 874 | 1074 | 1512 | 1669 | 1779 | 1843 | 2203 |
| ODA | 93 | 99 | 108 | 114 | 121 | 132 | 139 | 152 |
| Total export credits | 56 | 68 | 61 | 68 | 67 | 61 | 50 | 48 |
| Total private | 457 | 707 | 905 | 1330 | 1481 | 1586 | 1654 | 2003 |
| *of which:* Bank loans | 431 | 668 | 843 | 1053 | 1159 | 1271 | 1344 | 1742 |
| Bonds | 26 | 39 | 62 | 277 | 322 | 315 | 310 | 261 |
| Other | – | – | – | – | – | – | – | – |
| Multilateral | 135 | 168 | 192 | 230 | 268 | 327 | 359 | 432 |
| *of which:* Concessional | 72 | 83 | 92 | 98 | 112 | 131 | 145 | 155 |
| CMEA countries | – | – | – | – | – | – | – | – |
| *of which:* Concessional | – | – | – | – | – | – | – | – |
| OPEC countries | 26 | 40 | 51 | 108 | 106 | 102 | 122 | 146 |
| *of which:* Concessional | – | – | – | – | – | – | 15 | 24 |
| Other LDC'S | 6 | 6 | 12 | 8 | 4 | 29 | 28 | 27 |
| *of which:* Concessional | – | – | – | – | – | – | – | – |
| Other and adjustments | 2 | 3 | 4 | 15 | 14 | 11 | 10 | 12 |
| **Total Debt** | **774** | **1091** | **1333** | **1873** | **2061** | **2249** | **2362** | **2821** |
| *of which:* Concessional | 165 | 182 | 200 | 212 | 233 | 263 | 299 | 331 |
| Non-concessional | 609 | 910 | 1133 | 1661 | 1828 | 1986 | 2063 | 2490 |
| **DEBT SERVICE** | | | | | | | | |
| DAC countries and capital | | | | | | | | |
| markets | 62 | 87 | 144 | 538 | 346 | 412 | 402 | 548 |
| ODA | 5 | 5 | 3 | 4 | 5 | 5 | 5 | 5 |
| Total export credits | 14 | 9 | 17 | 18 | 16 | 17 | 16 | 18 |
| Total private | 43 | 73 | 123 | 515 | 325 | 390 | 381 | 526 |
| *of which:* Bank loans | 41 | 71 | 121 | 506 | 295 | 348 | 342 | 442 |
| Bonds | 2 | 2 | 2 | 10 | 30 | 42 | 39 | 83 |
| Other | – | – | – | – | – | – | – | – |
| Multilateral | 10 | 13 | 16 | 21 | 26 | 29 | 64 | 40 |
| *of which:* Concessional | 5 | 6 | 6 | 6 | 7 | 7 | 7 | 8 |
| CMEA countries | – | – | – | – | – | – | – | – |
| *of which:* Concessional | – | – | – | – | – | – | – | – |
| OPEC countries | 0 | 0 | 0 | 1 | 10 | 15 | 16 | 16 |
| *of which:* Concessional | – | – | – | – | – | – | 1 | 1 |
| Other LDC'S | 0 | 0 | 1 | 7 | 4 | 4 | 7 | 6 |
| *of which:* Concessional | – | – | – | – | – | – | – | – |
| Other and adjustments | 0 | 0 | 1 | 2 | 2 | 5 | 3 | 3 |
| **Total Debt Service** | **73** | **101** | **161** | **568** | **389** | **465** | **492** | **614** |
| *of which:* Concessional | 10 | 11 | 9 | 10 | 12 | 12 | 13 | 14 |
| Non-concessional | 62 | 89 | 152 | 557 | 377 | 454 | 479 | 600 |

*US $ Million*

| | 1975 | 1976 | 1977 | 1978 | 1979 | 1980 | 1981 | 1982 |
|---|---|---|---|---|---|---|---|---|
| **DEBT** | | | | | | | | |
| DAC countries and capital | | | | | | | | |
| markets | 260 | 203 | 212 | 243 | 285 | 345 | 446 | 619 |
| ODA | 28 | 27 | 26 | 31 | 30 | 34 | 38 | 35 |
| Total export credits | 42 | 42 | 7 | 21 | 19 | 49 | 77 | 263 |
| Total private | 190 | 134 | 179 | 191 | 236 | 262 | 331 | 321 |
| *of which:* Bank loans | 111 | 52 | 87 | 85 | 140 | 177 | 258 | 260 |
| Bonds | 79 | 82 | 92 | 106 | 96 | 85 | 73 | 61 |
| Other | – | – | – | – | – | – | – | – |
| Multilateral | 67 | 77 | 91 | 114 | 130 | 177 | 204 | 228 |
| *of which:* Concessional | 23 | 29 | 40 | 61 | 70 | 106 | 129 | 146 |
| CMEA countries | – | – | – | – | – | – | – | – |
| *of which:* Concessional | – | – | – | – | – | – | – | – |
| OPEC countries | – | – | – | – | – | 3 | 3 | 3 |
| *of which:* Concessional | – | – | – | – | – | 3 | 3 | 3 |
| Other LDC'S | – | – | – | – | – | – | – | – |
| *of which:* Concessional | – | – | – | – | – | – | – | – |
| Other and adjustments | – | – | – | – | – | – | – | – |
| **Total Debt** | **327** | **281** | **303** | **357** | **415** | **524** | **653** | **850** |
| *of which:* Concessional | 51 | 56 | 66 | 92 | 100 | 142 | 169 | 184 |
| Non-concessional | 276 | 225 | 237 | 265 | 315 | 382 | 484 | 666 |
| **DEBT SERVICE** | | | | | | | | |
| DAC countries and capital | | | | | | | | |
| markets | 24 | 32 | 39 | 31 | 45 | 59 | 66 | 114 |
| ODA | 4 | 5 | 6 | 5 | 5 | 8 | 8 | 8 |
| Total export credits | 7 | 19 | 20 | 6 | 8 | 10 | 14 | 23 |
| Total private | 12 | 8 | 14 | 19 | 33 | 41 | 45 | 83 |
| *of which:* Bank loans | 8 | – | 6 | 11 | 18 | 26 | 33 | 71 |
| Bonds | 4 | 8 | 8 | 9 | 15 | 15 | 13 | 12 |
| Other | – | – | – | – | – | – | – | – |
| Multilateral | 3 | 5 | 6 | 7 | 8 | 9 | 10 | 11 |
| *of which:* Concessional | 0 | 1 | 1 | 1 | 2 | 2 | 2 | 2 |
| CMEA countries | – | – | – | – | – | – | – | – |
| *of which:* Concessional | – | – | – | – | – | – | – | – |
| OPEC countries | – | – | – | – | – | 0 | 0 | 0 |
| *of which:* Concessional | – | – | – | – | – | 0 | 0 | 0 |
| Other LDC'S | – | – | – | – | – | – | – | – |
| *of which:* Concessional | – | – | – | – | – | – | – | – |
| Other and adjustments | – | – | – | – | – | – | – | – |
| **Total Debt Service** | **27** | **36** | **45** | **37** | **53** | **68** | **76** | **125** |
| *of which:* Concessional | 5 | 5 | 6 | 6 | 7 | 10 | 10 | 10 |
| Non-concessional | 22 | 31 | 39 | 31 | 46 | 58 | 67 | 115 |

*US $ Million*

| | 1975 | 1976 | 1977 | 1978 | 1979 | 1980 | 1981 | 1982 |
|---|---|---|---|---|---|---|---|---|
| **DEBT** | | | | | | | | |
| DAC countries and capital | | | | | | | | |
| markets | 129 | 154 | 181 | 269 | 408 | 459 | 457 | 631 |
| ODA | 63 | 72 | 88 | 110 | 106 | 108 | 108 | 141 |
| Total export credits | 26 | 32 | 30 | 57 | 113 | 91 | 109 | 195 |
| Total private | 40 | 50 | 63 | 102 | 189 | 260 | 240 | 295 |
| *of which:* Bank loans | 10 | 10 | 18 | 72 | 159 | 230 | 205 | 260 |
| Bonds | – | – | – | – | – | – | – | – |
| Other | 30 | 40 | 45 | 30 | 30 | 30 | 35 | 35 |
| Multilateral | 67 | 80 | 97 | 124 | 157 | 193 | 253 | 321 |
| *of which:* Concessional | 57 | 66 | 77 | 89 | 103 | 109 | 126 | 147 |
| CMEA countries | – | – | – | – | – | – | – | – |
| *of which:* Concessional | – | – | – | – | – | – | – | – |
| OPEC countries | – | – | – | – | – | – | – | – |
| *of which:* Concessional | – | – | – | – | – | – | – | – |
| Other LDC'S | 21 | 28 | 86 | 110 | 139 | 178 | 207 | 254 |
| *of which:* Concessional | 0 | 0 | 57 | 61 | 64 | 68 | 72 | 79 |
| Other and adjustments | 1 | 18 | 32 | 39 | 36 | 34 | 31 | 35 |
| **Total Debt** | **218** | **280** | **395** | **542** | **741** | **863** | **948** | **1241** |
| *of which:* Concessional | 120 | 149 | 242 | 282 | 294 | 305 | 324 | 383 |
| Non-concessional | 97 | 132 | 152 | 261 | 447 | 558 | 624 | 858 |
| **DEBT SERVICE** | | | | | | | | |
| DAC countries and capital | | | | | | | | |
| markets | 20 | 21 | 24 | 40 | 50 | 80 | 85 | 115 |
| ODA | 4 | 4 | 4 | 6 | 7 | 11 | 8 | 6 |
| Total export credits | 8 | 11 | 8 | 10 | 28 | 20 | 24 | 36 |
| Total private | 8 | 6 | 12 | 24 | 15 | 49 | 53 | 73 |
| *of which:* Bank loans | 3 | 1 | 2 | 8 | 10 | 44 | 46 | 65 |
| Bonds | – | – | – | – | – | – | – | – |
| Other | 5 | 5 | 10 | 16 | 5 | 5 | 7 | 8 |
| Multilateral | 4 | 4 | 5 | 6 | 9 | 13 | 18 | 24 |
| *of which:* Concessional | 2 | 3 | 3 | 3 | 3 | 4 | 4 | 5 |
| CMEA countries | – | – | – | – | – | – | – | – |
| *of which:* Concessional | – | – | – | – | – | – | – | – |
| OPEC countries | – | – | – | – | – | – | – | – |
| *of which:* Concessional | – | – | – | – | – | – | – | – |
| Other LDC'S | 4 | 3 | 7 | 7 | 11 | 16 | 19 | 19 |
| *of which:* Concessional | 0 | 0 | 0 | 0 | 0 | 0 | 0 | 0 |
| Other and adjustments | 1 | 0 | 2 | 4 | 5 | 6 | 4 | 3 |
| **Total Debt Service** | **28** | **28** | **37** | **56** | **75** | **115** | **126** | **161** |
| *of which:* Concessional | 7 | 7 | 7 | 10 | 13 | 17 | 14 | 12 |
| Non-concessional | 22 | 21 | 30 | 46 | 62 | 98 | 112 | 149 |

# PERU

*US $ Million*

| | 1975 | 1976 | 1977 | 1978 | 1979 | 1980 | 1981 | 1982 |
|---|---|---|---|---|---|---|---|---|
| **DEBT** | | | | | | | | |
| DAC countries and capital | | | | | | | | |
| markets | 2607 | 3026 | 3523 | 4025 | 4238 | 4753 | 4949 | 5323 |
| ODA | 206 | 212 | 255 | 368 | 442 | 541 | 586 | 607 |
| Total export credits | 1085 | 1207 | 1370 | 1753 | 1690 | 2000 | 2056 | 1780 |
| Total private | 1316 | 1607 | 1898 | 1904 | 2106 | 2212 | 2307 | 2936 |
| of which: Bank loans | 1264 | 1532 | 1825 | 1831 | 2044 | 2150 | 2240 | 2850 |
| Bonds | 2 | 1 | 3 | 3 | 2 | 2 | 2 | 1 |
| Other | 50 | 74 | 70 | 70 | 60 | 60 | 65 | 85 |
| Multilateral | 157 | 171 | 220 | 258 | 331 | 513 | 648 | 852 |
| of which: Concessional | 103 | 95 | 92 | 94 | 93 | 98 | 112 | 123 |
| CMEA countries | 195 | 229 | 601 | 703 | 707 | 785 | 819 | 822 |
| of which: Concessional | 144 | 180 | 528 | 637 | 654 | 737 | 748 | 710 |
| OPEC countries | 15 | 33 | 86 | 134 | 70 | 55 | 47 | 37 |
| of which: Concessional | – | – | – | – | – | – | – | – |
| Other LDC'S | 135 | 207 | 279 | 303 | 277 | 328 | 354 | 417 |
| of which: Concessional | 1 | 1 | 1 | 2 | 2 | 6 | 6 | 5 |
| Other and adjustments | 141 | 247 | 485 | 602 | 882 | 645 | 538 | 933 |
| **Total Debt** | **3251** | **3913** | **5194** | **6025** | **6507** | **7081** | **7356** | **8383** |
| of which: Concessional | 454 | 489 | 876 | 1100 | 1191 | 1382 | 1452 | 1453 |
| Non-concessional | 2797 | 3424 | 4318 | 4924 | 5316 | 5699 | 5904 | 6930 |
| **DEBT SERVICE** | | | | | | | | |
| DAC countries and capital | | | | | | | | |
| markets | 440 | 406 | 573 | 604 | 787 | 1343 | 1683 | 1196 |
| ODA | 13 | 13 | 16 | 25 | 13 | 31 | 34 | 28 |
| Total export credits | 259 | 224 | 245 | 251 | 312 | 454 | 554 | 515 |
| Total private | 168 | 169 | 312 | 328 | 462 | 859 | 1095 | 652 |
| of which: Bank loans | 157 | 157 | 297 | 313 | 441 | 853 | 1085 | 640 |
| Bonds | 3 | 1 | 0 | 0 | 0 | 1 | 0 | 0 |
| Other | 8 | 11 | 15 | 15 | 20 | 5 | 10 | 12 |
| Multilateral | 23 | 25 | 29 | 36 | 42 | 58 | 75 | 89 |
| of which: Concessional | 15 | 15 | 16 | 17 | 16 | 14 | 12 | 12 |
| CMEA countries | 20 | 16 | 36 | 39 | 37 | 58 | 99 | 162 |
| of which: Concessional | 12 | 5 | 23 | 12 | 15 | 39 | 82 | 131 |
| OPEC countries | 0 | 2 | 4 | 34 | 83 | 32 | 24 | 10 |
| of which: Concessional | – | – | – | – | – | – | – | – |
| Other LDC'S | 9 | 24 | 46 | 59 | 77 | 75 | 80 | 95 |
| of which: Concessional | – | – | – | – | – | – | – | 0 |
| Other and adjustments | 8 | 24 | 38 | 47 | 56 | 69 | 45 | 72 |
| **Total Debt Service** | **500** | **497** | **726** | **820** | **1081** | **1635** | **2005** | **1624** |
| of which: Concessional | 40 | 33 | 54 | 54 | 43 | 84 | 128 | 171 |
| Non-concessional | 460 | 464 | 671 | 766 | 1039 | 1551 | 1877 | 1453 |

179

US $ Million

| | 1975 | 1976 | 1977 | 1978 | 1979 | 1980 | 1981 | 1982 |
|---|---|---|---|---|---|---|---|---|
| **DEBT** | | | | | | | | |
| DAC countries and capital | | | | | | | | |
| markets | 2245 | 3023 | 4323 | 5389 | 6231 | 7133 | 8105 | 9368 |
| ODA | 391 | 464 | 561 | 770 | 755 | 949 | 1088 | 1169 |
| Total export credits | 949 | 1052 | 1532 | 1866 | 2222 | 2482 | 2767 | 2810 |
| Total private | 905 | 1507 | 2230 | 2753 | 3254 | 3702 | 4250 | 5389 |
| of which: Bank loans | 850 | 1095 | 1600 | 1794 | 2210 | 2460 | 2950 | 3915 |
| Bonds | 5 | 371 | 480 | 709 | 717 | 842 | 800 | 824 |
| Other | 50 | 41 | 150 | 250 | 327 | 400 | 500 | 650 |
| Multilateral | 339 | 472 | 608 | 852 | 1180 | 1501 | 2006 | 2300 |
| of which: Concessional | 85 | 96 | 117 | 179 | 254 | 310 | 308 | 310 |
| CMEA countries | – | – | – | – | 11 | 13 | 15 | 13 |
| of which: Concessional | – | – | – | – | 9 | 11 | 13 | 11 |
| OPEC countries | 17 | 17 | 47 | 74 | 69 | 61 | 58 | 56 |
| of which: Concessional | – | – | – | – | 3 | 7 | 6 | 8 |
| Other LDC'S | 37 | 32 | 25 | 19 | 14 | 13 | 8 | 9 |
| of which: Concessional | 3 | 2 | 2 | 2 | 1 | – | – | – |
| Other and adjustments | 52 | 252 | 101 | 1 | 1 | 0 | 0 | 166 |
| **Total Debt** | **2690** | **3796** | **5104** | **6336** | **7506** | **8721** | **10193** | **11911** |
| of which: Concessional | 479 | 562 | 680 | 951 | 1021 | 1277 | 1415 | 1498 |
| Non-concessional | 2211 | 3234 | 4424 | 5385 | 6485 | 7444 | 8778 | 10412 |
| **DEBT SERVICE** | | | | | | | | |
| DAC countries and capital | | | | | | | | |
| markets | 385 | 433 | 524 | 1069 | 1188 | 1070 | 1506 | 1584 |
| ODA | 15 | 11 | 24 | 30 | 45 | 44 | 58 | 61 |
| Total export credits | 208 | 227 | 293 | 379 | 456 | 440 | 460 | 407 |
| Total private | 162 | 195 | 206 | 660 | 688 | 586 | 989 | 1116 |
| of which: Bank loans | 150 | 171 | 145 | 476 | 395 | 362 | 735 | 895 |
| Bonds | 2 | 11 | 31 | 33 | 43 | 34 | 54 | 71 |
| Other | 10 | 13 | 30 | 150 | 250 | 190 | 200 | 150 |
| Multilateral | 31 | 45 | 60 | 89 | 120 | 146 | 174 | 240 |
| of which: Concessional | 9 | 9 | 9 | 10 | 10 | 12 | 12 | 11 |
| CMEA countries | – | – | – | – | 0 | 1 | 4 | 3 |
| of which: Concessional | – | – | – | – | – | 1 | 2 | 3 |
| OPEC countries | – | – | 2 | 2 | 11 | 16 | 6 | 7 |
| of which: Concessional | – | – | – | – | 0 | 0 | 1 | 1 |
| Other LDC'S | 8 | 8 | 10 | 7 | 11 | 3 | 7 | 3 |
| of which: Concessional | 1 | 1 | 1 | – | 1 | 1 | – | – |
| Other and adjustments | 1 | 0 | 0 | 0 | 1 | 0 | 0 | 0 |
| **Total Debt Service** | **424** | **487** | **596** | **1167** | **1331** | **1236** | **1697** | **1839** |
| of which: Concessional | 24 | 21 | 34 | 40 | 56 | 58 | 72 | 75 |
| Non-concessional | 400 | 466 | 562 | 1127 | 1275 | 1178 | 1624 | 1764 |

*US $ Million*

| | 1975 | 1976 | 1977 | 1978 | 1979 | 1980 | 1981 | 1982 |
|---|---|---|---|---|---|---|---|---|
| **DEBT** | | | | | | | | |
| DAC countries and capital markets | 51 | 50 | 66 | 82 | 101 | 112 | 104 | 114 |
| ODA | 51 | 46 | 53 | 61 | 65 | 64 | 56 | 70 |
| Total export credits | – | 4 | 13 | 21 | 36 | 48 | 48 | 44 |
| Total private | – | – | – | – | – | – | – | – |
| *of which:* Bank loans | – | – | – | – | – | – | – | – |
| Bonds | – | – | – | – | – | – | – | – |
| Other | – | – | – | – | – | – | – | – |
| Multilateral | – | – | – | – | – | – | – | – |
| *of which:* Concessional | – | – | – | – | – | – | – | – |
| CMEA countries | – | – | – | – | – | – | – | – |
| *of which:* Concessional | – | – | – | – | – | – | – | – |
| OPEC countries | – | – | – | – | – | – | – | – |
| *of which:* Concessional | – | – | – | – | – | – | – | – |
| Other LDC'S | – | – | – | – | – | – | – | – |
| *of which:* Concessional | – | – | – | – | – | – | – | – |
| Other and adjustments | – | – | – | – | – | – | – | – |
| **Total Debt** | **51** | **50** | **66** | **82** | **101** | **112** | **104** | **114** |
| *of which:* Concessional | 51 | 46 | 53 | 61 | 65 | 64 | 56 | 70 |
| Non-concessional | – | 4 | 13 | 21 | 36 | 48 | 48 | 44 |
| **DEBT SERVICE** | | | | | | | | |
| DAC countries and capital markets | 5 | 6 | 6 | 9 | 10 | 13 | 10 | 15 |
| ODA | 5 | 6 | 3 | 7 | 7 | 7 | 6 | 5 |
| Total export credits | – | 0 | 2 | 1 | 3 | 6 | 5 | 10 |
| Total private | – | – | – | – | – | – | – | – |
| *of which:* Bank loans | – | – | – | – | – | – | – | – |
| Bonds | – | – | – | – | – | – | – | – |
| Other | – | – | – | – | – | – | – | – |
| Multilateral | – | – | – | – | – | – | – | – |
| *of which:* Concessional | – | – | – | – | – | – | – | – |
| CMEA countries | – | – | – | – | – | – | – | – |
| *of which:* Concessional | – | – | – | – | – | – | – | – |
| OPEC countries | – | – | – | – | – | – | – | – |
| *of which:* Concessional | – | – | – | – | – | – | – | – |
| Other LDC'S | – | – | – | – | – | – | – | – |
| *of which:* Concessional | – | – | – | – | – | – | – | – |
| Other and adjustments | – | – | – | – | – | – | – | – |
| **Total Debt Service** | **5** | **6** | **6** | **9** | **10** | **13** | **10** | **15** |
| *of which:* Concessional | 5 | 6 | 3 | 7 | 7 | 7 | 6 | 5 |
| Non-concessional | – | 0 | 2 | 1 | 3 | 6 | 5 | 10 |

*US $ Million*

| | 1975 | 1976 | 1977 | 1978 | 1979 | 1980 | 1981 | 1982 |
|---|---|---|---|---|---|---|---|---|
| **DEBT** | | | | | | | | |
| DAC countries and capital | | | | | | | | |
| markets | 1212 | 1508 | 2246 | 3633 | 4594 | 5308 | 6422 | 7851 |
| ODA | 34 | 84 | 151 | 194 | 567 | 620 | 615 | 592 |
| Total export credits | 609 | 741 | 1139 | 1912 | 1905 | 1825 | 1808 | 1842 |
| Total private | 569 | 683 | 956 | 1527 | 2122 | 2863 | 3999 | 5417 |
| *of which:* Bank loans | 408 | 530 | 674 | 1253 | 1860 | 2605 | 3750 | 5180 |
| Bonds | 51 | 43 | 82 | 74 | 62 | 48 | 29 | 37 |
| Other | 110 | 110 | 200 | 200 | 200 | 210 | 220 | 200 |
| Multilateral | 62 | 117 | 179 | 283 | 418 | 536 | 604 | 1157 |
| *of which:* Concessional | 37 | 34 | 33 | 31 | 28 | 24 | 20 | 16 |
| CMEA countries | – | – | – | – | – | – | – | – |
| *of which:* Concessional | – | – | – | – | – | – | – | – |
| OPEC countries | – | – | 15 | 24 | 25 | 24 | 22 | 21 |
| *of which:* Concessional | – | – | – | – | – | – | – | – |
| Other LDC'S | 8 | 6 | 7 | 3 | 1 | 4 | 5 | 28 |
| *of which:* Concessional | – | – | – | – | – | – | – | – |
| Other and adjustments | 200 | 202 | 198 | 171 | 113 | 114 | 86 | 73 |
| **Total Debt** | **1482** | **1832** | **2644** | **4114** | **5151** | **5986** | **7138** | **9130** |
| *of which:* Concessional | 133 | 183 | 246 | 284 | 654 | 707 | 681 | 647 |
| Non-concessional | 1349 | 1649 | 2399 | 3830 | 4497 | 5280 | 6457 | 8483 |
| **DEBT SERVICE** | | | | | | | | |
| DAC countries and capital | | | | | | | | |
| markets | 230 | 288 | 322 | 436 | 785 | 1097 | 1461 | 1653 |
| ODA | 5 | 12 | 13 | 28 | 24 | 29 | 34 | 38 |
| Total export credits | 87 | 91 | 176 | 218 | 411 | 595 | 533 | 460 |
| Total private | 138 | 185 | 134 | 191 | 350 | 474 | 894 | 1154 |
| *of which:* Bank loans | 127 | 169 | 113 | 125 | 280 | 385 | 810 | 1060 |
| Bonds | 10 | 6 | 11 | 16 | 20 | 19 | 19 | 14 |
| Other | – | 10 | 10 | 50 | 50 | 70 | 65 | 80 |
| Multilateral | 10 | 10 | 15 | 24 | 42 | 67 | 84 | 145 |
| *of which:* Concessional | 5 | 5 | 6 | 6 | 6 | 6 | 5 | 5 |
| CMEA countries | – | – | – | – | – | – | – | – |
| *of which:* Concessional | – | – | – | – | – | – | – | – |
| OPEC countries | – | – | – | 1 | 2 | 3 | 3 | 3 |
| *of which:* Concessional | – | – | – | – | – | – | – | – |
| Other LDC'S | – | 2 | 2 | 4 | 2 | 1 | 0 | 2 |
| *of which:* Concessional | – | – | – | – | – | – | – | – |
| Other and adjustments | 11 | 4 | 6 | 7 | 12 | 12 | 10 | 10 |
| **Total Debt Service** | **250** | **304** | **345** | **473** | **844** | **1179** | **1558** | **1813** |
| *of which:* Concessional | 12 | 21 | 23 | 38 | 35 | 40 | 44 | 46 |
| Non-concessional | 238 | 283 | 322 | 434 | 808 | 1139 | 1514 | 1767 |

US $ Million

| | 1975 | 1976 | 1977 | 1978 | 1979 | 1980 | 1981 | 1982 |
|---|---|---|---|---|---|---|---|---|
| **DEBT** | | | | | | | | |
| DAC countries and capital markets | 173 | 311 | 371 | 632 | 479 | 568 | 478 | 352 |
| ODA | – | – | – | – | – | – | – | – |
| Total export credits | 173 | 311 | 371 | 632 | 479 | 568 | 478 | 302 |
| Total private | – | – | – | – | – | – | – | 50 |
| of which: Bank loans | – | – | – | – | – | – | – | 50 |
| Bonds | – | – | – | – | – | – | – | – |
| Other | – | – | – | – | – | – | – | – |
| Multilateral | – | – | – | – | – | – | – | – |
| of which: Concessional | – | – | – | – | – | – | – | – |
| CMEA countries | – | – | – | – | – | – | – | – |
| of which: Concessional | – | – | – | – | – | – | – | – |
| OPEC countries | – | – | – | – | – | – | – | – |
| of which: Concessional | – | – | – | – | – | – | – | – |
| Other LDC'S | – | – | – | – | – | – | – | – |
| of which: Concessional | – | – | – | – | – | – | – | – |
| Other and adjustments | – | – | – | – | – | – | – | – |
| **Total Debt** | **173** | **311** | **371** | **632** | **479** | **568** | **478** | **352** |
| of which: Concessional | – | – | – | – | – | – | – | – |
| Non-concessional | 173 | 311 | 371 | 632 | 479 | 568 | 478 | 352 |
| **DEBT SERVICE** | | | | | | | | |
| DAC countries and capital markets | 42 | 59 | 143 | 158 | 206 | 195 | 258 | 241 |
| ODA | – | – | – | – | – | – | – | – |
| Total export credits | 42 | 59 | 143 | 158 | 206 | 195 | 258 | 240 |
| Total private | – | – | – | – | – | – | – | 1 |
| of which: Bank loans | – | – | – | – | – | – | – | 1 |
| Bonds | – | – | – | – | – | – | – | – |
| Other | – | – | – | – | – | – | – | – |
| Multilateral | – | – | – | – | – | – | – | – |
| of which: Concessional | – | – | – | – | – | – | – | – |
| CMEA countries | – | – | – | – | – | – | – | – |
| of which: Concessional | – | – | – | – | – | – | – | – |
| OPEC countries | – | – | – | – | – | – | – | – |
| of which: Concessional | – | – | – | – | – | – | – | – |
| Other LDC'S | – | – | – | – | – | – | – | – |
| of which: Concessional | – | – | – | – | – | – | – | – |
| Other and adjustments | – | – | – | – | – | – | – | – |
| **Total Debt Service** | **42** | **59** | **143** | **158** | **206** | **195** | **258** | **241** |
| of which: Concessional | – | – | – | – | – | – | – | – |
| Non-concessional | 42 | 59 | 143 | 158 | 206 | 195 | 258 | 241 |

# REUNION

| | 1975 | 1976 | 1977 | 1978 | 1979 | 1980 | 1981 | 1982 |
|---|---|---|---|---|---|---|---|---|
| **DEBT** | | | | | | | | |
| DAC countries and capital markets | 139 | 133 | 131 | 165 | 164 | 136 | 98 | 76 |
| ODA | 139 | 132 | 130 | 163 | 161 | 133 | 96 | 75 |
| Total export credits | – | 1 | 1 | 2 | 3 | 3 | 2 | 1 |
| Total private | – | – | – | – | – | – | – | – |
| *of which:* Bank loans | – | – | – | – | – | – | – | – |
| Bonds | – | – | – | – | – | – | – | – |
| Other | – | – | – | – | – | – | – | – |
| Multilateral | – | – | – | – | – | – | – | – |
| *of which:* Concessional | – | – | – | – | – | – | – | – |
| CMEA countries | – | – | – | – | – | – | – | – |
| *of which:* Concessional | – | – | – | – | – | – | – | – |
| OPEC countries | – | – | – | – | – | – | – | – |
| *of which:* Concessional | – | – | – | – | – | – | – | – |
| Other LDC'S | – | – | – | – | – | – | – | – |
| *of which:* Concessional | – | – | – | – | – | – | – | – |
| Other and adjustments | – | – | – | – | – | – | – | – |
| **Total Debt** | **139** | **133** | **131** | **165** | **164** | **136** | **98** | **76** |
| *of which:* Concessional | 139 | 132 | 130 | 163 | 161 | 133 | 96 | 75 |
| Non-concessional | – | 1 | 1 | 2 | 3 | 3 | 2 | 1 |
| **DEBT SERVICE** | | | | | | | | |
| DAC countries and capital markets | 13 | 14 | 16 | 17 | 18 | 19 | 15 | 8 |
| ODA | 13 | 14 | 16 | 16 | 18 | 18 | 13 | 8 |
| Total export credits | – | – | 0 | 0 | 0 | 1 | 1 | 0 |
| Total private | – | – | – | – | – | – | – | – |
| *of which:* Bank loans | – | – | – | – | – | – | – | – |
| Bonds | – | – | – | – | – | – | – | – |
| Other | – | – | – | – | – | – | – | – |
| Multilateral | – | – | – | – | – | – | – | – |
| *of which:* Concessional | – | – | – | – | – | – | – | – |
| CMEA countries | – | – | – | – | – | – | – | – |
| *of which:* Concessional | – | – | – | – | – | – | – | – |
| OPEC countries | – | – | – | – | – | – | – | – |
| *of which:* Concessional | – | – | – | – | – | – | – | – |
| Other LDC'S | – | – | – | – | – | – | – | – |
| *of which:* Concessional | – | – | – | – | – | – | – | – |
| Other and adjustments | – | – | – | – | – | – | – | – |
| **Total Debt Service** | **13** | **14** | **16** | **17** | **18** | **19** | **15** | **8** |
| *of which:* Concessional | 13 | 14 | 16 | 16 | 18 | 18 | 13 | 8 |
| Non-concessional | – | – | 0 | 0 | 0 | 1 | 1 | 0 |

184

# RWANDA

|  | 1975 | 1976 | 1977 | 1978 | 1979 | 1980 | 1981 | 1982 |
|---|---|---|---|---|---|---|---|---|
| **DEBT** | | | | | | | | |
| DAC countries and capital | | | | | | | | |
| markets | 7 | 12 | 18 | 24 | 10 | 18 | 27 | 28 |
| ODA | 2 | 9 | 14 | 22 | 8 | 13 | 21 | 24 |
| Total export credits | 4 | 3 | 4 | 2 | 2 | 4 | 5 | 3 |
| Total private | 1 | 0 | 0 | 0 | – | 1 | 1 | 1 |
| of which: Bank loans | – | – | – | – | – | 1 | 1 | 1 |
| Bonds | 1 | 0 | 0 | 0 | – | – | – | – |
| Other | – | – | – | – | – | – | – | – |
| Multilateral | 16 | 25 | 37 | 53 | 79 | 104 | 118 | 134 |
| of which: Concessional | 16 | 25 | 37 | 53 | 79 | 104 | 118 | 133 |
| CMEA countries | – | – | – | – | – | – | – | – |
| of which: Concessional | – | – | – | – | – | – | – | – |
| OPEC countries | 3 | 3 | 8 | 9 | 10 | 11 | 11 | 11 |
| of which: Concessional | 3 | 3 | 8 | 9 | 10 | 11 | 11 | 11 |
| Other LDC'S | – | 8 | 11 | 15 | 28 | 28 | 24 | 22 |
| of which: Concessional | – | 8 | 11 | 15 | 28 | 28 | 24 | 22 |
| Other and adjustments | – | – | – | – | – | – | – | – |
| **Total Debt** | **25** | **49** | **74** | **101** | **127** | **161** | **180** | **195** |
| of which: Concessional | 21 | 45 | 70 | 99 | 125 | 156 | 174 | 190 |
| Non-concessional | 5 | 3 | 4 | 2 | 2 | 5 | 6 | 5 |
| **DEBT SERVICE** | | | | | | | | |
| DAC countries and capital | | | | | | | | |
| markets | 1 | 1 | 2 | 2 | 2 | 2 | 2 | 1 |
| ODA | 0 | 0 | 0 | 0 | 1 | 0 | 1 | 0 |
| Total export credits | 1 | 1 | 1 | 2 | 1 | 2 | 2 | 1 |
| Total private | 0 | 0 | 0 | 0 | 0 | 0 | 0 | 0 |
| of which: Bank loans | – | – | – | – | – | 0 | 0 | 0 |
| Bonds | 0 | 0 | 0 | 0 | 0 | – | – | – |
| Other | – | – | – | – | – | – | – | – |
| Multilateral | 0 | 0 | 0 | 0 | 0 | 1 | 1 | 4 |
| of which: Concessional | 0 | 0 | 0 | 0 | 0 | 1 | 1 | 4 |
| CMEA countries | – | – | – | – | – | – | – | – |
| of which: Concessional | – | – | – | – | – | – | – | – |
| OPEC countries | – | – | 0 | 0 | 0 | 0 | 1 | 1 |
| of which: Concessional | – | – | 0 | 0 | 0 | 0 | 1 | 1 |
| Other LDC'S | – | – | – | – | – | – | – | – |
| of which: Concessional | – | – | – | – | – | – | – | – |
| Other and adjustments | – | – | – | – | – | – | – | – |
| **Total Debt Service** | **1** | **1** | **2** | **3** | **2** | **3** | **4** | **6** |
| of which: Concessional | 0 | 0 | 1 | 1 | 1 | 1 | 2 | 5 |
| Non-concessional | 1 | 1 | 1 | 2 | 1 | 2 | 2 | 1 |

*US $ Million*

| | 1975 | 1976 | 1977 | 1978 | 1979 | 1980 | 1981 | 1982 |
|---|---|---|---|---|---|---|---|---|
| **DEBT** | | | | | | | | |
| DAC countries and capital | | | | | | | | |
| markets | 9 | 10 | 13 | 12 | 11 | 9 | 6 | 4 |
| ODA | 9 | 7 | 10 | 8 | 8 | 7 | 5 | 3 |
| Total export credits | – | 3 | 3 | 4 | 3 | 2 | 1 | 1 |
| Total private | – | – | – | – | – | – | – | – |
| of which: Bank loans | – | – | – | – | – | – | – | – |
| Bonds | – | – | – | – | – | – | – | – |
| Other | – | – | – | – | – | – | – | – |
| | | | | | | | | |
| Multilateral | – | – | – | – | – | – | – | – |
| of which: Concessional | – | – | – | – | – | – | – | – |
| | | | | | | | | |
| CMEA countries | – | – | – | – | – | – | – | – |
| of which: Concessional | – | – | – | – | – | – | – | – |
| | | | | | | | | |
| OPEC countries | – | – | – | – | – | – | – | – |
| of which: Concessional | – | – | – | – | – | – | – | – |
| | | | | | | | | |
| Other LDC'S | – | – | – | – | – | – | – | – |
| of which: Concessional | – | – | – | – | – | – | – | – |
| | | | | | | | | |
| Other and adjustments | – | – | – | – | – | – | – | – |
| | | | | | | | | |
| **Total Debt** | **9** | **10** | **13** | **12** | **11** | **9** | **6** | **4** |
| of which: Concessional | 9 | 7 | 10 | 8 | 8 | 7 | 5 | 3 |
| Non-concessional | – | 3 | 3 | 4 | 3 | 2 | 1 | 1 |
| | | | | | | | | |
| | | | | | | | | |
| **DEBT SERVICE** | | | | | | | | |
| DAC countries and capital | | | | | | | | |
| markets | 1 | 1 | 3 | 1 | 2 | 2 | 2 | 1 |
| ODA | 1 | 1 | 0 | 1 | 1 | 1 | 1 | 1 |
| Total export credits | – | 0 | 2 | 0 | 1 | 1 | 1 | – |
| Total private | – | – | – | – | – | – | – | – |
| of which: Bank loans | – | – | – | – | – | – | – | – |
| Bonds | – | – | – | – | – | – | – | – |
| Other | – | – | – | – | – | – | – | – |
| | | | | | | | | |
| Multilateral | – | – | – | – | – | – | – | – |
| of which: Concessional | – | – | – | – | – | – | – | – |
| | | | | | | | | |
| CMEA countries | – | – | – | – | – | – | – | – |
| of which: Concessional | – | – | – | – | – | – | – | – |
| | | | | | | | | |
| OPEC countries | – | – | – | – | – | – | – | – |
| of which: Concessional | – | – | – | – | – | – | – | – |
| | | | | | | | | |
| Other LDC'S | – | – | – | – | – | – | – | – |
| of which: Concessional | – | – | – | – | – | – | – | – |
| | | | | | | | | |
| Other and adjustments | – | – | – | – | – | – | – | – |
| | | | | | | | | |
| **Total Debt Service** | **1** | **1** | **3** | **1** | **2** | **2** | **2** | **1** |
| of which: Concessional | 1 | 1 | 0 | 1 | 1 | 1 | 1 | 1 |
| Non-concessional | – | 0 | 2 | 0 | 1 | 1 | 1 | – |

US $ Million

| | 1975 | 1976 | 1977 | 1978 | 1979 | 1980 | 1981 | 1982 |
|---|---|---|---|---|---|---|---|---|
| **DEBT** | | | | | | | | |
| DAC countries and capital markets | 380 | 1121 | 1385 | 1852 | 2730 | 2884 | 2369 | 2732 |
| ODA | – | 9 | 9 | – | – | – | – | – |
| Total export credits | 380 | 1082 | 1326 | 1752 | 2610 | 2724 | 2089 | 1982 |
| Total private | – | 30 | 50 | 100 | 120 | 160 | 280 | 750 |
| of which: Bank loans | – | 30 | 50 | 100 | 120 | 160 | 280 | 750 |
| Bonds | – | – | – | – | – | – | – | – |
| Other | – | – | – | – | – | – | – | – |
| Multilateral | – | – | – | – | – | – | – | – |
| of which: Concessional | – | – | – | – | – | – | – | – |
| CMEA countries | – | – | – | – | – | – | – | – |
| of which: Concessional | – | – | – | – | – | – | – | – |
| OPEC countries | – | – | – | – | – | – | – | – |
| of which: Concessional | – | – | – | – | – | – | – | – |
| Other LDC'S | – | – | – | – | – | – | – | – |
| of which: Concessional | – | – | – | – | – | – | – | – |
| Other and adjustments | – | – | – | – | – | – | – | – |
| **Total Debt** | **380** | **1121** | **1385** | **1852** | **2730** | **2884** | **2369** | **2732** |
| of which: Concessional | – | 9 | 9 | – | – | – | – | – |
| Non-concessional | 380 | 1112 | 1376 | 1852 | 2730 | 2884 | 2369 | 2732 |
| **DEBT SERVICE** | | | | | | | | |
| DAC countries and capital markets | 287 | 468 | 753 | 1399 | 1923 | 2015 | 2170 | 2120 |
| ODA | – | – | – | – | – | – | – | – |
| Total export credits | 287 | 463 | 745 | 1384 | 1897 | 1980 | 2122 | 2028 |
| Total private | – | 5 | 8 | 15 | 26 | 35 | 48 | 92 |
| of which: Bank loans | – | 5 | 8 | 15 | 26 | 35 | 48 | 92 |
| Bonds | – | – | – | – | – | – | – | – |
| Other | – | – | – | – | – | – | – | – |
| Multilateral | – | – | – | – | – | – | – | – |
| of which: Concessional | – | – | – | – | – | – | – | – |
| CMEA countries | – | – | – | – | – | – | – | – |
| of which: Concessional | – | – | – | – | – | – | – | – |
| OPEC countries | – | – | – | – | – | – | – | – |
| of which: Concessional | – | – | – | – | – | – | – | – |
| Other LDC'S | – | – | – | – | – | – | – | – |
| of which: Concessional | – | – | – | – | – | – | – | – |
| Other and adjustments | – | – | – | – | – | – | – | – |
| **Total Debt Service** | **287** | **468** | **753** | **1399** | **1923** | **2015** | **2170** | **2120** |
| of which: Concessional | – | – | – | – | – | – | – | – |
| Non-concessional | 287 | 468 | 753 | 1399 | 1923 | 2015 | 2170 | 2120 |

*US $ Million*

| | 1975 | 1976 | 1977 | 1978 | 1979 | 1980 | 1981 | 1982 |
|---|---|---|---|---|---|---|---|---|
| **DEBT** | | | | | | | | |
| DAC countries and capital | | | | | | | | |
| markets | 198 | 252 | 351 | 489 | 578 | 616 | 605 | 757 |
| ODA | 80 | 80 | 100 | 134 | 151 | 142 | 154 | 183 |
| Total export credits | 53 | 93 | 132 | 224 | 281 | 394 | 381 | 480 |
| Total private | 65 | 79 | 119 | 131 | 146 | 80 | 70 | 94 |
| *of which:* Bank loans | 50 | 65 | 105 | 120 | 135 | 70 | 50 | 78 |
| Bonds | 5 | 4 | 4 | 3 | 3 | 2 | 2 | 1 |
| Other | 10 | 10 | 10 | 8 | 8 | 8 | 18 | 15 |
| Multilateral | 63 | 79 | 105 | 155 | 202 | 263 | 346 | 392 |
| *of which:* Concessional | 48 | 61 | 76 | 117 | 157 | 196 | 254 | 291 |
| CMEA countries | 4 | 3 | 3 | 3 | 2 | 2 | 1 | 1 |
| *of which:* Concessional | 4 | 3 | 3 | 3 | 2 | 2 | 1 | 1 |
| OPEC countries | 10 | 27 | 26 | 20 | 21 | 17 | 68 | 80 |
| *of which:* Concessional | 1 | 3 | 5 | 4 | 10 | 10 | 65 | 76 |
| Other LDC'S | 2 | 2 | 14 | 23 | 22 | 23 | 15 | 38 |
| *of which:* Concessional | 2 | 2 | 6 | 9 | 10 | 15 | 13 | 36 |
| Other and adjustments | 1 | 2 | 8 | 20 | 35 | 34 | 38 | 41 |
| **Total Debt** | **278** | **366** | **507** | **711** | **860** | **955** | **1074** | **1309** |
| *of which:* Concessional | 135 | 149 | 193 | 272 | 337 | 377 | 503 | 599 |
| Non-concessional | 143 | 217 | 314 | 439 | 523 | 577 | 571 | 710 |
| | | | | | | | | |
| **DEBT SERVICE** | | | | | | | | |
| DAC countries and capital | | | | | | | | |
| markets | 32 | 37 | 52 | 74 | 99 | 151 | 78 | 67 |
| ODA | 9 | 6 | 4 | 6 | 7 | 9 | 7 | 4 |
| Total export credits | 11 | 18 | 33 | 36 | 52 | 66 | 42 | 42 |
| Total private | 13 | 13 | 15 | 31 | 40 | 76 | 29 | 22 |
| *of which:* Bank loans | 7 | 9 | 13 | 28 | 36 | 72 | 28 | 21 |
| Bonds | 1 | 1 | 1 | 1 | 1 | 1 | 0 | 0 |
| Other | 5 | 3 | 2 | 3 | 3 | 3 | 1 | 1 |
| Multilateral | 2 | 2 | 4 | 6 | 9 | 9 | 12 | 38 |
| *of which:* Concessional | 0 | 0 | 1 | 2 | 3 | 3 | 4 | 27 |
| CMEA countries | 1 | 1 | 1 | 1 | 1 | 1 | – | – |
| *of which:* Concessional | 1 | 1 | 1 | 1 | 1 | 1 | – | – |
| OPEC countries | 3 | 4 | 5 | 9 | 7 | 7 | 5 | 1 |
| *of which:* Concessional | 0 | 0 | 0 | 1 | 1 | 1 | 1 | 1 |
| Other LDC'S | – | – | 0 | 6 | 4 | 3 | 5 | 0 |
| *of which:* Concessional | – | – | – | – | – | – | – | 0 |
| Other and adjustments | 0 | 0 | 2 | 4 | 5 | 7 | 3 | 3 |
| **Total Debt Service** | **37** | **45** | **63** | **99** | **124** | **177** | **103** | **110** |
| *of which:* Concessional | 10 | 7 | 6 | 10 | 13 | 14 | 12 | 31 |
| Non-concessional | 28 | 37 | 57 | 90 | 111 | 162 | 91 | 79 |

# SEYCHELLES

| | 1975 | 1976 | 1977 | 1978 | 1979 | 1980 | 1981 | 1982 |
|---|---|---|---|---|---|---|---|---|
| **DEBT** | | | | | | | | |
| DAC countries and capital | | | | | | | | |
| markets | 5 | 4 | 4 | 7 | 17 | 27 | 28 | 37 |
| ODA | 2 | 1 | 1 | 4 | 11 | 16 | 17 | 19 |
| Total export credits | 3 | 3 | 3 | 3 | 6 | 10 | 11 | 10 |
| Total private | – | – | – | – | – | 1 | – | 8 |
| of which: Bank loans | – | – | – | – | – | 1 | – | 8 |
| Bonds | – | – | – | – | – | – | – | – |
| Other | – | – | – | – | – | – | – | – |
| Multilateral | – | – | 0 | 0 | 1 | 5 | 7 | 8 |
| of which: Concessional | – | – | 0 | 0 | 1 | 2 | 3 | 3 |
| CMEA countries | – | – | – | – | – | – | – | – |
| of which: Concessional | – | – | – | – | – | – | – | – |
| OPEC countries | – | – | – | – | – | 1 | 1 | 2 |
| of which: Concessional | – | – | – | – | – | – | – | – |
| Other LDC'S | – | – | – | – | – | – | 1 | 1 |
| of which: Concessional | – | – | – | – | – | – | 1 | 1 |
| Other and adjustments | – | – | – | – | – | – | – | – |
| **Total Debt** | **5** | **4** | **4** | **7** | **18** | **32** | **37** | **48** |
| of which: Concessional | 2 | 1 | 1 | 4 | 12 | 18 | 21 | 23 |
| Non-concessional | 3 | 3 | 3 | 3 | 6 | 14 | 16 | 26 |
| **DEBT SERVICE** | | | | | | | | |
| DAC countries and capital | | | | | | | | |
| markets | 0 | 1 | 0 | 0 | 1 | 1 | 3 | 2 |
| ODA | 0 | 0 | 0 | 0 | 0 | 0 | 0 | 0 |
| Total export credits | 0 | 1 | 0 | 0 | 1 | 1 | 1 | 2 |
| Total private | – | – | – | – | – | 0 | 1 | 0 |
| of which: Bank loans | – | – | – | – | – | 0 | 1 | 0 |
| Bonds | – | – | – | – | – | – | – | – |
| Other | – | – | – | – | – | – | – | – |
| Multilateral | – | – | – | 0 | 0 | 0 | 0 | 0 |
| of which: Concessional | – | – | – | 0 | 0 | 0 | 0 | 0 |
| CMEA countries | – | – | – | – | – | – | – | – |
| of which: Concessional | – | – | – | – | – | – | – | – |
| OPEC countries | – | – | – | – | – | 0 | 0 | 0 |
| of which: Concessional | – | – | – | – | – | – | – | – |
| Other LDC'S | – | – | – | – | – | – | – | – |
| of which: Concessional | – | – | – | – | – | – | – | – |
| Other and adjustments | – | – | – | – | – | – | – | – |
| **Total Debt Service** | **0** | **1** | **0** | **0** | **1** | **1** | **3** | **3** |
| of which: Concessional | 0 | 0 | 0 | 0 | 0 | 0 | 0 | 0 |
| Non-concessional | 0 | 1 | 0 | 0 | 1 | 1 | 3 | 2 |

*US $ Million*

| | 1975 | 1976 | 1977 | 1978 | 1979 | 1980 | 1981 | 1982 |
|---|---|---|---|---|---|---|---|---|
| **DEBT** | | | | | | | | |
| DAC countries and capital | | | | | | | | |
| markets | 131 | 121 | 153 | 210 | 250 | 254 | 247 | 231 |
| ODA | 48 | 44 | 49 | 61 | 72 | 97 | 93 | 121 |
| Total export credits | 67 | 65 | 50 | 67 | 72 | 71 | 71 | 70 |
| Total private | 16 | 12 | 54 | 82 | 106 | 86 | 83 | 40 |
| *of which:* Bank loans | 16 | 12 | 14 | 17 | 26 | 21 | 18 | 10 |
| Bonds | – | – | – | – | – | – | – | – |
| Other | – | – | 40 | 65 | 80 | 65 | 65 | 30 |
| Multilateral | 30 | 32 | 41 | 64 | 78 | 103 | 104 | 114 |
| *of which:* Concessional | 18 | 20 | 26 | 47 | 60 | 82 | 83 | 93 |
| CMEA countries | 1 | 0 | 0 | 1 | 2 | 2 | 1 | 1 |
| *of which:* Concessional | – | – | – | – | – | – | – | – |
| OPEC countries | – | – | 1 | 1 | 1 | 1 | 0 | 0 |
| *of which:* Concessional | – | – | – | – | – | – | – | – |
| Other LDC'S | 7 | 13 | 17 | 24 | 29 | 30 | 38 | 32 |
| *of which:* Concessional | 7 | 12 | 17 | 24 | 29 | 30 | 28 | 22 |
| Other and adjustments | – | – | – | – | – | – | – | – |
| **Total Debt** | **169** | **167** | **212** | **299** | **360** | **389** | **391** | **378** |
| *of which:* Concessional | 72 | 76 | 91 | 132 | 161 | 209 | 204 | 236 |
| Non-concessional | 96 | 91 | 121 | 167 | 199 | 180 | 187 | 142 |
| | | | | | | | | |
| **DEBT SERVICE** | | | | | | | | |
| DAC countries and capital | | | | | | | | |
| markets | 20 | 18 | 25 | 35 | 50 | 40 | 51 | 35 |
| ODA | 4 | 2 | 2 | 2 | 3 | 1 | 1 | 2 |
| Total export credits | 12 | 12 | 21 | 20 | 8 | 10 | 9 | 5 |
| Total private | 4 | 4 | 3 | 12 | 40 | 29 | 41 | 29 |
| *of which:* Bank loans | 4 | 4 | 3 | 2 | 10 | 7 | 13 | 8 |
| Bonds | – | – | – | – | – | – | – | – |
| Other | – | – | – | 10 | 30 | 22 | 28 | 21 |
| Multilateral | 1 | 1 | 2 | 2 | 3 | 2 | 3 | 3 |
| *of which:* Concessional | 1 | 0 | 1 | 1 | 1 | 1 | 1 | 1 |
| CMEA countries | 0 | 0 | 0 | 0 | 0 | 0 | – | 0 |
| *of which:* Concessional | – | – | – | – | – | – | – | – |
| OPEC countries | – | – | – | 0 | 0 | 0 | – | 0 |
| *of which:* Concessional | – | – | – | – | – | – | – | – |
| Other LDC'S | 0 | 1 | 0 | 0 | – | – | – | 3 |
| *of which:* Concessional | – | 0 | – | – | – | – | – | 2 |
| Other and adjustments | – | – | – | – | – | – | – | – |
| **Total Debt Service** | **22** | **20** | **28** | **38** | **54** | **43** | **54** | **41** |
| *of which:* Concessional | 5 | 3 | 2 | 3 | 4 | 2 | 2 | 5 |
| Non-concessional | 17 | 17 | 25 | 35 | 51 | 41 | 52 | 36 |

*US $ Million*

| | 1975 | 1976 | 1977 | 1978 | 1979 | 1980 | 1981 | 1982 |
|---|---|---|---|---|---|---|---|---|
| **DEBT** | | | | | | | | |
| DAC countries and capital | | | | | | | | |
| markets | 559 | 758 | 977 | 1197 | 1535 | 1512 | 1639 | 1860 |
| ODA | 91 | 83 | 92 | 108 | 94 | 98 | 77 | 62 |
| Total export credits | 348 | 395 | 415 | 539 | 736 | 785 | 966 | 1022 |
| Total private | 120 | 280 | 470 | 550 | 705 | 629 | 596 | 776 |
| *of which:* Bank loans | 30 | 60 | 58 | 53 | 156 | 145 | 130 | 350 |
| Bonds | 80 | 201 | 362 | 397 | 349 | 284 | 246 | 206 |
| Other | 10 | 19 | 50 | 100 | 200 | 200 | 220 | 220 |
| Multilateral | 158 | 167 | 166 | 181 | 174 | 180 | 174 | 169 |
| *of which:* Concessional | 26 | 26 | 25 | 23 | 21 | 19 | 16 | 14 |
| CMEA countries | – | – | – | – | – | – | – | – |
| *of which:* Concessional | – | – | – | – | – | – | – | – |
| OPEC countries | – | – | – | – | – | – | – | – |
| *of which:* Concessional | – | – | – | – | – | – | – | – |
| Other LDC'S | – | – | – | 7 | 7 | 6 | 4 | 3 |
| *of which:* Concessional | – | – | – | – | – | – | – | – |
| Other and adjustments | – | – | – | – | – | – | – | – |
| **Total Debt** | **717** | **925** | **1143** | **1385** | **1717** | **1699** | **1818** | **2032** |
| *of which:* Concessional | 117 | 109 | 117 | 131 | 115 | 117 | 93 | 76 |
| Non-concessional | 599 | 816 | 1026 | 1254 | 1602 | 1582 | 1725 | 1956 |
| **DEBT SERVICE** | | | | | | | | |
| DAC countries and capital | | | | | | | | |
| markets | 105 | 110 | 119 | 318 | 251 | 301 | 355 | 403 |
| ODA | 4 | 5 | 6 | 12 | 12 | 11 | 11 | 9 |
| Total export credits | 91 | 76 | 82 | 237 | 153 | 196 | 238 | 286 |
| Total private | 9 | 29 | 31 | 69 | 87 | 94 | 106 | 108 |
| *of which:* Bank loans | 4 | 10 | 4 | 16 | 20 | 27 | 34 | 30 |
| Bonds | 5 | 9 | 17 | 42 | 47 | 42 | 37 | 43 |
| Other | – | 10 | 10 | 12 | 20 | 25 | 35 | 35 |
| Multilateral | 19 | 22 | 24 | 27 | 29 | 29 | 30 | 31 |
| *of which:* Concessional | 3 | 3 | 3 | 4 | 4 | 4 | 4 | 4 |
| CMEA countries | – | – | – | – | – | – | – | – |
| *of which:* Concessional | – | – | – | – | – | – | – | – |
| OPEC countries | – | – | – | – | – | – | – | – |
| *of which:* Concessional | – | – | – | – | – | – | – | – |
| Other LDC'S | – | – | – | – | 2 | 2 | 1 | 1 |
| *of which:* Concessional | – | – | – | – | – | – | – | – |
| Other and adjustments | – | – | – | – | – | – | – | – |
| **Total Debt Service** | **124** | **131** | **143** | **344** | **282** | **332** | **386** | **435** |
| *of which:* Concessional | 8 | 8 | 9 | 15 | 15 | 15 | 15 | 13 |
| Non-concessional | 116 | 123 | 134 | 329 | 266 | 317 | 371 | 422 |

# SOLOMON ISLANDS (BR.) SALOMON, ILES (BR.)

*US $ Million*

| | 1975 | 1976 | 1977 | 1978 | 1979 | 1980 | 1981 | 1982 |
|---|---|---|---|---|---|---|---|---|
| **DEBT** | | | | | | | | |
| DAC countries and capital | | | | | | | | |
|   markets | 8 | 9 | 14 | 15 | 15 | 12 | 29 | 28 |
|   ODA | 8 | 9 | 9 | 10 | 11 | 11 | 9 | 9 |
|   Total export credits | – | – | 5 | 5 | 4 | 1 | 2 | 1 |
|   Total private | – | – | – | – | – | – | 18 | 18 |
|     *of which:* Bank loans | – | – | – | – | – | – | 18 | 18 |
|     Bonds | – | – | – | – | – | – | – | – |
|     Other | – | – | – | – | – | – | – | – |
| Multilateral | – | – | 0 | 1 | 3 | 7 | 11 | 16 |
|   *of which:* Concessional | – | – | 0 | 1 | 3 | 7 | 11 | 16 |
| CMEA countries | – | – | – | – | – | – | – | – |
|   *of which:* Concessional | – | – | – | – | – | – | – | – |
| OPEC countries | – | – | – | – | – | – | – | – |
|   *of which:* Concessional | – | – | – | – | – | – | – | – |
| Other LDC'S | – | – | – | – | – | – | – | – |
|   *of which:* Concessional | – | – | – | – | – | – | – | – |
| Other and adjustments | – | – | – | – | – | – | – | – |
| **Total Debt** | **8** | **9** | **14** | **16** | **18** | **19** | **40** | **44** |
|   *of which:* Concessional | 8 | 9 | 9 | 11 | 14 | 18 | 20 | 25 |
|     Non-concessional | – | – | 5 | 5 | 4 | 1 | 20 | 19 |
| | | | | | | | | |
| **DEBT SERVICE** | | | | | | | | |
| DAC countries and capital | | | | | | | | |
|   markets | 0 | 0 | 2 | 2 | 2 | 7 | 2 | 5 |
|   ODA | 0 | 0 | 0 | 1 | 1 | 1 | 1 | 1 |
|   Total export credits | – | – | 1 | 1 | 1 | 6 | 1 | 1 |
|   Total private | – | – | – | – | – | – | – | 3 |
|     *of which:* Bank loans | – | – | – | – | – | – | – | 3 |
|     Bonds | – | – | – | – | – | – | – | – |
|     Other | – | – | – | – | – | – | – | – |
| Multilateral | – | – | – | 0 | 0 | 0 | 0 | 0 |
|   *of which:* Concessional | – | – | – | 0 | 0 | 0 | 0 | 0 |
| CMEA countries | – | – | – | – | – | – | – | – |
|   *of which:* Concessional | – | – | – | – | – | – | – | – |
| OPEC countries | – | – | – | – | – | – | – | – |
|   *of which:* Concessional | – | – | – | – | – | – | – | – |
| Other LDC'S | – | – | – | – | – | – | – | – |
|   *of which:* Concessional | – | – | – | – | – | – | – | – |
| Other and adjustments | – | – | – | – | – | – | – | – |
| **Total Debt Service** | **0** | **0** | **2** | **2** | **2** | **7** | **2** | **5** |
|   *of which:* Concessional | 0 | 0 | 0 | 1 | 1 | 1 | 1 | 1 |
|     Non-concessional | – | – | 1 | 1 | 1 | 6 | 1 | 4 |

# SOMALIA

US $ Million

| | 1975 | 1976 | 1977 | 1978 | 1979 | 1980 | 1981 | 1982 |
|---|---|---|---|---|---|---|---|---|
| **DEBT** | | | | | | | | |
| DAC countries and capital | | | | | | | | |
| markets | 42 | 43 | 60 | 85 | 112 | 83 | 126 | 166 |
| ODA | 38 | 37 | 38 | 63 | 76 | 56 | 84 | 116 |
| Total export credits | 4 | 3 | 19 | 19 | 35 | 27 | 42 | 31 |
| Total private | – | 3 | 3 | 3 | 1 | – | – | 19 |
| *of which:* Bank loans | – | – | – | – | – | – | – | 19 |
| Bonds | – | – | – | – | – | – | – | – |
| Other | – | 3 | 3 | 3 | 1 | – | – | – |
| Multilateral | 47 | 59 | 72 | 101 | 131 | 175 | 268 | 311 |
| *of which:* Concessional | 47 | 59 | 72 | 101 | 127 | 166 | 211 | 253 |
| CMEA countries | 68 | 89 | 109 | 110 | 109 | 110 | 109 | 109 |
| *of which:* Concessional | 68 | 89 | 109 | 110 | 109 | 110 | 109 | 108 |
| OPEC countries | 44 | 62 | 98 | 146 | 218 | 267 | 298 | 291 |
| *of which:* Concessional | 44 | 62 | 98 | 146 | 218 | 267 | 298 | 291 |
| Other LDC'S | 35 | 40 | 69 | 107 | 109 | 114 | 105 | 101 |
| *of which:* Concessional | 35 | 40 | 69 | 103 | 104 | 110 | 101 | 97 |
| Other and adjustments | – | – | – | – | – | – | – | – |
| **Total Debt** | **236** | **293** | **409** | **549** | **679** | **749** | **906** | **978** |
| *of which:* Concessional | 232 | 287 | 387 | 522 | 635 | 708 | 804 | 866 |
| Non-concessional | 4 | 6 | 22 | 26 | 44 | 41 | 102 | 112 |
| **DEBT SERVICE** | | | | | | | | |
| DAC countries and capital | | | | | | | | |
| markets | 4 | 4 | 4 | 6 | 6 | 12 | 16 | 16 |
| ODA | 2 | 2 | 1 | 2 | 2 | 1 | 4 | 4 |
| Total export credits | 2 | 1 | 2 | 3 | 4 | 10 | 13 | 12 |
| Total private | – | – | 1 | 0 | 1 | 1 | – | 1 |
| *of which:* Bank loans | – | – | – | – | – | – | – | 1 |
| Bonds | – | – | – | – | – | – | – | – |
| Other | – | – | 1 | 0 | 1 | 1 | – | – |
| Multilateral | 0 | 0 | 1 | 1 | 1 | 6 | 13 | 15 |
| *of which:* Concessional | 0 | 0 | 1 | 1 | 1 | 1 | 2 | 4 |
| CMEA countries | 1 | 1 | 1 | 1 | 1 | – | 0 | 0 |
| *of which:* Concessional | 1 | 1 | 1 | 1 | 1 | – | 0 | 0 |
| OPEC countries | 0 | 0 | 0 | 0 | 2 | 2 | 0 | 2 |
| *of which:* Concessional | 0 | 0 | 0 | 0 | 2 | 2 | 0 | 2 |
| Other LDC'S | – | – | – | – | – | – | 1 | – |
| *of which:* Concessional | – | – | – | – | – | – | – | – |
| Other and adjustments | – | – | – | – | – | – | – | – |
| **Total Debt Service** | **5** | **5** | **6** | **8** | **9** | **20** | **31** | **33** |
| *of which:* Concessional | 3 | 3 | 3 | 4 | 5 | 4 | 7 | 10 |
| Non-concessional | 2 | 1 | 3 | 4 | 4 | 16 | 24 | 23 |

*US $ Million*

| | 1975 | 1976 | 1977 | 1978 | 1979 | 1980 | 1981 | 1982 |
|---|---|---|---|---|---|---|---|---|
| **DEBT** | | | | | | | | |
| DAC countries and capital | | | | | | | | |
|   markets | 435 | 456 | 529 | 667 | 766 | 930 | 1142 | 1328 |
|   ODA | 334 | 359 | 450 | 624 | 701 | 805 | 850 | 937 |
|   Total export credits | 91 | 91 | 75 | 42 | 63 | 83 | 175 | 219 |
|   Total private | 10 | 6 | 4 | 1 | 2 | 42 | 117 | 172 |
|     *of which:* Bank loans | 10 | 6 | 4 | 1 | 2 | 42 | 107 | 160 |
|     Bonds | – | – | – | – | – | – | – | – |
|     Other | – | – | – | – | – | – | 10 | 12 |
| Multilateral | 96 | 106 | 133 | 221 | 281 | 336 | 374 | 445 |
|   *of which:* Concessional | 67 | 73 | 99 | 186 | 245 | 302 | 343 | 412 |
| CMEA countries | 20 | 34 | 35 | 35 | 30 | 26 | 37 | 29 |
|   *of which:* Concessional | 16 | 19 | 18 | 17 | 15 | 14 | 11 | 9 |
| OPEC countries | 0 | 23 | 42 | 46 | 47 | 52 | 50 | 46 |
|   *of which:* Concessional | – | 21 | 26 | 31 | 33 | 41 | 40 | 37 |
| Other LDC'S | 66 | 73 | 59 | 69 | 70 | 72 | 72 | 103 |
|   *of which:* Concessional | 58 | 61 | 48 | 58 | 59 | 63 | 66 | 64 |
| Other and adjustments | – | – | – | – | – | – | – | – |
| **Total Debt** | **617** | **692** | **798** | **1038** | **1195** | **1415** | **1675** | **1950** |
|   *of which:* Concessional | 475 | 534 | 642 | 916 | 1053 | 1225 | 1310 | 1459 |
|     Non-concessional | 143 | 159 | 156 | 122 | 141 | 190 | 366 | 491 |
| **DEBT SERVICE** | | | | | | | | |
| DAC countries and capital | | | | | | | | |
|   markets | 98 | 103 | 90 | 58 | 48 | 52 | 63 | 102 |
|   ODA | 17 | 18 | 20 | 22 | 25 | 27 | 29 | 28 |
|   Total export credits | 63 | 78 | 64 | 31 | 22 | 24 | 25 | 32 |
|   Total private | 17 | 6 | 7 | 5 | 1 | 1 | 9 | 42 |
|     *of which:* Bank loans | 6 | 6 | 7 | 5 | 1 | 1 | 9 | 40 |
|     Bonds | 11 | – | – | – | – | – | – | – |
|     Other | – | – | – | – | – | – | – | 2 |
| Multilateral | 7 | 8 | 9 | 10 | 11 | 11 | 10 | 12 |
|   *of which:* Concessional | 4 | 4 | 5 | 5 | 6 | 5 | 5 | 7 |
| CMEA countries | 6 | 7 | 8 | 8 | 8 | 5 | 6 | 7 |
|   *of which:* Concessional | 5 | 5 | 5 | 4 | 4 | 2 | 2 | 2 |
| OPEC countries | 0 | 1 | 1 | 3 | 3 | 8 | 7 | 7 |
|   *of which:* Concessional | – | 1 | 1 | 2 | 1 | 3 | 4 | 5 |
| Other LDC'S | 27 | 7 | 25 | 10 | 12 | 15 | 11 | 12 |
|   *of which:* Concessional | 5 | 4 | 19 | 7 | 9 | 13 | 9 | 7 |
| Other and adjustments | – | – | – | – | – | – | – | – |
| **Total Debt Service** | **138** | **126** | **134** | **90** | **82** | **91** | **97** | **140** |
|   *of which:* Concessional | 31 | 32 | 49 | 40 | 45 | 50 | 49 | 49 |
|     Non-concessional | 107 | 94 | 86 | 50 | 38 | 41 | 48 | 90 |

*US $ Million*

| | 1975 | 1976 | 1977 | 1978 | 1979 | 1980 | 1981 | 1982 |
|---|---|---|---|---|---|---|---|---|
| **DEBT** | | | | | | | | |
| DAC countries and capital | | | | | | | | |
| markets | 679 | 723 | 940 | 1053 | 1144 | 1212 | 1713 | 1816 |
| ODA | 116 | 139 | 161 | 209 | 251 | 146 | 155 | 166 |
| Total export credits | 321 | 352 | 554 | 628 | 721 | 901 | 988 | 945 |
| Total private | 242 | 232 | 225 | 216 | 172 | 165 | 570 | 705 |
| *of which:* Bank loans | 242 | 227 | 220 | 206 | 167 | 135 | 520 | 650 |
| Bonds | – | – | – | – | – | – | – | – |
| Other | – | 5 | 5 | 10 | 5 | 30 | 50 | 55 |
| | | | | | | | | |
| Multilateral | 160 | 233 | 286 | 406 | 524 | 742 | 892 | 1099 |
| *of which:* Concessional | 144 | 215 | 258 | 340 | 409 | 540 | 682 | 803 |
| | | | | | | | | |
| CMEA countries | 127 | 130 | 152 | 146 | 150 | 143 | 162 | 157 |
| *of which:* Concessional | 90 | 85 | 101 | 97 | 108 | 104 | 125 | 120 |
| | | | | | | | | |
| OPEC countries | 477 | 719 | 885 | 1137 | 1513 | 1732 | 1943 | 2073 |
| *of which:* Concessional | 189 | 284 | 363 | 460 | 778 | 866 | 1012 | 1116 |
| | | | | | | | | |
| Other LDC'S | 78 | 78 | 112 | 130 | 164 | 225 | 214 | 202 |
| *of which:* Concessional | 76 | 78 | 106 | 121 | 148 | 172 | 163 | 151 |
| | | | | | | | | |
| Other and adjustments | 5 | 5 | 5 | 5 | 5 | 5 | 105 | 125 |
| | | | | | | | | |
| **Total Debt** | **1526** | **1890** | **2379** | **2878** | **3500** | **4060** | **5031** | **5473** |
| *of which:* Concessional | 616 | 802 | 988 | 1227 | 1693 | 1828 | 2187 | 2415 |
| Non-concessional | 911 | 1088 | 1391 | 1651 | 1807 | 2232 | 2844 | 3058 |
| | | | | | | | | |
| **DEBT SERVICE** | | | | | | | | |
| DAC countries and capital | | | | | | | | |
| markets | 93 | 87 | 84 | 46 | 30 | 28 | 52 | 33 |
| ODA | 8 | 6 | 5 | 2 | 6 | 5 | 4 | 5 |
| Total export credits | 74 | 72 | 70 | 32 | 22 | 23 | 48 | 28 |
| Total private | 11 | 9 | 9 | 12 | 3 | 1 | – | – |
| *of which:* Bank loans | 11 | 6 | 5 | 8 | 3 | 1 | – | – |
| Bonds | – | – | – | – | – | – | – | – |
| Other | – | 3 | 4 | 4 | – | – | – | – |
| | | | | | | | | |
| Multilateral | 13 | 13 | 15 | 17 | 17 | 19 | 25 | 18 |
| *of which:* Concessional | 11 | 11 | 13 | 15 | 10 | 12 | 17 | 13 |
| | | | | | | | | |
| CMEA countries | 10 | 6 | 8 | 9 | 13 | 11 | 1 | – |
| *of which:* Concessional | 6 | 5 | 6 | 4 | 4 | 6 | 1 | – |
| | | | | | | | | |
| OPEC countries | 48 | 46 | 35 | 37 | 32 | 31 | 19 | – |
| *of which:* Concessional | 7 | 4 | 11 | 9 | 2 | 3 | 5 | – |
| | | | | | | | | |
| Other LDC'S | 4 | 4 | 2 | 3 | 3 | 3 | 2 | – |
| *of which:* Concessional | 2 | 2 | 2 | 2 | 3 | 1 | – | – |
| | | | | | | | | |
| Other and adjustments | – | – | 0 | – | – | – | 30 | 40 |
| | | | | | | | | |
| **Total Debt Service** | **168** | **156** | **143** | **111** | **95** | **91** | **129** | **91** |
| *of which:* Concessional | 34 | 28 | 37 | 32 | 25 | 27 | 27 | 18 |
| Non-concessional | 134 | 127 | 107 | 79 | 70 | 64 | 102 | 73 |

# SURINAME

| | 1975 | 1976 | 1977 | 1978 | 1979 | 1980 | 1981 | 1982 |
|---|---|---|---|---|---|---|---|---|
| **DEBT** | | | | | | | | |
| DAC countries and capital | | | | | | | | |
| markets | 186 | 149 | 129 | 114 | 68 | 22 | 25 | 15 |
| ODA | 182 | 140 | 113 | 94 | 50 | 3 | 4 | 3 |
| Total export credits | 4 | 4 | 4 | 8 | 6 | 9 | 11 | 2 |
| Total private | – | 5 | 12 | 12 | 12 | 10 | 10 | 10 |
| of which: Bank loans | – | 5 | 12 | 12 | 12 | 10 | 10 | 10 |
| Bonds | – | – | – | – | – | – | – | – |
| Other | – | – | – | – | – | – | – | – |
| Multilateral | – | – | – | – | – | – | – | – |
| of which: Concessional | – | – | – | – | – | – | – | – |
| CMEA countries | – | – | – | – | – | – | – | – |
| of which: Concessional | – | – | – | – | – | – | – | – |
| OPEC countries | – | – | – | – | – | – | – | – |
| of which: Concessional | – | – | – | – | – | – | – | – |
| Other LDC'S | – | – | – | – | – | – | – | – |
| of which: Concessional | – | – | – | – | – | – | – | – |
| Other and adjustments | – | – | – | – | – | – | – | – |
| **Total Debt** | **186** | **149** | **129** | **114** | **68** | **22** | **25** | **15** |
| of which: Concessional | 182 | 140 | 113 | 94 | 50 | 3 | 4 | 3 |
| Non-concessional | 4 | 9 | 16 | 20 | 18 | 19 | 21 | 12 |
| **DEBT SERVICE** | | | | | | | | |
| DAC countries and capital | | | | | | | | |
| markets | 5 | 0 | 0 | 4 | 4 | 12 | 4 | 12 |
| ODA | 5 | – | – | 0 | – | 1 | 0 | 0 |
| Total export credits | 0 | 0 | 0 | 3 | 3 | 10 | 2 | 10 |
| Total private | – | – | – | 1 | 1 | 1 | 2 | 2 |
| of which: Bank loans | – | – | – | 1 | 1 | 1 | 2 | 2 |
| Bonds | – | – | – | – | – | – | – | – |
| Other | – | – | – | – | – | – | – | – |
| Multilateral | – | – | – | – | – | – | – | – |
| of which: Concessional | – | – | – | – | – | – | – | – |
| CMEA countries | – | – | – | – | – | – | – | – |
| of which: Concessional | – | – | – | – | – | – | – | – |
| OPEC countries | – | – | – | – | – | – | – | – |
| of which: Concessional | – | – | – | – | – | – | – | – |
| Other LDC'S | – | – | – | – | – | – | – | – |
| of which: Concessional | – | – | – | – | – | – | – | – |
| Other and adjustments | – | – | – | – | – | – | – | – |
| **Total Debt Service** | **5** | **0** | **0** | **4** | **4** | **12** | **4** | **12** |
| of which: Concessional | 5 | – | – | 0 | – | 1 | 0 | 0 |
| Non-concessional | 0 | 0 | 0 | 4 | 4 | 11 | 4 | 12 |

*US $ Million*

| | 1975 | 1976 | 1977 | 1978 | 1979 | 1980 | 1981 | 1982 |
|---|---|---|---|---|---|---|---|---|
| **DEBT** | | | | | | | | |
| DAC countries and capital | | | | | | | | |
| markets | 36 | 32 | 30 | 88 | 121 | 136 | 112 | 103 |
| ODA | 35 | 30 | 28 | 56 | 82 | 96 | 82 | 73 |
| Total export credits | 1 | 2 | 2 | 14 | 21 | 20 | 14 | 16 |
| Total private | – | – | – | 18 | 18 | 20 | 16 | 14 |
| *of which:* Bank loans | – | – | – | 18 | 18 | 20 | 16 | 14 |
| Bonds | – | – | – | – | – | – | – | – |
| Other | – | – | – | – | – | – | – | – |
| Multilateral | 9 | 18 | 24 | 33 | 53 | 68 | 79 | 101 |
| *of which:* Concessional | 8 | 12 | 15 | 17 | 30 | 39 | 38 | 41 |
| CMEA countries | – | – | – | – | – | – | – | – |
| *of which:* Concessional | – | – | – | – | – | – | – | – |
| OPEC countries | – | – | – | – | – | – | – | – |
| *of which:* Concessional | – | – | – | – | – | – | – | – |
| Other LDC'S | – | – | – | – | – | – | – | – |
| *of which:* Concessional | – | – | – | – | – | – | – | – |
| Other and adjustments | 1 | 1 | 1 | 0 | 0 | 0 | 0 | 0 |
| **Total Debt** | **45** | **50** | **55** | **121** | **174** | **204** | **191** | **204** |
| *of which:* Concessional | 43 | 42 | 43 | 73 | 112 | 135 | 120 | 114 |
| Non-concessional | 2 | 8 | 12 | 48 | 62 | 69 | 71 | 90 |
| **DEBT SERVICE** | | | | | | | | |
| DAC countries and capital | | | | | | | | |
| markets | 3 | 3 | 3 | 3 | 9 | 11 | 14 | 13 |
| ODA | 3 | 1 | 3 | 2 | 3 | 5 | 4 | 5 |
| Total export credits | 0 | 2 | 1 | 1 | 3 | 3 | 4 | 4 |
| Total private | – | – | – | 0 | 3 | 3 | 6 | 5 |
| *of which:* Bank loans | – | – | – | 0 | 3 | 3 | 6 | 5 |
| Bonds | – | – | – | – | – | – | – | – |
| Other | – | – | – | – | – | – | – | – |
| Multilateral | 1 | 1 | 2 | 3 | 3 | 4 | 5 | 8 |
| *of which:* Concessional | 1 | 1 | 1 | 1 | 1 | 2 | 2 | 2 |
| CMEA countries | – | – | – | – | – | – | – | – |
| *of which:* Concessional | – | – | – | – | – | – | – | – |
| OPEC countries | – | – | – | – | – | – | – | – |
| *of which:* Concessional | – | – | – | – | – | – | – | – |
| Other LDC'S | – | – | – | – | – | – | – | – |
| *of which:* Concessional | – | – | – | – | – | – | – | – |
| Other and adjustments | 1 | 0 | 0 | 0 | 0 | 0 | 0 | 0 |
| **Total Debt Service** | **6** | **4** | **5** | **6** | **12** | **15** | **19** | **21** |
| *of which:* Concessional | 4 | 2 | 4 | 3 | 4 | 6 | 6 | 7 |
| Non-concessional | 2 | 2 | 1 | 3 | 8 | 9 | 13 | 14 |

US $ Million

| | 1975 | 1976 | 1977 | 1978 | 1979 | 1980 | 1981 | 1982 |
|---|---|---|---|---|---|---|---|---|
| **DEBT** | | | | | | | | |
| DAC countries and capital | | | | | | | | |
| markets | 196 | 226 | 299 | 385 | 411 | 431 | 440 | 454 |
| ODA | 20 | 55 | 97 | 124 | 200 | 237 | 274 | 317 |
| Total export credits | 158 | 155 | 180 | 220 | 183 | 178 | 154 | 127 |
| Total private | 18 | 16 | 22 | 41 | 28 | 16 | 12 | 10 |
| of which: Bank loans | 18 | 16 | 22 | 41 | 28 | 16 | 12 | 10 |
| Bonds | – | – | – | – | – | – | – | – |
| Other | – | – | – | – | – | – | – | – |
| Multilateral | 20 | 69 | 136 | 179 | 251 | 311 | 353 | 379 |
| of which: Concessional | 16 | 42 | 64 | 74 | 89 | 95 | 102 | 106 |
| CMEA countries | 337 | 452 | 639 | 794 | 822 | 914 | 1007 | 1130 |
| of which: Concessional | 312 | 404 | 579 | 722 | 759 | 849 | 954 | 1043 |
| OPEC countries | 120 | 265 | 429 | 662 | 802 | 737 | 707 | 650 |
| of which: Concessional | 119 | 265 | 429 | 632 | 661 | 634 | 645 | 626 |
| Other LDC'S | 22 | 22 | 23 | 33 | 30 | 31 | 26 | 23 |
| of which: Concessional | 22 | 22 | 23 | 27 | 24 | 26 | 21 | 18 |
| Other and adjustments | 13 | 8 | 7 | 5 | 3 | 2 | 1 | 40 |
| **Total Debt** | **708** | **1041** | **1534** | **2057** | **2319** | **2426** | **2534** | **2676** |
| of which: Concessional | 489 | 788 | 1192 | 1579 | 1733 | 1841 | 1996 | 2110 |
| Non-concessional | 219 | 253 | 341 | 479 | 586 | 585 | 538 | 566 |
| **DEBT SERVICE** | | | | | | | | |
| DAC countries and capital | | | | | | | | |
| markets | 60 | 79 | 79 | 90 | 103 | 130 | 111 | 73 |
| ODA | 0 | 0 | 1 | 6 | 8 | 11 | 9 | 12 |
| Total export credits | 60 | 79 | 76 | 77 | 86 | 104 | 95 | 57 |
| Total private | 1 | 0 | 3 | 7 | 9 | 16 | 7 | 4 |
| of which: Bank loans | 1 | 0 | 3 | 7 | 9 | 16 | 7 | 4 |
| Bonds | – | – | – | – | – | – | – | – |
| Other | – | – | – | – | – | – | – | – |
| Multilateral | 1 | 2 | 5 | 9 | 17 | 24 | 31 | 37 |
| of which: Concessional | 0 | 0 | 1 | 1 | 2 | 2 | 2 | 6 |
| CMEA countries | 47 | 50 | 46 | 103 | 122 | 153 | 163 | 176 |
| of which: Concessional | 39 | 40 | 36 | 84 | 95 | 122 | 127 | 144 |
| OPEC countries | 3 | 5 | 6 | 72 | 139 | 131 | 113 | 98 |
| of which: Concessional | 1 | 3 | 4 | 31 | 91 | 84 | 68 | 53 |
| Other LDC'S | 2 | 2 | 2 | 3 | 3 | 4 | 3 | 3 |
| of which: Concessional | 2 | 2 | 2 | 3 | 3 | 4 | 3 | 3 |
| Other and adjustments | 4 | 5 | 3 | 4 | 2 | 1 | 1 | 1 |
| **Total Debt Service** | **117** | **142** | **141** | **282** | **386** | **442** | **423** | **388** |
| of which: Concessional | 43 | 46 | 44 | 125 | 199 | 223 | 209 | 219 |
| Non-concessional | 74 | 96 | 97 | 157 | 187 | 219 | 215 | 170 |

*US $ Million*

| | 1975 | 1976 | 1977 | 1978 | 1979 | 1980 | 1981 | 1982 |
|---|---|---|---|---|---|---|---|---|
| **DEBT** | | | | | | | | |
| DAC countries and capital markets | 1582 | 2207 | 2726 | 3155 | 3500 | 4546 | 5095 | 5897 |
| ODA | 130 | 111 | 102 | 114 | 83 | 72 | 58 | 46 |
| Total export credits | 1164 | 1473 | 1660 | 2047 | 2405 | 2974 | 3247 | 3521 |
| Total private | 288 | 623 | 964 | 994 | 1012 | 1500 | 1790 | 2330 |
| *of which:* Bank loans | 204 | 440 | 864 | 844 | 812 | 1250 | 1560 | 2100 |
| Bonds | – | – | – | – | – | – | – | – |
| Other | 84 | 183 | 100 | 150 | 200 | 250 | 230 | 230 |
| Multilateral | – | – | – | – | – | – | – | – |
| *of which:* Concessional | – | – | – | – | – | – | – | – |
| CMEA countries | – | – | – | – | – | – | – | – |
| *of which:* Concessional | – | – | – | – | – | – | – | – |
| OPEC countries | – | – | – | – | – | – | – | – |
| *of which:* Concessional | – | – | – | – | – | – | – | – |
| Other LDC'S | – | – | – | – | – | – | – | – |
| *of which:* Concessional | – | – | – | – | – | – | – | – |
| Other and adjustments | 333 | 321 | 329 | 349 | 375 | 378 | 348 | 323 |
| **Total Debt** | **1915** | **2528** | **3055** | **3504** | **3875** | **4924** | **5443** | **6220** |
| *of which:* Concessional | 169 | 148 | 154 | 190 | 185 | 177 | 143 | 126 |
| Non-concessional | 1746 | 2380 | 2901 | 3314 | 3690 | 4747 | 5300 | 6094 |
| **DEBT SERVICE** | | | | | | | | |
| DAC countries and capital markets | 285 | 428 | 549 | 807 | 848 | 1031 | 1265 | 1282 |
| ODA | 26 | 25 | 23 | 26 | 22 | 17 | 14 | 13 |
| Total export credits | 182 | 332 | 331 | 478 | 434 | 486 | 580 | 594 |
| Total private | 77 | 71 | 194 | 304 | 392 | 528 | 670 | 676 |
| *of which:* Bank loans | 42 | 54 | 168 | 264 | 362 | 498 | 590 | 596 |
| Bonds | – | – | – | – | – | – | – | – |
| Other | 35 | 17 | 26 | 40 | 30 | 30 | 80 | 80 |
| Multilateral | – | – | – | – | – | – | – | – |
| *of which:* Concessional | – | – | – | – | – | – | – | – |
| CMEA countries | – | – | – | – | – | – | – | – |
| *of which:* Concessional | – | – | – | – | – | – | – | – |
| OPEC countries | – | – | – | – | – | – | – | – |
| *of which:* Concessional | – | – | – | – | – | – | – | – |
| Other LDC'S | – | – | – | – | – | – | – | – |
| *of which:* Concessional | – | – | – | – | – | – | – | – |
| Other and adjustments | 42 | 43 | 45 | 55 | 53 | 61 | 60 | 58 |
| **Total Debt Service** | **327** | **471** | **593** | **863** | **901** | **1092** | **1325** | **1340** |
| *of which:* Concessional | 30 | 29 | 27 | 32 | 31 | 27 | 25 | 27 |
| Non-concessional | 297 | 442 | 566 | 830 | 870 | 1065 | 1300 | 1314 |

| | 1975 | 1976 | 1977 | 1978 | 1979 | 1980 | 1981 | 1982 |
|---|---|---|---|---|---|---|---|---|
| **DEBT** | | | | | | | | |
| DAC countries and capital | | | | | | | | |
|   markets | 379 | 463 | 566 | 602 | 727 | 720 | 802 | 736 |
|   ODA | 309 | 342 | 412 | 352 | 367 | 269 | 285 | 319 |
|   Total export credits | 48 | 92 | 130 | 219 | 333 | 429 | 501 | 407 |
|   Total private | 22 | 29 | 24 | 31 | 27 | 22 | 16 | 10 |
|     *of which:* Bank loans | 14 | 15 | 10 | 20 | 15 | 10 | 5 | 6 |
|     Bonds | 8 | 7 | 8 | 8 | 9 | 10 | 8 | – |
|     Other | – | 7 | 6 | 3 | 3 | 2 | 3 | 4 |
| Multilateral | 180 | 217 | 292 | 368 | 456 | 557 | 690 | 792 |
|   *of which:* Concessional | 100 | 128 | 181 | 236 | 305 | 378 | 497 | 592 |
| CMEA countries | 4 | 5 | 7 | 7 | 6 | 5 | 2 | 1 |
|   *of which:* Concessional | 4 | 5 | 7 | 7 | 6 | 5 | 2 | 1 |
| OPEC countries | – | 1 | 8 | 9 | 13 | 40 | 84 | 100 |
|   *of which:* Concessional | – | 1 | 8 | 9 | 13 | 40 | 84 | 100 |
| Other LDC'S | 273 | 289 | 329 | 379 | 391 | 412 | 373 | 363 |
|   *of which:* Concessional | 273 | 289 | 329 | 379 | 391 | 383 | 336 | 315 |
| Other and adjustments | – | – | – | – | – | – | – | 10 |
| **Total Debt** | **836** | **975** | **1202** | **1366** | **1592** | **1734** | **1950** | **2001** |
|   *of which:* Concessional | 686 | 765 | 937 | 983 | 1082 | 1075 | 1204 | 1326 |
|     Non-concessional | 150 | 210 | 264 | 383 | 511 | 659 | 746 | 676 |
| **DEBT SERVICE** | | | | | | | | |
| DAC countries and capital | | | | | | | | |
|   markets | 29 | 26 | 33 | 36 | 85 | 88 | 59 | 53 |
|   ODA | 9 | 9 | 9 | 11 | 8 | 8 | 7 | 3 |
|   Total export credits | 13 | 12 | 19 | 21 | 68 | 76 | 44 | 42 |
|   Total private | 8 | 5 | 5 | 4 | 9 | 5 | 8 | 8 |
|     *of which:* Bank loans | 7 | 3 | 3 | 3 | 8 | 4 | 7 | – |
|     Bonds | 1 | 0 | 0 | 0 | 0 | 1 | 0 | 7 |
|     Other | – | 2 | 1 | 1 | 1 | 0 | 0 | 1 |
| Multilateral | 9 | 10 | 14 | 16 | 20 | 25 | 34 | 38 |
|   *of which:* Concessional | 3 | 2 | 4 | 2 | 4 | 5 | 13 | 8 |
| CMEA countries | 0 | 0 | 1 | 1 | 1 | 1 | 4 | 3 |
|   *of which:* Concessional | 0 | 0 | 1 | 1 | 1 | 1 | 4 | 3 |
| OPEC countries | – | – | 0 | 0 | 0 | 1 | 2 | 7 |
|   *of which:* Concessional | – | – | 0 | 0 | 0 | 1 | 2 | 7 |
| Other LDC'S | 1 | 0 | 0 | 0 | 1 | 1 | 1 | 18 |
|   *of which:* Concessional | 1 | 0 | 0 | 0 | 1 | 1 | 0 | 15 |
| Other and adjustments | – | – | – | – | – | – | – | 0 |
| **Total Debt Service** | **40** | **36** | **48** | **53** | **108** | **115** | **99** | **119** |
|   *of which:* Concessional | 14 | 12 | 14 | 14 | 14 | 15 | 26 | 35 |
|     Non-concessional | 26 | 24 | 34 | 38 | 94 | 101 | 74 | 84 |

# THAILAND

US $ Million

| | 1975 | 1976 | 1977 | 1978 | 1979 | 1980 | 1981 | 1982 |
|---|---|---|---|---|---|---|---|---|
| **DEBT** | | | | | | | | |
| DAC countries and capital markets | 986 | 1128 | 1421 | 1937 | 3124 | 4067 | 5099 | 5645 |
| ODA | 196 | 230 | 297 | 468 | 574 | 833 | 936 | 1021 |
| Total export credits | 350 | 338 | 414 | 479 | 824 | 1095 | 1297 | 1474 |
| Total private | 440 | 560 | 710 | 990 | 1726 | 2139 | 2866 | 3150 |
| of which: Bank loans | 290 | 360 | 410 | 650 | 1284 | 1580 | 2250 | 2500 |
| Bonds | – | – | – | – | 42 | 99 | 136 | 170 |
| Other | 150 | 200 | 300 | 340 | 400 | 460 | 480 | 480 |
| Multilateral | 337 | 416 | 520 | 712 | 919 | 1159 | 1490 | 1931 |
| of which: Concessional | 117 | 115 | 132 | 192 | 246 | 283 | 287 | 298 |
| CMEA countries | – | – | – | – | – | – | – | – |
| of which: Concessional | – | – | – | – | – | – | – | – |
| OPEC countries | – | – | 0 | 2 | 4 | 14 | 21 | 55 |
| of which: Concessional | – | – | 0 | 2 | 4 | 14 | 21 | 55 |
| Other LDC'S | 1 | 1 | 1 | 0 | 0 | 0 | – | – |
| of which: Concessional | – | – | – | – | – | – | – | – |
| Other and adjustments | – | – | – | – | – | – | – | – |
| **Total Debt** | **1324** | **1545** | **1942** | **2652** | **4047** | **5239** | **6611** | **7632** |
| of which: Concessional | 313 | 345 | 430 | 662 | 824 | 1130 | 1245 | 1374 |
| Non-concessional | 1011 | 1200 | 1512 | 1990 | 3223 | 4109 | 5366 | 6258 |
| **DEBT SERVICE** | | | | | | | | |
| DAC countries and capital markets | 288 | 342 | 444 | 730 | 850 | 873 | 1109 | 1436 |
| ODA | 16 | 20 | 21 | 28 | 32 | 37 | 45 | 55 |
| Total export credits | 124 | 118 | 148 | 168 | 222 | 240 | 326 | 363 |
| Total private | 148 | 205 | 275 | 534 | 596 | 596 | 738 | 1018 |
| of which: Bank loans | 108 | 85 | 125 | 334 | 396 | 320 | 510 | 755 |
| Bonds | – | – | – | – | – | 6 | 8 | 13 |
| Other | 40 | 120 | 150 | 200 | 200 | 270 | 220 | 250 |
| Multilateral | 37 | 45 | 56 | 75 | 95 | 112 | 128 | 155 |
| of which: Concessional | 17 | 17 | 17 | 19 | 20 | 21 | 22 | 19 |
| CMEA countries | – | – | – | – | – | – | – | – |
| of which: Concessional | – | – | – | – | – | – | – | – |
| OPEC countries | – | – | – | 0 | 0 | 0 | 1 | 1 |
| of which: Concessional | – | – | – | 0 | 0 | 0 | 1 | 1 |
| Other LDC'S | 0 | 0 | 0 | 0 | 0 | 0 | 0 | – |
| of which: Concessional | – | – | – | – | – | – | – | – |
| Other and adjustments | – | – | – | – | – | – | – | – |
| **Total Debt Service** | **326** | **388** | **501** | **805** | **945** | **985** | **1238** | **1592** |
| of which: Concessional | 33 | 37 | 38 | 47 | 52 | 58 | 67 | 75 |
| Non-concessional | 292 | 350 | 463 | 758 | 893 | 927 | 1171 | 1517 |

US $ Million

| | 1975 | 1976 | 1977 | 1978 | 1979 | 1980 | 1981 | 1982 |
|---|---|---|---|---|---|---|---|---|
| **DEBT** | | | | | | | | |
| DAC countries and capital | | | | | | | | |
| markets | 130 | 148 | 291 | 552 | 706 | 705 | 662 | 563 |
| ODA | 52 | 50 | 73 | 125 | 165 | 160 | 143 | 153 |
| Total export credits | 57 | 78 | 202 | 347 | 391 | 431 | 464 | 359 |
| Total private | 21 | 20 | 16 | 80 | 150 | 114 | 55 | 51 |
| *of which:* Bank loans | 21 | 20 | 16 | 80 | 150 | 114 | 50 | 45 |
| Bonds | 0 | 0 | 0 | – | – | – | – | – |
| Other | – | – | – | – | – | – | 5 | 6 |
| Multilateral | 8 | 15 | 28 | 72 | 99 | 138 | 143 | 159 |
| *of which:* Concessional | 7 | 13 | 23 | 59 | 84 | 118 | 123 | 136 |
| CMEA countries | – | – | – | – | – | – | – | – |
| *of which:* Concessional | – | – | – | – | – | – | – | – |
| OPEC countries | – | – | – | – | – | – | 0 | 3 |
| *of which:* Concessional | – | – | – | – | – | – | 0 | 3 |
| Other LDC'S | – | – | – | 7 | 7 | 14 | 14 | 13 |
| *of which:* Concessional | – | – | – | – | – | – | – | – |
| Other and adjustments | – | 14 | 9 | 25 | 46 | 60 | 47 | 74 |
| **Total Debt** | **138** | **177** | **328** | **656** | **858** | **917** | **867** | **812** |
| *of which:* Concessional | 59 | 63 | 96 | 184 | 249 | 278 | 266 | 292 |
| Non-concessional | 79 | 114 | 231 | 473 | 609 | 639 | 601 | 520 |
| **DEBT SERVICE** | | | | | | | | |
| DAC countries and capital | | | | | | | | |
| markets | 21 | 29 | 36 | 46 | 49 | 72 | 53 | 27 |
| ODA | 3 | 4 | 2 | 3 | 5 | 4 | 2 | 2 |
| Total export credits | 15 | 22 | 30 | 36 | 26 | 48 | 41 | 22 |
| Total private | 3 | 3 | 4 | 6 | 18 | 21 | 10 | 4 |
| *of which:* Bank loans | 3 | 3 | 4 | 6 | 18 | 21 | 10 | 2 |
| Bonds | 0 | 0 | 0 | 0 | – | – | – | – |
| Other | – | – | – | – | – | – | – | 2 |
| Multilateral | 0 | 0 | 1 | 1 | 2 | 2 | 3 | 3 |
| *of which:* Concessional | 0 | 0 | 0 | 0 | 1 | 1 | 1 | 1 |
| CMEA countries | – | – | – | – | – | – | – | – |
| *of which:* Concessional | – | – | – | – | – | – | – | – |
| OPEC countries | – | – | – | – | – | – | – | 0 |
| *of which:* Concessional | – | – | – | – | – | – | – | 0 |
| Other LDC'S | 0 | – | – | – | 0 | – | 1 | 2 |
| *of which:* Concessional | 0 | – | – | – | – | – | – | – |
| Other and adjustments | – | 1 | 5 | 3 | 1 | 3 | 1 | 2 |
| **Total Debt Service** | **22** | **31** | **41** | **50** | **51** | **78** | **57** | **35** |
| *of which:* Concessional | 4 | 4 | 2 | 4 | 5 | 5 | 3 | 3 |
| Non-concessional | 18 | 26 | 39 | 46 | 46 | 73 | 54 | 33 |

*US $ Million*

| | 1975 | 1976 | 1977 | 1978 | 1979 | 1980 | 1981 | 1982 |
|---|---|---|---|---|---|---|---|---|
| **DEBT** | | | | | | | | |
| DAC countries and capital markets | 1 | 2 | 2 | 2 | 15 | 17 | 17 | 16 |
| ODA | 1 | 2 | 2 | 2 | 15 | 17 | 17 | 16 |
| Total export credits | – | – | – | – | – | – | – | – |
| Total private | – | – | – | – | – | – | – | – |
| of which: Bank loans | – | – | – | – | – | – | – | – |
| Bonds | – | – | – | – | – | – | – | – |
| Other | – | – | – | – | – | – | – | – |
| Multilateral | – | – | – | – | – | – | – | – |
| of which: Concessional | – | – | – | – | – | – | – | – |
| CMEA countries | – | – | – | – | – | – | – | – |
| of which: Concessional | – | – | – | – | – | – | – | – |
| OPEC countries | – | – | – | – | – | – | – | – |
| of which: Concessional | – | – | – | – | – | – | – | – |
| Other LDC'S | – | – | – | – | – | – | – | – |
| of which: Concessional | – | – | – | – | – | – | – | – |
| Other and adjustments | – | – | – | – | – | – | – | – |
| **Total Debt** | **1** | **2** | **2** | **2** | **15** | **17** | **17** | **16** |
| of which: Concessional | 1 | 2 | 2 | 2 | 15 | 17 | 17 | 16 |
| Non-concessional | – | – | – | – | – | – | – | – |
| **DEBT SERVICE** | | | | | | | | |
| DAC countries and capital markets | – | – | – | 0 | 0 | 0 | 0 | 0 |
| ODA | – | – | – | 0 | 0 | 0 | 0 | 0 |
| Total export credits | – | – | – | 0 | – | – | – | – |
| Total private | – | – | – | – | – | – | – | – |
| of which: Bank loans | – | – | – | – | – | – | – | – |
| Bonds | – | – | – | – | – | – | – | – |
| Other | – | – | – | – | – | – | – | – |
| Multilateral | – | – | – | – | – | – | – | – |
| of which: Concessional | – | – | – | – | – | – | – | – |
| CMEA countries | – | – | – | – | – | – | – | – |
| of which: Concessional | – | – | – | – | – | – | – | – |
| OPEC countries | – | – | – | – | – | – | – | – |
| of which: Concessional | – | – | – | – | – | – | – | – |
| Other LDC'S | – | – | – | – | – | – | – | – |
| of which: Concessional | – | – | – | – | – | – | – | – |
| Other and adjustments | – | – | – | – | – | – | – | – |
| **Total Debt Service** | **–** | **–** | **–** | **0** | **0** | **0** | **0** | **0** |
| of which: Concessional | – | – | – | 0 | 0 | 0 | 0 | 0 |
| Non-concessional | – | – | – | 0 | – | – | – | – |

# TRINIDAD AND TOBAGO

| | 1975 | 1976 | 1977 | 1978 | 1979 | 1980 | 1981 | 1982 |
|---|---|---|---|---|---|---|---|---|
| **DEBT** | | | | | | | | |
| DAC countries and capital | | | | | | | | |
| markets | 127 | 76 | 215 | 375 | 470 | 736 | 947 | 1069 |
| ODA | 19 | 19 | 17 | 18 | 18 | 18 | 10 | 10 |
| Total export credits | 28 | 21 | 19 | 18 | 133 | 286 | 464 | 517 |
| Total private | 80 | 36 | 179 | 339 | 319 | 432 | 473 | 542 |
| *of which:* Bank loans | 63 | 23 | 160 | 282 | 260 | 380 | 420 | 480 |
| Bonds | 17 | 13 | 13 | 51 | 51 | 44 | 43 | 42 |
| Other | – | – | 6 | 6 | 8 | 8 | 10 | 20 |
| Multilateral | 47 | 53 | 58 | 61 | 62 | 62 | 61 | 58 |
| *of which:* Concessional | 32 | 31 | 29 | 26 | 25 | 24 | 23 | 22 |
| CMEA countries | – | – | – | – | – | – | – | – |
| *of which:* Concessional | – | – | – | – | – | – | – | – |
| OPEC countries | – | – | – | – | – | – | – | – |
| *of which:* Concessional | – | – | – | – | – | – | – | – |
| Other LDC'S | – | – | – | – | – | – | – | – |
| *of which:* Concessional | – | – | – | – | – | – | – | – |
| Other and adjustments | – | – | – | – | – | – | – | – |
| **Total Debt** | **174** | **130** | **273** | **436** | **531** | **798** | **1008** | **1127** |
| *of which:* Concessional | 51 | 50 | 46 | 44 | 43 | 42 | 33 | 32 |
| Non-concessional | 122 | 80 | 227 | 392 | 488 | 755 | 975 | 1095 |
| **DEBT SERVICE** | | | | | | | | |
| DAC countries and capital | | | | | | | | |
| markets | 26 | 73 | 10 | 33 | 46 | 232 | 147 | 245 |
| ODA | 1 | 1 | 1 | 2 | 1 | 1 | 9 | 1 |
| Total export credits | 4 | 14 | 3 | 12 | 9 | 47 | 71 | 105 |
| Total private | 20 | 58 | 6 | 20 | 36 | 184 | 67 | 139 |
| *of which:* Bank loans | 19 | 49 | 4 | 16 | 29 | 170 | 60 | 129 |
| Bonds | 2 | 9 | 2 | 3 | 6 | 13 | 5 | 5 |
| Other | – | – | – | 1 | 1 | 1 | 3 | 5 |
| Multilateral | 4 | 6 | 6 | 9 | 10 | 11 | 11 | 9 |
| *of which:* Concessional | 3 | 4 | 4 | 5 | 5 | 5 | 5 | 3 |
| CMEA countries | – | – | – | – | – | – | – | – |
| *of which:* Concessional | – | – | – | – | – | – | – | – |
| OPEC countries | – | – | – | – | – | – | – | – |
| *of which:* Concessional | – | – | – | – | – | – | – | – |
| Other LDC'S | – | – | – | – | – | – | – | – |
| *of which:* Concessional | – | – | – | – | – | – | – | – |
| Other and adjustments | – | – | – | – | – | – | – | – |
| **Total Debt Service** | **30** | **78** | **17** | **42** | **56** | **243** | **158** | **254** |
| *of which:* Concessional | 5 | 6 | 5 | 6 | 6 | 6 | 13 | 4 |
| Non-concessional | 25 | 73 | 12 | 36 | 50 | 237 | 145 | 250 |

*US $ Million*

| | 1975 | 1976 | 1977 | 1978 | 1979 | 1980 | 1981 | 1982 |
|---|---|---|---|---|---|---|---|---|
| **DEBT** | | | | | | | | |
| DAC countries and capital | | | | | | | | |
| markets | 839 | 1148 | 1615 | 2126 | 2480 | 2557 | 2543 | 2617 |
| ODA | 606 | 664 | 800 | 978 | 1087 | 1086 | 1055 | 1090 |
| Total export credits | 167 | 232 | 444 | 570 | 714 | 920 | 968 | 1015 |
| Total private | 66 | 252 | 371 | 578 | 679 | 551 | 520 | 512 |
| *of which:* Bank loans | 50 | 210 | 330 | 537 | 634 | 510 | 480 | 470 |
| Bonds | 1 | 25 | 21 | 16 | 11 | 6 | 0 | 0 |
| Other | 15 | 17 | 20 | 25 | 34 | 35 | 40 | 42 |
| Multilateral | 178 | 235 | 285 | 327 | 380 | 440 | 514 | 587 |
| *of which:* Concessional | 82 | 90 | 92 | 92 | 91 | 96 | 98 | 111 |
| CMEA countries | 12 | 10 | 9 | 30 | 54 | 99 | 106 | 103 |
| *of which:* Concessional | 12 | 10 | 9 | 10 | 18 | 51 | 60 | 61 |
| OPEC countries | 51 | 73 | 176 | 223 | 310 | 404 | 393 | 404 |
| *of which:* Concessional | 51 | 71 | 118 | 156 | 184 | 236 | 278 | 297 |
| Other LDC'S | 0 | 0 | – | – | 5 | 13 | 24 | 41 |
| *of which:* Concessional | 0 | 0 | – | – | 5 | 12 | 16 | 31 |
| Other and adjustments | 12 | 11 | 10 | 9 | 8 | 7 | 8 | 15 |
| **Total Debt** | **1092** | **1478** | **2096** | **2716** | **3236** | **3520** | **3588** | **3768** |
| *of which:* Concessional | 755 | 840 | 1023 | 1240 | 1387 | 1484 | 1510 | 1601 |
| Non-concessional | 338 | 638 | 1073 | 1476 | 1849 | 2036 | 2079 | 2167 |
| | | | | | | | | |
| **DEBT SERVICE** | | | | | | | | |
| DAC countries and capital | | | | | | | | |
| markets | 112 | 129 | 163 | 212 | 323 | 424 | 436 | 458 |
| ODA | 32 | 31 | 31 | 43 | 57 | 53 | 59 | 50 |
| Total export credits | 69 | 78 | 102 | 117 | 158 | 182 | 190 | 254 |
| Total private | 12 | 20 | 30 | 53 | 109 | 188 | 187 | 154 |
| *of which:* Bank loans | 12 | 18 | 18 | 40 | 96 | 175 | 172 | 144 |
| Bonds | 0 | 0 | 7 | 7 | 6 | 6 | 6 | 0 |
| Other | – | 2 | 5 | 6 | 6 | 7 | 10 | 10 |
| Multilateral | 14 | 18 | 28 | 32 | 41 | 48 | 59 | 74 |
| *of which:* Concessional | 3 | 3 | 6 | 5 | 4 | 5 | 6 | 5 |
| CMEA countries | 2 | 2 | 2 | 8 | 5 | 16 | 9 | 12 |
| *of which:* Concessional | 2 | 2 | 2 | 5 | 2 | 5 | 5 | 5 |
| OPEC countries | 5 | 6 | 7 | 15 | 23 | 30 | 82 | 31 |
| *of which:* Concessional | 5 | 6 | 7 | 10 | 14 | 14 | 18 | 19 |
| Other LDC'S | 0 | 0 | 0 | – | – | 5 | 1 | 1 |
| *of which:* Concessional | 0 | 0 | 0 | – | – | – | – | – |
| Other and adjustments | 1 | 2 | 2 | 2 | 2 | 2 | 2 | 2 |
| **Total Debt Service** | **136** | **157** | **201** | **270** | **395** | **524** | **588** | **578** |
| *of which:* Concessional | 42 | 42 | 47 | 64 | 78 | 78 | 88 | 80 |
| Non-concessional | 94 | 115 | 155 | 207 | 317 | 446 | 500 | 498 |

## TURKEY

*US $ Million*

|  | 1975 | 1976 | 1977 | 1978 | 1979 | 1980 | 1981 | 1982 |
|---|---|---|---|---|---|---|---|---|
| **DEBT** | | | | | | | | |
| DAC countries and capital | | | | | | | | |
| markets | 2585 | 3120 | 3875 | 5260 | 9173 | 10826 | 10819 | 10521 |
| ODA | 1710 | 1678 | 1758 | 2059 | 2614 | 2972 | 3176 | 3358 |
| Total export credits | 815 | 966 | 1388 | 2246 | 3110 | 3620 | 4128 | 3165 |
| Total private | 60 | 476 | 729 | 955 | 3449 | 4234 | 3515 | 3998 |
| *of which:* Bank loans | 45 | 350 | 600 | 794 | 3000 | 3100 | 3150 | 3580 |
| Bonds | 15 | 36 | 34 | 61 | 49 | 34 | 5 | 18 |
| Other | – | 90 | 95 | 100 | 400 | 1100 | 360 | 400 |
| Multilateral | 747 | 980 | 1201 | 1462 | 1827 | 2184 | 2623 | 3079 |
| *of which:* Concessional | 416 | 489 | 573 | 650 | 763 | 731 | 660 | 626 |
| CMEA countries | 272 | 257 | 259 | 334 | 463 | 575 | 652 | 739 |
| *of which:* Concessional | 271 | 253 | 255 | 288 | 330 | 321 | 277 | 232 |
| OPEC countries | – | 9 | 27 | 282 | 168 | 253 | 318 | 521 |
| *of which:* Concessional | – | 9 | 12 | 11 | 40 | 238 | 303 | 504 |
| Other LDC'S | 8 | 22 | 26 | 32 | 27 | 24 | 19 | 14 |
| *of which:* Concessional | – | – | – | – | – | – | – | – |
| Other and adjustments | 3 | 2 | 2 | 6 | 109 | 10 | 61 | 112 |
| **Total Debt** | **3614** | **4390** | **5389** | **7376** | **11767** | **13870** | **14492** | **14987** |
| *of which:* Concessional | 2397 | 2429 | 2598 | 3008 | 3748 | 4262 | 4416 | 4719 |
| Non-concessional | 1218 | 1961 | 2791 | 4368 | 8019 | 9608 | 10076 | 10267 |
| **DEBT SERVICE** | | | | | | | | |
| DAC countries and capital | | | | | | | | |
| markets | 266 | 359 | 313 | 258 | 373 | 722 | 970 | 1649 |
| ODA | 91 | 101 | 100 | 56 | 57 | 76 | 135 | 170 |
| Total export credits | 164 | 214 | 144 | 154 | 244 | 301 | 343 | 395 |
| Total private | 12 | 44 | 69 | 48 | 73 | 346 | 493 | 1083 |
| *of which:* Bank loans | 10 | 42 | 61 | 35 | 63 | 340 | 460 | 990 |
| Bonds | 2 | 2 | 5 | 8 | 5 | 4 | 28 | 3 |
| Other | – | 1 | 3 | 5 | 5 | 2 | 5 | 90 |
| Multilateral | 52 | 66 | 92 | 123 | 159 | 195 | 225 | 293 |
| *of which:* Concessional | 22 | 20 | 20 | 24 | 27 | 30 | 28 | 28 |
| CMEA countries | 36 | 57 | 38 | 40 | 54 | 76 | 100 | 97 |
| *of which:* Concessional | 36 | 57 | 37 | 39 | 49 | 52 | 52 | 52 |
| OPEC countries | – | 0 | 0 | 66 | 144 | 123 | 21 | 25 |
| *of which:* Concessional | – | 0 | 0 | 1 | 1 | 9 | 19 | 23 |
| Other LDC'S | 4 | 4 | 7 | 6 | 7 | 7 | 7 | 6 |
| *of which:* Concessional | – | – | – | – | – | – | – | – |
| Other and adjustments | 1 | 1 | 1 | 0 | 0 | 0 | 1 | 2 |
| **Total Debt Service** | **359** | **488** | **451** | **492** | **737** | **1123** | **1324** | **2071** |
| *of which:* Concessional | 148 | 179 | 158 | 119 | 134 | 166 | 235 | 273 |
| Non-concessional | 210 | 309 | 293 | 373 | 602 | 957 | 1089 | 1798 |

*US $ Million*

| | 1975 | 1976 | 1977 | 1978 | 1979 | 1980 | 1981 | 1982 |
|---|---|---|---|---|---|---|---|---|
| **DEBT** | | | | | | | | |
| DAC countries and capital | | | | | | | | |
| markets | 101 | 117 | 149 | 200 | 198 | 217 | 181 | 215 |
| ODA | 86 | 84 | 88 | 99 | 92 | 92 | 67 | 58 |
| Total export credits | 15 | 27 | 44 | 70 | 74 | 98 | 107 | 152 |
| Total private | – | 6 | 17 | 31 | 32 | 27 | 7 | 5 |
| of which: Bank loans | – | – | 4 | 8 | 9 | 11 | 6 | 5 |
| Bonds | – | – | – | – | – | – | – | – |
| Other | – | 6 | 13 | 23 | 23 | 16 | 1 | – |
| Multilateral | 57 | 63 | 68 | 75 | 78 | 110 | 134 | 198 |
| of which: Concessional | 57 | 63 | 68 | 75 | 75 | 104 | 123 | 183 |
| CMEA countries | 27 | 47 | 41 | 39 | 57 | 56 | 56 | 22 |
| of which: Concessional | 27 | 37 | 35 | 32 | 30 | 29 | 29 | 11 |
| OPEC countries | 15 | 15 | 13 | 32 | 37 | 37 | 37 | 18 |
| of which: Concessional | 15 | 15 | 13 | 32 | 37 | 37 | 37 | 18 |
| Other LDC'S | 13 | 10 | 11 | 10 | 122 | 189 | 176 | 82 |
| of which: Concessional | 3 | 2 | 3 | 3 | 3 | 3 | 3 | 3 |
| Other and adjustments | – | – | – | – | – | – | – | 10 |
| **Total Debt** | **213** | **252** | **281** | **355** | **492** | **609** | **585** | **546** |
| of which: Concessional | 188 | 201 | 206 | 241 | 237 | 265 | 259 | 274 |
| Non-concessional | 25 | 51 | 76 | 114 | 255 | 344 | 326 | 272 |
| **DEBT SERVICE** | | | | | | | | |
| DAC countries and capital | | | | | | | | |
| markets | 15 | 11 | 16 | 6 | 11 | 11 | 17 | 12 |
| ODA | 2 | 1 | 4 | 0 | 1 | 1 | – | 1 |
| Total export credits | 13 | 9 | 11 | 3 | 9 | 5 | 13 | 5 |
| Total private | – | 1 | 1 | 2 | 1 | 5 | 4 | 6 |
| of which: Bank loans | – | – | – | 2 | 1 | 5 | 2 | 2 |
| Bonds | – | – | – | – | – | – | – | – |
| Other | – | 1 | 1 | 0 | – | – | 2 | 4 |
| Multilateral | 1 | 2 | 2 | 2 | 3 | 2 | 5 | 14 |
| of which: Concessional | 1 | 2 | 2 | 2 | 3 | 2 | 5 | 13 |
| CMEA countries | 1 | 2 | 10 | 5 | 3 | 1 | 0 | 10 |
| of which: Concessional | 1 | 2 | 6 | 5 | 3 | 1 | – | 5 |
| OPEC countries | – | – | 3 | 0 | 0 | 0 | – | 3 |
| of which: Concessional | – | – | 3 | 0 | 0 | 0 | – | 3 |
| Other LDC'S | 2 | 2 | 2 | 2 | 0 | – | 39 | 85 |
| of which: Concessional | – | – | – | – | – | – | – | 0 |
| Other and adjustments | – | – | – | – | – | – | – | – |
| **Total Debt Service** | **20** | **16** | **32** | **14** | **17** | **15** | **61** | **124** |
| of which: Concessional | 5 | 4 | 14 | 7 | 7 | 4 | 5 | 22 |
| Non-concessional | 15 | 12 | 17 | 7 | 10 | 11 | 56 | 102 |

*US $ Million*

| | 1975 | 1976 | 1977 | 1978 | 1979 | 1980 | 1981 | 1982 |
|---|---|---|---|---|---|---|---|---|
| **DEBT** | | | | | | | | |
| DAC countries and capital | | | | | | | | |
|   markets | 730 | 1029 | 1058 | 1362 | 2414 | 1593 | 1256 | 1117 |
|   ODA | – | – | 1 | 1 | – | – | – | 1 |
|   Total export credits | 480 | 779 | 807 | 861 | 1314 | 1193 | 846 | 656 |
|   Total private | 250 | 250 | 250 | 500 | 1100 | 400 | 410 | 460 |
|     *of which:* Bank loans | 250 | 250 | 250 | 500 | 1100 | 400 | 410 | 460 |
|     Bonds | – | – | – | – | – | – | – | – |
|     Other | – | – | – | – | – | – | – | – |
| Multilateral | – | – | – | – | – | – | – | – |
|   *of which:* Concessional | – | – | – | – | – | – | – | – |
| CMEA countries | – | – | – | – | – | – | – | – |
|   *of which:* Concessional | – | – | – | – | – | – | – | – |
| OPEC countries | – | – | – | – | – | – | – | – |
|   *of which:* Concessional | – | – | – | – | – | – | – | – |
| Other LDC'S | – | – | – | – | – | – | – | – |
|   *of which:* Concessional | – | – | – | – | – | – | – | – |
| Other and adjustments | – | – | – | – | – | – | – | – |
| **Total Debt** | **730** | **1029** | **1058** | **1362** | **2414** | **1593** | **1256** | **1117** |
|   *of which:* Concessional | – | – | 1 | 1 | – | – | – | 1 |
|     Non-concessional | 730 | 1029 | 1057 | 1361 | 2414 | 1593 | 1256 | 1116 |
| **DEBT SERVICE** | | | | | | | | |
| DAC countries and capital | | | | | | | | |
|   markets | 136 | 272 | 300 | 446 | 843 | 1295 | 869 | 518 |
|   ODA | – | – | – | – | 1 | – | – | – |
|   Total export credits | 110 | 237 | 255 | 296 | 332 | 445 | 764 | 410 |
|   Total private | 26 | 35 | 45 | 150 | 510 | 850 | 105 | 108 |
|     *of which:* Bank loans | 26 | 35 | 45 | 150 | 510 | 850 | 105 | 108 |
|     Bonds | – | – | – | – | – | – | – | – |
|     Other | – | – | – | – | – | – | – | – |
| Multilateral | – | – | – | – | – | – | – | – |
|   *of which:* Concessional | – | – | – | – | – | – | – | – |
| CMEA countries | – | – | – | – | – | – | – | – |
|   *of which:* Concessional | – | – | – | – | – | – | – | – |
| OPEC countries | – | – | – | – | – | – | – | – |
|   *of which:* Concessional | – | – | – | – | – | – | – | – |
| Other LDC'S | – | – | – | – | – | – | – | – |
|   *of which:* Concessional | – | – | – | – | – | – | – | – |
| Other and adjustments | – | – | – | – | – | – | – | – |
| **Total Debt Service** | **136** | **272** | **300** | **446** | **843** | **1295** | **869** | **518** |
|   *of which:* Concessional | – | – | – | – | 1 | – | – | – |
|     Non-concessional | 136 | 272 | 300 | 446 | 842 | 1295 | 869 | 518 |

# UPPER VOLTA

*US $ Million*

| | 1975 | 1976 | 1977 | 1978 | 1979 | 1980 | 1981 | 1982 |
|---|---|---|---|---|---|---|---|---|
| **DEBT** | | | | | | | | |
| DAC countries and capital markets | 32 | 43 | 60 | 90 | 100 | 105 | 81 | 104 |
| ODA | 29 | 39 | 52 | 64 | 57 | 47 | 25 | 42 |
| Total export credits | 3 | 4 | 8 | 24 | 27 | 49 | 48 | 52 |
| Total private | 0 | 0 | 0 | 2 | 16 | 9 | 8 | 10 |
| *of which:* Bank loans | – | – | – | 2 | 16 | 9 | 8 | 10 |
| Bonds | 0 | 0 | 0 | 0 | 0 | 0 | 0 | 0 |
| Other | – | – | – | – | – | – | – | – |
| Multilateral | 26 | 34 | 62 | 95 | 133 | 164 | 183 | 209 |
| *of which:* Concessional | 23 | 30 | 58 | 90 | 128 | 157 | 175 | 194 |
| CMEA countries | – | – | – | – | – | – | – | – |
| *of which:* Concessional | – | – | – | – | – | – | – | – |
| OPEC countries | 1 | 1 | 1 | 1 | 1 | 1 | 1 | 1 |
| *of which:* Concessional | 1 | 1 | 1 | 1 | 1 | 1 | 1 | 1 |
| Other LDC'S | 4 | 6 | 9 | 10 | 27 | 28 | 23 | 20 |
| *of which:* Concessional | 4 | 6 | 9 | 10 | 15 | 19 | 17 | 15 |
| Other and adjustments | – | – | – | – | – | – | – | 10 |
| **Total Debt** | **62** | **84** | **132** | **197** | **261** | **299** | **288** | **344** |
| *of which:* Concessional | 56 | 76 | 120 | 165 | 200 | 224 | 218 | 251 |
| Non-concessional | 6 | 8 | 12 | 32 | 61 | 75 | 70 | 92 |
| | | | | | | | | |
| **DEBT SERVICE** | | | | | | | | |
| DAC countries and capital markets | 7 | 5 | 5 | 7 | 7 | 10 | 7 | 13 |
| ODA | 3 | 3 | 2 | 3 | 4 | 4 | 1 | – |
| Total export credits | 4 | 2 | 3 | 4 | 2 | 3 | 6 | 10 |
| Total private | 0 | 0 | 0 | 1 | 2 | 3 | 1 | 2 |
| *of which:* Bank loans | – | – | – | 1 | 2 | 3 | 1 | 2 |
| Bonds | 0 | 0 | 0 | 0 | 0 | 0 | 0 | – |
| Other | – | – | – | – | – | – | – | – |
| Multilateral | 1 | 1 | 1 | 2 | 2 | 3 | 6 | 7 |
| *of which:* Concessional | 0 | 0 | 1 | 1 | 1 | 2 | 2 | 6 |
| CMEA countries | – | – | – | – | – | – | – | – |
| *of which:* Concessional | – | – | – | – | – | – | – | – |
| OPEC countries | 0 | 0 | 0 | 0 | 0 | 0 | 0 | 0 |
| *of which:* Concessional | 0 | 0 | 0 | 0 | 0 | 0 | 0 | 0 |
| Other LDC'S | 0 | 0 | 0 | 0 | 1 | 3 | 2 | 0 |
| *of which:* Concessional | 0 | 0 | 0 | 0 | 0 | 0 | 0 | 0 |
| Other and adjustments | – | – | – | – | – | – | – | – |
| **Total Debt Service** | **8** | **6** | **7** | **9** | **10** | **16** | **15** | **20** |
| *of which:* Concessional | 3 | 3 | 3 | 4 | 5 | 6 | 3 | 6 |
| Non-concessional | 4 | 3 | 4 | 5 | 5 | 10 | 12 | 14 |

*US $ Million*

| | 1975 | 1976 | 1977 | 1978 | 1979 | 1980 | 1981 | 1982 |
|---|---|---|---|---|---|---|---|---|
| **DEBT** | | | | | | | | |
| DAC countries and capital | | | | | | | | |
| markets | 451 | 502 | 532 | 545 | 665 | 759 | 970 | 1409 |
| ODA | 75 | 72 | 72 | 69 | 67 | 66 | 67 | 64 |
| Total export credits | 42 | 54 | 55 | 71 | 97 | 120 | 112 | 97 |
| Total private | 334 | 376 | 405 | 405 | 501 | 573 | 791 | 1248 |
| *of which:* Bank loans | 80 | 90 | 88 | 86 | 172 | 250 | 460 | 780 |
| Bonds | 234 | 266 | 287 | 279 | 269 | 263 | 266 | 403 |
| Other | 20 | 20 | 30 | 40 | 60 | 60 | 65 | 65 |
| Multilateral | 101 | 120 | 125 | 146 | 168 | 182 | 179 | 201 |
| *of which:* Concessional | 24 | 20 | 15 | 17 | 21 | 22 | 20 | 20 |
| CMEA countries | 1 | 1 | 0 | 0 | 0 | 0 | 0 | 0 |
| *of which:* Concessional | – | – | – | – | – | – | – | – |
| OPEC countries | – | – | – | – | – | – | – | – |
| *of which:* Concessional | – | – | – | – | – | – | – | – |
| Other LDC'S | 54 | 48 | 55 | 126 | 205 | 286 | 355 | 357 |
| *of which:* Concessional | 1 | 1 | 1 | 1 | 1 | 0 | 0 | – |
| Other and adjustments | 47 | 41 | 36 | 20 | 17 | 17 | 62 | 8 |
| **Total Debt** | **654** | **712** | **749** | **838** | **1056** | **1244** | **1565** | **1975** |
| *of which:* Concessional | 101 | 94 | 89 | 87 | 89 | 89 | 87 | 84 |
| Non-concessional | 553 | 618 | 661 | 752 | 967 | 1155 | 1478 | 1891 |
| | | | | | | | | |
| **DEBT SERVICE** | | | | | | | | |
| DAC countries and capital | | | | | | | | |
| markets | 182 | 146 | 196 | 388 | 117 | 149 | 166 | 222 |
| ODA | 6 | 5 | 4 | 5 | 6 | 5 | 6 | 6 |
| Total export credits | 9 | 11 | 14 | 18 | 30 | 26 | 47 | 39 |
| Total private | 167 | 130 | 178 | 365 | 81 | 118 | 114 | 178 |
| *of which:* Bank loans | 122 | 69 | 115 | 109 | 23 | 68 | 58 | 131 |
| Bonds | 40 | 56 | 58 | 249 | 50 | 36 | 41 | 30 |
| Other | 5 | 5 | 6 | 8 | 8 | 14 | 15 | 17 |
| Multilateral | 16 | 17 | 21 | 23 | 24 | 25 | 29 | 30 |
| *of which:* Concessional | 7 | 7 | 7 | 5 | 5 | 3 | 3 | 1 |
| CMEA countries | 0 | 0 | 0 | 0 | 0 | 0 | 0 | 0 |
| *of which:* Concessional | – | – | – | – | – | – | – | – |
| OPEC countries | – | – | – | – | – | – | – | – |
| *of which:* Concessional | – | – | – | – | – | – | – | – |
| Other LDC'S | 16 | 27 | 22 | 10 | 15 | 24 | 35 | 54 |
| *of which:* Concessional | 0 | 0 | 0 | 0 | 0 | 0 | 0 | 0 |
| Other and adjustments | 13 | 12 | 15 | 23 | 5 | 4 | 3 | 3 |
| **Total Debt Service** | **227** | **203** | **255** | **445** | **162** | **202** | **233** | **308** |
| *of which:* Concessional | 13 | 13 | 12 | 11 | 11 | 8 | 9 | 6 |
| Non-concessional | 213 | 190 | 243 | 434 | 150 | 194 | 224 | 302 |

*US $ Million*

| | 1975 | 1976 | 1977 | 1978 | 1979 | 1980 | 1981 | 1982 |
|---|---|---|---|---|---|---|---|---|
| **DEBT** | | | | | | | | |
| DAC countries and capital | | | | | | | | |
| markets | 6 | 7 | 7 | 10 | 12 | 10 | 7 | 6 |
| ODA | 6 | 7 | 7 | 9 | 9 | 8 | 6 | 4 |
| Total export credits | – | – | – | 1 | 3 | 2 | 1 | 2 |
| Total private | – | – | – | – | – | – | – | – |
| *of which:* Bank loans | – | – | – | – | – | – | – | – |
| Bonds | – | – | – | – | – | – | – | – |
| Other | – | – | – | – | – | – | – | – |
| Multilateral | – | – | – | – | – | – | – | – |
| *of which:* Concessional | – | – | – | – | – | – | – | – |
| CMEA countries | – | – | – | – | – | – | – | – |
| *of which:* Concessional | – | – | – | – | – | – | – | – |
| OPEC countries | – | – | – | – | – | – | – | – |
| *of which:* Concessional | – | – | – | – | – | – | – | – |
| Other LDC'S | – | – | – | – | – | – | – | – |
| *of which:* Concessional | – | – | – | – | – | – | – | – |
| Other and adjustments | – | – | – | – | – | – | – | – |
| **Total Debt** | **6** | **7** | **7** | **10** | **12** | **10** | **7** | **6** |
| *of which:* Concessional | 6 | 7 | 7 | 9 | 9 | 8 | 6 | 4 |
| Non-concessional | – | – | – | 1 | 3 | 2 | 1 | 2 |
| **DEBT SERVICE** | | | | | | | | |
| DAC countries and capital | | | | | | | | |
| markets | 1 | 1 | 0 | 1 | 3 | 2 | 1 | 1 |
| ODA | 1 | 1 | 0 | 1 | 1 | 2 | 1 | 1 |
| Total export credits | – | – | 0 | – | 1 | 0 | 0 | 0 |
| Total private | – | – | – | – | – | – | – | – |
| *of which:* Bank loans | – | – | – | – | – | – | – | – |
| Bonds | – | – | – | – | – | – | – | – |
| Other | – | – | – | – | – | – | – | – |
| Multilateral | – | – | – | – | – | – | – | – |
| *of which:* Concessional | – | – | – | – | – | – | – | – |
| CMEA countries | – | – | – | – | – | – | – | – |
| *of which:* Concessional | – | – | – | – | – | – | – | – |
| OPEC countries | – | – | – | – | – | – | – | – |
| *of which:* Concessional | – | – | – | – | – | – | – | – |
| Other LDC'S | – | – | – | – | – | – | – | – |
| *of which:* Concessional | – | – | – | – | – | – | – | – |
| Other and adjustments | – | – | – | – | – | – | – | – |
| **Total Debt Service** | **1** | **1** | **0** | **1** | **3** | **2** | **1** | **1** |
| *of which:* Concessional | 1 | 1 | 0 | 1 | 1 | 2 | 1 | 1 |
| Non-concessional | – | – | 0 | – | 1 | 0 | 0 | 0 |

# VENEZUELA

| | 1975 | 1976 | 1977 | 1978 | 1979 | 1980 | 1981 | 1982 |
|---|---|---|---|---|---|---|---|---|
| **DEBT** | | | | | | | | |
| DAC countries and capital | | | | | | | | |
| markets | 1949 | 4024 | 6031 | 9159 | 12071 | 13615 | 14710 | 16387 |
| ODA | 38 | 34 | 28 | 6 | 5 | 3 | 3 | 2 |
| Total export credits | 801 | 902 | 915 | 1166 | 1423 | 1654 | 1623 | 1751 |
| Total private | 1110 | 3088 | 5088 | 7987 | 10643 | 11958 | 13084 | 14634 |
| of which: Bank loans | 689 | 1811 | 3670 | 5860 | 8320 | 9900 | 11200 | 12900 |
| Bonds | 71 | 65 | 496 | 1255 | 1340 | 1582 | 1434 | 1234 |
| Other | 350 | 1212 | 922 | 872 | 983 | 476 | 450 | 500 |
| Multilateral | 299 | 311 | 290 | 279 | 249 | 216 | 180 | 151 |
| of which: Concessional | 153 | 151 | 143 | 133 | 115 | 101 | 82 | 71 |
| CMEA countries | – | – | – | – | – | – | – | – |
| of which: Concessional | – | – | – | – | – | – | – | – |
| OPEC countries | – | – | – | – | – | – | – | – |
| of which: Concessional | – | – | – | – | – | – | – | – |
| Other LDC'S | 0 | 1 | 1 | 0 | 0 | – | – | – |
| of which: Concessional | – | – | – | – | – | – | – | – |
| Other and adjustments | 8 | 4 | 1 | – | – | – | – | – |
| **Total Debt** | **2257** | **4340** | **6323** | **9438** | **12320** | **13832** | **14890** | **16538** |
| of which: Concessional | 191 | 185 | 171 | 139 | 120 | 104 | 85 | 73 |
| Non-concessional | 2066 | 4155 | 6152 | 9299 | 12199 | 13728 | 14805 | 16466 |
| **DEBT SERVICE** | | | | | | | | |
| DAC countries and capital | | | | | | | | |
| markets | 451 | 501 | 1040 | 1508 | 2716 | 4656 | 4975 | 5124 |
| ODA | 6 | 5 | 8 | 22 | 1 | 1 | 1 | 1 |
| Total export credits | 237 | 212 | 340 | 596 | 435 | 498 | 617 | 539 |
| Total private | 208 | 284 | 692 | 890 | 2281 | 4158 | 4357 | 4584 |
| of which: Bank loans | 131 | 205 | 240 | 654 | 1941 | 3600 | 4100 | 4220 |
| Bonds | 16 | 15 | 17 | 58 | 93 | 126 | 152 | 259 |
| Other | 60 | 65 | 436 | 177 | 246 | 431 | 105 | 105 |
| Multilateral | 44 | 48 | 66 | 53 | 57 | 50 | 51 | 39 |
| of which: Concessional | 24 | 23 | 26 | 23 | 28 | 24 | 27 | 16 |
| CMEA countries | – | – | – | – | – | – | – | – |
| of which: Concessional | – | – | – | – | – | – | – | – |
| OPEC countries | – | – | – | – | – | – | – | – |
| of which: Concessional | – | – | – | – | – | – | – | – |
| Other LDC'S | 0 | 1 | 0 | 0 | 0 | 0 | – | – |
| of which: Concessional | – | – | – | – | – | – | – | – |
| Other and adjustments | 4 | 4 | 3 | 1 | – | – | – | – |
| **Total Debt Service** | **500** | **553** | **1110** | **1562** | **2773** | **4707** | **5026** | **5163** |
| of which: Concessional | 30 | 28 | 34 | 45 | 29 | 25 | 28 | 17 |
| Non-concessional | 469 | 525 | 1075 | 1517 | 2744 | 4682 | 4998 | 5146 |

*US $ Million*

|  | 1975 | 1976 | 1977 | 1978 | 1979 | 1980 | 1981 | 1982 |
|---|---|---|---|---|---|---|---|---|
| **DEBT** | | | | | | | | |
| DAC countries and capital | | | | | | | | |
| markets | 209 | 231 | 335 | 710 | 898 | 843 | 773 | 646 |
| ODA | 164 | 185 | 204 | 286 | 338 | 365 | 345 | 329 |
| Total export credits | 45 | 46 | 81 | 214 | 325 | 298 | 268 | 212 |
| Total private | – | – | 50 | 210 | 235 | 180 | 160 | 105 |
| *of which:* Bank loans | – | – | 50 | 210 | 235 | 180 | 160 | 105 |
| Bonds | – | – | – | – | – | – | – | – |
| Other | – | – | – | – | – | – | – | – |
| Multilateral | – | – | – | – | 8 | 40 | 50 | 54 |
| *of which:* Concessional | – | – | – | – | 8 | 40 | 50 | 54 |
| CMEA countries | 280 | 250 | 200 | 600 | 900 | 1000 | 900 | 1100 |
| *of which:* Concessional | 280 | 250 | 200 | 600 | 900 | 1000 | 900 | 1100 |
| OPEC countries | – | – | 100 | 200 | 300 | 500 | 600 | 650 |
| *of which:* Concessional | – | – | 100 | 200 | 300 | 500 | 600 | 650 |
| Other LDC'S | – | – | – | – | 60 | 70 | 85 | 110 |
| *of which:* Concessional | – | – | – | – | 60 | 70 | 85 | 110 |
| Other and adjustments | 50 | 60 | 80 | 110 | 100 | 150 | 188 | 200 |
| **Total Debt** | **539** | **541** | **715** | **1620** | **2266** | **2603** | **2596** | **2760** |
| *of which:* Concessional | 444 | 435 | 504 | 1086 | 1606 | 1975 | 1980 | 2243 |
| Non-concessional | 95 | 106 | 211 | 534 | 660 | 628 | 616 | 517 |
| **DEBT SERVICE** | | | | | | | | |
| DAC countries and capital | | | | | | | | |
| markets | 7 | 43 | 16 | 13 | 71 | 140 | 106 | 40 |
| ODA | 2 | 1 | – | 6 | 7 | 3 | 2 | 1 |
| Total export credits | 5 | 41 | 16 | 1 | 43 | 57 | 51 | 19 |
| Total private | – | – | – | 6 | 21 | 80 | 52 | 20 |
| *of which:* Bank loans | – | – | – | 6 | 21 | 80 | 52 | 20 |
| Bonds | – | – | – | – | – | – | – | – |
| Other | – | – | – | – | – | – | – | – |
| Multilateral | – | – | – | – | – | – | 0 | 0 |
| *of which:* Concessional | – | – | – | – | – | – | 0 | 0 |
| CMEA countries | – | – | – | – | 15 | – | – | – |
| *of which:* Concessional | – | – | – | – | 15 | – | – | – |
| OPEC countries | – | – | – | 10 | 10 | 10 | 25 | – |
| *of which:* Concessional | – | – | – | 10 | 10 | 10 | 25 | – |
| Other LDC'S | – | – | – | – | 6 | 5 | 8 | – |
| *of which:* Concessional | – | – | – | – | 6 | 5 | 8 | – |
| Other and adjustments | – | – | 4 | 6 | 10 | 5 | 5 | 35 |
| **Total Debt Service** | **7** | **43** | **20** | **29** | **112** | **160** | **144** | **75** |
| *of which:* Concessional | 2 | 1 | – | 16 | 38 | 18 | 36 | 31 |
| Non-concessional | 5 | 41 | 20 | 13 | 74 | 142 | 108 | 44 |

# WALLIS AND FUTUNA

| | 1975 | 1976 | 1977 | 1978 | 1979 | 1980 | 1981 | 1982 |
|---|---|---|---|---|---|---|---|---|
| **DEBT** | | | | | | | | |
| DAC countries and capital | | | | | | | | |
| markets | – | – | – | 1 | 1 | 2 | 2 | 2 |
| ODA | – | – | – | 1 | 1 | 1 | 1 | 1 |
| Total export credits | – | – | – | – | – | 1 | 1 | 1 |
| Total private | – | – | – | – | – | – | – | – |
| of which: Bank loans | – | – | – | – | – | – | – | – |
| Bonds | – | – | – | – | – | – | – | – |
| Other | – | – | – | – | – | – | – | – |
| Multilateral | – | – | – | – | – | – | – | – |
| of which: Concessional | – | – | – | – | – | – | – | – |
| CMEA countries | – | – | – | – | – | – | – | – |
| of which: Concessional | – | – | – | – | – | – | – | – |
| OPEC countries | – | – | – | – | – | – | – | – |
| of which: Concessional | – | – | – | – | – | – | – | – |
| Other LDC'S | – | – | – | – | – | – | – | – |
| of which: Concessional | – | – | – | – | – | – | – | – |
| Other and adjustments | – | – | – | – | – | – | – | – |
| **Total Debt** | – | – | – | 1 | 1 | 2 | 2 | 2 |
| of which: Concessional | – | – | – | 1 | 1 | 1 | 1 | 1 |
| Non-concessional | – | – | – | – | – | 1 | 1 | 1 |
| | | | | | | | | |
| **DEBT SERVICE** | | | | | | | | |
| DAC countries and capital | | | | | | | | |
| markets | 0 | 0 | 0 | 0 | 0 | 0 | 0 | 0 |
| ODA | 0 | 0 | 0 | 0 | 0 | 0 | 0 | 0 |
| Total export credits | – | – | – | – | – | 0 | 0 | 0 |
| Total private | – | – | – | – | – | – | – | – |
| of which: Bank loans | – | – | – | – | – | – | – | – |
| Bonds | – | – | – | – | – | – | – | – |
| Other | – | – | – | – | – | – | – | – |
| Multilateral | – | – | – | – | – | – | – | – |
| of which: Concessional | – | – | – | – | – | – | – | – |
| CMEA countries | – | – | – | – | – | – | – | – |
| of which: Concessional | – | – | – | – | – | – | – | – |
| OPEC countries | – | – | – | – | – | – | – | – |
| of which: Concessional | – | – | – | – | – | – | – | – |
| Other LDC'S | – | – | – | – | – | – | – | – |
| of which: Concessional | – | – | – | – | – | – | – | – |
| Other and adjustments | – | – | – | – | – | – | – | – |
| **Total Debt Service** | 0 | 0 | 0 | 0 | 0 | 0 | 0 | 0 |
| of which: Concessional | 0 | 0 | 0 | 0 | 0 | 0 | 0 | 0 |
| Non-concessional | – | – | – | – | – | 0 | 0 | 0 |

*US $ Million*

| | 1975 | 1976 | 1977 | 1978 | 1979 | 1980 | 1981 | 1982 |
|---|---|---|---|---|---|---|---|---|
| **DEBT** | | | | | | | | |
| DAC countries and capital | | | | | | | | |
| markets | 157 | 107 | 112 | 91 | 127 | 122 | 171 | 178 |
| ODA | 36 | 28 | 31 | 38 | 41 | 41 | 35 | 28 |
| Total export credits | 121 | 79 | 81 | 53 | 86 | 81 | 136 | 150 |
| Total private | – | – | – | – | – | – | – | – |
| *of which:* Bank loans | – | – | – | – | – | – | – | – |
| Bonds | – | – | – | – | – | – | – | – |
| Other | – | – | – | – | – | – | – | – |
| Multilateral | – | – | – | – | – | – | – | – |
| *of which:* Concessional | – | – | – | – | – | – | – | – |
| CMEA countries | – | – | – | – | – | – | – | – |
| *of which:* Concessional | – | – | – | – | – | – | – | – |
| OPEC countries | – | – | – | – | – | – | – | – |
| *of which:* Concessional | – | – | – | – | – | – | – | – |
| Other LDC'S | – | – | – | – | – | – | – | – |
| *of which:* Concessional | – | – | – | – | – | – | – | – |
| Other and adjustments | – | – | – | – | – | – | – | – |
| **Total Debt** | **157** | **107** | **112** | **91** | **127** | **122** | **171** | **178** |
| *of which:* Concessional | 36 | 28 | 31 | 38 | 41 | 41 | 35 | 28 |
| Non-concessional | 121 | 79 | 81 | 53 | 86 | 81 | 136 | 150 |
| | | | | | | | | |
| **DEBT SERVICE** | | | | | | | | |
| DAC countries and capital | | | | | | | | |
| markets | 23 | 54 | 8 | 29 | 39 | 11 | 56 | 53 |
| ODA | 2 | 2 | 1 | 2 | 2 | 2 | 2 | 2 |
| Total export credits | 21 | 53 | 6 | 27 | 37 | 9 | 54 | 51 |
| Total private | – | – | – | – | – | – | – | – |
| *of which:* Bank loans | – | – | – | – | – | – | – | – |
| Bonds | – | – | – | – | – | – | – | – |
| Other | – | – | – | – | – | – | – | – |
| Multilateral | – | – | – | – | – | – | – | – |
| *of which:* Concessional | – | – | – | – | – | – | – | – |
| CMEA countries | – | – | – | – | – | – | – | – |
| *of which:* Concessional | – | – | – | – | – | – | – | – |
| OPEC countries | – | – | – | – | – | – | – | – |
| *of which:* Concessional | – | – | – | – | – | – | – | – |
| Other LDC'S | – | – | – | – | – | – | – | – |
| *of which:* Concessional | – | – | – | – | – | – | – | – |
| Other and adjustments | – | – | – | – | – | – | – | – |
| **Total Debt Service** | **23** | **54** | **8** | **29** | **39** | **11** | **56** | **53** |
| *of which:* Concessional | 2 | 2 | 1 | 2 | 2 | 2 | 2 | 2 |
| Non-concessional | 21 | 53 | 6 | 27 | 37 | 9 | 54 | 51 |

*US $ Million*

| | 1975 | 1976 | 1977 | 1978 | 1979 | 1980 | 1981 | 1982 |
|---|---|---|---|---|---|---|---|---|
| **DEBT** | | | | | | | | |
| DAC countries and capital | | | | | | | | |
| markets | 10 | 11 | 15 | 12 | 19 | 17 | 12 | 9 |
| ODA | 1 | 3 | 1 | 1 | – | – | – | – |
| Total export credits | 2 | 1 | 6 | 3 | 9 | 9 | 6 | 4 |
| Total private | 7 | 7 | 8 | 8 | 10 | 8 | 6 | 5 |
| *of which:* Bank loans | 3 | 3 | 3 | 3 | 5 | 3 | 2 | 2 |
| Bonds | 4 | 4 | 5 | 5 | 5 | 5 | 4 | 3 |
| Other | – | – | – | – | – | – | – | – |
| Multilateral | 6 | 8 | 13 | 20 | 25 | 34 | 39 | 44 |
| *of which:* Concessional | 6 | 8 | 13 | 20 | 25 | 34 | 39 | 44 |
| CMEA countries | – | – | – | – | – | – | – | – |
| *of which:* Concessional | – | – | – | – | – | – | – | – |
| OPEC countries | – | – | – | – | – | – | – | – |
| *of which:* Concessional | – | – | – | – | – | – | – | – |
| Other LDC'S | – | 2 | 2 | 2 | 6 | 6 | 6 | 7 |
| *of which:* Concessional | – | – | – | – | – | – | 0 | 1 |
| Other and adjustments | – | – | – | – | – | – | – | – |
| **Total Debt** | **16** | **22** | **30** | **34** | **49** | **57** | **56** | **60** |
| *of which:* Concessional | 7 | 11 | 14 | 21 | 25 | 34 | 39 | 45 |
| Non-concessional | 9 | 11 | 16 | 13 | 25 | 22 | 18 | 15 |
| **DEBT SERVICE** | | | | | | | | |
| DAC countries and capital | | | | | | | | |
| markets | 1 | 1 | 2 | 2 | 3 | 3 | 2 | 1 |
| ODA | – | – | – | – | – | – | – | – |
| Total export credits | 1 | 1 | 1 | 0 | 1 | 1 | 1 | 1 |
| Total private | 1 | 0 | 1 | 1 | 2 | 2 | 1 | 1 |
| *of which:* Bank loans | 0 | 0 | 0 | 1 | 1 | 2 | 1 | 1 |
| Bonds | 0 | 0 | 0 | 0 | 0 | 0 | 0 | 0 |
| Other | – | – | – | – | – | – | – | – |
| Multilateral | 0 | 0 | 0 | 0 | 0 | 1 | 1 | 1 |
| *of which:* Concessional | 0 | 0 | 0 | 0 | 0 | 1 | 1 | 1 |
| CMEA countries | – | – | – | – | – | – | – | – |
| *of which:* Concessional | – | – | – | – | – | – | – | – |
| OPEC countries | – | – | – | – | – | – | – | – |
| *of which:* Concessional | – | – | – | – | – | – | – | – |
| Other LDC'S | – | – | 0 | 0 | 0 | 1 | 0 | – |
| *of which:* Concessional | – | – | – | – | – | – | – | – |
| Other and adjustments | – | – | – | – | – | – | – | – |
| **Total Debt Service** | **1** | **1** | **2** | **2** | **4** | **5** | **4** | **2** |
| *of which:* Concessional | 0 | 0 | 0 | 0 | 0 | 1 | 1 | 1 |
| Non-concessional | 1 | 1 | 2 | 2 | 3 | 4 | 3 | 1 |

US $ Million

| | 1975 | 1976 | 1977 | 1978 | 1979 | 1980 | 1981 | 1982 |
|---|---|---|---|---|---|---|---|---|
| **DEBT** | | | | | | | | |
| DAC countries and capital | | | | | | | | |
| markets | 56 | 62 | 80 | 127 | 160 | 141 | 173 | 186 |
| ODA | 52 | 54 | 74 | 97 | 110 | 32 | 49 | 72 |
| Total export credits | 4 | 8 | 6 | 30 | 50 | 109 | 124 | 114 |
| Total private | – | – | – | – | – | – | – | – |
| of which: Bank loans | – | – | – | – | – | – | – | – |
| Bonds | – | – | – | – | – | – | – | – |
| Other | – | – | – | – | – | – | – | – |
| Multilateral | 22 | 40 | 69 | 101 | 132 | 168 | 213 | 278 |
| of which: Concessional | 22 | 40 | 69 | 101 | 132 | 168 | 213 | 253 |
| CMEA countries | 81 | 86 | 84 | 91 | 108 | 308 | 370 | 384 |
| of which: Concessional | 81 | 86 | 84 | 91 | 92 | 295 | 356 | 374 |
| OPEC countries | 41 | 34 | 53 | 113 | 151 | 276 | 386 | 481 |
| of which: Concessional | 18 | 33 | 51 | 113 | 151 | 276 | 383 | 478 |
| Other LDC'S | 49 | 48 | 56 | 67 | 75 | 91 | 81 | 77 |
| of which: Concessional | 49 | 48 | 56 | 67 | 75 | 91 | 81 | 77 |
| Other and adjustments | – | – | – | – | – | – | – | – |
| **Total Debt** | **248** | **271** | **342** | **500** | **627** | **984** | **1223** | **1406** |
| of which: Concessional | 221 | 261 | 334 | 470 | 560 | 862 | 1082 | 1255 |
| Non-concessional | 27 | 10 | 8 | 30 | 66 | 122 | 141 | 151 |
| **DEBT SERVICE** | | | | | | | | |
| DAC countries and capital | | | | | | | | |
| markets | 2 | 3 | 6 | 10 | 13 | 28 | 51 | 38 |
| ODA | 1 | 1 | 1 | 1 | 1 | 0 | 0 | 1 |
| Total export credits | 2 | 2 | 5 | 9 | 12 | 28 | 51 | 37 |
| Total private | – | – | – | – | – | – | – | – |
| of which: Bank loans | – | – | – | – | – | – | – | – |
| Bonds | – | – | – | – | – | – | – | – |
| Other | – | – | – | – | – | – | – | – |
| Multilateral | 0 | 0 | 0 | 1 | 2 | 4 | 5 | 9 |
| of which: Concessional | 0 | 0 | 0 | 1 | 2 | 4 | 5 | 9 |
| CMEA countries | 0 | 2 | 5 | 4 | 6 | 8 | 45 | 31 |
| of which: Concessional | 0 | 2 | 5 | 4 | 6 | 4 | 42 | 26 |
| OPEC countries | 1 | 0 | 2 | 3 | 1 | 4 | 5 | 7 |
| of which: Concessional | 0 | 0 | 1 | 1 | 1 | 4 | 5 | 7 |
| Other LDC'S | 2 | 3 | 1 | – | – | 3 | 3 | 3 |
| of which: Concessional | 2 | 3 | 1 | – | – | 3 | 3 | 3 |
| Other and adjustments | – | – | – | – | – | – | – | – |
| **Total Debt Service** | **5** | **8** | **13** | **18** | **23** | **47** | **110** | **89** |
| of which: Concessional | 3 | 6 | 7 | 7 | 11 | 15 | 56 | 46 |
| Non-concessional | 2 | 2 | 6 | 11 | 12 | 31 | 54 | 42 |

# YEMEN, DEM.

| | 1975 | 1976 | 1977 | 1978 | 1979 | 1980 | 1981 | 1982 |
|---|---|---|---|---|---|---|---|---|
| **DEBT** | | | | | | | | |
| DAC countries and capital | | | | | | | | |
| markets | 23 | 21 | 19 | 27 | 24 | 50 | 57 | 56 |
| ODA | 11 | 10 | 10 | 18 | 17 | 15 | 12 | 15 |
| Total export credits | 12 | 11 | 9 | 9 | 7 | 35 | 45 | 41 |
| Total private | – | – | – | – | – | – | – | – |
| of which: Bank loans | – | – | – | – | – | – | – | – |
| Bonds | – | – | – | – | – | – | – | – |
| Other | – | – | – | – | – | – | – | – |
| Multilateral | 4 | 13 | 24 | 63 | 84 | 117 | 135 | 167 |
| of which: Concessional | 4 | 13 | 24 | 63 | 84 | 117 | 135 | 167 |
| CMEA countries | 34 | 19 | 93 | 117 | 163 | 216 | 328 | 389 |
| of which: Concessional | 34 | 19 | 93 | 117 | 163 | 216 | 328 | 389 |
| OPEC countries | 25 | 36 | 45 | 62 | 71 | 82 | 93 | 123 |
| of which: Concessional | 25 | 36 | 45 | 62 | 71 | 82 | 93 | 123 |
| Other LDC'S | 34 | 69 | 75 | 85 | 85 | 84 | 84 | 82 |
| of which: Concessional | 34 | 69 | 75 | 85 | 85 | 84 | 84 | 82 |
| Other and adjustments | – | – | – | – | – | – | – | – |
| **Total Debt** | **120** | **158** | **257** | **354** | **427** | **549** | **697** | **817** |
| of which: Concessional | 108 | 147 | 248 | 345 | 420 | 514 | 652 | 776 |
| Non-concessional | 12 | 11 | 9 | 9 | 7 | 35 | 45 | 41 |
| **DEBT SERVICE** | | | | | | | | |
| DAC countries and capital | | | | | | | | |
| markets | 4 | 3 | 5 | 5 | 6 | 9 | 31 | 11 |
| ODA | – | 0 | 0 | 0 | 0 | 1 | 1 | 1 |
| Total export credits | 4 | 3 | 5 | 4 | 6 | 8 | 30 | 11 |
| Total private | – | – | – | – | – | – | – | – |
| of which: Bank loans | – | – | – | – | – | – | – | – |
| Bonds | – | – | – | – | – | – | – | – |
| Other | – | – | – | – | – | – | – | – |
| Multilateral | 0 | 0 | 0 | 1 | 3 | 4 | 5 | 6 |
| of which: Concessional | 0 | 0 | 0 | 1 | 3 | 4 | 5 | 6 |
| CMEA countries | 0 | 0 | 0 | 1 | 1 | 3 | 24 | 30 |
| of which: Concessional | 0 | 0 | 0 | 1 | 1 | 3 | 24 | 30 |
| OPEC countries | 0 | 0 | 0 | 0 | 1 | 4 | 5 | 6 |
| of which: Concessional | 0 | 0 | 0 | 0 | 1 | 4 | 5 | 6 |
| Other LDC'S | – | – | – | – | 2 | 1 | 4 | 6 |
| of which: Concessional | – | – | – | – | 2 | 1 | 4 | 6 |
| Other and adjustments | – | – | – | – | – | – | – | – |
| **Total Debt Service** | **4** | **3** | **6** | **6** | **13** | **22** | **68** | **59** |
| of which: Concessional | 0 | 0 | 1 | 2 | 7 | 14 | 38 | 48 |
| Non-concessional | 4 | 3 | 5 | 4 | 6 | 8 | 30 | 11 |

US $ Million

|  | 1975 | 1976 | 1977 | 1978 | 1979 | 1980 | 1981 | 1982 |
|---|---|---|---|---|---|---|---|---|
| **DEBT** | | | | | | | | |
| DAC countries and capital | | | | | | | | |
| markets | 5070 | 5881 | 7091 | 8402 | 9514 | 10706 | 10339 | 9265 |
| ODA | 538 | 543 | 605 | 680 | 666 | 579 | 485 | 439 |
| Total export credits | 1872 | 2208 | 2770 | 3308 | 4236 | 4517 | 4036 | 3970 |
| Total private | 2660 | 3130 | 3716 | 4414 | 4612 | 5610 | 5818 | 4856 |
| of which: Bank loans | 2042 | 2260 | 2800 | 3300 | 3600 | 4900 | 4980 | 4050 |
| Bonds | 18 | 17 | 16 | 14 | 12 | 10 | 8 | 6 |
| Other | 600 | 853 | 900 | 1100 | 1000 | 700 | 830 | 800 |
| Multilateral | 564 | 660 | 762 | 901 | 1170 | 1408 | 1522 | 1730 |
| of which: Concessional | 206 | 191 | 177 | 164 | 150 | 137 | 122 | 107 |
| CMEA countries | 299 | 355 | 963 | 1300 | 2389 | 1999 | 1882 | 1863 |
| of which: Concessional | 299 | 355 | 410 | 496 | 589 | 615 | 643 | 703 |
| OPEC countries | 143 | 309 | 382 | 439 | 462 | 1000 | 1400 | 1545 |
| of which: Concessional | – | – | – | – | – | – | – | – |
| Other LDC'S | – | – | – | – | – | – | – | – |
| of which: Concessional | – | – | – | – | – | – | – | – |
| Other and adjustments | – | – | – | – | – | – | – | – |
| **Total Debt** | **6077** | **7205** | **9198** | **11042** | **13535** | **15113** | **15144** | **14403** |
| of which: Concessional | 1044 | 1089 | 1192 | 1340 | 1406 | 1331 | 1250 | 1248 |
| Non-concessional | 5033 | 6116 | 8006 | 9703 | 12129 | 13782 | 13893 | 13155 |
| **DEBT SERVICE** | | | | | | | | |
| DAC countries and capital | | | | | | | | |
| markets | 1160 | 1252 | 1417 | 1524 | 2048 | 2863 | 2821 | 2822 |
| ODA | 67 | 64 | 66 | 62 | 56 | 41 | 37 | 32 |
| Total export credits | 533 | 458 | 528 | 580 | 890 | 1010 | 857 | 749 |
| Total private | 560 | 730 | 823 | 883 | 1103 | 1812 | 1927 | 2042 |
| of which: Bank loans | 459 | 557 | 610 | 680 | 850 | 1400 | 1720 | 1840 |
| Bonds | 1 | 1 | 3 | 3 | 3 | 2 | 2 | 2 |
| Other | 100 | 173 | 210 | 200 | 250 | 410 | 205 | 200 |
| Multilateral | 58 | 70 | 87 | 117 | 144 | 178 | 207 | 252 |
| of which: Concessional | 30 | 29 | 27 | 27 | 27 | 27 | 25 | 24 |
| CMEA countries | 18 | 20 | 99 | 130 | 397 | 180 | 198 | 207 |
| of which: Concessional | 18 | 20 | 45 | 39 | 47 | 57 | 64 | 81 |
| OPEC countries | 12 | 14 | 44 | 145 | 146 | 120 | 210 | 354 |
| of which: Concessional | – | – | – | – | – | – | – | – |
| Other LDC'S | – | – | – | – | – | – | – | – |
| of which: Concessional | – | – | – | – | – | – | – | – |
| Other and adjustments | – | – | – | – | – | – | – | – |
| **Total Debt Service** | **1248** | **1356** | **1647** | **1916** | **2735** | **3341** | **3436** | **3635** |
| of which: Concessional | 115 | 112 | 138 | 127 | 130 | 125 | 127 | 137 |
| Non-concessional | 1133 | 1243 | 1509 | 1789 | 2605 | 3216 | 3309 | 3499 |

# ZAIRE

US $ Million

| | 1975 | 1976 | 1977 | 1978 | 1979 | 1980 | 1981 | 1982 |
|---|---|---|---|---|---|---|---|---|
| **DEBT** | | | | | | | | |
| DAC countries and capital | | | | | | | | |
| markets | 1736 | 2014 | 2375 | 2961 | 3293 | 3452 | 3452 | 3363 |
| ODA | 146 | 168 | 205 | 239 | 316 | 431 | 506 | 573 |
| Total export credits | 945 | 1184 | 1464 | 1985 | 2135 | 2364 | 2346 | 2176 |
| Total private | 645 | 662 | 706 | 737 | 842 | 657 | 600 | 614 |
| of which: Bank loans | 640 | 650 | 690 | 720 | 805 | 600 | 535 | 550 |
| Bonds | 5 | 6 | 6 | 7 | 7 | 7 | 5 | 4 |
| Other | – | 6 | 10 | 10 | 30 | 50 | 60 | 60 |
| Multilateral | 78 | 116 | 206 | 317 | 384 | 469 | 474 | 528 |
| of which: Concessional | 49 | 67 | 128 | 213 | 289 | 346 | 358 | 414 |
| CMEA countries | – | – | – | – | – | – | – | – |
| of which: Concessional | – | – | – | – | – | – | – | – |
| OPEC countries | 70 | 132 | 187 | 188 | 186 | 238 | 259 | 222 |
| of which: Concessional | 20 | 47 | 101 | 101 | 98 | 88 | 95 | 93 |
| Other LDC'S | 13 | 66 | 85 | 95 | 95 | 89 | 78 | 89 |
| of which: Concessional | 3 | 56 | 75 | 86 | 87 | 85 | 74 | 68 |
| Other and adjustments | – | – | – | 7 | 7 | 6 | 6 | 4 |
| **Total Debt** | **1897** | **2328** | **2854** | **3569** | **3965** | **4253** | **4269** | **4206** |
| of which: Concessional | 217 | 337 | 510 | 639 | 790 | 950 | 1034 | 1148 |
| Non-concessional | 1680 | 1991 | 2344 | 2931 | 3176 | 3303 | 3236 | 3058 |
| | | | | | | | | |
| **DEBT SERVICE** | | | | | | | | |
| DAC countries and capital | | | | | | | | |
| markets | 183 | 108 | 133 | 159 | 184 | 385 | 182 | 123 |
| ODA | 7 | 5 | 8 | 4 | 12 | 35 | 16 | 18 |
| Total export credits | 96 | 66 | 77 | 110 | 130 | 239 | 112 | 80 |
| Total private | 80 | 37 | 48 | 45 | 43 | 112 | 54 | 25 |
| of which: Bank loans | 80 | 35 | 45 | 40 | 38 | 111 | 54 | 25 |
| Bonds | 0 | 0 | – | – | – | 1 | 0 | 0 |
| Other | – | 2 | 3 | 5 | 5 | – | – | – |
| Multilateral | 6 | 8 | 10 | 13 | 24 | 23 | 22 | 20 |
| of which: Concessional | 1 | 0 | 0 | 1 | 2 | 2 | 4 | 4 |
| CMEA countries | – | – | – | – | – | – | – | – |
| of which: Concessional | – | – | – | – | – | – | – | – |
| OPEC countries | 0 | 4 | 1 | 1 | 1 | 22 | 12 | 8 |
| of which: Concessional | 0 | 0 | 1 | 1 | 1 | 21 | 7 | 8 |
| Other LDC'S | – | – | 2 | – | 2 | – | – | – |
| of which: Concessional | – | – | – | – | – | – | – | – |
| Other and adjustments | – | – | – | 1 | – | 1 | – | 1 |
| **Total Debt Service** | **189** | **121** | **145** | **174** | **211** | **432** | **216** | **152** |
| of which: Concessional | 7 | 5 | 9 | 6 | 15 | 58 | 27 | 30 |
| Non-concessional | 182 | 115 | 136 | 168 | 196 | 374 | 189 | 121 |

# ZAMBIA

US $ Million

| | 1975 | 1976 | 1977 | 1978 | 1979 | 1980 | 1981 | 1982 |
|---|---|---|---|---|---|---|---|---|
| **DEBT** | | | | | | | | |
| DAC countries and capital | | | | | | | | |
|   markets | 681 | 743 | 850 | 922 | 1127 | 1295 | 1337 | 1423 |
|   ODA | 95 | 98 | 113 | 241 | 354 | 450 | 475 | 511 |
|   Total export credits | 322 | 377 | 437 | 457 | 544 | 528 | 527 | 572 |
|   Total private | 264 | 268 | 300 | 224 | 229 | 317 | 335 | 340 |
|     *of which:* Bank loans | 220 | 220 | 234 | 155 | 163 | 124 | 55 | 50 |
|       Bonds | 10 | 8 | 6 | 9 | 6 | 3 | – | – |
|       Other | 34 | 40 | 60 | 60 | 60 | 190 | 280 | 290 |
| Multilateral | 196 | 266 | 310 | 340 | 385 | 450 | 495 | 519 |
|   *of which:* Concessional | 51 | 50 | 48 | 46 | 74 | 102 | 121 | 128 |
| CMEA countries | 6 | 6 | 5 | 22 | 233 | 240 | 276 | 263 |
|   *of which:* Concessional | 2 | 2 | 2 | 2 | 2 | 1 | 1 | 1 |
| OPEC countries | – | – | – | – | – | 23 | 23 | 110 |
|   *of which:* Concessional | – | – | – | – | – | 23 | 23 | 110 |
| Other LDC'S | 275 | 312 | 330 | 375 | 377 | 376 | 337 | 313 |
|   *of which:* Concessional | 218 | 266 | 289 | 329 | 334 | 327 | 287 | 264 |
| Other and adjustments | 3 | 2 | 1 | 3 | 3 | 2 | 1 | 1 |
| **Total Debt** | **1160** | **1328** | **1496** | **1662** | **2125** | **2384** | **2469** | **2630** |
|   *of which:* Concessional | 366 | 416 | 453 | 618 | 764 | 904 | 906 | 1014 |
|     Non-concessional | 794 | 912 | 1043 | 1044 | 1362 | 1480 | 1563 | 1616 |
| **DEBT SERVICE** | | | | | | | | |
| DAC countries and capital | | | | | | | | |
|   markets | 87 | 113 | 176 | 226 | 191 | 239 | 193 | 115 |
|   ODA | 6 | 6 | 6 | 8 | 12 | 14 | 17 | 13 |
|   Total export credits | 66 | 77 | 62 | 75 | 56 | 123 | 74 | 56 |
|   Total private | 15 | 31 | 108 | 143 | 123 | 102 | 103 | 46 |
|     *of which:* Bank loans | 13 | 19 | 101 | 136 | 115 | 78 | 80 | 28 |
|       Bonds | 2 | 2 | 2 | 2 | 3 | 4 | 3 | – |
|       Other | – | 10 | 5 | 5 | 5 | 20 | 20 | 18 |
| Multilateral | 16 | 19 | 26 | 33 | 42 | 51 | 48 | 48 |
|   *of which:* Concessional | 5 | 5 | 5 | 5 | 6 | 6 | 6 | 3 |
| CMEA countries | 0 | 1 | 1 | 1 | 1 | 2 | 30 | 22 |
|   *of which:* Concessional | 0 | 0 | 0 | 0 | 0 | 0 | 0 | 0 |
| OPEC countries | – | – | – | – | – | – | 0 | 3 |
|   *of which:* Concessional | – | – | – | – | – | – | 0 | 3 |
| Other LDC'S | 10 | 9 | 9 | 9 | 12 | 9 | 10 | 2 |
|   *of which:* Concessional | – | – | – | – | – | – | – | – |
| Other and adjustments | 1 | 1 | 1 | – | 0 | 1 | 1 | 0 |
| **Total Debt Service** | **114** | **143** | **213** | **269** | **247** | **302** | **283** | **191** |
|   *of which:* Concessional | 11 | 11 | 11 | 13 | 18 | 21 | 24 | 19 |
|     Non-concessional | 103 | 132 | 202 | 256 | 229 | 281 | 259 | 172 |

# ZIMBABWE

*US $ Million*

| | 1975 | 1976 | 1977 | 1978 | 1979 | 1980 | 1981 | 1982 |
|---|---|---|---|---|---|---|---|---|
| **DEBT** | | | | | | | | |
| DAC countries and capital | | | | | | | | |
| markets | 142 | 104 | 115 | 123 | 137 | 254 | 471 | 780 |
| ODA | 14 | 12 | 11 | 13 | 14 | 5 | 42 | 91 |
| Total export credits | – | – | – | – | 5 | 8 | 166 | 386 |
| Total private | 128 | 92 | 104 | 110 | 118 | 241 | 263 | 303 |
| *of which:* Bank loans | – | – | – | – | – | 63 | 118 | 175 |
| Bonds | 128 | 92 | 104 | 110 | 118 | 178 | 125 | 88 |
| Other | – | – | – | – | – | – | 20 | 40 |
| | | | | | | | | |
| Multilateral | 22 | 18 | 14 | 12 | 8 | 5 | 58 | 81 |
| *of which:* Concessional | 22 | 18 | 14 | 12 | 8 | 5 | 16 | 25 |
| | | | | | | | | |
| CMEA countries | – | – | – | – | – | – | – | – |
| *of which:* Concessional | – | – | – | – | – | – | – | – |
| | | | | | | | | |
| OPEC countries | – | – | – | – | – | – | – | 42 |
| *of which:* Concessional | – | – | – | – | – | – | – | 42 |
| | | | | | | | | |
| Other LDC'S | – | – | – | – | – | – | – | – |
| *of which:* Concessional | – | – | – | – | – | – | – | – |
| | | | | | | | | |
| Other and adjustments | 11 | 11 | 10 | 269 | 369 | 413 | 347 | 254 |
| | | | | | | | | |
| **Total Debt** | **175** | **133** | **139** | **404** | **514** | **673** | **875** | **1157** |
| *of which:* Concessional | 41 | 34 | 29 | 27 | 24 | 10 | 58 | 158 |
| Non-concessional | 134 | 99 | 110 | 377 | 490 | 662 | 817 | 999 |
| | | | | | | | | |
| **DEBT SERVICE** | | | | | | | | |
| DAC countries and capital | | | | | | | | |
| markets | 1 | 1 | 1 | 1 | 4 | 1 | 47 | 111 |
| ODA | – | – | – | – | – | 0 | 0 | 1 |
| Total export credits | – | – | – | – | 0 | 0 | 11 | 40 |
| Total private | 1 | 1 | 1 | 1 | 3 | – | 36 | 70 |
| *of which:* Bank loans | – | – | – | – | – | – | 4 | 31 |
| Bonds | 1 | 1 | 1 | 1 | 3 | – | 32 | 34 |
| Other | – | – | – | – | – | – | – | 5 |
| | | | | | | | | |
| Multilateral | 6 | 5 | 4 | 3 | 4 | 4 | 4 | 5 |
| *of which:* Concessional | 6 | 5 | 4 | 3 | 4 | 4 | 4 | 0 |
| | | | | | | | | |
| CMEA countries | – | – | – | – | – | – | – | – |
| *of which:* Concessional | – | – | – | – | – | – | – | – |
| | | | | | | | | |
| OPEC countries | – | – | – | – | – | – | – | 1 |
| *of which:* Concessional | – | – | – | – | – | – | – | 1 |
| | | | | | | | | |
| Other LDC'S | – | – | – | – | – | – | – | – |
| *of which:* Concessional | – | – | – | – | – | – | – | – |
| | | | | | | | | |
| Other and adjustments | 1 | 1 | 1 | 4 | 8 | 38 | 25 | 28 |
| | | | | | | | | |
| **Total Debt Service** | **8** | **7** | **6** | **8** | **15** | **43** | **76** | **144** |
| *of which:* Concessional | 7 | 6 | 5 | 5 | 5 | 5 | 4 | 2 |
| Non-concessional | 1 | 1 | 1 | 3 | 10 | 37 | 72 | 142 |

DEVELOPING COUNTRIES AND TERRITORIES BY INCOME GROUP (a) AND SELECTED CREDITOR GROUPS (OPEC, CMEA)

## 62 LICs: Low-Income (b)

| | |
|---|---|
| * Afghanistan | * Malawi |
| Angola | * Maldives |
| * Bangladesh | * Mali |
| * Benin | Mauritania |
| * Bhutan | Mayotte |
| Bolivia | Mozambique |
| | |
| Burma | * Nepal |
| * Burundi | * Niger |
| * Cape Verde | Pakistan |
| * Central African Rep. | * Rwanda |
| * Chad | St. Helena |
| * Comoros | * Sao Tome & Principe |
| | |
| * Djibouti | Senegal |
| Egypt | * Sierra Leona |
| El Salvador | Solomon Islands (Br.) |
| * Equatorial Guinea | * Somalia |
| * Ethiopia | Sri Lanka |
| * Gambia | * Sudan |
| | |
| Ghana | * Tanzania |
| * Guinea | * Togo |
| * Guinea-Bissau | Tokelau Islands |
| * Haiti | Tonga |
| Honduras | Tuvalu |
| India | * Uganda |
| | |
| Indonesia | * Upper Volta |
| Kampuchea | Vanuatu |
| Kenya | Viet Nam, Soc. Rep. |
| * Lao PDR | * Yemen |
| * Lesotho | * Yemen, Dem. |
| Liberia | Zaire |
| | |
| Madagascar | Zambia |

## 39 LMICs: Lower Middle-Income (c)

| | |
|---|---|
| Belize | Morocco |
| * Botswana | Nicaragua |
| Cameroon | Nigeria |
| Colombia | Niue Island |
| Congo | Pacific Isl. (US) |
| Cook Islands | Papua New Guinea |
| | |
| Cuba | Peru |
| Dominican Republic | Philippines |
| Guatemala | Swaziland |
| Guyana | Thailand |
| Ivory Coast | Wallis and Futuna |
| Jamaica | West Indies (d) |
| | |
| Jordan | * Western Samoa |
| Kiribati | Zimbabwe |
| Mauritius | |

## 56 UMICs: Upper Middle-Income (c)

| | |
|---|---|
| Algeria | Malaysia |
| Argentina | Malta |
| Bahamas | Martinique |
| Bahrain | Mexico |
| Barbados | Nauru |
| Bermuda | Netherlands Antilles |
| | |
| Brazil | New Caledonia |
| Brunei | Oman |
| Chile | Panama |
| Costa Rica | Paraguay |
| Cyprus | Polynesia, French |
| Ecuador | Portugal |
| | |
| Falkland Islands | Qatar |
| Fiji | Reunion |
| Gabon | St. Pierre and Miquelon |
| Gibraltar | Saudi Arabia |
| Greece | Seychelles |
| Guadeloupe | Singapore |
| | |
| Guiana, French | Suriname |
| Hong Kong | Syria |
| Iran | Taiwan |
| Iraq | Trinidad and Tobago |
| Israel | Tunisia |
| Korea, Rep. (South) | Turkey |
| | |
| Kuwait | United Arab Emirates |
| Lebanon | Uruguay |
| Libya | Venezuela |
| Macao | Yugoslavia |

## 13 OPEC: Organisation of Petroleum Exporting Countries

| | |
|---|---|
| Algeria | Kuwait |
| Ecuador | Libya |
| Gabon | Nigeria |
| Indonesia | Qatar |
| Iran | Saudi Arabia |
| Iraq | United Arab Emirates |
| | Venezuela |

## CMEA: Council for Mutual Economic Assistance

| | |
|---|---|
| Albania | Korea, PDR |
| Bulgaria | Mongolia |
| Czechoslovakia | Poland |
| Germany, DR | Romania |
| Hungary | USSR |

---

* LLDC (36 Least Developed Countries).

a. The People's Republic of China is not included as a debtor country in any debt Tables.

b. LICs include countries and territories with 1980 GNP per capita under $600. In this Survey, however, data for the LICs include all of the LLDCs; hence, the two LLDCs which are LMICs (Botswana and Western Samoa) are excluded from data for the LMIC group.

c. LMICs include countries and territories with 1980 GNP per capita between $600 and $1200; UMICs include countries and territories with 1980 GNP per capita above $1200.

d. West Indies includes: Anguilla, Antigua, Cayman Islands, Dominica, Grenada, Montserrat, St. Kitts-Nevis, St. Lucia, St. Vincent, Turks and Caicos Islands, and the British Virgin Islands. St. Vincent and Turks and Caicos Islands are LICs; Antigua, Cayman Islands, Montserrat and the British Virgin Islands are UMICs, but all West Indies are grouped here together in LMICs.

# OECD SALES AGENTS
## DÉPOSITAIRES DES PUBLICATIONS DE L'OCDE